Quality: Achieving Excellence

Each book is carefully co-ordinated to complement *The Sunday Times* 'Business Skills' video training package of the same name, produced by Taylor Made Films Ltd.

Quality: Achieving Excellence

Edgar Wille

CENTURY
BUSINESS

This paperback edition first published in the UK 1993
by Century Business
An imprint of Random House UK Ltd
20 Vauxhall Bridge Road, London SW1V 2SA

Random House Australia (Pty) Ltd
20 Alfred Street, Milsons Point
Sydney, NSW 2061, Australia

Random House New Zealand Ltd
18 Poland Road, Glenfield
Auckland 10, New Zealand

Random House South Africa (Pty) Ltd
PO Box 337, Bergvlei, South Africa

First published in 1992 by Century Business

Typeset by ℳ Tek Art Ltd, Croydon, Surrey
Printed and bound in Great Britain by
Mackays of Chatham PLC, Chatham, Kent

A catalogue record for this book is available from the British Library.

ISBN 0–7126–5672–3

Contents

To
Ruth, David and Marion
my children
who grew up to be my friends

Acknowledgements

I am grateful to so many people who have helped in various ways in the preparation of this book.

Bill Pryce, Tim Evans, Ian Mitchell, Richard Smith and David Slater of the Employment Department and Valerie Hammond, director of Ashridge Management Research Group (AMRG), must have the credit for starting me on my journey through British industry. (See Appendix A for details of the 'Investors in People' initiative which was the basis of this journey.)

Many people at Ashridge gave me a helping hand. Anthony Mitchell, who also runs Anthony Mitchell Associates, a Quality Management Consultancy, debated the gurus with me. Kathryn Leishman taught me about statistical process control. Terrylynn Knott gave me a rest now and again from doing my own word processing. Margaret Dawson, the AMRG administrator, dug me out several times. Jackie Ashton sorted out my computer problems. Chris Conway and Martin Bennett participated in some of the organisational visits. Corinne Seymour, on an Ashridge award in connection with her work on the learning organisation, provided the basis for chapter 18, with the help of Michael O'Sullivan, Governor of Holloway Prison, George Harris, Personnel Director of Toshiba and Martin Wibberley, Director of Human Resources, Bosch. Rod Boyle helped particularly with BS5750.

Then there are the people who welcomed me into their organisations: Bob Knox of Stanbridge Precision Turned Parts, Colin O'Neill of Rothmans, Charles Daybell of Braintree District Council, Phil Steele of IBC Vehicles, David Clifford of Seaham Harbour Docks and a number of their colleagues. Also Paul Ruggier of Texaco and Chris Hodgkinson of ICL without whom there would have been no chapters 16 and 17.

Henry Neave of the British Deming Association showed a lively interest which was most encouraging. He clarified my understanding of variations enormously.

Elizabeth Hennessy, Martin Liu, Diana Eliot and Paula Jacobs of Century Business were a pleasure to work with on a very tight timescale. Lucy Shankleman of Century Business launched me on the writing of this book, saying it would be good for my career. As an over 60 I liked that.

EW

A Route Map to this Book

This book owes its origin to visits I made, on behalf of Ashridge and the Employment Department, to scores of organisations. Many of them follow the total quality approach, a revolution in business life.

Chapters 1 and 2 set the scene by looking at definitions of quality and sitting at the feet of the Quality gurus, such as W. Edwards Deming, Joseph M. Juran and Philip Crosby. The sources of some of my information are the subject of chapter 21, where I offer a sample of 69 books which might start you on your own voyage of discovery.

Chapter 3 takes the plunge and gets into the apparently technical subject of 'variations' discovering that in fact it is all about management responsibilities and the folly of nagging operators for what they cannot control. This chapter also links with chapter 9 where some of the techniques used at all levels in a total quality company, not least by shop floor workers, are briefly illustrated. A short chapter 10 fits BS5750 into the scheme of things.

Chapters 4 to 8 deal with how total quality management affects everything done in an organisation. The way in which the whole workforce becomes committed to quality and continuous improvement is discussed in chapter 4; the dangers of preoccupation with quotas, targets, goals and numbers management might spark off controversy in chapter 5. Chapter 6 sees quality achieved by the co-operation of a whole chain of suppliers and customers, both internal and external. Each awaits the results of the work of the other and each expects quality; so we don't have to wait till the end of the chain to get it. It is built in all the way.

Chapter 7 sees the effectiveness of organising people in self-directed teams and how this empowers them to be involved in the search for quality. No longer a question of leaving their brains at the door and just doing as they are told. Chapter 8 applies all these principles to the service industries, recognising that the staff are more on public display in such organisations, but that the principles of quality and how to provide it are still the same.

Chapters 11 to 18 then invite the reader to accompany me, in retrospect, on some of my journeys round British organisations involved in total quality management. Put together they make it clear that total quality is not an idealistic dream. It *is* happening. Progress is being made. My general feeling about what I saw is one of optimism.

This is reflected in chapter 20 on co-operation, where the principles set out would change not only the face of business, but of society as a whole.

EW

1. Introducing Quality

QUALITY IS ABOUT PEOPLE

The total quality approach is about people and attitudes. It's not about techniques and procedures as such. It includes them, and it needs them. However, it's people who actually use them, inspired with a simple idea that the purpose of work is to provide customers with something that will delight them and make them want to keep paying your salary, by buying the product or service you provide.

MANAGEMENT DEFINED

Providing quality is everybody's job in a company. A lead needs to come from management who should offer frameworks and a sense of purpose. Management can be defined as:

> *Risking yourself in the mobilising of resources and relationships to add value to the enterprise.*

Managers risk themselves because every decision, however well informed, is a risk. They don't know for sure that everything will turn out as they planned. The very word 'decide' implies risk. It comes from a Latin word meaning 'to cut off'. When you chop off the branch of a tree you have stopped any chance of it bearing fruit. When you decide on one course of action, you have blocked off another possibility.

Life is like this – but you try not to risk the business, you choose the best branches to retain and what seem inferior ones to remove. Quality is an essential branch to grow, some would say *the* essential one.

Of the rest of the definition 'relationships' is the most important word. 'Resources' seems to cover everything. People are there as well as money, materials, markets, machines and so on. The word 'relationships' brings people into concert to produce something that is greater than the sum of their individual contributions. We use the word synergy for it (i.e. one plus one equals three or more). The most important single function of management is to foster relationships; between all the stakeholders; suppliers, customers, community, government, as well as employees.

QUALITY IS ABOUT WORKING TOGETHER

Fostering relationships is vital when dealing with quality. Quality is a mindset, but it is not merely an individual mindset; it is a collective one. Quality is attained by people linked with each other. We speak of the chain of suppliers and customers. Everyone and every team is a supplier to someone and a customer of someone else. This applies both within the organisation and outside it. It is the key to quality.

If ever the quotation 'No man is an island' rings true it is in this area. Donne hadn't lived to see the significance of women in this crusade, but his idea is sound. Interdependence – true in every field of life and never more so than when seeking to produce quality goods and services. This is why when the *doyen* of quality gurus, W. Edwards Deming, produced his 14 points about quality, ten of them made explicit reference to people, and people were in the other four by implication.

Quality demands people's energies, enthusiasm and intelligence. It means that everyone in the enterprise is involved in producing the best, as defined by the customer, and perhaps even better than that – the best that the customers will want when they know they can have it.

The implication of this is that the gospel according to Frederick Winslow Taylor is dead. No longer can managers do the thinking and the 'workers' just do as they are told. Everyone's ideas and observational powers are required. Gone are the days when most employees were met by a notice in invisible ink as they came to work which said:

Please park your brains at the gate.

QUALITY NEEDS TECHNIQUES

Of course techniques are required. In Chapter 9, I describe techniques that help the whole workforce to use their brainpower productively – statistical process control, cause and effect diagrams, problem solving, Pareto charts, histograms and so on. These are the tools of self-control and of self-management. These make visible the process of achieving quality; the operators themselves can then monitor progress. They do not have to depend on supervisors.

Increasingly the role of managers and supervisors is changing so that they become the coaches, counsellors and guides for teams of workers in the art of managing and developing themselves and in making the best use of available techniques. We shall see many examples of this new role of management, from a wide range of companies with whom I have had close contact as part of my work for the Ashridge Management Research Group and the Employment Department (UK).

DEFINITIONS

Definitions are always a problem. They usually spring from *your* perception, which of course is wrong, and *mine* which is right! Actually there is often no right and wrong. This was the point made by Humpty Dumpty in *Alice through the Looking Glass* where words meant what he chose: 'The question is which is to be the master – that's all.' As long as we define how we are using words everyone knows where they stand, then we can go ahead and communicate. This is the purpose of words anyway, unless you are a politician dodging a tricky question.

The word 'definition' has a fascinating origin which has a lesson for us when we use it. It comes from a Latin word meaning 'to finish'. You can see it in the *fini* in definition. The word therefore means 'to determine the boundaries of something', to say where something finishes. In the case of words this means to specify their limits, how far we can take them. This will be particularly relevant

3

in the use of the word 'quality', where some gurus want to push the boundaries further than others. It is then not just a matter of words, but of the thinking behind their use.

(Readers will, I hope, bear with me and even share a little of my fascination with words, because they are the only tools we have to engage in this conversation – and I do want it to be a conversation, not a monologue, even though I have the advantage. Or perhaps I don't, because you can always stop reading.)

DEFINING QUALITY

Some of the definitions of quality are a bit uninspiring. BS4778 (1979) reads:

> *The totality of features and characteristics of a product or service that bear on its ability to satisfy a given need.*

This doesn't set many boundaries and leaves all kinds of unanswered questions. A given need. Given by whom, for whom? It is not what Dr Deming would call an operational definition, but at least it envisages people out there in the world with a need to be satisfied.

We are not working to satisfy our own need. Perhaps a product-led business tends to do this because it may still be in love with a product no one wants any more. Its abstract quality might be wonderful, but this is not what quality means in business terms. Gold taps are not quality when all the customer needs and wants are reliable brass ones. The definition does, therefore, have the benefit of directing our attention outside ourselves to the market-place which in the end defines quality.

FITNESS FOR USE

This is the definition offered by Joseph Juran, another of the quality gurus. It has the advantage of brevity and is therefore memorable. It can be used by anybody as an aid to thought. Is the item I am producing fit for use? Does it fit in with the customers' intention for its use? Will they find it works effectively, that they won't lose time and production while they wait for a replacement? Will it fit in with whatever else they are doing?

This last point is important. My heating engineer told me about a wonderful new boiler for a central heating system which was designed and produced by one company. It was economical and effective in hot water production. The only trouble was – it was too powerful for most existing systems. It was not fit for use.

The definers of 'fit' and 'use' are the customers, not the providers, though the latter by their marketing and selling efforts may have contributed to the definitions. 'Fitness', as in our example, means ability to fit into the total activity of the customer.

CONFORMANCE TO REQUIREMENTS

This is the favourite of the evangelist of quality, Philip Crosby. Its advantage is that it points outside ourselves to the customers and the market-place. Somebody requires something, whether goods or services. What they want is defined in their terms. They know what they want and are able to say what it is. That is made clear by the word 'conformance'; the customers have said what they require and the provider has to meet the specification. 'Which of you if your son ask for bread will give him a stone?' The biblical saying can extend to customers as well as sons.

The word 'conform' has the idea of taking the shape of something. In this case it is a question of fitting the mould in the customer's mind. The two main words in the Crosby definition are clear and unambiguous. Something either meets what is asked for or it does not. If you have stuck to the pattern provided by the customers, eliminated all defects, met all deadlines and ensured proper safe delivery, you have conformed.

However, disciples of Deming are less sure of the sufficiency of this definition. 'Requirements' is seen as a limiting word. It means that the provider may settle for just meeting the specification. However, this disregards the competitive nature of the market-place. Someone else may come up with something that is better suited to the underlying requirements of the customers.

The customers may not have the vision to imagine that

5

something better is a possibility, but when they see it, they will know that it is just what they have been searching for. You may lose future business if you don't pursue the path of improvement beyond customers' expressed wishes.

Continuous improvement

You have to be thinking all the time (and 'you' means everyone at every level in your organisation):

'There must be a better way to do this' or *'This would suit the customer better if . . .'.*

Continuous improvement is the key to gaining a competitive edge in today's market-place. The Japanese have a word for it – *kaizen*. It means continuously improving everything that everybody does, in every operation in every part of the organization at every minute of the day . . . and if you can think of any more 'everys' just drop them in. It is a word of much greater emphasis than the mere translation 'continuous improvement'.

It isn't only a matter of your ultimate customers. It is the whole chain of customers. If you are working in a plant and you have to provide the traditional widget as a component to the next bay in your work team, then they are your customer. Your widget must be fit for their purposes, so that they in turn can conform to the requirements of the next in line after them, and so on until the ultimate consumer is reached.

If as you work, however, you and your team see a way of reducing rejects or reworks by a little adjustment in methods or procedures, you make the change. Make sure, of course, that you need no one's authority, that you check with customers – the next in line and anyone else who is affected. You may also need to check with someone who is responsible for design or logistics. A major improvement may have to go back to the design board, although there are lot of little things that make a big difference which require no permission from anyone.

We shall later discuss the two different types of variation – one of which is systematic and needs managerial decision – the other being due to special, even one-off causes, which may be suitable for individual action.

The main point, though, is that everyone should be on the look-out for improvement – and improvement means going beyond the mere specification of your internal or external customers. If you can really improve the product or service, then maybe you will not merely satisfy your customers; you might even *delight* them.

DELIGHTING THE CUSTOMERS

John Macdonald and John Piggott in their book *Global Quality* have yet another definition, which encapsulates this aspect of delight.

> *Quality is delighting the customer by continuously meeting and improving upon agreed requirements.*

You may query how feasible this is. You can't let everyone go tampering with what the design department has come up with; you can't have declarations of unilateral independence amongst the work teams. Nevertheless we shall see how clear arrangements can be made to empower people to contribute to continuous improvement and to feel responsible for everything, so that in one sense everything is their job, or at least their concern.

Teamworking particularly helps this and creates the opportunity for multi-skilling, where all members of the team can undertake a variety of tasks and can stand in for one another. This broadens their horizons and enables them to apply their minds to a range of improvements. The team structure also encourages the sharing of ideas and the working out of how to implement the improvements.

ASSOCIATED QUALITY

Another factor in delighting the customer is the kind of quality action which accompanies the main task. Too often we have thought of quality in the purely manufacturing context. Now we extend it to services. Nonetheless there is a large service element in every offering made to customers, especially if we include the whole chain, our next in line internally as well as the external customer.

Cheerfulness in adversity and clear communication of what is needed or of potential difficulties or threats to the next in line, enhance ultimate quality indirectly, but are of themselves quality offerings to those we serve and support.

Then there are those parts of any organisation which are not directly involved in the manufacturing of the product or the provision of the service. Their opportunity to affect quality can be enormous. The invoicing section which bills a worthy customer for goods not required nor sent is guilty of eroding quality. Even worse if, as in an illustration given by Popplewell and Wildsmith in their novel about total quality called *Becoming the Best*, the error is compounded by putting them on the bad debt list and consequently losing a large and respected customer. These are breaches of quality, as are inaudible mumbles when answering the phone or indeed, long delays before answering.

EMPOWERED PEOPLE

Similarly, it is a quality action when an employee uses discretion to bend the normal rules a little to accommodate a long-standing customer's urgent needs. This is where the theme of empowering people is a significant one. Give people at the most junior level the knowledge, information and permission to use their common sense when the rule doesn't really meet the situation.

People should be able to give at least some information about something which is not strictly within their area. This can be done by encouraging employees to work in a broad context where they don't have only one narrow activity, but have a reasonable idea of where they fit in with what other people are doing. Thus BA baggage handlers can usually tell you something that will put you on the track of some other service you require, and are trained courteously to explain your rights and possible actions when your baggage has gone astray.

Another example which will be discussed later is that of Braintree District Council, which I visited during the Ashridge research. There we will meet a refuse collector who sees the job as providing a quality service, and who debates the merits and demerits of the British quality standard BS5750. Quality actions from the Refuse Department include a willingness to take the extra step even if one Monday you have some extra refuse, because you cleared out the attic. How it delights when the refuse collector says 'That's all right, mate', as he humps that awkward non-standard box into the waiting vehicle.

As Macdonald and Piggott put it:

> The customer's perception of quality includes more than the satisfaction obtained from the primary product or service. Their view of the company that provides the basic need will include how the original enquiry was handled on the telephone, the method of timing of delivery, the clarity and helpfulness of the operating instructions and the timeliness and accuracy of the invoice. Clearly if we are to delight the customer, quality management must be extended to the administrative areas.

OTHER DEFINITIONS

There are some other rather long-winded definitions of quality about. I give a couple here, not because you could ever remember them, but because in terms of logical thought they do cover a lot of ground.

Armand Feigenbaum defines quality as:

> The total composite product and service characteristics of marketing, engineering, manufacture and maintenance through which the product and service in use will meet the expectations of the customer.

There are several good thoughts here. The product or service is used and that is when its quality is tested. It is aimed to meet customers' expectations, but there is no thought here of going further to what he or she might be educated to expect, and therefore buy your product or service in preference to someone else's. There is some recognition that quality is a cross-functional, composite affair, but there is no reference to administration which can create the greatest customer dissatisfaction.

Another and rather general definition comes from John Groocock, who describes quality as:

> *The degree of conformance of all relevant features and characteristics of the product to all aspects of the customer's need, limited by the price and delivery he or she will accept.*

I suppose by referring to customer need rather than expectation the way is open for unexpected improvement which goes beyond what was thought possible.

A FAVOURITE DEFINITION

H.J. Harrington defines quality as:

> *Meeting or exceeding customers' expectation at a price that represents value to them.*

This gets the idea of going beyond what the customer knew they wanted.

In *Becoming the Best*, Popplewell and Wildsmith put a definition into the mouth of the hero of their novel – Neil Johnson, the company's chief executive. He encouraged a lot of debate to define quality at every level of the company. The definition arrived at was:

> *Quality is the degree of excellence by which we satisfy the needs of the customer.*

This led to a lot of employees saying they never saw a customer, which in turn led to discussion of the fact that everyone had a customer, the one served by the process – the next in line.

Furthermore, needs are impersonal; someone suggested making it more personal, so the definition finished up:

> *Quality is the degree of excellence by which we satisfy our customer.*

The 'our' of 'our customer' creates a personal link. I think I would like to retain the idea of delighting our customer. On balance, if I were awarding a prize for the best definition, it would go to Macdonald and Piggott for their:

Quality is delighting the customer by continuously meeting and improving upon agreed requirements.

THE CUSTOMER CHAIN

I have referred to this concept several times and will look at it in chapter 6. It is a crucial part of the concept of quality. It forges a chain in which many links build quality into the process of delivering a product or service. This goes all the way from conception and design to arrival at final destination and subsequent use.

Rarely does one person produce and deliver a product or service. Everyone has a supplier and a customer. Everyone is part of the simple process of receiving an input and transforming it into an output, which then becomes someone else's input. The next person's job is made much more difficult if the transformation of input into output by the previous person has not resulted in faultless input from the perspective of the next in the line.

If, however, it does meet or exceed the agreed requirements, not only is there a chance that work will be a delight for the receiving customers, but also the whole chain, with its many handover points, makes quality a more attainable goal. It is not a question of a once-for-all inspection at the end or at key points in the process. The process is broken down into a number of steps, simple to identify and easy to carry out. Quality is created incrementally and not in one mammoth leap, and because there is a series of handover points at which any dissatisfaction can be expressed by the recipient, inspection as a separate activity is virtually superfluous.

THE DEPENDENCY OF MANAGERS

Everything, we have said in this chapter, depends on people. Quality is a people issue. It needs people who have intelligence and who are empowered to act for themselves without a lot of supervision. In one sense everyone is a manager now. Everyone is a white-collar worker even if blue overalls are worn.

Unfortunately, management, especially senior management, see themselves as responsible for everything that goes on, and in a sense they are. The buck stops with the chief executive or the chairman. Thus the managerial hierarchy think they can co-ordinate everything in such a way that the company will fulfil its objectives. They will issue instructions and if everyone does as they are told, fulfils all the laid down procedures, then mistakes will be minimal and the customer will receive what is required.

This approach cannot succeed. Management have to empower people to do their own checking and co-ordination. They have to share their responsibility. They still have the ultimate responsibility, but they fulfil it by ensuring that people are trained and developed to meet the challenges of their own enhanced responsibilities.

This makes life tolerable for the people at the top, who can then get on with their policy-making activities. It makes life more interesting for the people lower down in the old fashioned pecking order. It reduces the amount of middle level supervision required and enhances everyone's status in the one-time lower orders. All are colleagues with a sense of responsibility and the opportunity to undertake meaningful intelligent work. This is not a question of altruism or being nice to people. It is the only way to survive and progress. To do otherwise would be to waste the vast talent untapped in most organisations.

Management are no longer in control of the complexity of modern business and industry, if they ever were. They have to recognise that they cannot run the business on their own, especially when it comes to ensuring that quality prevails and that continuous improvement is being harnessed to gain competitive edge.

INTERDEPENDENCE

Every single person is vital to the success of the operation. Each has to take responsibility for their part and its relation to all the others. To get it all right we have to lean on each other. It is no longer a matter of workers leaning on managers. Everyone's ability, creativity and intelligence has to be harnessed.

It is a completely different way of working, a different way of organising the business and will involve a substantial re-education effort. People will need to be re-educated in their own jobs; they'll need to understand that they are not working in isolation; that each job is part of a whole process and they have to know how they and the next person fit into it.

No one quality director can be wholly responsible for quality, poring over reports and charts which obscure as much as they reveal. Safety checks, audits, corrective actions, data analyses, none of these track the real issues; often they try to lock the stable door after the horse has bolted. However, if you make everyone responsible for quality and for continuous improvement; fire them with enthusiasm and give the training and the tools to handle it, you will have a committed workforce, mobilised to delight their customers within the enterprise and in the world outside.

IT'S HAPPENING

Quality then is about people. Quality is about working together. Quality uses techniques and gets everyone using them. Quality conforms to requirements, establishes fitness for purpose and above all delights the customer. Quality is produced by empowered people and in turn empowers customers by giving them what they want, and ultimately something beyond their expectations.

All very well, but does anyone do it? Is it happening? Is it feasible? If it's not even feasible, it's not worth writing about. If some organisations are there already, then it is worth writing about to spread the message and get more to join the trail of success – success for customers, for suppliers and for employees. Even if they are only part way there it's worth writing about. Didn't there used to be a saying 'I'd sooner see a sermon than hear one any day'?

Over the last two years I have been privileged to visit some 70 organisations and to have close discussion with as many again to find out what they are doing to link their people development policies and actions with the fulfilment of their business objectives. This was done as part of a project awarded by the Employment Department in the UK to Ashridge Management Research Group (AMRG). One of the outputs of this project was a book *People Development and Improved Business Performance* (Wille 1990). Another was a second project, in support of the 'Investors in People' programme (see Appendix A). These visits showed me that total quality was being adopted in many organisations. Some of the stories are told in chapters 11 to 18.

2. Listening to the Gurus

All subjects have their gurus; Einstein, Jung, Freud, Galbraith, Keynes, Popper and so on. Management has Peter Drucker. Customer care has Tom Peters. Lateral thinking has Edward de Bono. Mind mapping has Tony Buzan. No budding MBA can get an 'A' for a strategy assignment without reference to Michael Porter, or one on leadership without mentioning Warren Bennis.

QUALITY GURUS

A guru was originally a mystical teacher, to whom people went to have their thinking and their lives transformed. The word then came to describe any thinker or teacher who introduced transforming ideas. Quality is as such a system of thought and has its share of gurus.

Three in particular stand out although there are others not far behind. The three are W. Edwards Deming, now in his nineties, Joseph M. Juran, not much younger, and a relative stripling, Philip Crosby, who has been in the quality business for something like 40 years. He survived a heart attack and revolutionised his health by taking a total quality approach to the management of his own life.

When I first met Deming on one of his visits to Ashridge Management College (where he has often led the studies of the British Deming Association) I was somewhat awed to realise that I was in the company of one of the 10 most influential personalities on the world stage since the Second World War. This must be so for he was the major influence in the transformation of the Japanese economy from junk shop of the East to standard bearer of quality and conqueror of Western markets.

Juran must also claim a major share in this revolution. And Crosby must take his place alongside these two for popularising the religion of quality in a way that was accessible to American and Western companies. There are also another half dozen quality experts whose contribution is reflected in the book.

W. EDWARDS DEMING

Deming is an expert in statistics and quality control, who worked in the American Census Bureau and in industry on the American war effort. He had gone to Japan after the war at the invitation of the Japanese Union of Scientists and Engineers (JUSE) to help rebuild the Japanese economy on a peacetime footing. He gave a series of lectures on quality control to engineers and on management's tasks and responsibilities to top managers. Within five years Japanese industry was outperforming the Americans and people all over the world were clamouring for Japanese goods.

The Japanese took notice. The Americans had let quality slide once the war-time need for reliability had subsided. Japan has come to dominate the market in many areas, from motorcycles to consumer electronics, from steel to cameras.

Deming started out on the path of statistical method in collaboration with Dr Walter Shewhart, whose name is perpetuated in the Shewhart Control Chart. As Deming's experience grew, he became convinced that the opportunity for progress lay not in techniques, though these are important, but in management. Wherever he went he found himself talking about management, which had lost sight of quality in the endless search for quantity and cost cutting.

Yet in fact, as Deming has pointed out repeatedly, quality reduces costs (see figure 5.1, p. 61). If you think about it, it ought to be obvious that to do or make something right first time saves all the expense of redoing.

Deming came to popular notice in America as a result of a TV programme in 1980: *If Japan can, why can't we?* Since then he has been giving over 30 four-day seminars a year to American managers, to say nothing of his frequent excursions overseas. He is a guru who could claim, though he is too modest to do so, that thousands of disciples sit at his feet each year.

At the time of writing he still visits Japan most years for the presentation of the Deming Prize, which is a most prestigious award. The message is gradually getting through all over the world, with the Japanese unworried, because they believe that when the West catches up with where they are now, they will be several more years ahead.

THE DEMING PHILOSOPHY

There is a distinct philosophic, almost spiritual, fervour about the Deming message. It is based upon a system of beliefs about people and aspirations for their well-being. The people are employees and everyone who may be called a customer. Happy people, delighted by what you have provided, become loyal customers. They will continue to demand what you supply and you will be on the pathway to profit and growth.

Cutting costs by reducing quality may improve the financial numbers in the short term. Profit is often seen as the difference between numbers – revenue and expenses. If the profit is down, things which don't contribute visibly to the numbers, like training, research and development and customer service, tend to be cut. But without continually improving what you offer your customers you will lose their loyalty and short-term number improvements will backfire. It does not fool customers. Rafael Aguayo calls managers who take this short-term approach VNO managers (Visible Numbers Only).

Similarly, employees are often rewarded on the basis of numbers without regard to the quality of what is being produced or the customer loyalty it is losing. Productivity induced in this way is counter-productivity.

We shall look at other aspects of the Deming philosophy as we proceed. It never departs from the original Deming principle that statistical analysis is essential to the identification of errors and their causes. Nevertheless his main message concerns management and

17

people rather than particular techniques. He propounds a new way of looking at business life and indeed life in general. A popular formulation of Deming's perspective is set out in his *14 Points*, summarised below. They will keep on cropping up.

It is important to understand that the 14 points, which sometimes Deming calls obligations, are a way of thinking rather than writing on tablets of stone. From time to time Deming himself changes the phraseology to make them clearer. Henry Neave produced a good summary of them for the British Deming Association entitled *Deming's 14 Points for Management*. I am indebted to him for enabling me to make sure that I have 'got it right', and for permission to quote from this and his book, *The Deming Dimension*.

He writes of the *14 points:*

> *They are not a straightforward, well-defined list of instructions; they are not techniques; they are not a checklist; they are vehicles for opening up the mind to new thinking; to the possibility that there are radically different ways of organising our business and working with people.*

CONSTANCY OF PURPOSE

The first of the points stresses the need to keep at it. Continuous improvement of products and services cannot be switched on and off in the light of short-term needs. The striving for improvement must be consistent, inexorable and never ending; it affects everything in the company.

A NEW PHILOSOPHY

The second point describes quality as a whole new philosophy, involving a thorough and radical rethink which will not live with the commonly accepted levels of delays, mistakes, defective materials and defective workmanship. Deming says that this requires a total transformation of the western management style. Otherwise, industry will continue to decline. Continuous improvement of systems, processes and activities will not happen.

AWAY WITH MASS INSPECTION

The third point eliminates the need for mass inspection as a way to achieve quality. Quality has to be built into the product in the first place with statistical evidence available. At first people used to laugh at Deming, doubting whether workers could be relied upon to do their own inspection and to produce things properly in the first place. They have, however, been proved quite wrong.

RELIABILITY OF SUPPLIER

The fourth point ends the practice of awarding contracts to suppliers solely on the basis of price tag. Many companies go for the cheapest supplier. Deming would have us go for quality, without disregarding price. Often his fourth point is regarded as insisting on single sourcing – this is a matter of having one supplier with whom you build up a close relationship. Deming himself recognises that single sourcing may not always be possible and it may take time to reduce the suppliers sufficiently, but it is a distinct aim with advantages which far exceed possible disadvantages of being held to ransom by a single source. The very entertaining of such a thought shows that the quality of mind that Deming is teaching is not understood. The idea is to build a co-operative relationship with the supplier.

FOREVER IMPROVING

Deming's fifth point is never to be content with things as they are, never to give up seeking for better systems of operating, 'improve constantly and forever *every* process for planning, production and service'.

TRAIN AND TRAIN AND TRAIN

The sixth point is training. Training is absolutely fundamental to the Deming philosophy because new skills are required to keep up with the continual changes in materials and methods, design, machinery, techniques and service. Training is productive and not one of the things that should be cut when the financial situation is tight.

LEADERSHIP

The seventh point concerns leadership: leaders are there to help people to do a better job. They are responsible for putting the system right where necessary (and Deming believes that as many as 90 per cent of problems are system ones). The better the systems become, the more chance the workers have of doing a good job. Deming has no patience with the idea of browbeating people to do a proper job when, in fact, the system in which they are working is ill-equipped and ill-designed. To be forced by the system to do a poor job is demotivating indeed.

DRIVE OUT FEAR

The eighth point is succinctly stated as 'drive out fear'. This is a matter of getting away from the 'us and them' approach of confrontation between superiors and others. In fact the language of superiority is not used by Deming and his followers. Resentful compliance will not achieve good work. There have to be joint working relationships rather than management by blame. Quality will not be achieved where people come to work of necessity, but hate every moment of it.

PULL DOWN BARRIERS

The ninth point gets rid of barriers between departments and staff. A company is a system. In fact, the supplier company and customer are parts of the system. Any part of the system which fails will diminish the whole. Thus the people who handle the invoices, the researchers, the designers, the sales desk and the production people are one team as well as part of their own specific teams. Traditionally people have tended to work in their own little fortresses, often fighting their fellow employees instead of the competition. As Neave says it is important to use elementary statistical tools at all levels to provide a common language and mutual understanding.

ELIMINATE SLOGANISING

The tenth point proposes the elimination of slogans, posters or other exhortations to the workforce to do better. In this he is taking a different approach to Philip Crosby who runs zero-defect days and does go in for sloganising. Deming says that these kinds of exhortations create adversarial relations, and just to put up a poster saying 'Do it right first time,' or, 'Increase input by a certain percentage,' can be counter-productive, particularly where the process is set up wrongly. People can only do a good job if they are part of the chain which gives them good materials to start with and a system which works.

GET RID OF QUOTAS

Deming's eleventh point opposes quotas where numbers are often chosen quite arbitrarily as targets. Again it is much better to use statistical methods for continual improvement of quality and productivity which the workers and their team leaders can handle for themselves. Deming is against all measuring methods that pay bonuses when certain quotas have been reached. If the target is too high, you are giving the workers something very difficult to achieve, and it will only be achieved by corner cutting, lowering standards and ignoring the quality requirements. On the other hand, if the targets are soft and easily reached, then people may hang about doing nothing because they have reached their target and fear it will be raised. Better for everybody to work to the limit of their capacity with emphasis on quality.

This elimination of arbitrary numerical targets, quotas and bonuses is one of the most controversial of Deming's points. There are a lot of pressures for what is called 'performance management based on financial incentives'. This is called into question by the Deming approach.

PRIDE OF WORKMANSHIP

The twelfth point wants all workers to have pride of workmanship in their jobs. This means getting rid of annual merit ratings, or performance appraisal, and of management by objectives and a move from sheer numbers to quality. When Deming says no appraisal of performance, he does not mean that leaders and workers should not frequently get together to discuss the personal development of their skills, he means that traditional payment by rating is not conducive to quality. In fact he goes right back to schooldays when marks and competitive ratings were of the essence and meant that only a minority left school with their heads held high, feeling proud of their performance. Most people were marked as second-raters. The barriers to good workmanship also include poor tools, unreasonable targets, bad material and unsatisfactory systems.

SELF-IMPROVEMENT

The thirteenth point makes an appeal for a vigorous programme of education and for the encouragement of everybody in self-improvement. Deming makes the point that it's not enough just to have good people, but people who are improving, and this means education. He uses the word education rather than training as more fundamental. Education to Deming means personal improvement, personal development.

TRANSFORMATION IS EVERYBODY'S JOB

The fourteenth of Deming's points originally read in a 1985 version:

Clearly define top management's permanent commitment to quality and productivity and its obligation to implement all of these principles.

In keeping with what I've said above, that the points are not written on tablets of stone, in 1986, Deming offered a significant rewording:

> *Put everybody in the company to work to accomplish the transformation. The transformation is everybody's job.*

This change is characteristic of the way in which Deming listens to the discussions he sparks off at his seminars. The new rewording to involve everybody does not deny that top management's commitment is vital to continuous improvement of quality and productivity. Deming still believes that top management must take initiatives which go beyond pious aspiration. They must set up the system and the structure which will provide the framework for what, in his later version, Deming calls transformation. The emphasis is now on everybody having responsibility for improvement within their own areas, and in the context of the whole organisation.

DEADLY DISEASES

Deming has also produced a list of 'deadly diseases' of Western management, among which he includes emphasis on short-term profits and short-term thinking, and management by use only of visible figures with no recognition that unknown or unknowable ones may be important.

Deming is often thought of as essentially a statistician. He does start by discussing variability in results, but this leads into a whole management philosophy. (See chapter 3.)

JOSEPH JURAN

Joseph Juran is another nonagenerian, very active and much appreciated in Japan, and now in the United States. Juran's writings are very thorough, though some find them tedious. Nevertheless his 1954 visit to Japan made a significant contribution to what Deming had stated.

I first came across him when I bought a few hundred random second-hand books for £100. Among them was Joseph Juran's book *Managerial Breakthrough*, which defined the work of all managers as follows:

- To break through into new levels of performance, creating change, followed by holding the resulting gains.
- To control (prevent the wrong kind of change).

This philosophy of management echoes many of the points which we have already seen with Deming.

The two gurus, Deming and Juran, do not seem to me to be drastically different in their viewpoints. In *Out of the Crisis*, Deming refers several times approvingly to the work of Juran. In *Juran on Leadership for Quality* , there is only one reference to Deming. They have both contributed much; this book is more interested in their contributions than their supposed rivalry.

Managerial breakthrough

In his book, *Managerial Breakthrough*, Dr Juran defines control as the prevention of unfavourable change, which implies an accepted standard or norm. However, he says:

> It can be a cruel hoax, a built-in procedure for avoiding progress. We could become so preoccupied with meeting targets that we fail to challenge the target itself.

Challenging the target is what he means by breakthrough. It means potentially favourable change:

> A dynamic decisive movement to new, higher levels of performance.

He makes the distinction between 'improvement through better control by making sure standards are adhered to' and 'improvement through breakthrough where a whole system is changed'. This is very close to Deming's criticism of managers who blame workers for inadequate performance when actually it is the system itself which requires improvement. Breakthrough is the creation of good changes, whereas control is the prevention of bad changes. All managerial activity is directed at either breakthrough or control.

Juran uses the human biological organism as an analogy. The body devotes much energy to preventing change, with body temperature as a case in point. But the body also devotes energy to creating change, by exercise and general improvement.

Deming describes occasional and unpredictable deviation in processes as *special causes* of variation and predictable and relatively stable deviation as *common causes* of variation. Juran uses the terms *sporadic* for the former and *chronic* for the latter. It is the responsibility of management to address the chronic and not to blame the workforce for them. It is indeed helpful to recognise that these two giants in the field of quality arrived at similar conclusions via their own routes, both of which started off with a statistical approach. Juran also stresses that breakthrough activity tends to be long term, where control is short term and immediate.

COMPARING JURAN AND DEMING

Juran is the editor of *Juran's Quality Handbook*, which is periodically revised. It is easier to describe it by weight than by number of pages, though these run well in excess of a thousand. Juran has been highlighting managerial responsibility for quality since the 1940s with emphasis on the fact that although techniques are useful, it's people who produce quality. He was probably the first of the gurus to emphasise that quality was achieved by communication, management and people. Like Deming, he emphasises that massive training is essential and has to involve the whole workforce, that senior management have to be committed, and that improvement has to be continual.

Juran is clear that the 'pursuing of departmental goals can sometimes undermine a company's overall quality mission.' Like Deming, Juran believes it is more important to concentrate on the flow of the process and make sure you get it right rather than specific targets and management objectives.

He too is against campaigns to motivate the workforce to solve the company's quality problems by doing perfect work. Such slogans don't set achieveable goals or provide plans to meet them and resources to carry them out. Many believe that Juran was the first to bring a whole number of unconnected approaches into an integrated philosophy.

Juran has a systemic approach to company-wide quality management. It begins with quality policies and goals. It goes on with plans to meet them. Then it provides resources which enable progress to be evaluated and action taken. Finally it motivates and stimulates people to believe in, meet the goal, and improve on it. This is summed up in the Juran trilogy: quality planning, quality control and quality improvement.

Juran sees danger in single sourcing for key purchases. He believes that having several sources keeps the suppliers on their toes. He is, however, in agreement with the idea of maintaining a close relationship with the suppliers.

He does not believe that 'quality is free' or that there is a point where conformance to requirements may be more expensive than what is gained from adhering to these standards.

JURAN'S TEN STEPS

As Deming has his 14 points, so Juran has his ten steps:

1. Build awareness of the need and opportunity for improvement.
2. Set goals for it.
3. Set up an organisation to reach those goals with a quality council in the lead.
4. Training.
5. Problem solving projects.
6. Report progress.
7. Recognise people who produce good quality work.
8. Ensure that everybody is informed about the results.
9. Keep a score of it all.
10. Maintain momentum by making annual improvement part of the company's regular processes.

The Crosby approach

Philip Crosby is an evangelist and a populariser who goes in for quite a bit of razzamatazz in arousing interest in quality. He is a frequent broadcaster and a very persuasive speaker. Even though his original contributions are not as great as those of Deming and Juran, he is probably the man who has brought total quality to more companies than anyone else.

In principle most of his message harmonises with the other two gurus, but his approach is less rigorous. He does seem to give the impression that exhorting workers to turn out a perfect product is meaningful, even though most of the problems are systemic rather than operator-created.

Crosby does teach continuous improvement. His aim is to secure zero defects which is sometimes thought impractical. However by zero defects he means defects as perceived by the customer. Deming and Juran would criticise this by saying that it tends to rule out the possibility of going beyond what the customers know they want. In a sense 'zero defects' is not good enough.

Crosby goes in for the celebration of zero-defect days on which the workforce sign a pledge to aim for work which has no defects. Deming and Juran would query the value of that kind of thing.

Crosby's definition of quality is 'conforming to requirements', which again suffers from the criticism that you can conform to requirements without a ceaseless search for improvement.

It has to be said that Crosby has a lot of experience in working on quality in-company. He founded Philip Crosby Associates (PCA), a world-wide company which runs quality colleges. He has sold the company but still operates as a consultant.

The four absolutes

Like the other gurus, Crosby has his steps and points. He has four absolutes of quality which are at the root of all his, and PCA's, courses.

- Have a definition of quality, understood by everybody, as part of a common language facilitating communication: 'Quality has to be defined as conformance to requirements, not as goodness.'

- Have a system by which to manage quality and a performance standard which is unambiguous: 'The system for causing quality is prevention, not appraisal.'

- 'The performance standard must be zero defects, not "That's close enough".' In other words, we mustn't plan errors into our operation like the company that one year said it was 'going to halve fatal accidents'.

- 'The measurement of quality is the price of nonconformance to requirements.' That is, all the expenses of doing things wrong from the customer's perspective. (There is also the price of conformance – what is necessary to make things come out right, essential inspection, education and prevention. But these are part of doing a good job anyway.)

Whether you agree with Crosby in detail or not, he has succeeded in creating popular awareness of quality on a grand scale.

CROSBY'S 14 STEPS

His 14 steps, summarised below, emphasise:

1. Commitment from management.
2. A quality improvement team to run improvement programmes (though it's still part of everyone's job).
3. Quality measurement displayed so that everybody can evaluate what is happening and do what is necessary.
4. A definition of the cost of quality used as a management tool.
5. The provision of a method of raising quality awareness so that everyone has an operational definition of conformance to requirements.

6. A systematic method of resolving problems that have been identified in the earlier steps.
7. Launching a zero–defects programme.
8. Training supervisors to lead the quality improvement programme.
9. Having a zero–defects day to help all employees realise that things are changing.
10. Goal setting to turn the pledges that employees are encouraged to make into specific improvement goals.
11. Setting up a means by which, when employees meet a situation they need to communicate to the manager, there is a channel for doing it. Without this, the pledge to improve things and go for zero defects becomes meaningless.
12. Showing appreciation of those who participate.
13. Setting up quality councils.
14. 'Do it over again.' This is to emphasise that quality improvement programmes never end.

The 14 steps are intended as guidelines, but a lot of people who follow Crosby tend to treat them, as indeed Deming's 14 points and Juran's ten, as if they were gospels. In the strict sense of the word 'gospel' meaning good news, they probably are, but they are not absolute laws without the following of which quality cannot happen. Particularly in the case of Crosby, some companies exclude the zero-defects day and some of the stirring up of excitement that Crosby tends to go in for.

Crosby emphasises the ongoing management of quality, but his 14 points don't have the same amount of emphasis on the principles of breakthrough and control or handling variation with statistical process control that we get from Juran and Deming.

Crosby's books make a good read because to a large extent they are novels with live characters grappling with quality in companies. His book *Quality Without Tears; the art of hassle-free management* has a good deal of straightforward guidance, again taking you through his 14 steps.

SUMMING UP THE GURUS

All three of these gurus are really talking about management. That is what quality is about. The purpose of a business is to create and keep a customer. There is only one way to do this, by giving the customers what they want, and that is a definition of quality. Running a business, therefore, is all about quality. In one way there is no other topic.

3. The Principle of Variation

In the past, and maybe still in many companies, it has been the custom for supervisors to nag the operators for greater speed, higher productivity, less defective work and reduced wastage. The attitude is that if only the workers would try harder, do their best, be careful, concentrate on the job in hand, then output would increase in quality and in quantity.

This chapter explores the view expressed by Deming, Juran and others that this attitude, which makes going to work such a miserable business for many, stems from a misunderstanding of what causes variations in output. A clearer grasp of the fact that there are two sources of variation in outputs would show the folly of blaming people for what they cannot control.

Variations through special or sporadic causes can often be put right by operators. Once these stabilise, however, improvement is possible only by tackling the system, and that is the ultimate responsibility of management. The systemic variations may represent ongoing problems which need addressing, or they may be opportunities to seek ever higher standards of excellence, even though there is no current problem.

IS POOR QUALITY THE OPERATOR'S FAULT?

The reason for poor quality is often not the unwillingness of workers, but the system under which the work is carried out. Incoming material may be defective and operators are trying 'to make a silk purse out of a sow's ear'. Perhaps maintenance is rushed because the quota system means there isn't time to stop production to do it properly.

Such circumstances are outside the control of the operator, who may none the less be bullied because of the poor quality output. The issues are systemic and are the responsibility of management to put right, with help from the operator who may well know best what needs doing.

Rafael Aguayo lists some of these things which affect quality, yet are quite outside operator control. He includes the layout of the plant, the room temperature and the amount invested in research, development and training.

> They don't buy the equipment, tools, and raw materials or determine the design of the product. They don't develop the reward system or the organisational structure. In short they don't determine 90 per cent of the things responsible for the quality of the product.

He goes on to challenge management for holding the workers responsible for all the defects. Only management can provide the framework in which the operators can do a quality job and take pride in it. They will then contribute to the continuous improvement process with a stream of suggestions on how things might be further improved.

There will be some things the operator can do something about. Given the right training, employees can respond to and reduce the number of mistakes which are due to their own carelessness; they can make sure they are working when they should be, that they don't hold things up by being late and that they don't try to make the equipment do what it is not designed to do.

Nevertheless, both Deming and Juran believe that most of the variations in the processing of work are due to the system, which management should address. A small proportion are due to the errors of the operators. Yet it is they who are so often blamed; exhorted to do better and bombarded with slogans.

Special causes of variation

Writers on quality categorise the causes of *variation* of goods or services in two main classes:

- Those which the worker is able to deal with.
- Those which require management action.

Deming describes *special causes* of variation as unpredictable or unusual circumstances in a process, which may be due to individual or group mistakes or some exceptional failure of material or equipment. Often the operators can do something about these special causes. Juran describes them as *sporadic*. On process control charts they show up as major high or low points thus displaying a state of unpredictability. (See chapter 9 for examples.) Get rid of the cause and the process settles down to a steady range of predictable variations within the limits of what the system allows it to achieve. *This is described as being in statistical control.*

Common causes of variation

The variations which remain once the results are stable in this way cannot be improved by intervening. Such variations are inherent in the system and to reduce them requires that something be done to improve the process, with action to enable the operators to work within it.

This second category of variations is described by Deming as *common causes* and by Juran as *chronic waste*. The special causes may be dealt with by 'firefighting' activity; but common causes or chronic waste have to be dealt with fundamentally. No amount of bullying or exhortation will change these variations. Try as they might the workers cannot change the shape of the graph. The predictable ups and downs will still occur.

This stable condition still needs comparing with customer specifications. It may or may not be within them, but with special causes out of the way, the continuing 'stable' variations can be addressed. Something can be done to change the system, either to get it into conformity with customer requirements or to improve beyond these. As Juran puts it, chronic waste is an opportunity for improvement. You can improve the supply arrangements, the maintenance arrangements, the complaints procedures, the customer care awareness and so on. A new process is established which will get nearer to the elusive goal of perfection.

Once the system is in statistical control, its predictability enables one to work, for example, to get the control limits closer together and therefore enhance the ability to meet or exceed customer requirements. In some cases the control limits have been brought so close that they have represented a level six times better than that the customer would accept. This means that variations outside the new limits on the chart may still be within the customer's requirements and the scope for maintaining quality is high. The whole system has been tightened and if this is continued in a methodical way continuous improvement will be the result. It is important however to avoid tampering, where although the process is in control, common causes of variation are mistaken for special causes, leading to haphazard chases after every individual variation in sight.

This systemic change has to be tackled by management. It will tend to be more long-term than dealing with the unpredictable special causes. Management should harness the knowledge and experience of the operators who can provide it, based upon their closeness to the job. Usually, however, it is only management who can change the processes in a way which will enable the workers to produce less variable output.

ANALOGY FROM THE SWIMMING POOL

Recently I was doing my mile swim in the Ashridge pool, which I use as a think tank as well as a health centre. It occurred to me that what I was doing provided an analogy to the theme of variations.

I am a slow swimmer, but a persistent one and am quite proud of my mile, as I'm in the second half of my sixties. Yet it does irk a little when I see the younger people and some of those in their fifties swimming two or even three lengths to my one. I therefore went in for some self exhortation. I ordered myself, just as do supervisors on the shop floor, to try harder, to put more effort into it.

I was not swimming correctly. I was not using the techniques I had learned years ago at school. My hands were not correctly parting the water; my legs were not coming properly together, nor were they co-ordinating with my arms. So I gave myself training and eradicated these common causes; I modified my system. After a week or two, instead of doing five lengths in five minutes I was doing seven. After that my rate settled down and I have been unable to improve it at all. Mere effort produces the odd spurt, but over the mile or even half mile there is no real change.

My improvement at first had been a matter of tackling common causes by changing my co-ordination system. There were no special causes at work, such as going in to swim with a hangover or trying fancy strokes. Such special causes could have been dealt with by desisting from such conduct.

So my swimming rate is in statistical control or stable state. The rate will not go up a second time unless I again change my swimming system, the relationship between my body and the water. I will probably need some proper lessons, so that I no longer swim only the breast stroke and with my head sticking up out of the water. I can improve my rate only by adopting a new system, swimming with my head under the water much of the time and using a variety of strokes. Sporadic effort will not do it. The problem is chronic and therefore needs a total revision of methods and procedures.

When I have achieved the second of these system changes, I will again become dissatisfied and will need to change the system by further enlargement of my stroke repertoire. There is a long way to go before there is no further room for improvement.

This constant setting up of systems, enabling people to work within new limits and achieve stability within them is the main meaning behind the term 'continuous improvement', so often used in quality discussions.

ANALOGY FROM A SLIMMING DIET

Just to reinforce the idea of variations and how to handle them, another idea came to me on the same swim. The pool really was a think tank that day.

When first working at Ashridge, I found the meals provided for those working on programmes, tutors and nominees, delicious and tempting. My girth began to show the results. The bathroom scales groaned under the added weight. My eating system might have been in statistical control, but the limits were unacceptable. Two friends separately and in the same week spoke of the benefits they had gained by a vegetarian diet. Always ready to try anything, I thought I would give it a go. I found that I enjoyed my food as much as ever, but with a lower fat and calorie intake my weight dropped. Day after day the pounds disappeared. This was a system change, but quite soon the fall in weight ceased.

Each day, give or take a pound or two, the scales told the same story. I was in statistical control or in stable state once more, albeit within a more satisfactory system with more acceptable limits. If I don't change my regime further, I shall remain between 173 and 175 pounds.

Now that may be all right, but I would still like to lose another six pounds. So what system am I going to use? Well I remember for some ten years keeping my weight under control with the aid of the Royal Canadian Air Force exercises; so if I resume these, perhaps I will be able to get my weight within new limits and achieve a new and better level of statistical control, which will conform more closely with my requirements.

THE FOLLY OF NAGGING

Of course these analogies are not perfect, but may help understanding. The reader will readily think of others. Take for example the audio typist who has to achieve a required speed in spite of the variation in clarity of the person dictating. It is absolutely useless for a supervisor to rebuke a typist for low output when he or she is being required to wrestle with the vagaries of a system which does not train dictators to enunciate clearly and indicate punctuation and new paragraphs, as well as spelling out obscure proper names.

This is the 'common cause' of the typist's variations. If it had happened only sporadically, when the dictator was in a great hurry, for instance, it would have been a special cause, easy to identify and put right, but this permanent variation from acceptable limits will require a new system, involving the retraining of the dictator.

The outcome of nagging, of insisting on higher output in spite of the regularly variable quality of the dictating, can only send quality of output into deeper decline. The typist will not even try to cope with the poor dictation. He or she will just do the best they can. It will go back to the dictator, who will complain about the high error rate, but he or she has set up the system of indistinct input and can expect nothing better until a new approach to dictating is learned.

TWO-MINUTE CUSTOMER CARE

Nagging, bullying or hustling will always result in a decline in quality. Viki Holton, of Ashridge, told me the story of the way in which a customer care department set up a system for dealing with customer queries. Every complaints clerk in a certain company was given two minutes in which to deal with a query. It was held that this was long enough to extract the precise nature of the problem, answer it if it was simple and straightforward, pass it on to an expert if this was not feasible or promise that someone would get back to the complainant within a fixed period. The time of each enquiry was automatically logged and the printouts regularly scrutinised.

What happened when a customer wanted to let off a little steam? didn't get to the point very quickly or in any way took up more than the two minutes allowed to the clerk? The customer would have to be interrupted, hustled to get to the point, and not given the understanding ear which helps to create customer loyalty.

Some clerks were even known to say: 'I'm sorry sir, but I am allowed only two minutes on each enquiry. So may I take your name and address and get someone to call you back.' Such frankness hardly did much for quality customer care. The other ruse was to transfer the customer to the first name that came to mind as the dreaded two minutes approached. This led to the customer being passed round the organisation with ever increasing frustration and a waste of everyone's time.

I suppose this two minute rule and the recording of it would be called quality control by some. But it broke every rule of quality. It was concerned only with one facet – time. It was not concerned with whether, in Crosby terms, it conformed to customer requirements; whether, in Juran terms, it was fit for use. And it certainly did not delight the customer.

Clearly when they exceeded two minutes a call the clerks were the victims of a poor system. If the extent to which they exceeded it was averaged out, it would be found that there was a consistency about the level of variation. It was in statistical control, but not achieving the levels which had been arbitrarily set by the system. The system needed changing, rather than the clerks needing discipline.

DEMING'S SOLUTION FOR THE HUSTLED TELEPHONIST

Deming gives a way to change the system in a very similar situation. After I had written about the two minute story above, I found a story in Deming's *Out of the Crisis* of a woman in his class at New York University Business School who had worked for an airline as telephone reservation and information representative. She had to cover 25 calls an hour.

She was instructed to be courteous and not rush customers who called. Failure to achieve her quota or to be courteous would be failure; but could she justly be held accountable for it? A statistical control chart would show a persistent and consistent pattern of variation. Nothing she could do would alter it. Either she departed from standards of courtesy or she failed to meet her time budget. The system set her up to fail. That was management's fault. They alone could have changed her terms of reference and the support arrangements she needed.

No provision was made in the 25 calls an hour rule for the

regular inability of the computer system to deliver information with sufficient speed or of the frequent need to consult directories manually. This was on straightforward enquiries, not the more complex ones, which from the start obviously needed to be referred elsewhere.

Deming offers some suggestions for improving the system itself. This would use the computer to monitor all the calls the telephonist undertook, including the delays through information not being immediately available. Presumably this would have to include time taken to placate a particularly irate customer.

Then Deming would have the supervisor plot the clerks' activity on a control chart. It would probably be found that there was a stable pattern of time taken, where the variations were predictable and where nothing the operators did could really alter things. Management would then get down to dealing with the system, defining when a call was to be referred to a specialist and developing procedures which would ensure that customer satisfaction was the prime criterion of success, yet also having regard to the need to minimise costs.

The plotting of information would also reveal where special or individual causes were responsible for variations, such as frequent spikes on the chart well outside the generally stable system, or someone whose individual chart was not in statistical control. These would indicate the the operator was in need of some special help or training or in extreme cases not suitable for this kind of work. Experience shows, however, that this is a minority of cases and that the system is the key cause of variations.

VARIATION A KEY MANAGEMENT ISSUE

The title of this chapter may have created an expectation of a study of statistical process control. 'Variations' in a heading doesn't look as if it is going to get to the heart of management practice. Yet in fact it has already had us traversing a wide range of examples of how to transform the working of a company.

I was puzzled when I first heard that the key to the Deming philosophy was 'variation'. But if you think about it you can say that this is all that management is about. It is about reducing unwanted change and ensuring beneficial change. This goes well beyond variations on a statistical control chart, proper use of which, however, will help the change processes in the wider sense.

Managers have to enable those they lead, producers of goods and providers of services, to maintain the standards which the customer depends on. Simultaneously they have to create systems which will enable improvements to be made to meet needs which the customer may not yet be aware of.

Reducing unwanted change is reflected in attention given to getting rid of special causes shown up on statistical control charts. When we have done that and our activity is in statistical control or stable state we still have to be sure that our new limits enable the employees to conform to customer requirements. We then go beyond this to deal with consistent and predictable variations which do not disturb the customer but signal an opportunity for improvement. This is the philosophy of *kaizen* or continuous improvement. (See chapter 1.)

If we recognise that change is essential to business success, then we should not be surprised that an apparently boring subject like variation is also central to competitive advantage.

LEADERSHIP NOT SUPERVISION

This is the substance of the seventh of Deming's 14 points. It links with the twin division of variations. The principal job of managers is *not* control, making sure that workers do what they have been empowered to do. That is up to the workers themselves, especially with help from their fellow team members. In the main the operators inspect their own work and deal with many of the special causes of variation, though some will require managerial attention.

A major role of management lies in the area of common causes of variation. These provide opportunities for improvement to the systems within which everyone else works.

As illustrated in the previous chapter, Juran saw the main task of management as breakthrough – 'change, a dynamic, decisive movement to new, higher levels of performance'.

Improvement can come through closer adherence to procedures. Juran gives an example of filling customer's orders within seven days. Factors such as blunders, shortcuts, gambles, failure to record correctly or forgetfulness may prolong the period to nine days. These are special causes which can be put right by getting back to the procedures.

But if someone comes up with a new approach based on a new concept or new machinery or procedures there may be a radical improvement down to under two days. This is changing the system; it is the area where quantum leaps are made, but even these build on the incremental steps taken at all levels within the enterprise.

These breakthrough activities should be at the top of managerial priority lists. While management are nagging the operators or getting involved in apportioning blame, they are not paying attention to the areas where they make their real contribution. While they are inducing fear in the operators, they are not harnessing their talents to help in the significant breakthroughs.

Quality a holistic issue

The theme of variation and failure to distinguish between those variations which are within the control of the operator and those which require management attention is a good illustration of the way in which quality issues lie at the root of many company problems and opportunities.

When variation is not understood, statistical information is misinterpreted. This results in a bad effect on people's morale, a misdirection of corrective effort and a misapplication of managerial contribution.

Thus a chapter which aimed at dealing with the statistical issue of variation in achieving quality standards has found itself involved in the whole range of issues by which a company succeeds or fails, nearly all of which concern how you treat people. Give people a sound system and appropriate training and generally they will deliver the goods or services at a quality which meets or exceeds the customer's expectations.

4. Everybody on Board

As we have seen, whatever you talk about when dealing with quality it will always come back to people. In the previous chapter an unpromising subject like statistical variation led us back to people. The majority of the errors and defects stem from the system, yet it's often the operators who get blamed. Only management, however, can change the system. The workforce can point out what needs doing and how, but they haven't the authority to change work flow, supplier arrangements, maintenance schedules, procedures and rules.

This chapter maintains that one of the keys to quality is to empower and encourage people to give input from their knowledge and experience. It is they who actually do the job and know all the idiosyncrasies of the system. They know the weaknesses of machines, the phone responses of customers; it is they who have to wrestle with cryptic instructions or complex computer forms. They are the people to consult if you really want to do a good quality job.

THE LEGACY OF TAYLOR

Instead, companies all over the world are still living in the shadow of Frederick Winslow Taylor. About a hundred years ago he saw the poverty of the workers and the back-breaking effort which had to go into getting such a poor return. He also saw that it meant a poor return to the owners. So he came up with 'scientific management', intending it to benefit both parties.

Jobs would be carefully analysed and broken down into the

minutest of their component parts. A worker would then concentrate on one particular function which became quicker and easier to perform. Taylor genuinely cared about the workers. They would have an easier life and earn more money, while the bosses would have higher productivity.

But there was a price to pay. Workers were not supposed to think about their work. Thinking workers were not time-efficient. Let specialists, called managers and engineers, do the thinking. Let the workers park their brains at the factory gate. This was efficiency.

Initially the workers and management were pleased, but in due course soul-destroying repetition took over from the pride of workmanship, which even the least skilled jobs had required in former days. Interest and sense of responsibility waned and the workers became cyphers with no real interest in their jobs.

Bosses manipulated the numbers quite frequently, when they saw wages rise as workers became more skilled and efficient. The rates would change and so new pressures were introduced to encourage faster work for the same reward. Workers responded by developing norms well below their capacity (and woe betide any colleague who exceeded these). Malicious compliance grew as operators learned to beat the system, while appearing to apply it.

The well-meaning efforts of Taylor gave rise to many decades of confrontation and disharmony between the workforce and management. Mistrust and suspicion prevailed between the parties. 'Labour' had no incentive to feel any pride in the product or service or any sense of ownership in the job or organisation.

REVERSING TAYLORISM

Total quality management seeks to reverse all this, by restoring to people a sense of responsibility for what they do and giving them the opportunity to contribute to improving performance, whatever their level.

As Juran points out (1989), quality requires the participation of all employees. They need to become artisans again. Jobs need redesigning to make this possible. The Taylor system was, in Juran's view, based on the low level of education of the workforce:

The subsequent rise in educational levels has made that premise obsolete. It is now feasible to increase the delegation to the workforce, provided that the jobs are redesigned so as to make it possible for the workforce to accept the delegation.

He comments that under the Taylor system the 'experience and creativity of the workforce were major unemployed assets of the companies'.

PRIDE OF WORKMANSHIP

A number of Deming's 14 points (discussed in chapter 2) are in the same vein.

Number twelve for example:

Remove barriers that rob the hourly worker of his right to pride of workmanship.

Pride of workmanship means that when variations are of the common cause type and the system needs to be changed by management, the operators are part of the process of change. They are the true experts, whose opinion is recognised as worthwhile and whose insights are based on close observation. They have learned over many years 'through the job' and in partnership with the specialists they can form an unassailable team.

Pride of workmanship means accountability and responsibility in a real sense; operators should be held accountable, when they have the tools, the scope and the authority without which accountablility is a mockery. Blaming people for variations which are outside their control completely fails to understand accountability. The avoidance of this is one of the reasons why understanding variations is of such significance to the managing of a business.

The recognition of every worker as part of the decision-making team is fundamental to total quality. An asset long neglected, the worker is now seen as essential to competitive advantage. Where this is so the workforce are empowered, self-managing and given tools for thought and action. They know they can make a difference. They are expected to contribute to innovation and improvement; making suggestions is part of their job.

This is the real world

No doubt some managers will feel cynical about this perspective. When I have discussed it with some of the old school I have been told to get my feet on the ground and that 'in the real world' it is just not like that.

'In the real world' is one of those killer phrases used to stultify rational debate. It is all too easy to be driven into a corner by them, because they are uttered with such confidence. That is why I am glad I was able to visit so many companies and see the success of these more enlightened attitudes.

In fact Martin Wibberley of Bosch in Cardiff has banned the words 'unskilled' and 'semi skilled' from the company vocabulary as an affront to the intelligence of the workforce. (See chapter 18.)

This attitude can and does work, but it means a change in managerial thinking, a new respect for all employees as colleagues and a flight from the 'us and them' mentality. It means this on both sides; when management begin to change, the operators must try to submerge their understandable mistrust, and the managers must prove themselves worthy of trust.

This isn't soft talk, nor is getting people to work together a soft skill. It all relates to hard necessity, often to company survival. But it can happen and is happening 'in the real world'.

Single status

This jibe about the need to live in the real world was doubtless frequent in the days when single status or common conditions of service were first discussed. The other word used – 'harmonisation' – is particularly expressive, fitting into the wider aims of establishing a workforce who work in unity for common objectives.

Yet single status or harmonisation is a fact of life in many companies now. The absence of special parking places for top management may seem a nuisance to a busy chief executive arriving at noon after external meetings all morning; but is it any less of a nuisance to the worker who comes in at shift change time and has to park far away? Both can use the walking time for the improvement of their health and a bit of thinking!

In the single status companies I visited I found no irritation on the part of senior management. Eating in the same place as everyone else has provided opportunity for gaining a sense of greater involvement with the workforce. Bosses are seen as ordinary people after all. The distance between levels of staff is bridged, and cohesion encouraged.

Companies I visited often had identical pension and private insurance schemes for all staff. In one large company the managers all transferred into a less prestigious scheme so that everyone could have the same terms. The company driver, no longer regarded as just the MD's chauffeur, told me of this with great pleasure.

This single status approach has no direct bearing on quality, but it is a quality approach in its own right. It contributes to the ethos of an organisation where pride in workmanship and ownership of results prevail.

SELF-INSPECTION

The reversal of Taylorism by total quality approaches is seen where the workforce inspect quality as part of their job rather than have products or services inspected externally at a later stage. In the case of service industries the latter is all too often after customers have experienced poor quality treatment.

Deming's third point is to cease to be dependent on mass inspection to achieve quality. Quality should be built into the product or service in the first instance. This is a people issue, as we shall see in chapter 12 when we look at the work of the teams in Rothmans where every worker is involved in recording delays and their causes subsequent study.

At Stanbridge Precision Turned Parts everyone understands the statistical control charts on the visual display units. When what appears to be a special cause begins to emerge, eager discussion takes place on whether to stop immediately and put things right or wait and see if a little more time will produce self-correction. (See chapter 11.)

Similarly, workers at the Seaham Harbour Dock Company know when to call in their falconer to stop the contamination of stored products by seagulls. (See chapter 15).

DRIVE OUT FEAR

This is the eighth of Deming's 14 points. Crosby is on the same wavelength, stressing involvement of all work groups in corrective action and never-ending improvement which cannot happen in an atmosphere of fear. Juran also believes that the workforce must be fully informed on the purposes of all action. They must be involved in everything from quality planning to quality control to quality improvement (the 'Juran trilogy').

Deming has the air of an evangelist when he calls upon managers to 'drive out fear'. The man who started out as a statistician makes the most stirring calls to humanistic action, albeit for very practical business reasons.

In his classic *Out of the Crisis* he gives many quotations from people about their jobs in companies where total quality does not predominate. There are fears that the next annual rating may not provide a needed 'raise'; fears of being held guilty of treason if they dare to put forward an idea; fear to shut down production on a line for an essential overhaul, because the production figures would suffer. This last concern contrasts strikingly with those companies, many of them Japanese, which permit *any* worker to stop the line rather than go on turning out a defective product.

Then there is fear of not having an answer for the boss, when the reason for some difficulty is demanded; fear to admit a mistake; fear to ask the reasons for a decision; fear of not reaching the daily quota; fear of contributing to a team effort, because someone else may get the credit and the rating; fear of reporting a problem, because it might mean temporary shutdown of equipment.

There are still managers who do not understand that people need to be respected. If you accept the principle of democracy no person has the right to despise or bully another just because he or she has a different level of decision making authority. Some managers still believe that the only way to get workers to produce is to introduce some sense of fear.

Even Juran believes that fear can bring out the best in people in certain circumstances. So say Macdonald and Piggott – they also have a sly dig at Deming who can create fear at his seminars when he berates managers who ask what he considers are silly questions!

SLOGANISING

Juran is strongly against 'campaigns to motivate the company's workforce to solve the company's quality problems by doing perfect work'. As he sees it, depending on motivation by slogans is management abdication unless they agree 'specific goals, establish specific plans to meet these goals or provide the needed resources'. Blaming operators for poor quality work is pointless in the absence of effective systems, and slogans can make no difference.

Philip Crosby cannot be held responsible for all the sloganising which follows in the wake of his campaigns. However his razzamatazz – with special zero-defects days and people signing the pledge to strive for zero defects – acknowledges insufficiently the distinction between the two types of variation studied in the previous chapter. (Though ICL seemed to make it work as we show in chapter 17.)

'Eliminating slogans, exhortations and targets for the work force' is the tenth of the Deming points. This flows from the two types of variation. If the problem is systemic, what is the use of urging the workforce to do better without changing the system? It will only infuriate them or make them cynical.

Deming quotes one such slogan 'Your work is your self-portrait. Would you sign it?' He counters: 'No, not when you give me a defective canvas to work with, paint not suited to the job, worn out brushes.' Again, we are being directed to an understanding of the true role of the manager to provide the framework in which people can produce quality goods and services.

Posters are mentioned such as 'Getting better together', when no one listens to worker suggestions or invites them to full participation in the journey toward total quality.

Even 'Do it right first time,' while excellent as the aim of the company as a total team, is useless when directed just at operators, who are wrongly assumed to be the cause of the problems. It is just as likely that they are being provided with faulty material or unreliable machinery. Deming is emphatic that such posters are being largely directed at the wrong people. They do nothing to transform attitudes; in fact they demotivate.

Quotas and targets similarly can be impediments to progress. They frequently require from people results over which they have little or no control.

TRAINING FOR RESPONSIBILITY

This is a key issue in enabling people to move out of the Taylor mode into the acceptance of responsibility and involvement in the achievements of their organisation.

It is training which will enable the workforce to contribute to the process of continuous improvement. Training will enable them to deal with the variations that lie within their range of authority, to deal with simple special causes and then go on to help both their team and their manager to work out what needs to be done.

A variety of statistical tools need to be understood and utilised at all levels of the company. These make participation, ownership of the job and pride in workmanship feasible. I found it quite humbling in my early visits to British companies to have people with little formal education explain what they were working on in complex statistical terms that were fast losing me. I was thus challenged to gain at least some working understanding.

This kind of training gives people pride in their own abilities; it enhances their own self-confidence and cultivates teams with individual strengths that complement each other.

Deming's sixth point is a simple one: 'institute training on the job'. I prefer the term 'learning through the job'. Learning goes deeper than training; 'through the job' takes the learning right into the heart of the work that is being accomplished.

'Sitting by Nellie' is a UK term for the haphazard kind of training where you sit by someone else and eventually get the hang of things. It is still widely practised. A more formal kind of training takes time and means temporary loss of production. Short-term thinking doesn't like that; although the temporary loss will be recouped many times over.

Another problem with such unstructured training is that it can instil bad habits. Short cuts may be taught to achieve quotas at the expense of quality. Customer satisfaction and competitive edge are not likely to get uniformly stressed in a company which won't spend money and time on formal training.

EDUCATION AND LIFE-LONG LEARNING

Training deals with skills, but it must go beyond just how to perform a particular operation. It must be set in context. It must enable the learner to know why activities are undertaken and what customer expectations are. Only then can the trainee contribute to quality work.

Deming's thirteenth point, in one of its versions, runs: 'Institute a vigorous programme of education and self-improvement.' Education goes beyond training and seeks to bring out people's potential. Education is linked with a Latin word which means to 'lead out'. Training, on the other hand, is derived from an old French word meaning to 'drag behind in an orderly fashion'.

However, development is probably the most comprehensive word. It too comes from the old French and originally meant 'to unwrap, so as to reveal the germ' of something. It is this wider end of the learning process that Deming has in mind. He is looking for the growth of a workforce who can respond to new things; who can be creative, thoughtful and innovative. The human asset is one which does not depreciate, but rather appreciates in value as it matures.

During my visits to British companies, I was impressed with the work at Lucas where any employee can be supported to learn anything related to work. If it is related to the current job it is regarded as part of the company's normal responsibility. Anything else, so long it has some connection with work, is supported. There has been a high take up. The company rationale is that it needs an adaptable, flexible workforce who will be able to cope with whatever the future may bring forth. Minds which are exercised over a wide range of subjects and skills are more likely to meet that future in a way which optimises its potential.

Some skills being acquired in Lucas are in the realm of foreign languages, so that with closer links with the rest of Europe, people will be ready to seize business opportunities. Wider global opportunities are envisaged too, for example a group of people undertook to learn Japanese so that they could get closer to Japanese people with whom they were already doing business.

Rover and Ford are also investing in people in ways which encourage their overall learning, rather than just the attainment of job-related skills.

When Deming speaks of self-improvement he is also applying to the individual the philosopy implicit in *kaizen* or continuous improvement. It is up to everyone never to be content with what they know and what they can do. There is always more. This is a life quality approach which will have untold repercussions on the quality of life at work and the outcomes of that work.

There is no doubt, from the issues we have looked at in this chapter, that quality is fundamentally about developing people's skills and potential. It concerns the human contribution, which, aided by machines, statistics, procedures and structures, nevertheless goes beyond them. Quality is the most human of subjects. It rests on people; it is defined by people and it can delight people, both customers and providers.

5. Beware of Management by Numbers Only

Let us admit straight away that numbers do matter. Costs have to be controlled, a company has to know what it is producing, how much and of what quality. It has legal obligations which involve numbers. But this is different from managing by numbers only. This chapter will address this issue.

The eleventh of Deming's 14 points advocates leadership in place of quotas on the factory floor, and the elimination of management by objectives, by numbers, by numerical goals.

This has created a good deal of controversy, causing some to say the Deming should stick to his statistics and not meddle in management. It must nevertheless be remembered that statistics led him into managerial considerations, as indeed it did for Juran.

QUOTAS – ENEMIES OF QUALITY

The reasons for objecting to managing by visible numbers lie in several directions.

Take quotas first. They usually make no distinction between the different kinds of variation, whether they are specific, and controllable by the worker or whether they are systemic and therefore the reponsibility of management.

Many quotas are set quite arbitrarily. A decision taken in the boardroom to double turnover in two years may be the translation of the chairman's optimism into policy. Perhaps it gets pushed through on the basis of fear. One of the board members dares to raise objections of a realistic nature. The chairman responds: 'Not you; I thought when I appointed you that you were going to be entrepreneurial and bold; now you're joining the negative thinkers who can always find a hundred reasons for doing nothing. I expected better of you.'

The board member is young and has family responsibilities which quickly flash before his eyes. So he gives in, the decision is recorded and the pressure to achieve it soon permeates every level of the company with everybody knowing its impossibility, but no one daring to say.

Another way of setting quotas is to take the previous year's figures for some activity and just add a percentage. This too can be meaningless, based on hope, not analysis. MBAs are taught analysis at business schools, and then told to forget it when they get into the 'real world'.

This attitude is prevalent at all levels. Quotas are set on a company-wide basis which take no account of special local circumstances. Rafael Aguayo tells the story of an excellent salesperson who was continually under target. Closer examination revealed that her area included the home base of one of the main competitors. It was always going to underperform by comparison with other areas.

Aguayo and Deming both bring out another folly of quotas. They are often set at the average for the whole factory. It is evident that some people are going to be above them and some below, otherwise it wouldn't be an average. As Aguayo puts it: 'We can't all be above average can we?'

Another negative influence of quotas is that people stop work when they have achieved them, for fear that the quota and the pressure will be increased if they exceed it. If the quota has been based on an average then the effect will be to drive production levels down. Those whose performance was responsible for the high average on which the quota is based now have to perform at the new average level, or suffer the wrath of their peers. They dare not do what they did before. In some companies the abolition of quotas must sound like blasphemy. But it is a good illustration of the fact that when you talk quality you are talking of nothing less than a revolution in the way of doing business. All manner of idols fall.

If the quota is set too high then quality will fly out of the window. Short cuts will be taken; defective material will be passed; self-inspection will be skimped; everything will be ruled by the stampede to get the quota out of the door. How much of it comes back as reject is neither here nor there. The quota has been met.

Deming also berates piecework. People get paid for the number of items they turn out and therefore concentrate on quantity not quality. There is no piecework in Japanese factories.

Quotas, piecework and management by measured objectives are all substitutes for everyone working in teams within stable systems, with a common objective to delight the customer and secure the further success of the company and therefore of their own livelihood.

RATING BY APPRAISALS

Appraisals for ranking, rating and rewarding people are seen as divisive and demotivating by those who share Deming's perspective. Divisive because they focus on individuals rather than teams, the true units of quality performance. Demotivating because they usually fail to enhance people's sense of worth. Someone is told that he or she is slightly below average. Apart from our misgivings about averages, this will be taken as a vote of no confidence and can have a disastrous effect on a person's work.

This kind of approach creates winners and losers and motivates no one. If you are in the top quartile you're a winner. Everyone else is a loser, as Aguayo comments when talking of appraisals for rating and ranking people.

This is probably one of the most opposed parts of the teaching of the quality gurus, particularly of Deming. Many managers believe you have to rank and rate people to keep them motivated. Conferences are run on 'performance management', encouraging individual incentives and bonuses for measured performance. I spoke at one myself and asked the audience of human resource specialists why this term 'performance management' was being hijacked to describe incentive, bonus and other reward schemes aimed at relating people's personal achievements to money and other benefits. Surely all management is performance management, not simply that part which aims to manipulate people to work harder by offering rewards.

The Economist for 18 January 1992 carried an article on Performance Related Pay (PRP) which declared that 'belief in its efficacy is based more on faith than hard evidence'. The Institute of Manpower Studies (IMS) found no correlation between PRP and profit growth. There was doubt whether it motivated people to perform better. It could destroy a collegiate atmosphere.

Some writers actually talk of joy in work as motivational. Consultant Roger Harrison put his reputation on the line with a book subtitled *Love in the Workplace*. However soft this may sound, if you think about it, aren't joy and love what even the most hardbitten of us seek out of life? Our worklife is a big part of life, it cannot be separated from the rest of what we are and what we do, so why shouldn't we find some love and joy at work? I retired once for about three weeks. I wouldn't still be working if there wasn't more to it than monetary reward.

As Herzberg recognised we all need money, but he called it a hygeine factor. Our real kicks come from the content of our work and the fellowship we find with others in carrying it out.

Conventional appraisal systems designed for merit rating deny this in practice. They often administer a different kind of kicks. I remember the near terror with which they were approached by managers in the Pakistan State Manufacturing Industries where I was working in 1986. The basis was mainly an attempt to fix numbers to achievement or lack of achievement. The system was judgmental and destructive of good working relationships, unless your boss was easy-going when it was meaningless anyway. There were a few bosses who approached it positively as an opportunity to aid the development of their staff, but that was not how it was generally seen.

PERSONAL MERIT VERSUS TEAM PERFORMANCE

If you are trying to inspire the whole workforce to work as a team, pull together to achieve quality in product and service, accept the interdependence that goes with that approach and optimise the synergies, how then can you proceed to put them on an individual rack for variations in performance, many of which may be systemic, over which they have no real control?

Henry Neave, director of research of the British Deming Association, has some helpful ideas about this matter of performance appraisal in *The Deming Dimension*. He points out that the term 'appraisal' means different things to different people. According to him Deming uses the term to cover schemes which involve judging and ranking people, ignoring the fact that 'most of the variations in performance come from the system in which people live and work, rather than from the people themselves'.

DEVELOPMENT REVIEW

Regular free, frank discussions, on individual development needs (including where people fit into the team and defining roles and functions) are seen as useful by Neave and Deming. My own experience would echo that view. I wrote a manual on how to carry out that kind of developmental review for the Pakistan Institute of Management and seven State Manufacturing Industries. When I managed the Training School of Compower, the British Coal Board's Computer Company, the staff used to put me under pressure to get on with the development discussions because they found them helpful. So I would go along with Henry Neave's perspective.

JUDGMENTAL REVIEW

What is being opposed as detrimental to quality, co-operation and teamwork is the judgmental review. This doesn't mean that there is no place for discipline, but if there is a need for rebuke it should be dealt with straight away and not saved up for an annual reprimand.

Neave and Deming quote Lao Tze who 26 centuries ago said: 'Reward for merit brings strife and contention.' In merit rating of people, because there will be different views of what they can be held responsible for, many will leave the interview smarting under a sense of injustice. The situation will not be one where everyone wins and pulls together. The danger is that everyone will look after their own interests, to get a good rating. The needs of the group and even of the company as a whole will be secondary.

Performance appraisal for rating people will smother innovation, because innovation is risky. People will tend to get rewarded for conforming, for pleasing the boss, rather than for sticking their necks out in support of what they see as best for the enterprise. Much of the judgement will be on short term criteria. And none of it really examines the circumstances under which the performance varied. Attempts to explain that the system caused the variation will be considered excuse making.

Similarly the interdependences without which nothing can be achieved will not normally get a fair hearing. Barriers between departments can be a potent preventer of achievement. They are part of the system which impedes results. The usual response to pointing this out is that it is part of your job to be political and exercise influence where you have no authority; you just haven't been good enough at that part of your job. You haven't been tough enough, persuasive enough, farsighted enough, quick enough on your feet. How does any of this help the growth of teamwork and a company which is united in the aim of delighting customers with quality in the terms that they define?

GOAL SETTING

We have already seen that quotas are based on false premises which ignore the fact that if the systems set up by management are not sound, all the goodwill in the world on the part of the workers will not produce quality goods or services. Looking at goal setting as a whole this fallacy is then compounded by all kinds of absurdities, some of which are now illustrated.

Henry Neave tells of a nuclear plant which averaged 12 serious accidents a year. The edict came one year from top management that the rate was to be halved this year! (In other words we had 12 accidents last year; this year we plan to have only six.)

It is this kind of thing that fuels Crosby's zero defects campaign. He asks how you can plan to have defects. There is nothing wrong with his view that you can't plan to have any defects at all, that the only acceptable standard is zero; but some distinction between sources of imperfection needs to be made, otherwise you are getting people to pledge what does not lie within their power to deliver. It also has to be borne in mind that Crosby defines a defect as something which does not conform to customer requirements. He is not talking of perfection.

Aguayo tells the story of a personnel director who was given two significant goals: to reduce employee turnover and increase the use of training. She noticed that the least capable people and those with the least education stayed the longest, because they couldn't easily get other jobs. So she recruited people with minimum education and put them all through the training two or three times. The chairman commended her for meeting both her goals. But how much damage had she done to the company?

Aguayo also tells the story of a company which set plant production quotas it just couldn't meet. But there was no escape, so the numbers were faked. This had the effect of making the inventory numbers lower than the records said, every time they were counted. Theft was suspected; as a result a very expensive security system was installed.

Deming tells of a conversation he had with a postal service official who was vexed by the number of mistakes his sorters were making. Deming asked how they were paid. The answer was on the basis of sorting 15,000 pieces of mail a day. Obviously the highway to error-making.

We must all have seen in our business lives the way in which goals are set. I remember in one organisation in which I worked there was a scurry every month to explain the variances from budget. I didn't understand then the folly of the exercise, that we were putting all deviations into the same pot, irrespective of whether they were normal fluctuations of a system in statistical control or more fundamental problems involving the whole system.

How are some of these budgets set? At the the time next year's budgets are being set, someone says: 'I reckon we could increase sales by five per cent next year'. No analysis, just a gut feeling, which either leads to a lot of pressure on everyone or is ignored. If it leads to pressure then this is the way in which quality suffers and customers, the arbiters of quality, don't even get what they want, let alone something better.

SQUEEZING COSTS

Another aspect of the numbers game is that of sqeezing costs to increase profits. It has to be done from time to time, and anyway there must be a limit to what is spent. There is never enough money to do everything we would like to do. There has to be some prioritising of expenditure, but the process of containing costs leads sometimes to very unwise steps.

Companies will change suppliers to the cheapest provider of a particular component. Although it is the cheapest and helps initially to keep costs down, its product may be inferior or not fit in with the rest of the system. Goods then begin to be returned under warranty. The hoped for higher margins are not obtained. The cost of replacing faulty parts involves attention to the whole of the finished article, taking it apart and putting it together again. This far outweighs the cost of doing it right to begin with, using high quality parts, fit for use, as Juran would say.

All this seems so obvious. Why do intelligent, well trained managers ignore these truths? Nothing short of a total revolution in the way we think about and do business will put it right. For this reason it is not enough to set up statistical systems for quality control, to get everyone talking quality and even doing their own inspection. Unless we take a total view of how the business is run at every level and in every function we shall fall well behind our competitors in the market-place.

INCREASING COSTS BY REDUCING QUALITY

We have been giving examples of interfering with financial figures under the illusion we are improving the situation, but all we are doing is sacrificing quality and reputation for apparent short-term gain. Of course it is difficult in times of recession, but even then we don't help ourselves by a reputation for shoddy goods or services. We mortgage the future without improving the present situation.

In any case there is a large cost in not aiming for quality. You have to carry out all these reworks and accompanying support activities, credit notes and telephone discussion or meetings, to say nothing of the diminishing of employee morale as they see the standards slipping.

When you have to rework products they incur cost twice. You pay for the initial manufacture or assembly and then you pay again when the job is repeated. Five per cent reworks at each stage of a process through nine steps means about a third of production is lost. This agrees with the IBM estimate that not doing things right first time accounts for 30 per cent of their products' manufacturing costs.

All this runs counter to the view that quality is expensive and too much attention to it will erode profits. Figure 2.1 suggests the reverse is true.

THE COST OF QUALITY

Crosby has plenty to say about the cost of quality in his various books and his colleges study them in depth. He stresses the need to go beyond treating such costs as just a means of measuring defects on the production line. Knowledge of the cost of quality is a management tool.

He divides the cost of quality into two categories

- The price of nonconformance (PONC).
- The price of conformance (POC).

PONC includes all the costs of doing things wrong. This will include the effort involved in correcting sales orders when they come

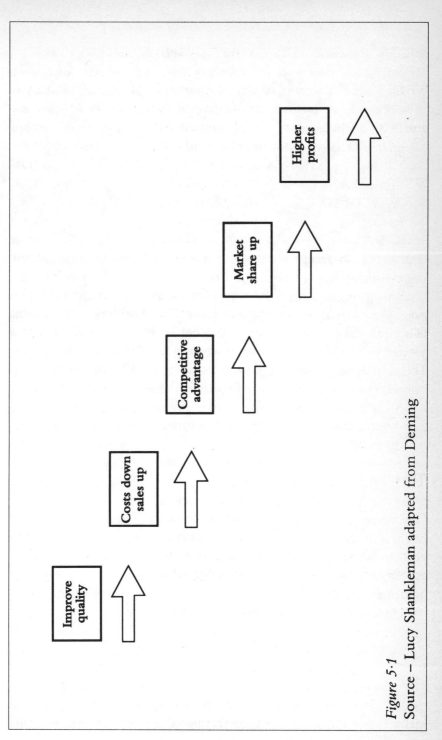

Figure 5·1
Source – Lucy Shankleman adapted from Deming

in from the field staff, sending products to the wrong address, sending out innacurate invoices, giving the wrong discounts, sending out the wrong product and so on – all this in addition to reworks and the non-measurable cost of the disgruntled customer.

POC includes the cost of prevention and appraisal. Crosby summarises the cost of quality as comprising the following:

- Prevention.
- Appraisal.
- Failure.

The first is an acceptable cost, so long as the best method is used. And nothing can better a quality conscious workforce who are continually doing their best to prevent defects occurring and a perceptive management who ensure that the workforce are working within a system which doesn't saddle them with defects beyond their power to prevent. Included in prevention are all the costs of training people in quality procedures and philosophy, of joint activities with suppliers, of preventive maintenance, of studies of process quality, checking drawings and reviewing specifications.

Appraisal is the cost of of conducting tests, inspections and planned evaluations in checking out the suppliers and ensuring that all specifications are in line with the customers' requirements. This includes a study of what the customer said was wanted, how marketing, design and engineering have interpreted this and all the procedures and processes about to be set in motion to meet the requirements. Appraisal should be carried out as close as possible to the point of origin.

Failure costs are those connected with any product or service which does not conform to the customer requirements, such as those we have discussed above. Absolutely everything which fails is involved here, whether it is the output of a machine, a pencil, a voice or a computer.

It is failure which costs the most and which clearly indicates that the price of error is enormous. Crosby recommends the measuring of the failures to bring home the seriousness of the issue. He doesn't mean that there should be a measurement with the type of accuracy needed for the company accounts. If you can measure 80 per cent of the failures, there will be enough to shock everyone into the action they can take and to achieve considerable improvements.

QUALITY ATTITUDES

Treating cost of quality figures as if they were a precise part of the company accounts is to miss the point of the calculations, which is to alert everyone to the need to act within their capacity and authority. The key to success is the creation of a workforce (managers and operators) who are unceasingly aware of the need for quality. Awareness of cost is one of their motivators. If everything done in the company is built on teamwork, trust, and putting the customer first, including the internal customer, with everyone participating and feeling it is their company then the present is likely to be more secure and the future positively rosy.

This has been the experience of Bob Knox, of Stanbridge Precision Turned Parts, whose story I tell in chapter 11. In 1991 he went for the Ford Q1 award and was one of a very few automobile companies to prosper in a recessionary year, even to the point of taking on extra staff. IBC Vehicles were also busy recruiting when so many companies were laying off workers. (See chapter 14.)

And if you do manage to get temporary respite through buying cheaper and inferior supplies, what about the customers who don't complain, but quietly take their business elsewhere, or perhaps not so quietly, telling all their business acquaintances on the way. Various figures are bandied about on this issue, but in general it is reckoned by market researchers that satisfied customers might tell another six or so people about it, but that dissatisfied customers will tell at least another 20.

6. *Teaming up with Customers and Suppliers*

When I said you always come back to people when you talk about quality, I had employees in mind. There would be no employees, however, without customers. Therefore this chapter looks at the relationships between customers and suppliers, recognising that they are internal to an organisation as well as external.

Customers are the reason behind everything that everybody in a company does. This is not exclusive to companies either, as will be demonstrated in chapter 13 when we look at the work of Braintree District Council. The people who live there and pay for the services in one way or another are regarded as customers. They are to be shown respect and given good service.

FACE TO FACE WITH THE CUSTOMER

Whatever the organisation, the customers are part of the production line or service process. This is even true of the end users or final consumers of a product or service.

When Jan Carlzon, boss of the Scandinavian Air Lines (SAS), revived its fortunes in the early 1980s he inspired people with his vision of an upturned hierarchy. The traditional hierarchy is represented by a triangle with the chief executive at the apex and the masses of front line workers at the base. In between are the various ranks of supervisor and manager. Carlzon turned the triangle upside down and said that he and the management were there to support the front line workers. And they in turn were there to support the topmost part of the upturned triangle – the customers.

The customers were the reason for everything. Their loyalty to SAS depended on the thousands of 'moments of truth' when the front line employees, cabin staff, check-in people, waiters and waitresses, porters, information providers and sweepers were face to face with their public. These employees had the power to make the public feel good about flying with SAS. Top and other senior management had few of these moments of truth. Their job was to provide the front liners with the framework within which they could offer quality service and make the end users feel part of a family.

This is an approach which has spread through many companies. British Airways has had great success with its own customer care programme, where everyone was trained to see the customer as their personal responsibility. No one could say: 'I don't know; it's not my job'. It was up to everyone to know enough to be able to guide people to the information they required. Training was provided to make this possible.

This all makes good sense as well as adding pleasure to doing a job. The joy of life is largely about relationships. If you can have satisfying relationships at work with colleagues and customers, then a large chunk of your waking hours is going to be filled with enjoyment. More times than not you will arrive at work with a sense of anticipation rather than reluctance. There will be some personal fulfilment awaiting you.

I am in the real world and millions of people can echo these sentiments. Unfortunately many more cannot. It is they who do not have the opportunity to provide the quality goods and services which make work worthwhile and customers happy.

QUALITY IMPLICIT IN SUPPLY AND DEMAND

The whole of business is about supply and demand. I have something you want. You have something I want. I supply you with the product or service and you provide me with money in return. If you make no demand there is no exchange. Nothing happens. If what you have requested doesn't materialise or arrives in a form which varies from your request, you will be unhappy and will demand redress or vow never to come to me again. This view doesn't have to be graced with the description 'economics'. It's just plain common sense. Yet how many companies neglect it, eager to get their part of the exchange, but wanting to give as little as possible in return.

Quality is an attitude of mind, which actually believes that you are entitled to what you have asked for, even if your asking is the impersonal picking up of something that takes your fancy in a supermarket.

You could say that providing quality to the customer is an ethical issue. It might even be elevated to a moral issue. This has been done in Mary Kay Cosmetics. Wherever you go in that organisation you will see the golden rule displayed: 'Do to others as you would have them do to you'.

Providing quality is good business too. In fact you can say it is the foundation of business, even if sometimes it has to be enforced by law. Trust, however, is a better route than law enforcement. The best companies are those where self-interest and high principles coincide. The meeting point is quality.

EVERYONE'S GOT A CUSTOMER

In many business activities most of the workers never see the end user. In this sense they never meet the customer and may find it difficult to be motivated by the thought of serving this unknown, invisible ultimate employer. They are toiling in factories, perhaps on quite a small part of the operation and it would take a rare gift of imagination to be able to think 'customer' in those circumstances.

That's where a new piece of 'imagineering' has come in over the last few years. Imagineering is where imagination is used to engineer a new vision and new consequences. You envision where you want to be and then engineer the steps needed to get there. The vision is of a workforce obsessed with the idea of satisfying and even delighting the customer by providing and exceeding expectations.

Nevertheless some practical steps have to be interposed if this vision is to be fulfilled.

The customer/supplier chain concept does just this. Operators don't have to make the leap from their own work straight to the unseen end user. Everyone who does any kind of productive work has someone who needs the result of their labours. That someone is a customer who can be seen, spoken to and negotiated with. Such a customer can complain directly if your work cannot be used or creates difficulties by being shoddy or late. Such customers can also say thank you directly when you have gone out of your way to make life easier, by the way you have provided what they need.

Most of these customers will be internal – the next in line. As Richard Schonberger (1990) puts it they are 'a group of people connected by work flow'. If people in an enterprise recognise the need to pass on the best possible product or service to the next in line then a spirit of teamwork and co-operation can be established across functional barriers. Teams of teams are established. And work becomes worthwhile.

I could be worried at this stage that readers might think I was going over the top, but for one factor which I describe later on in this book. A new way of working or a return to an old one where people were dependent on each other as they ran the life of the village. I've seen it with my own eyes. It makes me optimistic about the future.

THE CUSTOMER CHAIN

Thus we see that in a manufacturing plant there is a whole chain of customers, needing the results of others' work. Materials come in (there the plant is the external customer of a supplier). The Stores Department checks them and stores them in the most appropriate place, to suit their immediate customer, the driver of the fork lift truck. This will be crucial if they are working on a 'just-in-time' basis, as there will be no time to be lost; the fork lift driver's customer will be waiting to take the first steps towards transforming the raw material into the product to be bought by the ultimate customer.

The recipients of the material may be people who transfer the material into a hopper and thence on to a conveyor belt. A good system is essential, and with careful placing by the fork lift driver everything is running smoothly – more satisfied customers. In spite of automation there are still people who have to observe and control some parts of each operation.

In seeking to please their colleagues, people are likely to make each step of the process a quality one. Every one of, say, 20 steps in a process, from raw material to finished product, is treated in this personal way as between members of one team composed of many interlocking teams. What is the result? Twenty infusions of quality which, joined together by the chain of customers produce a final quality product, which will at least satisfy and at most delight the external customer. It is easier to build in quality a step at a time between people who are known to each other, than to engage in mere propaganda, exhorting workers to think of the customer. The ultimate customer is not very real to them, but their colleagues are.

CUSTOMER AS VISIBLE REALITY

It's a bit like the Christian idea that asks how you can love God whom you can't see if you don't love your brother whom you can? How can you serve up quality to the external customer whom you can't see, if you don't first serve it up to your colleague, next in line, whom you can see?

The customer chain concept turns quality into a personal reality for everyone. It is also a distinct improvement on the old hierarchical approach. Under this the only real customers anyone had were bosses. You worked to provide them with their requirements. Quality was what they didn't shout at you about. It is quite a shift to think of the most important customer as the one who receives the fruit of your labours, whose own work you are helping or hindering.

Henry Neave shows how this has an effect on organisational structure. Vertical reporting lines matter less and horizontal connecting lines matter more. Information and communication increasingly follow these horizontal lines and enable ideas for improvement to flow. The internal customer/supplier concept helps to produce an organic structure, created by relationships which already exist rather than by someone drawing organisation charts to represent formal authority.

THE END CUSTOMER

Ultimately this customer stream (to vary the analogy) flows beyond the company and reaches the people who created the demand and who are going to do the paying. These are the external customers. They may consist of several layers, or form different links of a chain. There may be wholesalers, then retailers, before we get to the final consumer who drives away with the product to enjoy it at home. Even in the home the children may really be the ultimate customers. They will be delighted by the present their parents have bought them. Or they may treat the house to wails of disappointment if the item breaks down the first time it is used.

Increasingly it is being felt, as we saw from Jan Carlzon, that the customer should figure at the top of the company hierarchy, and be regarded as part of the family.

Deming says that the consumer is the most important part of the production line, ranking higher than the supplier, vital though good supplier relationships are. He considers that the consumer is more important than the raw material. It is easier to replace the supplier, even though long-term relationships are preferred, than it is to find a new consumer, or reclaim one you have lost.

THE SUPPLIER CHAIN

The previous paragraph is not belittling the role of the supplier. It is simply emphasising the overriding primacy of the customer. Nonetheless, without a sound relationship with suppliers quality will not be achieved. The supplier is part of the production line, too.

The supplier chain is the customer chain in reverse. Every customer needs a supplier. Every customer needs to be able to communicate to the supplier in an unequivocal way what is required and expected. If the two can co-operate there is some chance that expectations and needs will be met. If each customer in the chain receives from each supplier inputs which meet or exceed expectations then the end user will receive a high quality end product.

Most of these suppliers are inside the company, but there are also external suppliers. If the quality of their input is poor then the whole chain will suffer and the ultimate consumer will have grounds for complaint. In its progress through the chain there will be a cumulative effect. Things will get worse; errors and defects will be compounded as efforts are made to correct and compensate for elements which do not truly fit.

The traditional way of ensuring that the external supplier sent in quality materials was mass inspection, by either a high level of sampling or total inspection. This is costly in time and money and still may not identify everything which is unsatisfactory. Some of the figures quoted for faulty incoming material are disturbing indeed. Steel delivered to automobile manufacturers of which eight per cent had to be rejected is one example.

PART OF THE FAMILY

In recent years many companies have made considerable efforts to make their external suppliers 'part of the family'. Instead of playing one off against another and selecting them on the basis of price tag alone, they enter into alliance with them. They jointly work out what is needed and what standards are to be applied. This is not a soft option. There can still be demanding standards and some tough talking when these are not met. At least, though, the suppliers know where they stand. They do not feel that the sword of Damocles is hanging over their head all the time, so that if a cheaper supplier is found they will be cut off from a significant part of their revenue. In return they make sure they they conform to their customer's requirement, ensure it is fit for use and even able to delight.

Marks and Spencer have had this kind of close relationship with suppliers for years. They are rigorous in their demands, but in exchange the suppliers have a sense of security.

I visited a Northern Foods factory in Grantham, which is almost totally devoted to providing Marks and Spencer with convenience foods. The long arm of Marks and Spencer reaches right into the levels of hygeine required so that the purchasers in the stores can have every confidence that the products are safe. There had to be two changes of protective clothing during my visit, depending on the nature of the operation. It is absolutely essential to keep out harmful bacteria. All these precautions were agreed between the contracting parties. The opportunity for taking short cuts was non-existent. The staff accepted this and there was no sense of being oppressed by a discipline imposed by a powerful customer.

This kind of relationship also enables the contracting supplier to invest in plant and equipment with a sense of confidence. Employment is secure. All stakeholders benefit. Quality lies at the heart of managing for excellence; it affects every part of all companies in the chain and benefits the local community. The customer organisations no doubt drive hard bargains, but their main criterion is not price. It is uniformity and reliability, as required by ever more discriminating end purchasers. This is particularly significant with food where health is at stake.

Stanbridge Precision Turned Parts (chapter 11) is another case in point. In gaining the Ford Q1 award, it accepted the inspection of the Ford engineers who examined everything Stanbridge did, including plans for continuous improvement. If the long arm of Ford reached into the supplier, Stanbridge could also ask questions about what Ford was doing where it affected them. The relationship was co-operative rather than colonial.

PRICE NOT THE PRIME SUPPLIER FACTOR

The fourth of Deming's 14 points concerns sources of supply. He is quite directive about the need to 'end the practice of awarding business on the basis of price tag'. He is all for minimising total cost, but this follows automatically if you buy good materials which live up to their claims. There are no costs of correction or adapting poorly fitting components.

Deming goes as far as recommending a single source for any one product. This builds mutual loyalty and trust, which begets reliability and uniformity. Such long-term relationships keep companies 'on their toes' more effectively than by maintaining an atmosphere of insecurity and uncertainty which will not encourage straight dealing; on the contrary it provides fertile ground for deception and short cuts.

Juran accepts the need for co-operation with suppliers to ensure a good relationship, but prefers to maintain more than one source of supply in order to avoid vulnerability through the failure of one of the suppliers. Even where these gurus vary, their ultimate intent is the same. Certainly neither of them would wish to force the supplier's price down so they could not provide the required quality economically. Thus quality means a more humane way of working than the ruthless drive for low prices which has characterised so much business life.

Deming says 'Price has no meaning without a measure of the quality being purchased'. He considers that American industry and the US Government are being cheated 'by rules which award business to the lowest bidder'. He considers that when purchasing tools and other equipment, organisations should be thinking long term and aiming to minimise net cost per hour or year, not just basing decisions on today's price. It is not only a question of initial cost, but of maintenance and durability.

It is also foolish to keep switching suppliers for temporary price advantage. The fit between suppliers and other elements in the total product inevitably vary between different suppliers. Things are likely to fit less well and rejects may accumulate with frequent switching. Issues such as precise colour match can be significant. Uniformity and reliability are much more likely to be achieved by sticking with a supplier of known capability, who has served well. The overall cost will thus be less than that incurred by chopping and changing all the time for short-term gain, mainly based on initial cost.

Another aspect of the problem of supply is that buyers in many companies have been conditioned to the lowest bid syndrome. Their terms of reference often require that they take this approach. Sometimes the Purchasing Department is not in close enough touch with the needs of the user departments and is operating on different criteria. This is a case of where functional barriers need to be completely broken down. Producing departments are in this case the customers and they look for a quality service from the Purchasing

Department, one which conforms to their requirements, is fit for use and even exceeds expectations. They cannot afford to go for the lowest initial price.

Cost of supplies has to be seen on a holistic basis. What is being purchased has to be seen in the light of its total contribution to the whole process for which it is being used.

The specifications to which a purchasing department works have to make clear all these needs, and the interrelationships of what one supplier provides with other provisions. It is a much more sophisticated process than negotiating on the basis of driving a hard bargain. It is much more in the direction of win-win negotiation, as recommended by Fisher and Ury in *Getting to Yes*.

LONG-TERM RELATIONSHIPS WITH SUPPLIERS

A good long-term relationship means that suppliers understand what the material is being used for. They do not just mechanistically comply with specifications, but understand the subtleties of fit with other elements in the customer's process. It is a sound principle to stay with a supplier who has come to know your business.

Another angle on long-term supplier relationships is the need to have *kaizen* (continuous improvement) within your company matched by a search for continuous improvement by the suppliers, continuous improvement which will mesh with the improvement activity within your company. Ford required a commitment to continuous improvement to be spelt out and accepted by Stanbridge before awarding the Q1 flag of quality. (See chapter 11.)

You would never get this enthusiasm for continuous improvement and the investment in innovation from a supplying company which was in fear of being dropped at any time.

A number of companies who have opted for long-term relationships have also found that the administration is easier, with fewer problems over invoicing and checking.

JOINT PROJECT TEAMS

The most successful way of achieving the integration of the external supplier with a customer company is for them to group their key managers together as a project team. They work out together in some detail what the customer wants to achieve, both at the earliest stages and throughout the design and development work. The designers and engineers from both enterprises serve on this project team along with the sales and purchasing experts, the production specialists and research departments. They all pull together to ensure that something can be produced which enables the customer to make optimum use of what the supplier provides. The fit between the two is worked out jointly. There is partnership.

In addition to the major issues of design and fit, the accompanying features will be mutually agreed. These include tolerances, cleanliness of production and the manner of delivery to a particular part of a specific factory. Nothing is too detailed to be considered. It is because of this need for close harmony that Deming proposes single sourcing. Then the partnership is absolute – there is real knowledge and understanding on both sides.

INTERNAL PARTNERSHIPS

If this concept of partnership between external supplier and customer is important then it surely must be of value within the company. Easier, too, one would have thought, because all parties serve under the same ultimate banner.

The internal politics of a company, however, can be as bitter and divisive as any relationship outside the company. Departments often regard themselves as companies within companies and indeed the financial discipline of being a profit, cost or responsibility centre as well as creating commercial rigour has a downside. It can make departments see things only from their own perspective and not from the angle of serving the company as a whole.

It is clear that if the ultimate customer is to be given quality then internal barriers have to come down and all departments have to be 'singing from the same hymn book'. They will maintain their own perspective as a valid contribution, but they will aim to arrive at the kind of consensus which shows that they really believe that the whole is more important than the parts.

Breaking down departmental barriers

This principle is emphasised in the ninth of Deming's 14 points, which aims to break down barriers between departments. It envisages all employees working as a team. They each try to see the problems that their specific activities may create for the others.

This idea has been around for a few years, yet while writing this book I was involved in conversation at a conference, first with a production person and then separately with a sales manager from the same company. Neither of them had a good word to say of the other department. They both accepted continual feuding as being part of the nature of things that would never alter.

Companies which really commit themselves to the total quality approach certainly seem to be less afflicted by inter-departmental warfare. They are trying to see things from a customer perspective and they set in motion procedures to encourage internal working together. Juran particularly recommends the formation of multi-functional project teams to ensure that all perspectives are taken into account in the design, development, creation and delivery of a product or service.

If barriers are not broken down you can have a range of departments each doing a highly competent job, seen on their own, yet their efforts are not contributing to a coherent whole. Each department is optimising its own activity, but is not understanding how to optimise the whole organisation.

Communicating across functions

If this cross-functional partnership is going to succeed there must be good communication across the divide, which then disappears. An outstanding example of this is where salespersons are seen as the eyes and ears of the company, not just sellers of goods and services. They meet a lot of people and learn a lot about what is going on. There should be procedures for ensuring that this vital information is caught and used. Relatively junior members of the sales force may often come across information strategically important to the whole company. Training must create awareness of such situations and knowledge of how to ensure the company gets the benefit.

No one department or manager, however senior, has the right to make last-minute alterations without consulting everyone who might be affected. Innovation and entrepreneurship are not the partners of inconsistency and changeability.

Japanese companies are notorious for the time they take in trying to use all information to get internal consensus and impatient Westerners are often frustrated by being kept waiting for an answer to their own business proposals while this debate goes on. Once the debate is over, however, the Japanese move with breathtaking speed, because all the dangers have been foreseen, thought through and overcome. Everyone knows how far ahead they get in straight competition with most Western firms, with far fewer delays due to traditional teething troubles.

WHO IS THE CUSTOMER AND WHO IS THE SUPPLIER

One feature of our consideration of the customer/supplier chain is the ambiguity as to who is a supplier and who is a customer. This arises both internally and externally.

I was recently discussing the growth of agencies which arrange the letting of properties for people, who, for example, have to spend a few years in other countries as part of their career development. They become the customers of the agency who finds a suitable tenant. They become landlords and pay for this service. Once the agency has brought landlord and tenant together, then the tenant is the customer of the landlord and pays for a service – a roof over his or her head. Nonetheless the agency needed people to pass to the landlord and although no money exchange occurred between tenant and agency, yet the tenant asked the agency to supply the service of finding a roof, and so in a sense was a customer. It's all very blurred isn't it?

In all cases some kind of exchange is taking place. Each wants something from the other and is prepared to exchange something, money, product or service for it. When you look at business like this then the chain of suppliers and customers being intimately linked makes sense. It is inherent in the relationship. It is the corollary of human interdependence.

Total quality picks this up because it seeks every possible way of ensuring that customers get what is required or something better. That is why this book on total quality seems to be more about management as a whole than about a separate facet called quality. Because the purpose of a business is to get and keep a customer, and quality is a key route for doing this, we therefore have to discuss all aspects of business management in discussing quality. It becomes a focus which makes us do what we should have been doing anyway to survive or grow.

7. *Working in Teams*

At the beginning of this book I offered a definition of management. It is worth revisiting in the light of our study of the practice and theory of managing for quality, with managing shared by all employees. In a sense every employee is a manager. The definition is:

> *Managing is risking yourself in the mobilising of resources and relationships to add value to the enterprise.*

I mentioned that the word 'relationships' didn't feature in my original definition. Its insertion arose from a meeting with David Cox, ex-managing director of Ind Coope Brewery at Burton on Trent. We were discussing the revolution which he had inspired at the brewery in the mid 1980s. I trotted out my definition. He indicated general approval, but said there was something missing. It was the word 'relationships'.

RELATIONSHIPS

Everything we have considered so far supports this definition. There have been relationships between managers and the shop floor, revolutionised by the passing of the old hierarchies and the need for thinking workers. There have been relationships between outside suppliers and the firm, to work together for common objectives. There have been relationships across internal functions breaking down barriers to create an internal chain of suppliers and customers. You could say that quality is all about people's relationships. Defining quality in terms of customer requirements supposes a human relationship.

INTERLOCKING TEAMS

We now pick up the theme of relationships by viewing employees in their mutual relationships as members of teams. We have seen in the chain concept the idea of the whole company as one big team, passing the result of activity on from one to the next in a co-operative way. Now we consider the way in which each step along the way in a quality organisation is the outcome of team effort, rather than of rugged individualism. This is the feature of total quality crucial to its success in mobilising everyone's energies behind the concept.

David Cox attributes the success of the changes at Burton Brewery to the reorganisation of all functions into interlocking teams. The leader of any one team served as a member of another team concerned with the linking of several processes; the leader of that team in turn served in a team with other interlinking functions. The whole organisation looked something like figure 7.1, reproduced with permission from David Cox's book *Exploiting Change*.

Some of the teams, for example the executive team, were at a higher level than others, but the whole point of the figure is that it does not represent a reporting structure, rather one of relationships. Ideas, plans and information about action flow up, down and across to ensure that everything is integrated with one common purpose.

The team leaders serving on another team were what Rensis Likert called 'linking pins'. Even if sometimes it worked out that one team had more influence than another, because it was concerned with a number of functions, the approach was psychologically different from the normal hierarchy. People felt freer to suggest and propose, whatever their formal level. It was a team, a contrast to the normal organisational chart which portrays relatively isolated individuals calling other individuals to account, issuing orders, making decisions and personally deciding how far to consult others.

Wellins, Byham and Wilson in *Empowered Teams* have similar ideas. Members of self-directed operations or line teams are also members of specialist support teams such as the software team, training team or budget team.

Figure 7·1 The full ICBB organisation structure diagram as at Spring 1988

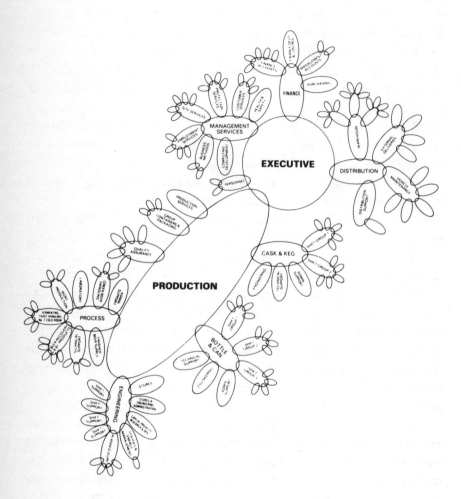

This approach is in line with systems thinking, where everything in a sequence of activity is affected by everything else. Change one aspect and you have to think of all the other aspects of the process which need changing. If every operations team is represented at every other part of the system awareness of the whole system has the opportunity to grow. Tampering with one part of the system without regard to other parts can only create problems.

A related benefit derived from operations or line team members also serving on support teams is that the specialist departments, themselves run on a team basis, are then in touch with the basic producer (line) teams. The operations team member is also able to help line teams understand the support teams' problems. This is one way of implementing the view that 'staff' departments should be consultants to the 'line'.

This is relevant to human resource management departments. It is increasingly recognised that managers have responsibility for developing their 'subordinates' (unacceptable word). The human resource specialist acts as a consultant to the manager, providing coaching and material to enable the manager to fulfil this development function.

Wellins and his colleagues tell of some companies where the training members of operations teams are assisted by also being members of the training teams which provide their operational teams with guidance on available training. In some cases training team representatives will also be involved in the delivery of training within their teams. This certainly ensures that the training is relevant.

The same approach applies to other team representatives. For example the budget team representative on a line team has a special role when budgets are being worked out. This helps the other members of the team to exercise their responsibility, not to abdicate from it.

This approach of line operations team members serving on support teams and bringing back the knowledge and expertise they gain helps to develop the concept of shared leadership, where while there will probably always be team leaders, the distance between them and the rest of the team is an ever diminishing one.

If you accept such a team approach the words 'subordinate' and 'employee' disappear in favour of 'team member' or something more personal and equal. Throughout the world the employees of Mars are called associates.

THE DYNAMICS OF TEAMWORKING

The dynamics of teamworking are entirely different from the standard hierarchy. Everyone has the right to be listened to, even if the experience of leaders may give them added weight, and informal leaders will emerge with persuasive powers. In the end a leader has to decide or take an issue to someone more competent to handle it, but it will not arbitrary or secretive.

And this again *is* the real world. It happened at Burton Brewery and continues years after its establishment. It is the basis of Rothmans, the successes of Nissan and Komatsu in County Durham, Bosch in Cardiff, Toshiba in Plymouth, Holloway Prison in London and Sony in Bridgend. It is universally successful in Japan, but it cannot be attributed merely to a more collective type of culture, because wherever Japanese firms set up in other countries, as in the UK, it works just as well.

Human beings are gregarious and where this is given scope, people rise to the opportunity to fulfil their inner needs in the world of work. In Maslow's hierarchy of needs you don't get to self-actualisation without first experiencing the esteem of others and the sense of belonging.

It can be argued that self-actualisation is not the apex, that it depends on the participation of others. As Martin Buber has shown, there is no 'I' without a 'thou'. George Mead and others of the 'symbolic interactionist' school of thought have demonstrated how the essential 'I' is constructed out of millions of interactions with others. Each day as we interact with others we are slightly changed. I am still I, but an enriched I if I truly allow other influences into my life.

THE PROOF OF THE PUDDING

The proof of the pudding is in the eating. Teamworking was the key to success in every company I visited where total quality was the main concern. When Bedford Commercial Vehicles became IBC Vehicles, the 1,250 employees were organised into 130 teams as outlined in chapter 14. The press shop, body and paint, and final assembly all worked in teams of about 12 people and the administrative support teams were a bit larger. Team leaders were appointed on the basis of ability to weld the groups together and a free flow of ideas was encouraged. After ten years of losses everyone knew their jobs were on the line. They needed to ensure that their teams worked, just to survive.

They learned willingly to monitor their own work. They learned statistical process control, so that the information boards were meaningful to them. They put up their own results in a clear manner. Daily meetings became a feature to create the kind of harmony that would make for a successful day.

Within one year there was a small profit. This reversal of ten years of failure must be partly due to the new way of working.

I was particularly impressed at Nissan Motor Manufacturing in County Durham at the way in which no one seemed in a particular hurry to leave at five o'clock in the afternoon. The department where I was at that time seemed to want to clear up outstanding matters, so that they could start with a clear run in the morning. There was none of the traditional stampede for the door. Doug Lorraine, responsible for training, suggested that a sense of working for the team involved everyone supporting everyone else. This was particularly noticeable at eight o'clock every morning. For about ten minutes, no one appeared to be doing any work. They were all at their team meetings. That was work and got the day started well.

An interesting by-product of these Nissan meetings was that people hardly ever arrived late. That would let the team down and make the latecomer open to peer criticism. That wasn't the purpose, but it illustrates the power of teamworking. It achieves what exhortations from foremen and even pay docking never could.

SELF-DIRECTED WORK TEAMS

The key feature of the teams set up in pursuance of quality is that they are self-managing – self-directed. This doesn't mean that they are leaderless – far from it – but the role of leaders is to elicit their talent and weave together their ideas and energies to achieve what mere orders never could.

The Tom Peters video *Leadership Alliance* illustrates self-managed teams at work. The firm is Johnsonville Foods, a Wisconsin sausage company. Teams of about eight people have their own budgets and authority to work out best how to do their jobs. They even recruit new members of the team, choosing those with qualities favourable to co-operation. The subtleties of team dynamics have to be maintained in spite of personnel changes.

Wellins, Byham and Wilson offer an excellent definition of self directed teams in their book, *Empowered Teams*:

> *Self-directed work teams are small groups of people empowered to manage themselves and the work they do on a day to day basis. They are different from other types of teams or 'teamwork' you may be using in your organisation, in that self-directed teams are formal, permanent organisational structures or units that perform and manage work. Typically members of self-directed work teams not only handle their job responsibilities, but also plan and schedule their work, make production related decisions, take action to solve problems and share leadership responsibilities.*

Such teams are based on the premise that those closest to a job know best how it should be done and are most likely to have ideas on improving performance. There is no better way of securing worker participation in organisational objectives and a sense of owning the work. The achievements of a self-directed work team are likely to jell with those of the whole company. There are checks and balances in the diversity always found in any group. There will be disagreements and variations of perspective, but these are just what you need to ensure that no one voice has all the say, unchecked by alternative possibilities.

THE DIFFERENCE FROM OTHER TEAMS

The distinction between project teams, football teams, quality circles and self-directed work teams is considerable. The normal team pulls together for a common purpose but does not by definition have the shared self-governance of the kind of team we are talking about.

Most of the other teams are of a temporary nature or come together from time to time to perform a particular operation or play a specific game. Take a sports team, say a football team: they are together only during the practices and at the actual match. The self-directed work team is together the whole of its working days for as many shifts as it works in a week, a month and a year. It is responsible for the whole of a segment of the firm's operations. It delivers a completed item or set of items, product or service, to its customer, the next in line or the external customer.

Though at different levels of competence and expertise, they work together daily solving the problems which arise, finding opportunities for continuous improvement, which they carry out where feasible, or alternatively propose to those who can. Particularly significant is the fact that within wider pre-set parameters they plan and control their activities. They do their own scheduling and act in a way contrary to the Taylor division of people into thinkers and workers. They are all thinkers and they are all workers.

One of the outstanding features of the self-managed team is the way in which people learn to do a number of jobs, so that the most effective team is completely multi-skilled. Everyone can perform all the operations. This means that if anyone is unavoidably absent, the show goes on. There is no hold up while a spare person with a particular skill is found to fill the gap.

I saw examples of this at Rothmans (see chapter 12). Two team members went off with the team leader to have discussions about faulty material with a supplier of aluminium foil. The rest of the team covered for them and the work went on. This enables everyone to have a more interesting job, both because there is more variety in what they normally do and because of the opportunity it affords to participate in specific managerial roles. There is no question of a team leader saying: 'You get on with your work and leave me to get on with the managing'.

NEW UNION ATTITUDES

The self-directed team approach also means that the traditional divide between management and 'labour' is eroded. This sometimes causes tension initially, particularly where old style trade unions fear an erosion of their power. They used to claim to be the channel of communication between the workers and management on anything which could remotely be called policy.

There are signs that this attitude is changing. Unions are becoming increasingly interested in pressurising management to pay more attention to the training and development of staff. There is less sole concentration on an annual round of basic wage bargaining and a recognition that many other issues affect worker well-being. There are an increasing number of single union agreements, or where there are several unions, they will often agree to speak to management with one voice. Their members would not forgive them if opportunities to have a plant established in their location were lost through union politics. Progress is sometimes slow, but in my opinion a sense of reality is creeping into union activity. Bill Jordan's words quoted in chapter 20 illustrate this.

IBC Vehicles is an illustration of a company which would not have survived if the union had been intransigent. Instead it recognised the logic of survival and agreed to a non-confrontational approach, which has served everyone well. (See chapter 14.)

Self-directed teamworking is real participation, whereas some of the institutional type of participatory arrangements are more cosmetic than real. The ordinary worker does not get involved in a wider range of responsibility. Sometimes it is a matter of union officials having worker seats on the board or on a second tier of the board. This is proxy participation. It makes little difference to the quality of daily work life. It does little to enhance the self-respect and skill range of the individual worker. Being a responsible member of a self-managing team, however, does. This is direct participation.

Some senior managers who read these words may be doubtful

whether such an approach is feasible in their companies. Perhaps this is the opportunity to display managerial courage, to show belief in staff and skill in advocacy. Self-fulfilling prophecies can be very powerful and if managers show confidence that staff can accept the responsibilities, then in time there is every hope that they will. It does mean a total change from the old 'us and them' attitude. It means persisting in the belief that the new approach can work and resisting the temptation to feel that you are the fount of all wisdom who must always tell others what to do.

FROM INDIVIDUAL TO COLLECTIVE WORKING

Changes in the relationships between management and unions have been signalled in human resource literature as a move from the collective approach to a more individual one (Storey 1989). This reflects the move from a total concentration on collective bargaining. Collective bargaining had egalitarian overtones; it sought to ensure that all the members were treated on a fair basis.

Now individual diversity is being recognised and there is a move toward a recognition of difference so long as the base line is equitable. Also, with growing decentralisation, there is increasing acceptance of the principle of subsidiarity, where everything in business life is handled at the most local level possible. Individuals are counting for more in their own right and are less influenced by unions which in the past claimed the right to speak for them. This is what is meant by human resource writers who speak of the move to a more individual climate in personnel issues, by which they here mean industrial relations issues.

As the individual becomes more liberated, however, there grows a move toward a new form of collectivism in which the individual gains in power, influence and opportunity to contribute, by co-operation and joint activity with colleagues. In that sense I find myself at variance with those who say we have now moved into the era of individual primacy in human resource management. We are in fact on the verge of the new collective era, where people realise the fullness of their individualism by a varied range of joint activity. That way the individual *and* the group win and there need be no conflict between the two concepts.

Of course we are not there yet. The human resource or personnel world is ringing with discussions of performance management, by which (as we saw in chapter 5) is meant a range of ways of rewarding individual achievement, by which people stand out as superior to their fellows, and are rewarded with incentive payments and individual bonuses. We saw how Deming attacks these approaches, regarding them as divisive and destructive of team cohesion. *The Economist* (18.1.92) commented that some see Performance Related Pay (PRP) as 'antithetical to teamwork'.

IN PLACE OF THE RAT RACE

Once you recognise the cohesion of the team and the dependence of every member on all the others, then it is less than fair to pick on some as producing superior performance. They are all 'members one of another' and achieve most by recognising this old biblical concept in the secular world. This doesn't mean a dull uniformity where the unique features of the individual are no longer appreciated. Rather the reverse, when a team says: 'Oh, Fiona can handle that; she's really good at it.'

Of course some will emerge as informal leaders and will coach and counsel their colleagues, thus making life easier for everyone. Coaching and counselling and enabling others to perform more effectively, as Colin O'Neill pointed out at Rothmans (see chapter 12), is the key activity of managing. Wellins and his colleagues report how Beckon, Dickinson and Co. of North Carolina found that when they moved from the traditional supervisory model, the new style team leaders spent 60 per cent of their time in coaching and training, compared with 10 per cent for the previous traditional supervisors.

Some members of the teams with such capacities will tend to go on to formal team leadership themselves. Rothmans makes a point of ensuring that such people receive the training which enables them to apply for the position of team leader when one becomes vacant.

Such team leaders are first among equals. With the hierarchy becoming flatter and middle management having fewer levels, the rat race and ceaseless anxiety about promotion has to diminish.

People have to find their motivation in more interesting work and membership of the working group. It really does mean a transformation of working life.

Quality circles

Quality circles should not be confused with self-directed teams. They were defined by David Hutchins in 1980 on the basis of work by Kaoru Ishikawa and Jeff Beardsley as:

A small group of between three and twelve people who do the same or similar work, voluntarily meeting together regularly for about an hour a week in paid time, usually under the leadership of their own supervisor, and trained to identify, analyse and solve some of the problems in their work, presenting solutions to management, and, where possible, implementing the solutions themselves.

This definition was officially adopted as a standard in the UK by the National Society for Quality Circles (NSQC).

The original idea was that quality circles should be work group based, rather than cross-functional. People should work together on their own areas where they really are the experts. They have been successful in Japan, where they have fitted into the structure of total quality as a whole. Where, as often in the West, they have been seen as quick fixes and unrelated to a total quality programme, they have often fizzled out.

Another factor is that quality circles need to differentiate between special causes of variation and systemic ones. The latter are of more general contribution to improvement, so long as they are not just interfering with something already in statistical control and management will pay serious attention to their recommendations.

In one sense quality circles are extra to the daily work, though closely related to it. They address specific problems and not the whole activity of a work team. In this they vary from the self-directed work team which is totally involved in the whole job. This obviously has value in securing special attention for a specific problem, but is not so deeply embedded in day-to-day work as the self-directed work team.

Quality circles depend very much on the enthusiasm of a few members and if the membership changes substantially they often fade away. This is a pity because they can make a valuable contribution, though they are not the major part of total quality as they have often been perceived. They should spring out of the wider concept as one of a number of mechanisms and techniques for the creation and maintenance of quality.

When Stanbridge Precision Turned Parts (see chapter 11) were applying for the Ford Q1 quality award, they had to provide evidence that they were involved in the quality circle kind of activity. They initiated improvement teams as their version of the quality circle and these run side by side with the ordinary working teams.

WORK LAYOUT

A significant factor in the effectiveness of teamworking in the manufacturing world is the way in which the production facility is laid out. The Western world probably first became aware of this when the press began to report what was going on at Kalmar in Sweden, where Volvo had introduced a totally new way of working.

They moved away from the traditional assembly line where workers performed in endless repetition a few simple operations as the vehicle or other product passed slowly by them. Volvo built a new plant in which the key factor was ferrying around the cars on mechanical carriers to various teams of workers, who would be responsible for a complete aspect of the finished product. They reduced costs by 25 per cent compared with conventional plants and defects were down by 90 per cent.

They have since gone further and the story has been told of how, as a press headline puts it: 'Volvo's new assembly plant has no assembly line'. In place of the assembly line the plant at Uddevalla is based on six workshops which surround a central parts warehouse. The teams in each of the workshops build whole cars. This goes a long way towards meeting Deming's appeal for the restoration pride of workmanship. Such pride is collective as well as individual.

In a smaller way the arrangements at Rothmans are of production equipment surrounding the central facilities, which I have dubbed 'bungalows' (see chapter 12). The physical layout facilitates the team approach. It makes it almost inevitable.

One of the challenges we have to respond to is how to achieve similar improvement to work layout to encourage teamworking in the support facilities and administrative functions.

THE NEED FOR FLEXIBILITY

Another significant contribution from the self-directed team is in meeting the need for flexible production. Stan Davis introduced the term 'mass customisation', where the use of computers enables mass production to cope with highly individualised items. The flick of a few computer keys and the equipment could adjust, for example, from small garments to outsize ones.

A flexible workforce organised in teams which are multi-skilled is obviously more able to respond to the frequent adaptations required by such a process. A mind is required which can cope with frequent changes. The mass assembly line approach had that type of flexibility scrubbed out of it. It was seen as a positive disadvantage. Not so any longer when discriminating customers define quality in terms of ability to meet their specific and often non-standard needs.

As mass customisation gathers momentum, the number of changes to meet customer demand each day will grow. Quality is about responsiveness to customer need and the flexible, multi-skilled, self-directing team is the best organisational form for providing it. People who share in managing their own activities don't need to be told all the time what to do. Thus the frequent adaptations come easily to them and the customer is satisfied. Quality prevails.

COMPETENCIES FOR TEAMWORK

When teams are choosing replacements for people who have moved on, or when any team vacancy is being filled, they need to know which knowledge, skills, attitudes and aptitudes they should be looking for. The catch-all word nowadays is competencies.

There is much debate as to whether personal traits should be included, but in teamwork they are very important. They can be developed, unless someone has a disposition totally at variance with them. Competence theorists would also say that traits can be related to behaviours which can be learned. We enter an area of controversy here, but it is true that we do need what Deming calls operational definitions. They enable us to describe what a suitable team worker will do in various situations.

When selecting new team members many organisations involve the whole team in group discussions and simulations so that there is some opportunity for prospective members to reveal something of themselves in the interpersonal situations which are the essence of team life.

EMPATHY

Whatever it might mean in terms of actual behaviours, I would say that a prime capacity is empathy. This is different from sympathy. Sympathy means feeling at one with another person and in harmony with what he or she is going through. It is a word usually used in connection with some kind of suffering or a cause that is being fought for.

Empathy on the other hand does not imply any agreement, any feeling of unity with or liking for the subject of it. It simply means that you have the ability to stand in the shoes of the other person and imagine what it must feel like to be them. You can then shape your course appropriately and deal with problems with a likelihood of solving them.

If, in the days leading up to World War Two, statesmen had been able to empathise with Hitler, while being totally out of sympathy with his objectives, they might have better understood what to do at an earlier stage, before he had acquired the power to be the menace he became. They would have understood what motivated him, how he could play on the fears of other people. However much they loathed his approach they would have been equipped to handle him. They would not have been surprised or fallen for promises he had no intention of keeping.

The advantage of a real team is that not everyone will have equal amounts of empathy in their make up, but between them they will be able to fathom out the motivation of people with whom they have to deal. Different members of the team may understand different categories of people. There will be a wealth of human understanding which can be utilised for the meeting of problems, which nearly always have a human component.

It is also important for the members of a team to be able to stand in each other's shoes and understand the point of view of others even where they do not share it.

Behaviours which manifest the empathetic quality will include willingness to listen to the ideas of others, to reserve judgment until they have heard the other person out. How can they stand in the other person's shoes unless they do this?

In discussions the empathetic person will be able to offer help, suggestions, advice and ideas of such a character and in such a way that they are likely to be accepted. Similarly they will be more likely to know when to offer help, even though it has not been asked for. When someone offers suggestions they will understand his or her viewpoint and be able to assess the value of the ideas better.

There is a wide range of individual behavioural competencies involved in the single word empathy, but if once it is grasped and its related behaviours learned, it is probably the most crucial of all.

Quality has been the main theme of this chapter. It is about working methods, competencies and relationships which enable a team to provide customers, internal and external, with their unique requirements.

8. Service and Support Quality

Discussion of quality tends to take its cue from manufacturing. This chapter will concentrate on service activity. The principles of quality are largely common to both services and manufacturing as we shall see, though some differences will become apparent.

Measuring quality is more difficult in the service area than in manufacturing. The evidence is likely to be anecdotal rather than based upon scientific measurement. You can measure the acidity of a sample of food; but it is less easy to measure the acidity of a customer's complaint about a store assistant's attitude.

The number of complaints can be catalogued and, more to the point, how rapidly they were dealt with to recapture lost reputation. Writing in the *Financial Times* (10 January 1992), Christopher Lorenz refers to Richard Whitley's book, *The Customer Driven Company*. A plea is made for the adoption of 'measurement and research techniques which are available to transform many intangible aspects of a service into tangibles'. This involves measuring every possible customer and employee attitude and acting on the results.

QUALITY RESPONSE TO DISASTER

Nonetheless, there is nothing to better prompt action on the spot by the one who is face to face with the public. A serious complaint can sometimes be turned into a benefit. Simon Gulliford of Ashridge Management College tells the story of a holiday he and his family had when he was a boy. They stayed at a small hotel in Bournemouth. Dinner was a special occasion. Then the waiter spilt the custard all over father's best suit. Hardly quality service!

Without hesitation, however, the manager fixed father up with a new suit from the best tailor in town, and he had the soiled one properly cleaned. It was all done really fast; the Gullifords were treated like royalty for the rest of their stay.

The manager could have dithered and tried to escape with the minimum correction cost and profuse apologies. At worst he might have blamed the waiter or even tried to make out it was all Mr Gulliford's fault. Instead he made full and quick restitution with a courtesy and concern that created a spirit of friendship. The result was that for years the Gulliford family came to this same hotel at Bournemouth for their holidays. One costly mistake, put right in a costly, but unreserved manner and that manager secured the long-term loyalty of a customer. It recouped the cost many times over.

FACE TO FACE WITH THE CUSTOMER

Failure to provide quality is even more obvious in service industries and support functions than in manufacturing, because the provider is usually in the customer's presence.

As Jan Carlzon has described it, many more of the providers of service experience those 'moments of truth' when they are face to face with the customer. Many more people are now employed in the service industries than in manufacturing, even though manufacturing is still the foundation of prosperity.

We have all experienced examples of bad quality service. I hope too we can remember good service, though with human perversity we are more likely to remember the bad. Or is it perverse? We are paying; so we have a right to expect good service. Sometimes, however, we get that extra 'bit' that really adds to the pleasure. Deming's idea of delighting the customer!

A PERSONAL EXPERIENCE OF DISCRETION NOT EXERCISED

I think back over my own experiences. No doubt you can do the same. I think of an Electricity Board which claimed their strictly legal right of charging me for reading my meter (I had been unable to make arrangements for anyone to be present when they wanted to read it). Eventually they found me at home and read the meter; this was followed by a bill for £9.50. Their estimated readings had in any case been in excess of the actual.

I told them that I had no intention of paying, that they had discretion to remit it and that it would make for good customer relationships to do so. For several bills there was no reponse; the charge still appeared and I deducted it when paying. I wrote again and received a curt reply informing me that the charge would continue to appear on my bill until I paid it.

At that point I wrote to tell them I was writing a book on total quality. If they didn't respond positively I would reproduce their curt letter in my book. I never did get a reply, but I did get a credit note cancelling the £9.50, although without a covering letter. Still they did cancel it, so I haven't reproduced the letter. If they had taken the Bournemouth hotel approach I might even have been telling a story which commended them. As it was they ungraciously gave into my insistence.

Why bother to tell the story? Because there is a lesson to be learnt from it. It is about giving quite junior people discretion – empowerment. I assume that there are precise procedures for dealing with fruitless calls to read meters. After a certain number of calls and non-responses, make sure that customers stay in for the meter man. Threaten them with a kind of fine and when at last the meter gets read impose the fine.

Presumably a junior person applied the rule. When I wrote on several occasions another person or persons ignored my letter. Eventually a more senior person signed a letter putting me in my place. I was just a faceless nuisance.

Who was to blame? Was it a special cause where the individual was the sole cause? Or was it systemically caused, because management hadn't given discretion to people and trained them for it? It would not have taken a very senior person to see that it might have been wise to exercise discretion and cancel the charge. This is how a quality relationship is built up. But in Deming terms you have to drive out fear if junior people are going to feel comfortable about making a liberal interpretation of the rules.

OTHER EXAMPLES GOOD AND BAD

I can tell a recent story about a good response. I paid twice by mistake for some attention to my heating system. Back on Christmas Eve came the cheque with a little note: 'I am so glad you appreciated the work I did on your heating. But there is really no need to show it by paying twice.' A little humour goes a long way.

Then on the other side there are some check-in people at the supermarket who ignore your presence as they deal with your goods and talk to their neighbours at the next desk. I believe this is improving. I suspect someone has arranged for it to be covered in employee training.

I think of the motor repair specialist who couldn't solve the mystery of the noisy exhaust system he had sold me, but who took it all to pieces and put it together again without charge, although he could have argued that it was out of warranty. I always go there now. He even remembered my name when he met me after an absence of some months. Those are the little things that make a customer feel good.

I think back to a few years ago when motorway service stations were the last places one would have chosen to eat. The service was often surly and the food inevitably poor. Yet apparently the service message is getting through and great improvements have occurred. The food is better due to systemic decisions, but the attitude must have been the subject of training.

I'm sure we all can tell stories good and bad about restaurants where you can't attract attention to pay your bill. This must be a custom loser, when people are waiting to be seated.

A GOOD ELECTRICITY STORY

I will now tell a good story about an Electricity Board retail shop, to make amends for the bad one. My washing machine was leaking badly. I could have bought a new one from the shop, but it would have taken nearly a week because it had to come from a central store. The last day for ordering for Tuesday delivery was Friday. This was Friday but I was expecting a call from the Hoover service man the next day to see if it was worthwhile repairing my old machine. Therefore, if it couldn't be repaired and I wanted a new one I would have to order on Saturday and wait till Thursday.

The sales lady came up with an excellent solution. I could order a new washing machine there and then, and if the Hoover man was able to repair my machine I could ring up and cancel the order. That is exactly what I did, but because of the initiative shown I have a good feeling about the shop and will no doubt return.

I have just one reservation left. Why does it have to take so long to get the equipment out of the central store? Is this for the convenience of the Electricity Company or of the customer? Does the customer exist for the supplier or the supplier for the customer? Nevertheless, I do have a soft spot for the lady who used her initiative.

WHO IS RESPONSIBLE FOR BAD QUALITY SERVICE?

The examples we have been talking about have tended to concern the end user's experience. They have been about how you and I as purchasers of services and goods from stores and public utilities, perceive the quality of the service we get. A lot of the examples illustrate the way people treat us, what kind of attitude they display and how they use their initiative. They have certainly not involved actions that can easily be measured.

It would be difficult to create a statistical process control chart about discourteous behaviour. First it is subjective in its definition, though you could say that what the customer perceives as discourteous is discourteous. Second it is a case where no variation is acceptable. There's just no room for treating customers with rudeness or indifference. Does this mean that every case of discourteous behaviour is the responsibility of the person who displays it? Or can it be the fault of the system, which is the responsibility of management? The principle that tends to apply in manufacturing is that less than 20 per cent of the problems are due to the worker; more than 80 per cent are the responsibility of management. Management are the only people with the authority to change the framework within which workers operate. Does this apply in services?

If people are discourteous are management truly exempt from responsibility? Who recruited these discourteous people? Who put them into a straitjacket of inflexible procedures supported by fear, so that they cannot use initiative? Management. Who failed to give them good induction training and subsequently gave them little opportunity to grow in understanding and skill? Who presumed that they could be used as 'unskilled labour', who neither need nor can use training? Management. Who failed to watch closely enough what was going on, so that they could encourage more satisfactory and satisfying attitudes? Management. So perhaps it *is* a case of the 80/20 rule again.

WHO REPRESENTS QUALITY TO THE CUSTOMER?

Where the customer is face to face with the provider of a service in a store, bank, post office, ticket office, or on the phone to a public utility or government department, it is that front line person who is perceived as the bearer of quality or the one who fails to give it. So that if quality is to be defined in the terms of the customer, there is after all a difference between responsibility for quality in the manufacturing and that in the service field.

Perhaps as far as the customer is concerned it is the shop assistant or ticket person who is responsible. The customer rarely sees the manager and will hardly ask the question: 'Is this a systemic problem, which management should address?' Just now and again some people might ask whether a shop assistant, who is obviously very junior, is receiving the right training, but generally it is the assistant who will be blamed. We have to accept this if customers are the definers of quality.

PRINCIPLE OF VARIATION IN SERVICES

What about the idea we discussed in chapter 3, however, that eventually you get the work of production into statistical control. It is stable. The variations are predictable and will not be changed by personal effort; only a change of system will do that. What Deming calls common causes are now responsible for these variations. They may lie within tolerances acceptable to the customer; and in that case the aim is to get them to new levels of excellence and to go beyond current levels of customer expectation. Or it may be that a policy is being followed or equipment used which creates situations unacceptable to the customer. In either case the action lies with management and changes in the system. The operator can't do this or improve the situation by better personal service; the framework has to be changed.

These principles also apply to services. There are still two kinds of variation in the process – those due to special and unusual circumstances and others due to the system. The system may need changing either to exceed current customer expectations and enhance competitive edge; or to deal with a fault of design or policy.

However in the service area it is less easy to distinguish the various categories. In the *Financial Times* article mentioned above, Christopher Lorenz cites various examples of unsatisfactory service he has received from companies generally renowned for quality in the airline, hotel and mail courier businesses. He tells of being billed in error for services, followed by threatening letters from the Paris office in French and no acknowledgement of his protestations. He goes on to talk of food defects in certain hotel chains and related airlines and says they were so widespread that they could not arise from human error but from 'some sort of system fault'. All the efforts of airline staff to make you happy will be wasted if you have to line up for hours at inadequate ticket desks or if when you get on board there is not enough leg room. Again says Lorenz, 'systems faults' must be responsible.

Lorenz refers again to Richard Whitley's book and comments that it is not enough to get thousands of staff to behave impeccably in their moments of truth; 'product and service quality are intertwined in an intimate fashion'. 'Every aspect of the product and service must be designed, produced and delivered correctly.' This is improving the system to meet faults. Lorenz also emphasises the fact that, 'last year's excellent service may become tomorrow's also ran'. In other words the other kind of system attention which seeks to exceed the expectations of the customer is necessary if you are to have competitive edge.

ZERO DEFECTS IN SERVING THE CUSTOMER

All this being granted, how far can the concept of the process being in statistical control be relevant to face-to-face service to the customer? Can there be variations in relation to discourteous behaviour? Can you say our discourtesy level is predictable and stable. Now we'll hand over to our system experts to see if they can find new and lower levels of discourtesy, where our front line staff are only half as rude. Won't the customers be pleased? Surely on issues of service there must often be not only the search for zero defects, but a recognition that nothing less than the most rigorous definition of zero defects is good enough.

Similarly there is no room for variations in those areas of public service where safety is a prime consideration. You can't talk about the process being in statistical control when you are dealing with people's life and limb. One death is one too many. Only military generals can talk in that way on the field of battle, when they calculate acceptable casualty levels. But in normal peacetime life, zero defects of the most rigorous nature alone will do. We have already mentioned the organisation which aimed to halve serious accidents in the following year. Did they plan to have some?

ROSANDER – SERVICE QUALITY GURU

I had reached this stage in my thinking when I remembered I had a book on my shelves entitled *The Quest for Quality in Services*, by A.C.Rosander. He is a veteran in the field of quality, with a statistical background like Deming and Juran. I pulled it off the shelf and sure enough all the points I had been discovering for myself were dealt with at length. Like Deming in *Out of the Crisis* he is somewhat discursive, but his headings make it easy to find your way around. It is a standard text on quality in the service context.

Deming includes a whole chapter on service organisations and quality in *Out of the Crisis*. He recognises the differences between services and production, particularly the fact that in the service industries many more employees have direct contact with 'masses of people'. He also mentions the large volume of transactions; the vast amount of paper used; the enormous load of processing; great numbers of small money exchanges; all linked with great numbers of small items to be handled. This all results in a tremendous opportunity for making mistakes.

Deming still emphasises the need for management to create the right conditions for people to reduce the number of errors and to increase the pleasure of the customer. He lays great stress on care in hiring and training, not only of the people directly engaged in selling, but of all those who have contact with the public. He cites the way in which a Japanese company gives special training to the person who travels in the lift (or elevator) with the customers. Two months' training is given in order to prepare her to answer questions by the travellers, which may cover a range of issues about the company and its products. The elevator lady is a prime information source.

Rosander is quite specific on the differences between the production and services categories. He complains that concentration on the quality of products has pushed quality of services into the background. Yet as we have seen, the first thing most people think of in relation to quality is some experience with shopping, travelling or public utilities, in which the product itself may play only a small part. The Juran Institute is now giving seminars devoted to quality in the services area.

Rosander makes the point that the manufacturing company buys materials to make a product. The service organisation buys materials to provide a service. The latter will often be judged on the way in which it can bring together a number of products and intangible benefits to provide a total package. Quality provision means that this is done with maximum flexibility to meet the customer's varied needs and not the convenience of the supplier, who may try to restrict the number of options.

In general it is more difficult to measure services than products. Services have the following characteristics:

- They cannot be stored.
- They cannot be inspected or examined – they largely depend on words and expressions during an interaction.
- They cannot be determined beforehand – they consist largely of responses in the situation.
- They do not have a lifetime – they happen there and then in that moment of truth. They depend on the attitude of the person rendering the service at the time. That person is often one of the lowest paid and most junior of the staff.

A GALLUP POLL ON SERVICE QUALITY

A Gallup Poll carried out in the US in 1985 questioned over 1,000 people about quality of services in banking, insurance, government, hospitals, airlines and auto repairs. Employee attitude, behaviour or competence were cited by 67 per cent as the main quality factor; 81 per cent of the reasons for specifically poor quality lay in this same area. This means that the front line person, who is not the developer of the system, is held responsible by the customer for poor quality service. This supports the perception that was dawning on me before I remembered Rosander, that in services the front line operator does have to accept responsibility, though management in the background have to be held to account for not training them better.

The Gallup Poll highlighted the factors which constitute quality service. Under behaviour were included: acting promptly, listening carefully, making clear explanations, getting on with people and showing ability to do the job. Adjectives describing good attitudes included: courteous, friendly, kind, alert, concerned and responsible. There was also concern that the server should appear clean and tidy and dress appropriately.

WILL NINETY PER CENT GOOD BEHAVIOUR DO?

It is obvious that merely being in statistical control of service quality is unacceptable. Ninety per cent courtesy will not do, nor will 90 per cent clean or 90 per cent getting on with people. The system and the individual work together and continuous improvement is not something which can be delegated to management to achieve by action on the system. The individual is responsible, though management can help this to be understood and lived by. Ultimately management are responsible – they do the recruiting and establish the working ambience.

These days, one often meets the tendency of service workers to blame the computer. 'It's the computer you see.' We are less likely to be fooled by that excuse now. I am writing this on a powerful computer. My grandchildren are adept at computers. We know that the computer only acts in accordance with what people tell it to do.

In some parts of the services sector such as transportation and health, the cost of poor quality decisions can be fatal. A faulty computer can lead to an air accident or a train crash. Someone has the responsibility for monitoring such possibilities. Management can establish better systems which make it less likely that such errors will occur, but at the end of the day the person charged with doing the work has to accept responsibility. Zero defects and no variation is the only possible standard.

MARKET RESEARCH

Can service quality be measured? A lot of it is certainly anecdotal. You can't measure it in the same way as temperature, acidity, moisture content and so on. Perhaps there is a similarity between number of rejects and number of complaints, except that the physical state of a defective product is measured and can be placed in a specific category. It is more difficult to categorise complaints with precision.

However if quality is about customer perception, skilfully conducted market research can be utilised to find out what the customer is thinking. This will give some clear indications of what can be done. Rosander suggests making regular surveys of all customers, including lost ones. It is not enough to follow up only complaints if you want to have a balanced picture on which you can base sound decisions for the future. A body of accurate knowledge needs to be built up, as Lorenz and Whitley advocate.

Such customer surveys need to be carried out professionally by a reputable market survey firm, which can identify a reasonable sample and ask questions which produce useful answers, which are designed not to influence the respondent, perhaps unwittingly, to secure the answers it would like to hear.

WHAT CAN BE MEASURED?

A number of service elements can be measured. Wherever they can they should be, at least on a sample basis, with sufficient frequency to know the broad direction, before the complaints start rolling in. Errors in typing and completing forms and invoices create an enormous amount of work in their correction, particularly if they get as far as the customer, who may be so disgusted as to take his or her business elsewhere.

None of these measures should be used to apportion blame, but to direct training emphasis. If someone is untrainable that will emerge later and is a different issue. You will never get people to improve by making criminals of them; the object must be to help them to achieve success, with belief in them for as long as possible.

When it comes to measuring attributes like honesty, reliability and helpfulness it is a matter of observation, of getting to know people. This is part of the managerial or team leader role. Accurate observation is a characteristic of the self-directed work team. Peer pressure is a wonderful educator. The fact that it cannot be quantified (John is honest at a scale of 7 out of 10, Janet is rude at a scale of 6 out of 10), does not make the observation any less accurate. Life would be impossible if this were not so.

SERVICE IN MANUFACTURING

In this chapter we have been making distinctions between services and manufacturing. We have to bear in mind, however, that direct factory production is only part of the work of a manufacturing plant. There are a whole range of support functions, such as budgeting, accounting, purchasing, personnel, administration, storekeeping, transportation, packaging and despatch. Without these the manufactured goods would never be completed or reach their destination. Therefore quality of service must be included in what goes on at a manufacturing plant.

The measuring and observing we have discussed above has to be carried out for those services which make manufacturing possible. These also have a great bearing on the timeliness with which the goods reach the customer, and the condition in which they arrive and, indeed, whether they arrive at all. In 'just-in-time' systems this is critical, though the system is designed to make it easier. In addition to the tangible products there are many intangible facets which accompany the goods; without these the service is unlikely to meet, and certainly not exceed, the expectations of the customer.

It is important that at the manufacturing plant the control of quality for the intangibles is not neglected, just because it is on a different basis in many respects from the quality considerations for manufactured products.

Because quality in the factory has been associated with engineering we tend to think that its methods provide the only way to measure quality. If we stay with our initial definitions of quality we will see that this is not so. 'Fitness for use', 'meeting or exceeding the expectations of the customer', such definitions put the meaning and implementation of quality firmly in the customer's terms. In service and support areas in particular the customer will express quality experiences in narrative terms which can provide unambiguous lessons as a guide for the future.

9. Techniques for Quality

One aspect of the quality movement that impresses me is the way in which operations staff have absorbed the principles of statistics in order to control their own work, particularly when working in self-directed teams. It is certainly a revolution in business life when it is considered important for everybody in a plant to have the opportunity to be trained in basic statistics.

This chapter will outline briefly some of the main tools by which workers or associates can record and monitor what is going on and take remedial action when required. In doing so we shall get a better idea of the principles of variation which were set out (without too much statistical detail) in chapter 3.

I am particularly grateful to Henry Neave for the clear way in which he explains statistical charts in his book *The Deming Dimension*. Material produced by Alex Knight and Kathryn Leishman at Ashridge Management College has also been helpful.

THE STATISTICAL PROCESS CHART

The key statistical tool is the process control chart, developed in the thirties by Walter A. Shewhart (who was Deming's mentor). It provides a visual image of what is happening. At Stanbridge visual display units present the situation in relation to any machine so that special problems can be highlighted.

Before we look at the process control chart we consider briefly the run chart. Although this is the basis of the process control chart, it would not give sufficient information to be really useful. It simply

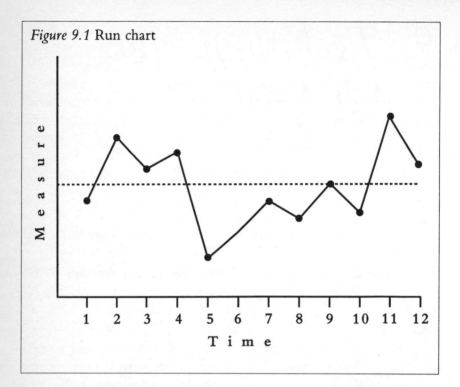

Figure 9.1 Run chart

plots samples, at intervals of time, of what the process is producing, whatever it might be. It might relate to the time customers waited in line before being seated at table in a restaurant; how long it took before the drinks order or meal order was taken and so on. This kind of information would have to be specially charted and would normally be part of a survey. With manufacturing processes and many distribution activities the information would be produced automatically. It would look like figure 9.1.

However, this does not tell us enough. It does not indicate whether these ups and downs are serious or not, although we might guess that numbers 5 and 11 need watching. We need the plotting to be compared against something. Here is an example of a process control chart. (Figure 9.2.)

You can see at a glance that superimposed on the run chart are two lines called the upper and lower control limits. These limits are drawn in such a way that a measurement would only be outside the limit once in a thousand times if the sources of variation are merely

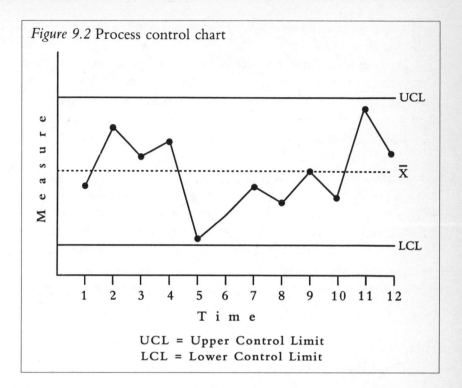

Figure 9.2 Process control chart

UCL = Upper Control Limit
LCL = Lower Control Limit

random fluctuations. So if the limits are breached it is most likely that some special cause, something that is not a random fluctuation is happening. The random fluctuations within the limits are inevitable, though a change to the system might reduce them. As we saw in chapter 3 this would be the responsibility of management.

To make the variations more meaningful and to make the pattern clear, a mean line is charted mid-way between the two limits. When the variations move up and down in a fairly regular manner yet stay within the limits the process is said to be within statistical control (that is stable). This is the position in figure 9.2.; even points 5 and 11 are within the limits, so that any action taken to deal with them would be 'tampering'.

(There are two kinds of control chart. One is called the $\overline{X}$ chart; it measures the mean of each sample and reveals any tendency for drift. The other, the $\overline{R}$ chart, measures the range of each sample, the largest measurement minus the smallest. It reveals the the tendency of the process to behave more or less randomly. For our purpose here, which is simply to get a broad idea, we will not worry unduly about the distinction.)

However now look at a different chart in figure 9.3; something is happening. It is in statistical control but it seems to be hovering near the lower limit. As long as it is within limits, however, we will not intervene. If we 'tamper' we shall establish new limits and new means and in time will have corrupted the whole process.

Bill Scherkenbach tells how a machine at Ford Motor Company for turning out transmission shafts was fitted with an automatic compensating device to change the setting whenever the shaft diameter was deemed too large or too small. When as an experiment the compensating device was turned off the variation was in fact reduced. The compensating device did not take account of the fact that the process was already in control. Its ups and downs represented the lowest variability of which it was capable under the present system. Every time compensation took place it was in fact

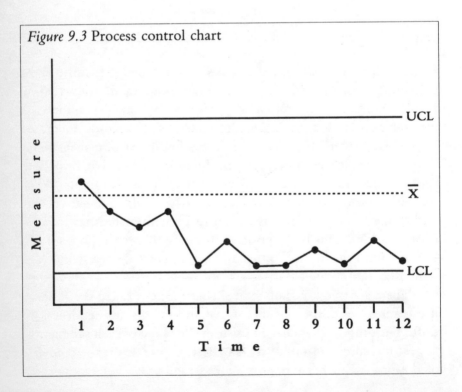

Figure 9.3 Process control chart

changing the mean and the limits and creating extra variability from the original limits. There were no special causes. To reduce the variability would require a change to the system, to address what Deming calls 'common causes'.

The variations which occur while process performance is in statistical control or stable are the result of a multitude of small random fluctuations. To get these to zero is impossible given the nature of matter, a concept we are understanding better with the advent of chaos theory. Even Crosby is not referring to these when he speaks of zero defects, though the smaller these can be made by improving the system the more likely you are to delight the customer.

Figure 9.4, however, is a cause for concern. The process is not in statistical control. $\overline{X}$ has shot right over the upper limit. Some special cause may be at work, an irregular cause of variation. This does call for attention, for if not dealt with some serious loss of

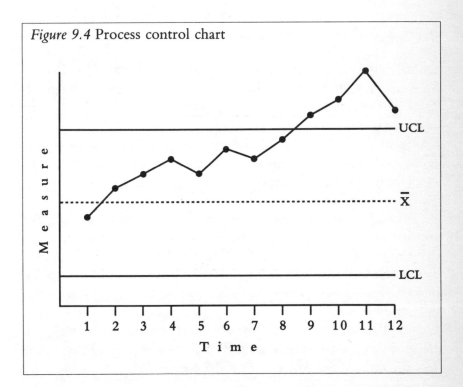

Figure 9.4 Process control chart

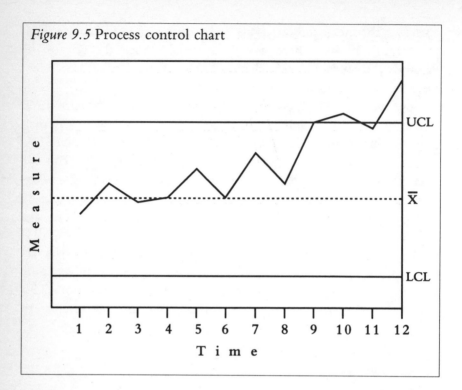

Figure 9.5 Process control chart

quality might occur. It could mean a variety of things. That is what the team must find out. It could mean a change in machine setting, an employee unfamiliar with the specification, or the introduction of material from a different supplier.

Figure 9.5 (also $\overline{X}$) could indicate three different operators who set up the machine and operate at different levels. Figure 9.6 ($\overline{R}$) could be a case of an inexperienced worker who eventually learns the job and gets into control.

In each of the cases 9.4 to 9.6 action has to be considered. The purpose of the public display of the charts near the machine is so that the trained workers, especially if they are members of a self-directed work team, can themselves deal with some of the special causes. They cannot change the system, address the common causes, though they may well have suggestions to management on the best way to do that. The process control chart simply provides a quick visual way of answering the question 'Is this process behaving the way it usually does, or has something changed?'

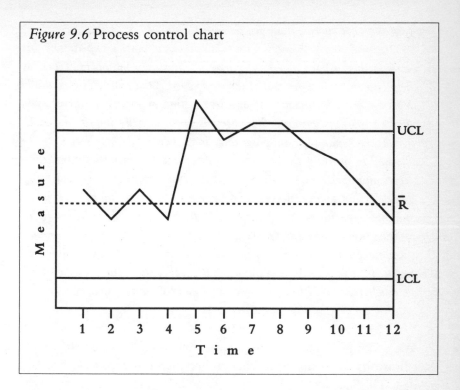

Figure 9.6 Process control chart

EXAMPLES OF PROCESS CONTROL CHART USAGE

Most repetitive processes can be tracked by these charts. The aim may be to check on the size of a part being machined, labour time used to produce a part, speed and accuracy of information processing, (say in a bank), checking on a telephone ordering system, late departures in airlines and railways, lost baggage, overbooking and underbooking in airlines. In the case of some personalised services an out-of-control chart may reveal that something has changed in the environment and the service needs to adjust to this.

Alex Knight in an Ashridge programme note makes some useful observations on how to interpret a process control chart:

Just because a process is 'in control' it does not necessarily mean it is within tolerances or up to the standard of the customer's expectations. Being 'in control' is a characteristic of the process, whereas the 'tolerances' of specification are a characteristic of the design.

If the design tolerances, specifications or customer's expectations are too high then a particular process may be physically incapable of meeting the requirement 100 per cent of the time, even if the process is statistically under control. No amount of objective setting or incentive schemes will improve the situation until the process is fundamentally improved.

As an example, suppose that in a bank the manager sets the maximum queuing time to two minutes and the process control chart shows an upper control limit (UCL) to be two minutes 45 seconds, then it is clear that some customers will have to wait longer than two minutes and improvement can only be achieved by fundamentally modifying the process. Rewarding the tellers for the times they meet the two-minute rule and punishing them for exceeding it can only be destructive. Of course if the process were not under statistical control, the problem would be much worse. This is because even more of the customers would be waiting longer than the specified time.

Alex Knight goes on to comment on the need to make specifications meaningful, neither tighter nor looser than is actually needed. This is a system problem, but in handling it we need to bear in mind the telephone clerk with two minutes per telephone enquiry.

There are a number of other tools used, especially by self-directed work teams and quality circles, in addition to the control chart. I set out below a brief description of some of them.

CAUSE AND EFFECT DIAGRAM

This is most frequently called the fishbone diagram, though sometimes the Ishikawa diagram, after the man who developed it, Kaoru Ishikawa. These diagrams (see Figure 9.7) are used in problem-solving sessions as a means of trying to identify the most likely causes of the problem and trying to decide which possibility to investigate first.

The head of the fish is the effect which is undesirable, the cause of which is being searched for. One then works back along the 'spine' and upward and downward along subsidiary bones. These are usually labelled people, money, materials, machines or whatever

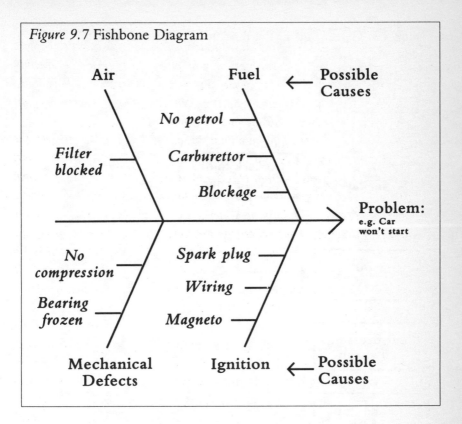

Figure 9.7 Fishbone Diagram

is appropriate to the area under consideration. Further bones lead off the subsidiary ones within the limits of space. The fishbone diagram gets discussion going, with a focused approach to searching for the cause of the problem. It points out where extra data is needed and keeps the discussion on course.

FLOW DIAGRAMS

Flow diagrams are familiar to those who work with computers. They encourage systems thinking with all the interdependent links being shown by the connecting arrows. Flow diagrams can be used to display what *should be* happening, with an alternative showing what is *actually* happening. Figure 9.8 illustrates the skeleton of a flowchart, which as the description suggests, shows the flow of the action.

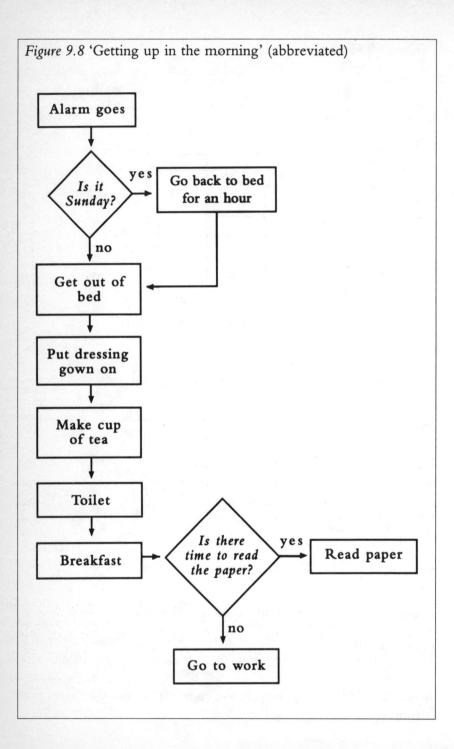

Figure 9.8 'Getting up in the morning' (abbreviated)

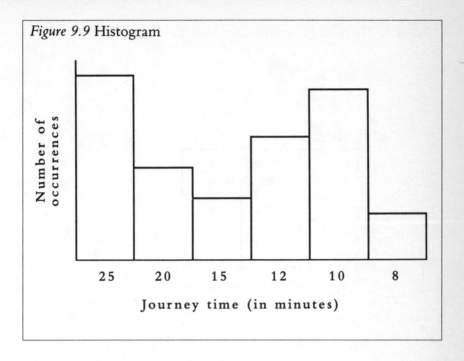

Figure 9.9 Histogram

HISTOGRAMS

Illustrated in figure 9.9, these measure how frequently something happens, whether it is time taken over a journey at different times of the week or the number of sales at different times of the year. Joining the tops of the columns produces a graph which can show trends.

PARETO DIAGRAMS

Looking a bit like histograms, these put the results of investigating an issue into some kind of priority order (see Figure 9.10). They are likely to reveal that 80 per cent of the problems come from 20 per cent of the causes, a principle to which Pareto gave his name.

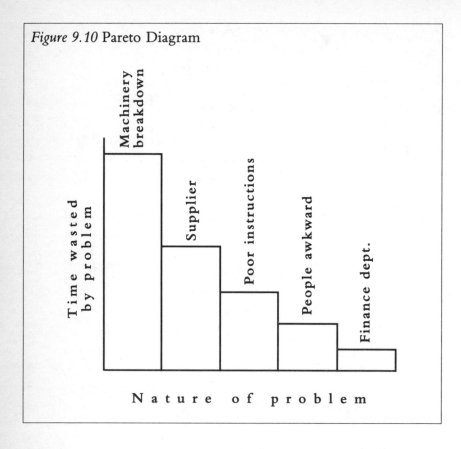

Figure 9.10 Pareto Diagram

SCATTER DIAGRAMS

These are a method of charting the relationship between two variables (see Figure 9.11). They might be used to plot the relationship between the extent of a worker's training and the number of defects, between light levels and computer errors or between moisture content and durability. Figure 9.11 illustrates this.

THE VALUE OF THE TECHNIQUES

This chapter has been concerned to give just a taster of the techniques of controlling work and solving problems, as used in the pursuit of

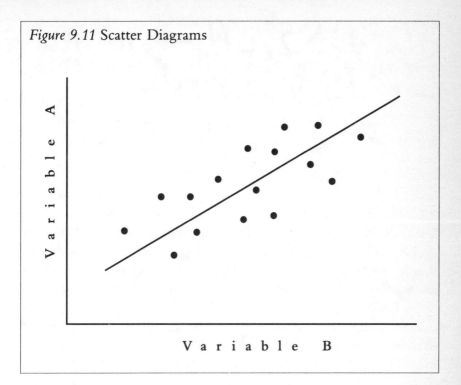

Figure 9.11 Scatter Diagrams

quality, by self-directed work teams and similar working groups.

They are simple enough to use. They do not require a degree in statistics, but they add to the likelihood of results being uniform, which is the key to quality in the customer's terms.

Another significant feature is the amount of interest they generate. No longer do workers just come to work and do as they are told. They have a role to play, an opportunity to be part of a team which wrestles with problems. The popularity of puzzles of one kind and another shows that people appreciate something to tease their brains. And if they get some of that at work it means that they will actually enjoy the job. Thus the use of these techniques is motivational. It was therefore necessary to say something about them from this motivational perspective as well as from the operational point of view. I hope enough has been said just to give the flavour of the new way of working.

10. BS5750 – Sound Procedures

No book on total quality published in the UK would be complete without some information about the BS5750 series, the standard of the British Standards Institute, which is virtually identical with the international standard series ISO9000 and the European standard series EN29000.

Increasingly accreditation under this standard is being insisted upon as a condition of being accepted as a supplier by many of the most reputable firms. We need to be clear about what it offers and what it does not. It does not accredit companies as total quality firms, but it does mean that procedures are followed in a firm which gives a framework which facilitates the introduction of total quality management (TQM).

A colleague at Ashridge, Rod Boyle, has helped me with this chapter and he makes it clear that

> BS5750 is not a product specification standard, but a management standard system, relating to HOW quality is provided. It provides a framework of procedures with which to achieve quality, but it is a means to an end and should not be seen as anything more. It is geared to the achievement of quality of production, not the production of quality.

ITS ORIGINS

BS5750 was first published in 1979 as the quality assurance standard intended to cover manufacturing industries, especially engineering. It was revised in 1987 and harmonised with the ISO9000 and

EN29000 series standards and is now applicable to a diversity of industries, so that a company accredited under BS5750 is automatically accredited under ISO9000 series and hence recognised internationally as meeting quality standards.

ITS PRINCIPLES

The guiding principle of the standard is the same as that of total quality in general. Goods and services are produced *right first time*, with everybody in the organisation having a part to play. The entire organisation is expected to be committed to quality as defined in the procedures.

The Employment Department has issued a booklet: *Total Quality Management and BS5750 – the links explained* (published by the former Training Agency, undated, but obtainable from the Department at Moorfoot in Sheffield). This defines quality in the BS5750 sense as

> *Fitness for purpose and safe in use. Quite simply, it is the service provided or product designed and constructed to satisfy the customers' needs.*

This requires sensitivity to reality and to the needs of the marketplace. It does not aim for perfection, but simply for all goods and services consistently to meet an agreed standard.

Tolerances determined by the customers are acceptable. They need only be tight enough to meet the customers' needs. BS5750 doesn't go beyond into Deming-Land and talk about exceeding the customers' expectations. If there are any legal requirements to be met, of course, there is no tolerance there.

BS5750 claims, according to the Employment Department paper, to be a common-sense approach which gets you to set down the following points on paper in an organised way:

- What you do.
- Justification of what you do.
- Evidence that you do what you say.
- A record of what you did.

BS5750 requires all aspects of an organisation's operations to be covered: the inputs, what is done with these inputs and the resulting outputs. Its aim is certainly not the mere counting of failures and defects as in traditional quality control and the inspectorial approach, which as we have said bolts the stable door after the horse has fled. It starts with a clear description of what the customer needs and finishes with a description of how those needs are met.

It covers by implication all the facets of business activity, the procedures relating to the whole supplier/customer chain within the organisation, and, indeed, all activity from initial supplier to end consumer:

- Design and product development.
- Procurement of materials and components.
- Process, programme or project planning and development.
- Actual production.
- Such inspection, testing and examination as is still required.
- Packing and storage.
- Sales and distribution.
- Installation and operation in customers premises.
- Technical assistance and maintenance.
- Disposal after use, where applicable.
- Marketing and market research

THE STRUCTURE OF BS5750

There are three parts to BS5750. Organisations have to meet the one which is appropriate to their activity. There is an additional two-sectioned part O which gives guidance on choosing the appropriate part to go for and how it fits in with overall quality management. The details of the three parts may be summarised as follows:

Part 1
This is the most comprehensive award and is appropriate where the standards are specifically expressed by the customer. It covers managerial responsibility, the quality system, contract review, design control, document control, purchasing, process control,

inspection, testing, measuring and related equipment, control of non-conforming products and services, corrective action, handling, storage, packaging and delivering, quality records, training, servicing and statistical techniques.

Part 2
This is concerned with quality assurance in production and installation; it does not cover design control and servicing.

Part 3
This is the most limited of the series of standards and is concerned only with quality assurance at final assurance and test stage. It is the furthest of the series from total quality management, but it is saying that if you have not gone the whole way to building quality in as you go along, then at least your final inspection will take place in an ordered and reliable manner. It is a case of 'half a loaf is better than none'. Those who start by getting part 3 accreditation may go on to the fuller accreditation.

It is clear from the above that when an organisation says it has BS5750 accreditation, it needs to be asked how far it has been taken. Often external customers will express a view as a condition of a contract.

BENEFITS OF BS5750

It gives a minimum language with which suppliers and customers can communicate. Suppliers can use it to demonstrate that they have in place a quality assurance system which protects and preserves product quality. This goes some way to producing co-operation between supplier and customer, but not in itself as far as chapter 6 of this book proposes, where supplier and customer enter into a close alliance, so that they are members of one family. Nevertheless, it could lead in that direction.

Following the procedures will lead to many of the benefits of total quality management in terms of reducing rework, retraining and corrective action and lost orders. Many regard BS5750 as a good starting point on the route to total quality management.

LIMITATIONS OF STANDARDS

As this book has made quite clear the goal of total quality management is one that never can be reached. It is an endless journey. There is always a better way. Continuous improvement is of the essence. It is not surprising then that there is no BS, EN, or ISO standard for total quality. It would be difficult to establish a standard for a mindset, for commitment, for empowerment, for *kaizen*, for leadership, for teamwork, collaboration, pride in work, creative thinking by all, and moreover a standard which takes on board all of these and others simultaneously.

The formal standards therefore go as far as they can in this direction, but in the nature of things are bound to be more mechanistic than would be the case if the full quality revolution had taken place. Because they restrict themselves to what they can realistically contribute to, BS5750 and the other standards have to deal with procedures and things which can be documented. There is therefore the danger that it may be applied bureaucratically, without the engagement of hearts and minds. People may then feel that as they have BS5750 they are all right; they are a quality organisation. They may mistake the form for the substance.

I don't think we can blame BS5750 for this, but we need to be aware of the limitations. It's a bit like the whole question of law. How wonderful it would be if everyone did the right thing from the heart because they wanted to. However, we live in the real world.

What BS5750 and the other standards instil as a procedural code, total quality management inspires as a way of life and thought. BS5750 has standards of what is desirable; total quality is a strategy for doing things right. BS5750 focuses on the actual product or service with some recognition of the steps to be taken; total quality follows through in depth all the company-wide steps which lead to the offering of a product or service to the external customers or end consumers. BS5750 offers processes; total quality a management way of life and philosophy.

BS5750 doesn't really cover continuous improvement, except by implication, and it requires no specific commitment to employee involvement, which we have seen is central to total quality. The goal of BS5750 is to pass the test and get the award. The goal of total quality is never to let up in the search for doing things better and better and better and . . . that is, continuous improvement.

BS5750 in a company can be quite low key, run by a few experts as a procedure to which people are instructed to work. There is no inherent ownership by everybody. There is no emblazonment of it throughout the company. It does what it has to do. It is a worthy step along the road, but it should not be seen as a destination. To be fair it makes no other claims for itself. No more than any law or code reckons to be a transforming power in the lives of people or organisations.

Getting BS5750 accreditation

The British Standards Institute can be approached by any organisation intending to get accreditation. Its address is:

BSI Quality Assurance
Business Development
P.O. Box 375
Milton Keynes
MK14 6LL

The pursuance of registration by an organisation will probably require help from a consultancy, experienced in the area, to set up the procedures. I would recommend that a consultant be appointed who has the wider vision of total quality and both recognises the value of BS5750 and can see beyond it to the fuller purpose. Any consultants who are totally absorbed in the procedures, rather than seeing them as stepping stones to greater things, will not be to the ultimate benefit of the organisation. Having said that, they do need to be adept at the procedures.

Before the final application takes place there are accredited bodies, including BSI QA themselves and Lloyds Register QA, who will make an initial assessment and indicate weaknesses which need to be corrected before the final audit.

Once having been accredited, there are twice-yearly audits in order to retain the award. Failure in these means losing it.

ASSESSING BS5750

I suppose one could sum up a reasonable attitude to BS5750 by saying: 'Just because you want to hitch your wagon to a star, there is no reason why you should not drive it efficiently on the earth.' The standard is already making a major contribution to improving quality. It is also required as a qualification for business by many customers. Just because you are convinced that you want to go much, much further is no reason for ignoring it.

Be aware the standard's limitations, exceed it by all means, but use it on its own terms for what it is. If it tends itself to be short term, it does not prevent you from being long term in your perspective. If it does not attempt to cover all the wider issues of a totally committed workforce, it may nevertheless be used to give them some of the tools with which to check their own work. BS5750 is no more the whole of total quality than statistical process control is. We must use everything which will help, but with our eyes open and a vision which is inexhaustible.

11. Stanbridge gets the Q1 award

This chapter is the first of a number which will illustrate the principles we have been studying. We shall see them in action within organisations, starting with Stanbridge Precision Turned Parts in Luton UK.

GROWING THE COMPANY

The story of Stanbridge Precision Turned Parts illustrates what a small company can do in establishing primacy through quality.

The first time I met Bob Knox, managing director of the company, he had been told there was only one way forward and that was to grow. He didn't particularly want the company to grow. After the hard graft of the early years, he was now able to lead something like a normal life, with time for family and golf.

However he had decided to develop the company so as to gain the Ford Q1 award, a prestigious accolade which could be obtained only by following the most stringent quality procedures. It carried with it the right to fly the Q1 flag and was respected by everyone in the automobile business.

My immediate reaction was to assume that Bob had, by default, made his decision and was now committed to growth. I envisaged his weekends spent working and his return to a life of business pressure such as he had left behind. However, when 18 months later, I attended the ceremony at which the parliamentary private secretary to the Prime Minister unfurled the flag of quality, I realised that total quality in fact reduces the pressures on management and shares responsibility more evenly throughout the company.

It certainly increased the prosperity of this company and its 66 employees, six of whom were new recruits, taken on in a recession, to be trained ready for an expected upturn. Among some 70 companies making components for the larger motor manufacturers, Stanbridge was one of only a handful who were weathering the 1991 recession without alarm and despondency. A reputation for quality was the key to this.

INTRODUCING STANBRIDGE

Stanbridge Precision Turned Parts make the small parts which are essential to automobile manufacture, for example the small turned parts associated with a carburettor. If the quality is not maintained you'll either get too much or too little petrol coming through – the resultant mechanical breakdown throwing any manufacturing deficiencies into stark relief. Too much of that would mean disaster for Stanbridge.

Bob Knox is a friendly sort of man who works very closely with all his staff; he knows remoteness won't get results. Bob heads a small management team. He personally attends to the sales and to growing international business. The company is already in the USA (east and west coast), France, Brazil, India, Australia, New Zealand and Holland. The company's turnover in 1990 was £3 million.

Achieving the Q1 award is dependent upon ensuring that all employees understand statistical process control and problem-solving techniques. A full-time training officer must be appointed, a training area set aside, and improvement groups established. Before a contract is signed to supply a customer, the firm has to foresee the things which could go wrong in terms of quality and agree the actions that will be taken should they arise. Clear standards of what is meant by quality have to be agreed.

THE Q1 SYSTEM

Q1 is different from BS5750. BS5750 makes a good springboard for attaining Q1 standards, but Q1 goes well beyond procedural documentation, to focus on attitudes and results.

The Q1 award is made to suppliers by Ford for consistency of quality in parts supplied. Proven commitment to improve the quality of these parts is also required. There is no ceiling to what is meant by improvement. A never-ending journey is implied. You never arrive at perfect quality. Ford Quality Assurance Engineers have to be satisfied that the process of continuous improvement is built into the culture. It has to be evident that all employees check for themselves what they are producing, swiftly rectifying errors and eliminating them at source, thus dealing effectively with rejects and defects.

UNDERSTANDING/COMMITMENT/QUALITY PLANNING

Stanbridge management had to accomplish the following:

- Attend specific seminars on statistical methodologies.
- Communicate a commitment to quality to the rest of the employees and provide evidence that a plan had been developed to guide this effort.
- Ensure that defect prevention and continuous improvement were understood and provide evidence that these principles were high priority management issues.
- Ensure that the management team understood the concepts of variability, statistical control, capability and over-control.
- Provide evidence that there was an attempt to understand quality in customer terms and to obtain customer feedback (including visits to customer facilities and investigating the cause of returned products).
- Implement a disciplined approach to quality planning, as found in the Ford Quality Planning Guidelines.

TRAINING

- Provide training in statistical methodology to all employees.
- Ensure a qualified statistical specialist was continually available as a training resource.
- Prepare training manuals or guidelines on statistical techniques and make them available to all staff.
- Make available training in advanced statistical techniques.

MANAGEMENT CONTROLS/IMPLEMENTATION

- Have a strategy for pursuing continuous improvement and implementing quality planning and statistical process controls.
- Support the strategy by actions such as preventive maintenance of equipment, statistical activity to prevent defects and reduce variations, employee involvement groups (or quality circles) and monitoring quality costs?
- Encourage a participative management style.
- Monitor training progress and its effectiveness.

Management have to give assurance that better ways of monitoring the improvement statistics are being continuously developed. They are also asked to provide examples of how managers use statistical thinking to manage the operations.

A very important question concerns the way in which the customer chain concept is actively promoted, because as we saw in chapter 6 this ensures that everyone recognises visible customers.

RESPONSE TO QUALITY CONCERNS

A further category in the Ford review of its suppliers' relates to 'response to quality concerns'. What happens when products are returned, and when customer warranty or field service issues arise? Are such problems turned into opportunities?

The Ford review also deals with suppliers monitoring how their product is used at Ford plants, so that there is a two-way involvement.

THE RESPONSE OF STANBRIDGE MANAGEMENT

Stanbridge management gave impressive evidence of the action they had taken. Training shines through every line. Training courses and seminars attended are specified; the use of outside consultants is described, together with cross-functional teams.

Stanbridge had to provide qualitative evidence that this learning was taking place as an integral part of the job, as well as setting out a wide range of training activities including 'off the job' statistical training. Team building training, machine operating and machine setting in the new context were included.

Such training makes employees marketable outside, but the potential for losing staff is offset, to a certain extent, by the *esprit de corps* that quality builds up. It provides a reward in its own right and creates reluctance to move on to an 'unknown quantity'. (Some employees did feel, however, that the very pressures caused by success made it difficult to maintain the training momentum.)

QUALITY SYSTEM SURVEY REPORT

Before the Q1 award is made, a fuller report is signed by the Ford quality engineer awarding marks for a series of aspects of the whole process.

Planning for quality
This involves clear organisational arrangements for planning quality into the products and reaching agreement with the customer on what defines quality; methods of reviewing design and process changes, updating of operating instructions and analysing faults are also evaluated.

Statistical methods
Control charts and process logs, together with operator and supervisor behaviour, are checked out in relation to statistical

methods employed; continual improvement methods are expected, not least that there are arrangements for those who supply the supplier to be brought into the chain of quality.

Documentation
The documentation for auditing, quality-related functions, monitoring and all other aspects of production is checked for clarity and soundness.

Testing and measurement
Measurement is crucial in the quality process; it is therefore essential to have the appropriate instruments and procedures, together with a ready understanding of them by everyone. Great emphasis is placed on being able to ensure that faulty and sound products do not get mixed. This is being practical, although the ultimate aim is to ensure there are no faulty products.

Customer
All members of the organisation are required to understand the precise requirements of the customer and to exercise a disciplined approach to problems which may arise.

General
Records of tests, rework documentation and packing arrangements which will preserve quality are examined. Environmental standards, such as cleanliness of paintwork and surroundings, housekeeping and working conditions are also assessed to see if they are such as to encourage quality working, on the grounds that non-quality surroundings are not conducive to quality working.

Although Stanbridge got its award, it was not an accolade for perfection. There remained, on the award documentation, a list of things to be done, under the heading 'Areas of guidance for improvement'. Total quality is a never-ending journey, with mileposts along the route to encourage the traveller to continue.

One of the areas noted as needing improvement concerned the fact that the managing director needs to delegate more, so that delays in meeting orders do not occur in his absence. This was seen as a quality issue.

QUALITY IMPROVEMENT TEAMS

All too often, people think of total quality as meaning mainly the running of quality circles. This is only one element of the process. To gain Q1, Stanbridge had to make their quality circles more effective. They restarted them as quality improvement teams, and ensured that lack of training which stalled an earlier attempt was no longer an issue.

Q1 involves continual self-assessment and continual evaluation of the process as well as the outcomes. Q1 looks for a culture change, and because the improvement sought is never-ending, the goal-posts are constantly shifting; everyone has to adapt constantly.

One of the strategies used in helping the improvement teams to function effectively is to bring in an outside consultant to contribute some discipline to the process. The discipline includes encourage-ment to 'Congratulate your team on a job well done'.

Self-monitoring and self-knowledge are essential to the quality programme at Stanbridge. It is not enough to rely on the statistical process control facilitator. Everyone must take responsibility for their own work, both individually and jointly as team members. This is implicit in a Team Oriented Problem Solving (TOPS) system which is used by the Stanbridge quality improvement teams. Everyone was issued with a training manual and was expected to understand it.

PARTNERSHIP BETWEEN SUPPLIER AND MANUFACTURER

The quality manager would once have been described as the quality controller, but now everyone is a quality controller. When quotations are being made to customers, there is an advanced planning quality team who, as a team, look at the specifications and capabilities of the machines employed to make the part. This enables them to make a feasibility and capability statement to send with the quotation. If the machine is not capable of operating at the required tolerance, this is openly stated and the customer is invited to consider whether the tolerance is too high. It is a joint decision between Stanbridge, the supplier, and the customer.

This partnership between supplier and customer is fundamental to the success of total quality. Thus it is not merely a matter of the main manufacturer having a well-trained workforce, but of all its suppliers, such as Stanbridge in relation to Ford, being similarly well trained.

An attitude survey of customers – the various automobile companies Stanbridge supplies – was taken. It included those who were the most likely to complain, so that the strengths and weaknesses of Stanbridge could become apparent. Quality customer care is a matter of growing in empathy so that you stand in the customers' shoes and share their expectations.

QUALITY MEANS EVERYTHING

Total quality is what it says, total. At Stanbridge it is not just the components which have to have quality built in, but quality exists in relation to every aspect of the business.

Stanbridge really do follow the working environment aspects of the Q1 document. They do paint the surroundings, because first impressions and tidy areas help to keep the staff working up to standard. The paint brush has moved on to the goods van which promotes the image of Stanbridge when it moves around the Luton area on its delivery schedule.

The Q1 teams cover the whole organisation and all employees are fully involved. There were difficulties at the beginning of the programme; the main one was the fact that the prospect of change itself was rather unnerving. However the obvious benefits to the viability of the company eventually won people over. The operations manager feels that total quality has ultimately consolidated the best of Stanbridge's past and enhanced the family spirit. The managing director did his utmost to convey to people how vital they were to the success of the business.

OPTIMISM

Bob Knox is optimistic about future business. Stanbridge expect their international connections to grow. They have gained a large contract from a European firm because their manufacturing is cheaper and there are only two others in the UK who can compete with them.

A LEARNING CULTURE

The company is not resting on its laurels. Q1 is a beginning not an end. Stanbridge recognise that they always have to be aware of their competitors and the developments taking place in technology. They make it their business to have a learning attitude, listening to the market-place, and watching out for technological development some of which could threaten them if they did not maintain awareness.

I found Stanbridge to have a learning culture in every respect. There is training to enable everyone to be part of the quality crusade in practical ways. There is development activity to help everyone in the organisation, and thereby enable the organisation as a whole to grow. There is the power of continuous improvement in which learning to do things better never ceases and everyone in the company is engaged in constant dialogue to satisfy customer needs more effectively.

This all added up to Stanbridge Precision Turned Parts being well on the way to becoming a learning organisation in which 'learning equals working' and is not a separate activity undertaken by a training department. Learning is everyone's business and happens through the job, off the job and beyond the job. Thus Stanbridge prepare themselves to adapt to whatever circumstances lie ahead. They face the future with confidence and quality represented by Q1 is the key to this.

12. Growing People at Rothmans

The story of Rothmans, the international tobacco firm, is very much about quality from the people perspective. Teamworking is the key quality issue for them.

Colin O'Neill, responsible for people development at the two Rothmans plants in Darlington and Spennymoor in County Durham, outlined the Rothman priorities in quality:

> *Growing people, giving them accountability and responsibility, taking them from baby to full adult is the key activity of organisations, and managers are the people with the key role in this growing of people. In fact you can say they have no other function.*

This may sound a little extreme until you actually visit the plants and see how everything is shaped around the group working, which is characteristic of total quality management.

What's involved in the job

At Darlington and Spennymoor the physical configuration of the manufacturing departments is based on the need to get people working in groups. Each group performs a relatively independent set of activities which form a whole task with a visible start and finish.

Cigarette manufacture starts once the blended tobacco has been processed (it is called 'cut rag') and it is fed through pipes to the various workstations. There machinery links it with the paper which turns loose tobacco into cigarettes. From another group, the filters flow and are joined with the unfiltered cigarettes.

The completed cigarettes work through the machinery and are mechanically packed in small packages of 20 each, which are then packed into bundles of 200, as you would buy at a duty free shop. The appropriate labels are printed on them. Then a number of such bundles of 200 are put into boxes and collated into position by machinery. The boxes finally leave on the conveyor belt for the distribution area.

TEAM ENVIRONMENT

Some 18 people comprise a team or group, including a team leader who is known as the 'group manager'. In each of the two sites there are half a dozen making and packing groups. In the middle of the equipment on which each group is working is a 'bungalow'. It contains the group manager's office and the office of the administrator, responsible for ordering resources, and a small testing room for quality assurance. The biggest area is the rest area or tea bar, where the operators, fitters and other staff can eat and relax during breaks as well as using the area for meetings and problem solving. These rest areas are, wherever possible, designed by the workers themselves.

The areas of work surrounding the 'bungalows' are six large squares, or diamonds, each with a special colour to give group identity. The layout supports the interlinking of everybody's activities. Everyone belongs to a distinct group as well as to the whole plant.

KEEPING LOST TIME DOWN

The work of operators and fitters is concerned with keeping the machinery turning and producing cigarettes of the designed quality. Everybody needs a sense of urgency to avoid time lost: even a minute lost costs hundreds of pounds. Where it is lost they record it on input forms for computerised analysis. There is friendly competition between the groups to see who can get the best figures.

This group working creates a sense of ownership, which an impersonal full assembly line could not.

COMMUNICATIONS

The reporting structure runs straight from the group manager to the group members, with the group members themselves each accepting responsibility for being interchangeable and standing in for each other.

With such interlinking, communications are the most important aspect of the work. Everybody has to be clear about the objectives of what they are doing, have a constant supply of feedback, and have the opportunity to feed in the facts about the process and their interpretation of it.

As part of the communication need, everything in the group manager or team leader's office is open to anybody, not only what is displayed but most of the filing cabinets. Immediate information is also recorded by each machine, being later aggregated by computer.

STATISTICAL PROCESS CONTROL

Everybody has training in statistical process control, using a Ford interactive video package of four discs. It is associated with two case studies and after a test, leads to a diploma. Using statistical process control methods, everybody is involved in problem-solving. Instead of the group managers being there to solve problems for them, they are there to coach and guide the team in making their own analysis of problems and arriving at their own solutions.

MAINTENANCE

Maintenance provides an example of the way in which the team gets involved. Annually there is a major service of the whole of a machine, and the group workers take a keen interest in what is being done and use the opportunity to clean every part of the machine with great pride. There is no question of 'It's not my job'. This major service takes a full week.

There is a shorter service of eight hours every month. Prior to that service, there is a pre-maintenance meeting of those involved with the machine that is going to be serviced, attended by operators, fitters and a technical expert. It examines all the problems that have come up and helps to highlight where any special attention is needed. The problems are mainly breakdowns, faulty supplies, quality defects and bottlenecks. Multi-skilling makes it possible for a relief crew to stand in while such meetings occur. This is essential because of the continuous process nature of the work.

FAULT LOGGING

Areas of high downtime are continually monitored and faults investigated. Everybody is responsible for logging downtime if it is more than a few seconds. In fact, while I was there, somebody very quickly avoided more than three seconds downtime by rapid rethreading of some paper; another stopped a log jam of cigarettes descending into the machine.

If a lot of waste is being generated, the fault sheet, attached to each machine and maintained by the operator, will identify the nature of the waste. This is all logged on to a computer sheet and linked with other people's waste data. The figures are presented, not only in money and percentages, but in the actual number of lost cigarettes, because that is psychologically clear to the operators at a glance. These figures are discussed at weekly and monthly meetings.

If the problem appears to be one generated in the leaf and stem processing room, where the raw tobacco is cut and steamed to the appropriate moisture level, then discussions take place between the group and the Leaf Department about the nature of the cut rag that is coming through.

MOTIVATION

There are no incentive payments, although the salary rate is reckoned to be good. Everyone seems to accept that bonuses destroy group working. People will vary in their bonus, yet everybody's job is important, and with multi-skilling everybody tends to do each other's job.

Colin Dunn, a group manager, explained how BS5750 procedures were now being installed, and already accreditation had been achieved. BS5750 is itself an exercise in communication and can create a challenge. It is a matter of conforming to specification. The procedures themselves are made to come alive by the variables which the company feeds into them. I was shown the visual quality index, with 114 parameters which could earn demerits, and there was a great keenness to avoid these demerits.

There is also a keen interest in competitive comparison analysis. The analytical lab for the company as a whole will buy in samples from various companies, and compare the various group manufacturing standards with these external companies. There is a continual stimulus to beat the competition, both internally and externally. The demerits involved in such comparisons could relate to such matters as loose ends in the individual cigarettes. Problem solving involves thinking about things like this. Quality assurance specialists come in as part of the team to help investigate, but the prime responsibility for quality lies with the groups themselves. Some faults might need major changes and a managerial decision, but even then the operators would advise.

The involvement of the operators is quite different from the old days when the workers would simply have reported the problem and waited for decisions or actions to be handed down to them.

GROUP BUDGETING

The budget for the month and the year is all clearly set out and shared by everybody. This includes waste figures and estimated downtime; it includes time for maintenance, for cleaning, for training and briefing. The groups set their own budgets and submit them to senior management as covering their requirements. The budgets are always set on the basis of what is achievable, maintaining a balance between pessimism and optimism.

GROUP MANAGER AS TRAINER

As well as leading meetings the manufacturing group managers establish a positive working climate by involvement of the group through briefings and informal talks in such matters as:

- Budgets.
- Housekeeping.
- Safety.
- Absenteeism.
- Quality.
- Performance.

Training and development is part of the actual job rather than something separate from it. There is an ongoing educational process led by the group manager, involving everybody in the group in mutual education.

At Spennymoor I saw an example of this training element of the group manager's job in one of the groups. Bob Dolan, a group manager at Spennymoor, explained that they liked the style of the open group working areas because everybody could see what everybody else was doing – very much a part of the philosophy at Rothmans. Problems were not to be hidden, but exposed so that they could be solved.

FLIPCHARTS ON THE FACTORY FLOOR

The training activity that Bob Dolan shared related to the removal of special relief teams and he had a series of flipcharts which had been used at a meeting the previous day. The main flipchart indicated that with the dissolution of relief teams, all work was to be equally shared by all members of the group.

There followed a list of the jobs that had to be shared.

- Quality inspection.
- All aspects of group cleaning.
- Tray handling and trolley movement.

- Two-hundred bundle inspection.
- Rework and all stripping.
- Waste removal and recording.
- Assistance in brand change procedures.
- Preparation of BS5750 requirements.

TRAINING FOR EVERYONE IN BS5750

Another flipchart in Bob Dolan's office referred to BS5750. The reference manuals were there for all to look at, and anyone could initiate action to follow the principles.

This flipchart talked about getting things right first time by prevention and detection. It also emphasised continuous improvement and the fact that the next stage in the process is in effect, the customer.

DEVELOPING GROUP MANAGERS

We asked Dan Gibson, training consultant, how group managers came to acquire the skills needed to be able to exercise such influence in the teams. We began to understand a little of what Colin O'Neill had said at the start that organisations existed to grow people.

Dan Gibson said he had previously worked in production in Rothmans and after a period away in Scotland in other work, had returned to set up the pre-management cadre. This was a matter of developing, ahead of time, managers who would soon take over the role of group managers. Existing managers eventually retired or would be moved into other other types of work, at no disadvantage to themselves, to make room for new managers to cut their teeth.

In developing the themes of the pre-management cadre programmes, Dan Gibson took us back into the history of how Kingston Polytechnic had helped them develop the six principles of group working which are set out in a handbook.

THE SIX PRINCIPLES OF GROUP WORKING

The main objective that Rothmans hoped to achieve through group working is stated in the handbook as 'to create an environment which will encourage the involvement and commitment of all in the organisation toward achievement of the aims of the organisation to the benefit of both'. It considers that while the factory layout does not by itself achieve the objective, it does provide a framework and creates a climate which allows people to:

- Contribute to all aspects of group operations.
- Develop a sense of belonging and association.
- Develop themselves as individuals.
- Through dependence on and trust of other group members, grow into a strong and self-motivated team with the ability to achieve success.

It points out in its preface that people are what group working is all about. The position of the machines can help, but that is not the key.

The six group working principles are as follows:

Principle 1 – The basic organisational unit is the primary work group.
Principle 2 – Work group members share the same conditions of employment and have working conditions which complement group working structures.
Principle 3 – Each group is led by a designated manager possessing leadership skills.
Principle 4 – Working arrangements between members of the same work group are flexible.
Principle 5 – Each work group is, as far as possible, responsible for planning its own work, evaluating the results of its performance, and comparing these results with its agreed standards.
Principle 6 – Each group performs a relatively independent and significant set of activities which form a 'whole task', with a visible start and finish.

A key factor in the work of these groups and therefore of the managers is to find out what people think is wrong and seek their help in putting it right.

GROUP WORKING ACROSS CULTURES

For a time Dan Gibson had been operations manager at the Rothmans plant in Yemen. Although the culture was totally different, he found that teamworking and trust could be developed in this different environment. It was a matter of helping people to get a sense of ownership of what they were doing and to realise that they had skills that others appreciated. In the different culture the coaching and counselling had to be less overt, but it was still quite acceptable to develop the theme of using people to solve their own problems.

THE PRE-MANAGEMENT CADRE

The cadre is a matter of training in advance of vacancies; training for positions that don't yet exist. It was felt essential to do this ahead of forthcoming retirements. People were invited to apply for selection as group managers or team leaders. There was no age or craft limit. Anyone could apply. Some available information would be investigated about their timekeeping and attendance, because obviously it is essential that the group leader should set a good example. Flexibility and willingness to tackle anything is a key issue in selecting people to be part of the management cadre. One particular capability upon which great emphasis is placed is ambassadorial skill; the ability to interact well with others and represent the group or the company.

Those who passed the initial screening on these basic issues, and most did, were given a series of tests of verbal ability, then numeric and diagnostic skills (including lateral and logical thinking) before going on to interviews.

The pre-management cadre programme

The programme of 30 days' training for the pre-management cadre was spread over six months and run by members of the Spennymoor and Darlington staff, some trainers from the Aylesbury HQ and some from a firm of consultants.

There was a lot of practical work as well as theory on the role of the manager, presentation skills, report writing, financial appreciation, team building, marketing and sales, planning, personnel, interviewing, selection and appraisals. High priority was given to quality assurance and total quality management, logistics, engineering, health and safety. There was a particularly long session on problem solving and decision making, linked with customer care and quality.

The idea was to give the group managers a tool kit with which to go back, and as soon as possible, start using what they had learned. They had to appreciate that they were first among equals and not remote bosses. They had to recognise the crucial role of teamwork in what they were going to do when they got their jobs as group managers.

Interpersonal skills

The very nature of group working means that interpersonal skills receive the greatest amount of emphasis. Everybody has to learn how to elicit information from team members, how to engage in open questioning, and to know the subtle differences between coaching and counselling.

Great emphasis is placed on the ability to empathise with other people. It is also important to be content not to seem infallible. The group manager does not know everything and will work *with* the team rather than impose solutions on it; nevertheless doing so without abrogating responsibility.

The role of the team leader as seen in Rothmans is one of taking chances on the ability of others and yet seeing that the group doesn't fall on its face. Initially this approach is more time-consuming but it is deep rooted and lasts longer.

OPENNESS WITH PROBLEMS

People at Rothmans are allowed to make mistakes as a means of learning. It is not shameful to have a problem. It is something to share with the group.

As part of the open approach everyone is encouraged to be involved with suppliers and, where possible, customers. On one of my visits a problem had arisen with the packing; the aluminium foil had not been up to standard. The group manager, through the Purchasing Department, arranged for the supplier's experts to come in to discuss the situation.

At the meeting the group leader summarised the problem, and then called on the operator to explain it in detail. This would not have happened in the past, but now the person on the shop floor dealing with the issue had the opportunity to lead the discussion. After all, people on the shop floor are best placed to assess their own problems. The operators are similarly involved in any internal discussions when problems arise with non-manufacturing groups or with the Leaf Department.

COMMON CONDITIONS OF EMPLOYMENT

Feeling is important as the reason for the common conditions of employment which exist at Rothmans. The 'us' and 'them' syndrome is disposed of.

- There is no reserved car park except for disabled people.
- There are no organisational barriers.
- Everybody receives a number of free shirts and trousers a year, with free laundering and replacement. This provision means that most people wear them, although it is not strictly compulsory, and it helps to remove barriers.
- Everybody shares the same restaurant.
- Everybody has the same sick pay.
- Everybody has the same pension basis.
- Everybody has the same private hospital insurance arrangements.

MAKING CHANGE WORK

Running a factory like the two in the north-east is, for Rothmans, a matter of making change work all the time and never accepting that finality has been reached. The process of involving everybody is the key area. If you get this process right, then the output will follow.

The job of the group manager is seen by Colin O'Neill as primarily counselling, coaching and helping people learn. Managers are managers simply because they have knowledge and experience to share. The rest of the team have the skills.

In order to be self-managing, groups need more knowledge; and it is the task of the manager or leader to give this, or more often to elicit it where it already exists in people. When people have a problem, the group leader doesn't say: 'Ah, this is what you must do', but rather discusses it, either collectively or individually, to get ideas out into the open.

LEARNING FOR THE GROUP

In traditional manufacturing, Colin O'Neill pointed out that the manager is usually too busy to listen to the shop floor workers. Then you get the manager saying the workers don't understand, and the workers saying that the manager doesn't listen to them. Actually the process of listening and sharing and benefiting from the shop floor workers' knowledge takes some of the load off the manager's shoulders. There is then less danger of being too busy.

Similarly, when it comes to decision making, too many managers jump straight in with solutions, instead of recognising that the person who raises the issue owns the problem and must own the decision. Therefore non-directive coaching is a sound way to handle the matter.

The purpose of an organisation like Rothmans is to develop people to enable them to work together to achieve a target and to maintain and improve quality. People development in this context is not about taking individuals and making them personally more effective, though that might be involved, but rather about making the group more effective. Some individuals might go away and get information, knowledge or understanding on behalf of the group, but it is always group-orientated rather than individualistic. The objectives are related to the team and not to the individual. Knowledge is power and traditionally is often monopolised by people for their own purposes. In a proper group working approach, knowledge is gained in order to give it away, but the more you give it away, the more it grows.

A lot of the training consists of practical exercises to enable people to work together and support each other. Only the team can grow, not just the most skilful members.

PEOPLE LIKE LEARNING

Colin O'Neill told us that he never met anybody who really did not want to make a contribution. The trouble is that all too often we cap them, stifle their energy and curiosity and prevent them from learning; we then have a lot of untapped resources. Summing up the job of the group manager or team leader, and its impact on the team, he says:

> 'Every manager enables, empowers and facilitates. The manager is a team developer, a broad planner and organiser in conjunction with the team, a teacher of problem solving, a communicator and a releaser of initiative. The team learns and the team leader learns, and all are developed.'

Everything that happens in the Rothmans plants is directed toward quality. It is embedded in the whole principle of group working. People need to own the principles of quality at all levels and they need to work together on their implementation. The well-led and largely self-directed team is clearly illustrated at Rothmans as fundamental to quality.

13. Braintree Means Public Service Quality

We might not immediately associate total quality management with the running of a large local authority in Essex (UK), but as Chris Conway and I interviewed employees, ranging from the chief executive to a refuse collector, we found the question of quality paramount. This chapter illustrates how public service can link with total quality.

The traditional image of a local authority has been of a rather impersonal organisation run by a lot of faceless bureaucrats. Even if this were ever true of some authorities, it's just not like this any more in many of them, and certainly not in Braintree. Charles Daybell, the chief executive, says: 'Braintree is a business and the local people are both the shareholders and the customers.'

British local authorities have been undergoing transformation from organisations which directly provide services to enabling bodies, ensuring that services are available. They have moved from hierarchical and central control to management by contract and influence; from direct management of services to devolved management; from uniform and standardised services to customer orientation, with emphasis on quality and choice; from standard to flexible employment structures. Many of these changes will find an echo in any business.

'BRAINTREE MEANS BUSINESS'

The district slogan is 'Braintree means Business', and when we went to see how they were doing, we found that everyone we spoke to who worked for the council had the same general ideal. They all spoke of the 'customers'. Everyone we met – telephone operator, chief executive, refuse collector, receptionist, personnel director, group accountant, swimming pool manager, planner, environmental health officer – shared the same approach. They all expressed how they saw Braintree in their own particular words, but there was a common thread. The variety of responses suggested that there was no question of an orchestrated response to our enquiries.

Braintree district comprises some 236 square miles from the outskirts of Chelmsford to the Suffolk border. It was one of the homes of the great Courtauld company and suffered the loss of 4,000 jobs when the company closed its local plant. Business opportunities have come to Braintree as a result of the council's attitude toward economic development and private investment.

The council is responsible for emptying 44,000 refuse bins a week, and for 38,000 housing repairs and 2,500 planning applications annually. There are 900 employees to ensure that a wide range of services is carried out, supplying some of them directly and ensuring that others are provided by outside bodies.

A GOOD PLACE TO LIVE AND WORK

Charles Daybell puts it:

> 'Our job is working together to run "Braintree plc". The authority is owned by the local people, represented by the councillors and served by all the employees.'

The council's key objective is to ensure that the district is a high quality place to live and work in; to attract businesses to set themselves up in the locality and to encourage people to come and live there; and to support these aims by making sure that the environment provides the opportunity for a good quality of life.

After 'customer', 'quality' was the word most frequently used by all the people we interviewed. Peter Tattersley, assistant director of environmental services, said:

'Quality is doing what you say you'll do; and it goes beyond BS5750'.

Braintree is an authority which works to BS5750 in a number of fields, but aims to go beyond it in the search for quality, especially in areas where procedures and rules could impede action.

Trevor Jefferis runs the Riverside Pool and Squash Courts and the smaller swimming pool at Halstead. A down-to-earth London East-Ender, he explained:

'My job is to make people happy and this means looking after a lot of little things, which often give more pleasure than some of the big things – little things like fixing up bubble machines for the children in their small pool.'
'I see my job' he continued, 'as giving a complete leisure experience from the moment people drive into the car park to the moment they leave.'

He said you could measure this too.

'When people drive in there is no litter in the car park to make them feel they don't want to swim here. The lights are all on; there are no missing light bulbs; the sign posts are clear and the shrubs don't overflow on to the footpath; the windows are not broken and there is no graffiti. The receptionist is friendly; the showers aren't too hot or too cold; the keys in the lockers work; and the vending machine hasn't got a sign "out of order" written across it. It did happen once; so I had one of the attendants selling crisps to make up for it. I got told off for that by one of the accountants, but Charles Daybell tells us to have a go and even if you make mistakes you don't have to worry. You can always learn from them.'

We asked him where he learnt all this. He said it was a matter of common sense. You got on and did things and if they worked then you knew you were on the right track.

QUALITY IN THE PRINTROOM

Mike O'Shea, director of corporate services, illustrated what quality meant by the story of the printroom:

> 'It used to be rather tatty and the equipment was old. So we brought new equipment, but this meant halving the team of six. I consulted with them and they asked that all of them should be interviewed for the three jobs. Other jobs were found for the unsuccessful candidates. The whole place was refurbished. If you work in tat, then tat is what you get.'

The team felt so renewed by the new environment that they decided to call themselves 'Phoenix Printing'.

Mike said that the effect of getting the environment right was the same for the town as a whole:

> 'If you let the town get filthy, people develop a "don't care" attitude; you even get more crime.'

BRAINTREE'S MISSION

Braintree has a mission statement – and a vision statement too. They feel that if they write down where they want to be, this is a significant step on the road to getting there. The culture, the quality concern, the customer care, the people development will all flow from it – and people development in Braintree means everyone who lives and works there. So Braintree aims to:

- Secure the best possible conditions for all who live in our district to lead a high quality of life.
- Focus on our customers and provide the quality services they require.
- Ensure all our staff are given opportunities for development, through training, appraisal, respect and support.
- Operate the council in a business-like manner with clear accountabilities, and ensure that targets are met.

THE BRAINTREE VISION

The vision is of a district which:

- is prosperous, clean and socially balanced;
- meets the basic needs of all in our community for affordable housing and a range of housing choice, for worthwhile employment and for security, health and welfare services and personal mobility;
- retains, respects and enhances its attractive environment, particularly its countryside, villages, historic buildings and conservation areas;
- while retaining its traditional character provides a range of modern industry on quality business parks, encourages initiative and enterprise as well as quality shopping, arts, leisure, education and welfare facilities;
- has thriving town centres at Braintree, Witham and Halstead. Town centres which are safe, convenient, accessible and attractive to shoppers and those who live and work there;
- meets the demand for efficient movement of road traffic, but not at the expense of safety and environmental conditions (particularly in the towns and villages) or the neglect of public transport;
- meets the particular leisure, welfare and housing needs of the young and the elderly;
- exhibits a real pride and respect on the part of all sections of the community, public and private, in its surroundings, with clean and tidy streets, parks and open spaces and property that is well maintained.

The Braintree vision illustrates powerfully how quality can be a key issue in a service industry, and indeed, in a public authority.

QUALITY IN BRAINTREE

The quality aim in Braintree is 'to deliver defect-free products and services to our customers, both internal and external, on time and within budget.'

Charles Daybell speaks of a 'defect-free district'. The district is on the path to total quality and to certification under BS5750 using in part Philip Crosby's organisation for training in quality. John Reeve, refuse collector and union convenor says:

'We are very concerned about quality control in the Refuse Collection Department. We accept BS5750 and think quality is very important in our job. The customers want all the rubbish moved, with none of it left on the path, and they want us to call every week. Things like that are what quality means for us.'

John also told us how the chief executive had spent a day on a dustcart with them and further days with other teams. This was good for the motivation of the team and no doubt good for Charles Daybell, too, as a member of a 'learning organisation'.

The 'Quality Improvement Award' scheme has been set up to involve all the employees in focusing on quality. Quality includes the way that customers are dealt with on the phone or face to face; anyone who telephones the District Office will straightaway hear the effect of the training in quality, by the way the phone is answered.

Peter Tattersley told us:

'In the Environmental Services Department we are developing quality assurance systems under the guidance of BS5750. We negotiate quality standards with the staff in a specific way. We have key service indicators to measure customer satisfaction. We actually encourage complaints so that we can put right anything that goes wrong. For every ten that grumble only one or two complain and so we don't find out. So we actually think it is good to get more complaints, at least to start with. Then we can make some progress to the defect-free standard.'

Braintree is realistic about quality though. Charles Daybell says that they do not provide gold plated taps when brass ones are perfect for the job.

An attractive brochure produced by Braintree District Council is the *Quality Life Catalogue* where the customers are informed of the services on offer for their home, their health, their environment, their leisure time, their rights, their community, their district.

Braintree District Council is not an elitist organisation. The district offices in the Causeway have an internal architecture which reflects collegiality between customers and providers alike. The general public wanders in and finds a welcoming style of furnishing. Rounded counters for receptionists and pay-in desks look comfortable; they have no sense of threat or officialdom about them. There is plenty of space and the children will be seen playing in what is after all *their* council office, but it is all so structured that the noise is not excessive.

The telephonists and the receptionists have genuine smiles to make everyone feel at home. The selection of people for these jobs has obviously been carefully carried out and they have been trained in quality service.

A CHANGE CULTURE

Quality doesn't mean standing still. Braintree sees change as of the essence in a progressive district. The change culture is fed by finding out what people want and responding with changed approaches. If quality is at best delighting customers and at least conformance to requirements, you need to know what will delight and what the requirements are.

The computer section ran a customer survey, prior to developing its first business plan. The customers were all the other departments in the council, emphasising the concept of the chain of suppliers and customers.

Robin Carsberg, responsible for the computer area, observes:

'We thought we were good at things until we asked, but we discovered a number of aspects needing improvement. One of the ways in which we responded was setting up a help desk and monitoring the way in which it has been used. We also set up user groups so that we could learn together how to establish a better service. Asking for feedback is now a regular feature of our work. It makes the customer feel valued too.'

DEVELOPING THE EMPLOYEES

Braintree takes a quality approach to the development of its employees. At any one time ten per cent of the staff are on educational activity, often with part-time day-release, in pursuit of various qualifications. In addition, some four per cent are engaged in any year in off-the-job skills training. However the emphasis is on the learning that goes on all the time as part of the service provision and the development of the new culture.

Training and development takes place at all levels for the Braintree District Council employees. You could say it is total employee development. The total quality approach in any case involves everyone, as does the related customer concept, which everyone we met talked about. While there is plenty of classroom learning it is likely that some 90 per cent of learning at all levels takes place through the job.

LEARNING TOGETHER

Roger Barrett, planning director, said Braintree was not a hierarchical organisation.

'It thrives on informal relationships. People are encouraged to network and work in teams across boundaries. The classroom training gives them the tools to make this effective, as in running meetings and generally communicating well.'

The cross-function network is a valuable way of getting feedback about the impact of what you are doing, and feedback is fundamental to doing more effectively. Life in Roger Barrett's team means that business is not conducted by individuals in isolation.

In order to learn from the feedback and through everything they do in the job, Roger says that people have to be trusted and given a lot of scope for exercising discretion.

'A case officer now deals with a majority of planning applications that come to him without reference upwards and takes responsibility for

making the recommendations for final approval by the council, with full backing from me.'

Delegation and trust are of the essence in 'learning through the job' so as to be capable of quality decisions. Mike Bailey was talking about learning through the job when he said:

'We are after continuous improvement in Braintree in everything we tackle. We have a system of job enrichment and we really believe in delegation. We give people scope to be entrepreneurial, to push out the boundaries, to test things out, to spread their wings and take on new things without fear. We've got an experimental environment where mistakes are there to be learned from.'

MANAGER AS DEVELOPER

Managers are all reminded that they have the prime responsibility for ensuring that training takes place and is relevant to the needs of the individual and the department or section. A quality approach is taken to training to ensure that it is 'fit for use', as one of the quality definitions puts it. One choice sentence in the handbook reads:

It is hoped that managers see training activities as priorities, even when faced with operational pressures.

All managers who feel they have some skills to offer are invited to take part in the delivery of the in-service training programmes. Before doing so, however, they are expected to attend the 'Training of Trainers' course.

No one comes on a course without having been briefed on the reason for attending. Great emphasis is also placed on debriefing, without which it is said that money will be wasted. Managers are made responsible for the relevance of the training. This makes for quality training.

STAFF PERFORMANCE APPRAISAL

Central to the development of staff at Braintree is the appraisal system. Everybody's progress in their job is assessed and their need for training analysed in discussion with the people to whom they report.

A well designed brochure is distributed, which begins with the statement:

> *Developing staff to meet objectives is crucial to the success and efficiency of the council. The appraisal system is a tool to help you, but its effectiveness depends on the importance you place on it.*

The approach suggested is honest and factual and offers help in giving and receiving appraisal. Its aims are as follows:

- To improve performance and job satisfaction.
- To identify training needs.
- To establish a framework in which targets for improvement are established and communication between the chief officers and their staff enhanced.

The process is similar to any good appraisal system, but the book gives appraisers some good advice, which begins:

> *Do you base your assessments on personality rather than on performance? Do you ignore the quiet person who contributes without fuss? Do you put haloes round your favourites, or black marks on trouble makers?*

It is an open system where the appraisee signs the form summarising the discussion and is given a copy. The form has to be typed or handwritten by the appraiser and not by any third party. There is nothing unique about all this, but Braintree does belong to the more open end of the appraising spectrum, as one would expect from its general philosophy. It does not follow the type of appraisal denounced by Deming as divisive and demotivating.

Peter Tattersley illustrates his use of the appraisal system for staff development:

> 'There was this redundant gardener with very little schooling. At appraisal he showed enthusiasm for a vacant post as dog warden. Under normal circumstances he would never have stood a chance, but appraisal brought out his suitability, by his attitude. It was then a simple matter to give him help by training him to write reports and letters and go and talk to schools. He is doing an extremely good job.'

Mike Legget, assistant director of housing, had this to say about appraisal:

> 'I see it as a two-way process. I learnt from one of my staff who told me at appraisal that I tend to move too fast on new things without winning support first. I found this useful.'

EVALUATING TRAINING AND DEVELOPMENT

Charles Daybell saw success in training and development of staff as going beyond particular aspects of training to the total success of the business.

> 'We evaluate business outcomes, as well as individual skills. The success of training and development is involved in the successful achievement of the corporate objectives. We set service targets and evaluate how far they are achieved – Are the rent arrears reduced? Are all the dustbins emptied? Is there a backlog of planning applications? What proportion of our staff have we retained? and so on. While we do set out to ensure that our customers feel able to complain, the overall numbers are less important than assessing how we dealt with the justified complaints. What did we learn? So it's rather what percentage of complaints did we successfully correct?'

Thus training and development is evaluated by its impact on the quality of the service given to the customers.

THE DUAL LEARNING ORGANISATION

There is an even wider sense in which Braintree as a district may be considered a learning organisation. Not only is work a learning and growing experience for the employees, but there is a sense of growth, improvement and learning about the whole business of Braintree. The council members, the council employees and the 'customers' served by the council are seen as part of one great partnership. This is made explicit by the council's attention to communications.

It is illustrated by what this study has described of the culture, mission, vision, quality service attitudes and business approach of Braintree. The authority is the enabler of wealth creation and the facilitator of quality of life development. It lies at the centre of a web of relationships between many of the elements which go to make up a community. It aims not to govern but to help release the energy of people to grow to the fullness of their potential; it provides an environment conducive to such growth.

QUALITY THROUGH COMPLAINTS

Two leaflets produced by the council deal with complaints procedures. This may sound a boring thing with which to end an exciting case study; but it sums up the Braintree approach.

First there is the guide for the people who live and run businesses in the Braintree district. It is attractively presented and entitled 'I would like to make a complaint'. It says that the council's complaints procedures

> are central to our philosophy of getting closer to you – the customer. We place great emphasis on the prompt and efficient handling of complaints, so that when you tell us of things which have gone wrong we can take action quickly to put them right.

The leaflet recognises that complete customer satisfaction may not always be possible, but the council aims to give a quality service and to respond to any complaints within seven days – and if this is not possible to keep the complainant posted. Precise detail is given about who to contact and what they will try to do, with a right of appeal to the local ombudsman. Each of the departments is described with a list of the directors; also a list of the district councillors and their addresses. There is a sense of positive encouragement to complain and a distinct will to pursue the path toward total quality.

Parallel with this green leaflet there is a red one for the employees called 'Our aim is quality'. It presents the *core values* of Braintree District Council:

1. *We are customer orientated.*
2. *We believe in the abilities of the individual.*
3. *We must be responsive and responsible.*
4. *We believe in quality.*
5. *We are action orientated.*

It then sets out a code of practice on complaints procedures for staff and a separate one for councillors, thereby joining the council members and the council employees together as one team. Both these codes give precise details of everyone's responsibilities and how to provide the best response to complaints. They are summed up in the introduction:

> *The council's aim is to give a high quality service to the public – OUR customers. The only job we have is to provide the best service we can. Customers are not a hindrance; they are our life blood. Without them we would also be without a job.*
>
> *So we have adopted the five core values which we should all try to remember. You will see them on notice boards and flexi machines throughout the offices and they are listed at the back of this booklet.*
>
> *What do they mean? In a nutshell they mean THINK CUSTOMER. Think of a way round a problem so that the customer benefits. Find a reason why we CAN do something, not why we can't. Imagine yourself on the other side of the counter or at the other end of the telephone. Because that's where complaints come in.*
>
> *What is your first impression of someone with a complaint? A nuisance? But supposing it were you who were complaining. That*

would be different wouldn't it? There would be some justification then.

Well there's the truth of the matter. Everyone who complains feels he has grounds to do so. Not many people actually ENJOY complaining. To a customer with a complaint we owe the courtesy of investigating the problem, apologising if we are wrong and putting the matter right as quickly as we can. The more satisfied customers we have, the better our reputation and the easier our job will be.

The leaflet also implies that Braintree aims to be a learning organisation when it says that the basic aim of the new procedures is to ensure that

we deal with complaints efficiently and sympathetically, WHILE AT THE SAME TIME LEARNING FROM THEM.

No doubt when it comes to paying for the services Braintree people grumble like the rest of us, but they do appear to have opportunity to own the services and participate in their development. This chapter has emphasised that total quality is much wider than the manufacturing and engineering arena.

14. Quality and Teamwork Save Bedford

This is a study of quality as the key to saving a company and it illustrates the way in which trade unions supported the total quality approach to help save their members' jobs. This is also one of two case studies with Japanese input involved in the companies.

For ten years up to 1989 the old Bedford Commercial Vehicle Company had been making a loss. This was reversed and the launch of a new vehicle initiated. At a time when other companies were laying off staff, Bedford was overwhelmed by recruitment to get ready for the new product. This was in stark contrast with much of British industry.

Bedford has long been known as a manufacturer of trucks and vans. In 1986 it was faced with bankruptcy. There were problems associated with variable quality and industrial unrest and losses had reached £½ million a week.

Although it was owned by General Motors, there was a limit to how long the parent corporation could sustain the situation. With General Motors' 46 per cent stake in Isuzu, a joint venture was a natural development.

THE NEW COMPANY

A new company was formed in September 1987, fully independent of both General Motors and Isuzu but with General Motors having a 60 per cent share ownership and Isuzu having 40 per cent. The new company took the name Isuzu Bedford Commercial Vehicles, and is known as IBC Vehicles.

The board reflects the 60/40 split of ownership, but the Japanese influence is strong. There are four Japanese people involved at Luton, including the president. The other three are advisory, with no actual direct authority, but obviously a great deal of influence.

THE NEW CONTRACT OF EMPLOYMENT

When the new company was formed, there was some hard negotiation with the trade unions, but in the end £½ million a week loss was something that couldn't be argued with, and as a result, a new contract of employment, which introduced new principles, was agreed. Central to this new contract was a recognition that old attitudes of confrontation between management and the workforce must go. Written into the contract was a commitment to the principles of co-operation, openness and trust as the only way to ensure a quality product, which would sustain profit and jobs.

This was largely achieved, according to Phil Steele of the Personnel Department, although, of course, there were always some pockets of doubt. A major change of this nature could not happen overnight; there was still room for improvement.

TRAVELLING HOPEFULLY

Even when I met the late Tony Jackson, who was personnel manager, in February 1990, the signs for the future were good. Here was a man reared in the old fashioned school of personnel management, who in spite of a sickness which proved terminal, was radiating a joy at the transformation that had come over the company, and a resolution to do all that he could to inspire its progress.

He said that the circumstances, though radically changed, did not mean that perfection had been reached. It was always a matter of travelling hopefully. Business was never a matter of arriving, but constantly readjusting to the requirements of circumstances. In order to do this, you had to have a flexible organisation in which everybody was committed to work together to ensure the highest quality. The principle of continuous improvement was clearly appreciated at the start of the new era.

EARLY PROFIT

At the beginning of the new company a series of business plans were developed which envisaged a loss in the first year, followed by a small profit and then real progress. In fact, they made a profit in year one and doubled the anticipated profit in year two. Phil Steele puts this down to the totally changed way of working, though the move forward was not achieved without some pain.

SIMPLICITY OF APPROACH

A fundamental idea behind the new contract, which could only be a framework, was that the whole workforce should accept and own the new approach and see quality and customer satisfaction as their prime aim. There were initially 1,250 people, building up to 1,750 in the first 12 months. They had to want to be with the company; they couldn't be threatened into change. As Tony Jackson said in 1990, the hearts of the people had to be won.

The basic framework of the contract and of the agreements that flowed from it was one of simplicity. It did not attempt to cover every small thing by written rules. Great significance was given to day-to-day trust and to teamworking.

TEAMWORK

Teamworking became central to the new quality culture. The 1,250 manufacturing staff in employment in 1990 were divided into 130 teams, with up to 12 people in each, in all parts of the operation, press shop, body and paint, final assembly. Regular team meetings were established, team leaders were appointed with quality and efficiency to improve on a continuous basis as their key themes.

CONTINUOUS IMPROVEMENT

An inventory and production system was set up to concentrate on continuous improvement. Statistical process control was spread through the company with everybody gradually learning to understand it, use it and engage in the self-monitoring associated with it, just as the quality gurus have taught. 'Just-in-time' inventory methods were also adopted. A suggestion scheme was introduced and the company ensured that it actually worked, with financial rewards of a tangible nature being given. Even local managers had the right to make small awards in connection with the suggestion scheme if a particular suggestion was not quantifiable, but was moving in the right direction.

HARMONY

This teamworking approach reflected some of the principles which have proved so successful in Japan, but it was recognised that you could not automatically transfer a way of working, based on the Japanese culture, to a Western situation. In Japan the company is seen by the worker as an extension of the family, and the company president is the grandfather of the clan. Loyalty and effort to the firm is like loyalty and effort for one's family, and the pride that goes with that. So there is no complaining about half-hour physical exercise at the beginning of the day, nor about singing the company song.

In a British context, this would probably feel embarrassing. Nevertheless, many of the fundamental principles have been adopted and westernised. There is a meeting first thing in the morning as a means of getting into harmony, to use the Japanese word, with each other. This is a brief time when each team talks about the essentials of the day.

FLATTER MANAGEMENT

The development of teamworking has flattened the management pyramid and pushed decision making down to the lowest possible level, so that assistant managers have the authority to make many decisions previously made higher up the tree.

Where team leaders are eminently successful, then they may be transferred once their work is established, so that they can bring their new skills to bear in another team.

LEARNING THROUGH THE JOB

Training takes place at all levels of the organisation, and is considered a daily activity, particularly in the field of communicating. Training through the job is seen as vital. Communicating is a particularly important skill to learn as it is fundamental to the running of the teams.

THE TOP TEAM

The development of the team approach is not only for the shop floor, but is powerful at the top. Thirty top executives led by the five most senior, including the Japanese president and the vice president, finance, manufacturing and personal directors, have been going away at the beginning of the year for 1½ days to plan for the year ahead and discuss how objectives are to be achieved. The first of these meetings made decisions on capital expenditure for the future and how the small loss that might be incurred could be overcome, as any loss was bad for morale. In the event, of course, there was no loss.

The initial formation of the top executive team included an Outward Bound type of experience, where comradeship was enhanced by doing difficult things in the outdoors together. IBC Vehicles illustrates the point made by all the quality gurus, that top commitment is vital.

COMMUNICATIONS

The objectives worked out at the annual executive conference are cascaded down to everybody. Twice a year everyone in the whole factory stops work and comes to a conference room – the day shift in one meeting and the night shift in another – to receive a progress review of the company; the current situation, the future hopes, the financial background, and the opportunities for new ideas and new products. At the June meeting of the executive group, progress reports from all the other teams are considered. All this concern with proper communicating and the cascading of information is seen as developmental in itself, both for those at the senior level and for those further down the chain, who have to pass the communications along in the regular communicating, as distinct from the twice yearly jamborees. It also inspires a sense of belonging.

A POSITIVE APPROACH

The company has talented management people, and Phil Steele said the aim is to take the shackles off them to broaden them and enable them to make further progress. There is no question of treating people as machines, because this would be a self-fulfilling prophecy. If high quality is to be maintained it has to be through people who understand what quality means and who are not satisfied with anything less.

The salary negotiations, although not agreeing the highest wages in the car industry, have been carried through with a minimum of problems and the company has lost no time of any significance through industrial action in the period since the changes.

UNION REPRESENTATION

There is a company joint council of sixteen members, five managers and eleven trade unionists from five different unions. The only qualification about the union representation is that however many unions are represented, they will agree and speak with one voice and elect a single spokesperson. This is somewhat different from the traditional Japanese single union approach, but it expresses the same idea.

COMMON CONDITIONS

Similarly, the single status or harmonised approach to employment conditions is followed. There are no special parking arrangements for anybody, not even for the president. There is no clocking in. There is a sick pay scheme for the shop floor, as well as for the office staff, on the grounds that the one should be trusted as much as the other. Trust breeds worthiness of trust as, Tony Jackson said shortly after the new company came into existence. The staff all eat from the same kiosk areas and use the same microwave ovens. The pension is on the same basis. The only difference lies in the actual salaries paid. The move away from the 'them and us' attitude which used to characterise so much of British industry is a regular feature in companies which adopt total quality management.

PRAISE

The executive group who meet every January made some open resolutions one year. One of these very senior managers made the resolution, and made it public, that he would be careful to praise the good things all the time, and would not engage in any putdowns because these were demotivational and negative. Even if an idea is not particularly good, it should not be derided.

MANAGERIAL ORGANISATION

Of the managers below the 30 executives, 51 are assistant managers, and below that are the supervisors who now have a strategic input. Their ideas on the direction of the company and their particular part of the business are actively sought and received with genuine interest. The role of general foreman has been dropped, and team leaders have assumed a much greater role.

APPRAISAL

The appraisal scheme is not just for managers – all staff are involved. There are special awards for performance; training needs are analysed; readiness for promotion is considered. Training is available, not only to do what needs to be done currently, but to enable people to move on to the team leader role and more senior roles. People are sent on courses where appraisal reveals needs, but they can initiate a request to have some special experience.

In order to enable team leaders and supervisors to carry out appraisal discussions, everybody is trained in counselling and appraisal activity if it forms part of their function.

MULTI-SKILLING

Within the teams there is a move towards multi-skilling. The company would not claim to be there yet; it takes time to train people to widen their skills, but the attitude of flexibility and willingness to avoid the 'It's not my job' syndrome is making rapid progress. There are no job descriptions to shackle people, so that multi-skilling tends to grow organically rather than be imposed.

CULTURE CHANGE

All in all a culture change has been achieved, and the company is now much more open; problems are openly discussed. Phil Steele said that the personnel policies developed are no longer mechanical sets of rules, but rather an expression of what is felt to be right. In my discussions with IBC there was little emphasis on what would conventionally be called management development, but because of the need to nurture the culture change, the top 30, the next 51, and the supervisors were very much involved in activity which affected their own development.

The team approach means that everybody not only has the opportunity, but also the need to develop. At IBC it is very difficult to separate management development from people development and company development.

SHARED VISION

Because of the holistic approach to the activity of the company, IBC finds training and development integrated with the business itself.

The way in which the top management considers itself and its objectives annually by its away days and then shares the business objectives with all the employees, is certainly in the direction of the UK 'Investors in People' Initiative. (See Appendix A.) There is a vision at the top, and it is shared all the way down.

LEARNING EVERY DAY

The exercise of appraisal throughout the company for staff at all levels means that the training needs for everybody are clearly identified. Many of them are met through the job itself. The team approach means that every day is a learning experience in which people share insights with one another.

RIGOROUS RECRUITMENT

Recruitment is being taken very seriously to ensure that the people who join IBC are of a calibre whose skill can be enhanced by continuous development and training. Right from the start this is a matter of significant concern for all managers and team leaders, supported by the Personnel Department.

EVALUATION

IBC is pragmatic about evaluating progress in training for quality. The impact of specific training is linked with the great emphasis on communication, openness and trust. The existence of teams is seen as a way of daily learning and sharing. Collective synergies are developed by such teamwork, and it is very difficult to separate the training activity from the total trading activity. There is doubt as to whether any sophisticated evaluation techniques applied to specific training activity would add much to the effectiveness of the company.

However, everything that is done is constantly evaluated to ensure that the way the company is organised and the way people learn leads to continuous improvement in every activity. Where continuous improvement is an active policy permeating the whole company ethos and activity, then evaluation runs side by side with it. Individuals evaluate their own contribution, and their team leaders help them do this. If you know that things are better, that there is improvement not only in the bottom line, but in all the ingredients that weld together into the bottom line, then you know that you are on course.

A company like IBC that believes in continuous improvement, believes in teamworking, believes in communication and enhancement of performance, knows whether it is learning or not. Learning is its very breath, and the outcomes are clear to see – a quality product in the customer's terms.

15. Seaham Harbour Dock Company Takes the Long View

Those of us who like to sit on a cliff top and look far out to sea could find few better places than David Clifford's office at the Seaham Harbour Dock Company, where he is the managing director. The lovely Durham coastline stretching out for miles is a symbol of the envisioning of the future Chris Conway and I were there to talk about.

There has been a harbour at Seaham since 1828, when the Marquess of Londonderry built it as an outlet for the coal from his mines in the north-east. Today the port of Seaham (now part of Anglo United plc), is still thriving and handling a wide variety of products.

A SMALL COMPANY WITH BIG IDEAS

Although a small company (with a turnover of £4.5 million and 80 employees), it is the second largest employer in the area with about 700 jobs relying indirectly on its success. Devolution of authority and the development of people are its key routes to quality. This chapter shows how binding a company together with a sense of purpose helps to create quality service as perceived by the customer.

David Clifford believes that the development of the organisation is dependent on releasing the contribution of the whole workforce. This strategic view has not always prevailed at the dock. The 'us and them' attitude used to thrive at Seaham. The change is reflected in common conditions of employment for all the employees.

Management used to stay in their offices, we were told. But when David Clifford was appointed general manager in 1977, he initiated a new approach, by walking around the quays and talking to people. 'It was a long and painful process but it worked' and management by walking around is now the practice of all the managers at the port. It is the kind of business in which success depends upon that kind of relationship.

A MASSIVE DIVERSITY OF SKILLS

The 150 acre self-contained site encompasses many different operations and skills. Not only is there a lighthouse, but a coal disposal site, the dock itself and a five-mile railway system complete with engines and rolling stock.

There is also a wide range of crafts; electricians, fitters, boilersmiths, turners, stevedores and drivers of fork lift trucks, cranes and mechanical grabs. Also, there are the skills associated with the 200,000 square feet of warehousing, such as the computerised weighbridge, stock control and its management. Because of this diversity a multi-skilled and flexible workforce is essential to successful operation at Seaham. On one occasion, when they were shorthanded and had a deadline to meet, David Clifford donned his overalls and gave a hand in unloading a ship.

HOW THE DOCK IS MANAGED

The management structure of the company reflects David Clifford's belief that individuals should take responsibility for their own area of work.

The operations director, the company secretary and David as managing director form the management board of the company. In addition all eight managers act as a management committee which meets formally once a month and informally every week. David

Clifford has increasingly pulled back from the day-to-day activities of the port. On one of our visits his management committee was carrying out the annual round of wage negotiations while he talked to us.

This principle of delegating as far down the line as possible gives people a sense of responsibility for the quality of the work. It is in harmony with ensuring that all employees know they can make a clear contribution to the success of the business.

At the same time, flatter structures within the company have resulted in twelve grades being reduced to four categories of employee other than manager and foreman supervisor – craftsman, operationally skilled, labourers and trainees.

Getting started with a new strategy

'We now have a more efficient and effective operation capable of responding and developing to meet future needs.'

These are the words of David Clifford on his organisation's search for a strategy for the future. In this search he was determined to involve as many people as possible in the process of developing and communicating a vision of where the company was heading.

To kick-start things, he decided that outside assistance was required. Thus, Seaham gained the distinction of being the first UK company to take up and complete the UK Employment Department's Business Growth Training Option 3 Initiative.

The essence of this scheme is that it provides substantial financial help towards securing the services of a management consultant over a one-year period. It aims to develop managers so that they have the ability to focus on key business issues and achieve business objectives.

Under the aegis of Option 3, Seaham acquired expert advice on planning for change as well as facilitating progress in a way whereby the employees feel a sense of ownership of the changes. Management training, both on and off the job, was designed and implemented.

THE DEVELOPMENT OF THE BUSINESS PLAN

In the beginning David Clifford and his managers held brainstorming sessions to identify their mission and then proceeded to divide up the objectives for further action.

From this a detailed business plan took shape. The next stage involved individual training and development needs analysis which started with the middle managers and went on to the supervisors during a difficult period for the company.

KEY RESULT AREAS REVIEWED

The process of creating a strategy involved identifying key result areas for individual managers, starting with the managing director himself. What does he have to do? To whom does he report? What does he delegate? From this type of question, a template was produced with which individuals could measure their own key result areas.

Each key result area was associated with the company's overall mission and objectives. People were asked if they had sufficient authority and resources to do the job. This determination to empower people to do things without constant reference up and with minimum supervision is a major aspect of the management philosophy at Seaham Harbour. The current phase of this activity is re-examining the company's objectives, reviewing everything that is done and evaluating success.

KNOCKING DOWN THE BARRIERS TO WORKING AND LEARNING

Some projects have been designed with the additional aim of providing an opportunity for teamworking, because as David Clifford notes: 'When people are busy, the barriers go down. It's when they have more time that artificial barriers often re-establish themselves.'

Every Friday there is a lunch-time meeting of the managers over sandwiches in David Clifford's office. They discuss the week's events and share information and opinions. It may be a specific 'hot topic' such as safety, but mostly the general operations of the port are discussed. The lunch period has been chosen because it tends to be quiet, and it provides the atmosphere of informality which aids free exchange of opinion.

The more formal monthly meeting provides the forum for reporting activities and receiving reports such as the financial figures from the finance director. The brief for the monthly meeting is prepared by each manager after they have met with their own managers and supervisors. Good ideas which have been generated are put forward to the monthly management meeting, and 'good ideas get put into effect so that people know that others are listening to them'.

This process is continually developing and improving the skills of employees which is central to being an investor in people. Development is not seen as an elitist activity, but as a matter of total employee development.

'We use our monthly management meetings as learning opportunities and giving people the freedom to make decisions, and by implication, mistakes – that's the best way to develop.'

Each manager brings a different supervisor to the monthly meeting on a rota basis, and this initiative has worked well, involving more people in the decision-making process at Seaham. In addition, the full minutes of the meeting are widely distributed all around the port. The minutes form a central element in communicating. They are written in a helpful way with sections, for example, on health and safety, quality, warehouse operations, engineering, in fact covering all parts of the harbour's operations. The minutes contain an open invitation to make suggestions (or indeed, complaints). This invitation has been readily taken up by the workforce who have made suggestions ranging from modifications to the dock's sea gates to the provision of litter bins on the site.

On a day-to-day basis, the foremen/supervisors are involved in organising the day's activities, and while, inevitably, there are variations in management styles between different departments, the foremen make a point of networking together to achieve a smooth linkage of operation between departments; they are customers and suppliers to each other. This method of working also enables employees to contribute to identifying and meeting their own job-related development needs. This development of the whole workforce is an enabling factor in bringing about major change within an organisation, not least in the pervasive issue of quality.

GOING FOR QUALITY

'Quality affects everything, really.' So says Brian Foster, the warehouse manager and quality representative. The motto of Seaham Harbour is 'total cargo care', and quality has been a key feature of the change programme which has transformed the business.

The warehouse operation at Seaham involves the management of the 200,000 square feet of warehouse space and ten acres of open storage. The work of these areas, together with the weighbridge, stock control and the bagging and palletising plant were assessed and passed first time by auditors from the British Standards Institute for the award of Part 2 of BS5750.

This standard requires all personnel to work systematically to a documented procedure. Brian Foster led the management team in the initial formation of the procedures of the warehouse, and now has a lead role in developing the quality initiative so that it will eventually take in all parts of the company.

WHAT QUALITY MEANS AT SEAHAM

The cargoes handled at Seaham are diverse; coal, coke, limestone, urea, fertilizer, dolomite, soda ash, scrap, pig iron, magnetite and grain are all exported from the dock. The imported products are anthracite, technical urea, coal, coke, ferrule alloys, refractory materials, fertilizer, sand, salt, phospate rock, sulphur and animal feeds. With this wide range of products being handled, a quality approach becomes essential.

The mixing of one product with another and the consequent

contamination could have serious consequences; a major quality issue is avoiding this. The dock handles animal feeds, which are inspected by the Ministry of Agriculture, Fisheries and Food (MAFF) who have strict regulations regarding their storage, and Seaham claims the best record in the United Kingdom for this type of storage.

One of the major potential contaminants of animal feed is bird excreta, which can cause the salmonella virus to develop in the feed. In their effort to prevent this form of contamination, the warehouse employs a contractor and his falcon to come in one day per month, and this is sufficient to frighten off the offending birds.

The quality approach at the warehouse involves a shared knowledge of the products handled, temperature control and the handling of potentially dangerous substances. It also means involving the customer who values the skill and knowledge of the warehouse manager and his staff. In fact, on many occasions the latter provide a sort of free consultancy to their customers.

Quality versus price

One of the problems which deregulation of the docks has brought about is that a small operator can quickly set up in competition and undercut on price. Seaham Harbour has found that the issue is not necessarily price – though it endeavours to be as competitive as possible – but quality. Quality concerns of an operational nature can have greater significance to the customer than financial issues. They ultimately have financial implications.

The quality of the products' storage means that the customer will return because of the reputation of the port. Brian Foster has said, 'We are working as a team and the result is that our customers receive a standard of service that precisely meets their specifications – you've got to be customer orientated now.' In this teamworking there is ongoing learning as the group searches continuously for more effective ways of maintaining the standards. It is a clear case of learning through the job and learning together to achieve total quality. It is also never-ending learning because it involves the search for perfection.

FORMAL RECOGNITION OF LEARNING

So how did Brian Foster get where he is today? He realised that his learning through the job needed to be supplemented. To achieve greater proficiency, he attended several events on warehouse management organised by National Association of Warehouse Keepers (NAWK). He has been able to take advantage of membership to keep up to date with the latest developments in this field, and also to network with other warehousemen in action learning groups.

This shared learning is further enhanced by Seaham's membership of the quality forum of the North Durham Corporation and the British Quality Association. Incidentally, Brian finds it necessary to order two copies of his NAWK newsletter as one always 'disappears' and is avidly read by his staff.

The penultimate word on quality is with Brian Foster.

'Quality is becoming a way of life for everyone here at the port. Due to the enthusiastic support and commitment we have behind us, from top management down through every department, our quality assurance programme has made a significant cultural impact on the company.'

However, David Clifford has given a firm indication of things to come on the quality front.

'The BS5750 registration achieved for the warehouse is only the beginning of our programme. Work is now well under way to extend this to cover all port and railway activities and eventually to achieve the ultimate goal of total quality management.'

ASSESSING THE NEEDS OF PEOPLE

It is no surprise to find training needs discussed as a regular standard item on the agenda for both the monthly and weekly management meetings. At Seaham each individual's training needs are assessed (as they must be under BS5750). The quality initiative has reinforced training and vice versa.

Another contribution has been from appraisal – not in the formal sense but in an ongoing review of key result areas with supervisors. This assists with the analysis of development needs. As an adjunct to this review process, through-the-job experience is enhanced by informal mentoring.

Under the earlier regulation by the National Dock Labour Board (NDLB) the sense of ownership and responsibility for the whole operation was stifled by demarcation and other restrictive practices. This atmosphere was not conducive to people being empowered because managers themselves felt helpless in the face of the legislation, which had become something of a controlling factor: 'You could only manage as far as they let you.'

The post-NDLB environment has meant a complete sea change for the management of the dock.

CUSTOMER RELATIONSHIPS

Commitment to the customer has resulted in flexibility and an enhancement of the staff's investigative skills, including new solutions to quality problems. People are seeing quality service as doing more than the customer expects and as an example, Andrew Ridley (Foster's assistant) has instituted giving customers the dock's internal record sheets so they can use them to reconcile their own stocks.

This open approach to customer relationships has involved the sea-going crews as well as the shipping agents who are based at Seaham. Customer complaints are taken seriously too: 'If you get a complaint, you do something about it.' Andrew reviews trends in complaints to see how the system can be tightened up. This propensity to innovation and initiative exemplifies what can happen when people's creative energies are liberated by a forward-thinking management.

Andrew Ridley's pride in the bagging plant, which he described to us with evident affection as 'my baby' evinced a desire to continue improving existing installations and procedures. For example, ten rather windblown acres of open storage are prone to dust problems – Andrew's solution was to invent his own sprinkler system which has considerably cut down this nuisance.

181

RELEASING PEOPLE'S POTENTIAL

Throughout his time at Seaham, Andrew has been the constant focus of his manager's attention in terms of his training needs and development. He has put Andrew into situations where he can learn through the job, whilst being actively supported and not just left to get on with it.

The commitment to continuous development is a central feature of what goes on at Seaham. This development is not confined simply to the managers of the port. When a person is recognised as having potential, that person is given a chance. David Clifford, for instance, insisted on promoting a telephonist to warehouse clerk as he saw her potential. She was given a period of time to acclimatise and learn the job before her performance was reviewed. Thus, faith in people based on sound analysis has formed a large part of people development at Seaham Harbour.

SEAHAM AND THE COMMUNITY

When a company has been established for over 160 years, strong links with the community are formed. Courage is then needed to introduce change. Changing the image of the port in its relationship with the community has been a major concern.

Quality management at Seaham also includes relationships with the community. An imaginative example has been the Seaham Harbour Coastal Centre. This building was formerly the Seamen's Mission and based on the quay has a good view of the port and the coastline. Used primarily to encourage local schoolchildren to learn about industry, it is also available for use by other interested parties such as further education students and adult groups. A schoolteacher is allocated to the running of the centre on behalf of the local authority and David's personal assistant administers it.

Another innovation has been an annual open day. In 1989 this featured ten NATO ships in the dock, and raised £8,000 for charity. The open day is an occasion when the townspeople of Seaham and the partners, children, and families of the dock's employees can visit the harbour and find out what goes on there. This understanding can be vitally useful in maintaining good relations between the company and the town dependent on it for its livelihood.

Seaham Harbour Dock Company provided many insights into a small company as a major innovator. The changes are real and not cosmetic. They fundamentally alter the way people perceive themselves and their jobs. There is a ceaseless search to contribute to the needs of customers and of the location as a whole, conforming to the requirements of the populace and seeking to exceed their expectations. This is quality for Seaham.

16. Quality with Texaco at Pembroke Oil Refinery

Texaco has a major oil refinery at Pembroke in Wales. Indeed it is one of the most advanced in Europe, and with capital costs high, and productivity critical to cost-effectiveness, quality in everything done is essential.

A QUALITY SYSTEM

An oil refinery is a process plant in which you get a very clear physical picture of what a system is about. Everything in the process flow affects everything else. A fault in one area can bring the whole plant to a stop. This is a clear analogy to understanding any business activity as a system. There cannot be little fortresses carrying on their part of the company's activities in complete isolation from each other. This is why the concept of the chain of customers and suppliers is so important in total quality.

So Texaco have built up an organisation in which the end product and the technical skills that stage by stage deliver the product are orientated towards quality. Quality in safety, quality in technical correctness, quality in environmental awareness. It was this preoccupation with quality that led the *Sunday Times* to commission the filming of a video on quality at Pembroke.

Quality is not related only to the main product, such as petrol. Getting more useful total product out of each barrel of crude oil is also a significant issue. It can make all the difference to the profitability, and therefore effectivess, of the company. Texaco can now convert almost 50 per cent of crude oil into petrol, with a further 40 per cent into other useful products such as jet fuel, home heating and diesel. This doubles the efficiency achieved in the early 1960s. This was borne out by a 1991 study of refineries throughout Europe. In four years the refinery moved from fifteenth on a rating of critical categories to second. This is a result of the co-operation of a whole range of people from designers and engineers to operators and technicians. It might be thought that using the word quality to describe overall business performance is stretching things a bit, but if the ultimate customer is to receive a product at a price that is acceptable, then productivity and efficiency matter too; they are part of the chain of quality.

SHUTDOWN 1990

All process operations, particularly where hydrocarbons (oil, fossil fuels, etc.) are involved, have a potential for danger. There are governmental regulations and substantial self regulation.

Whole areas of a process plant have to be closed from time to time so that major maintenance can take place. A key decision is how long these shutdowns take, and how often they should occur. Good quality preventive maintenance avoids unscheduled shutdowns, which lead to production losses.

In 1990 all production units were shut down in a phased manner to facilitate inspection and maintenance work. In addition, extensive revamp work was undertaken to increase the capacity of the refinery's catalytic-cracker unit.

It was decided to operate Shutdown 1990 as a project in its own right incorporating the quality management philosophy.

Total quality has to reach into every part of the company. It is not possible to have just one project on a total quality approach in isolation from the rest of a plant or company. The whole company and certainly the whole plant have to be involved in the total quality process. Pembroke are in no doubt about this.

PLANNING THE SHUTDOWN

In the case of the Texaco shutdown project, planning started 15 months prior to the operation, with the selection of people who would work well in teams. This is an example of a long timescale of preparation designed to save time when the actual work is done. These new teams followed the participative approach, thrashing out problems in meetings and learning to work together.

There was also a lot of listening to the staff, who operate the equipment every day. They were invited to be part of the project and to have a sense of ownership in return for which they gave expertise and commitment.

There was a detailed analysis of tasks, pre-planning of each part of the project and writing it down in detail.

Fundamental to all of this, and without which planning would not have achieved its objective, was making sure that full consultation occured continuously. Everybody, regardless of specialisms, shared the planning, listing and preparation. Nevertheless, there were specialists who could be consulted outside the individual teams. Information and knowledge was made available without the erection of barriers. This hierarchy went out of the window and individual responsibility came in.

IMPLEMENTING THE SHUTDOWN

The shutdown and revamp operation was also a success. It was completed on schedule (eight weeks) and within budget (£50 million).

Vast numbers of people were involved in the shutdown operation. Texaco normally employs around 650 staff at the plant, with 250 regular contractors, but at the peak of the shutdown period, working around the clock, close on 3,000 people were involved in the project. So high was the quality of the action that during the whole shutdown there was only one accident, a minor one where somebody's foot slipped through the scaffolding planks. It was felt that the reasons for this high safety record were the planning and preparation that had gone into the project. Most industrial accidents happen because people improvise, don't know where to get the right tools or from whom to seek advice.

The shutdown operation had a real impact on the normal work of the plant. Normal maintenance, part of the prevention aspect of total quality, is more effective because people became used to following fine detail in planning and using computerised procedures. Links were forged. People became more co-operative. They came to understand each other's jobs and work for other members of the team.

Measuring performance is involved in any operation. Texaco is already talking about and establishing even more challenging targets for the whole team to aim for.

BS5750 – Tool for supporting total quality

While total quality means an attitude of mind, it will not succeed just by good thinking, though that must lie at its root. Documented procedures are essential and can be achieved by following the BS5750 or ISO900 standards.

Areas of the refinery have been accredited with the BS5750 award, as they demonstrate written procedures and practices to ensure they operate to approved standards. Texaco believes this is important. It forms an excellent framework or foundation for a quality management system. However the company emphasises that it does not cover more than 30 per cent of what is involved in a total quality process. It covers what is often described as the 'quality assurance' element of total quality but does not involve all facets covered in this book, though it can be used to support them.

As at the end of 1991, Texaco's registration under BS5750 at Pembroke covered the blending, storage and testing of finished products, including gasoline, kerosene, diesel and fuel oil. Plant manager Guy Birmingham stresses that this achievement was a total team effort. Inspectors from the British Standards Institute visited Pembroke in October 1991, planning to spend three days auditing procedures and activities. But it took them only two days to be satisfied that the BS5750 requirements were being almost entirely met. Texaco was given 42 days to make good a few deficiencies, but within two weeks had met all the requirements.

David Harries, quality assurance manager, comments on the way in which the success was due to a concerted effort by all staff which operated across departmental boundaries. He sees the award as giving customers confidence that Texaco will meet their need – i.e., give them quality. Everyone has to be properly trained for their work and a yardstick against which to measure performance is provided. Harries sees BS5750 as a 'very powerful tool for letting us evaluate where we are and for *helping us move toward total quality*'. BS5750 is a tool to be used in the journey towards total quality. It is not the final goal.

THE COMPANY-WIDE TEXACO QUALITY PROCESS

This account of Texaco and its 1990 Shutdown has looked at a specific experience, but the challenge got total quality moving forward fast. It has removed barriers to communication, it has embedded the concept of continuous improvement, of teamworking, of ownership, commitment and collegiality. It is an example of the company-wide impact of the quality process.

In the company as a whole quality is inspired by top commitment. A quality council has been established with senior executives, aiming to practice as well as preach, as its members. Their programme includes the following:

- Developing a strategy and programme for continuous improvement.
- Setting up quality action teams (QATs) and employee involvement teams (EITs).
- Emphasis on teamwork.
- Helping everyone involved to define their roles and co-ordinate their activities.

Texaco's quality statement reads:

> *To create a continuous improvement process which unites Texaco in its commitment to a quality culture and focuses our efforts to meet or exceed customers' expectations by:*
> - *Inspired leadership*
> - *Employee participation*
> - *Teamwork*

Top management in Texaco are committed to quality. They are on record as saying:

> *Our renewed focus on quality leads directly to better productivity, improved service, and employees who discover a new-found pride in their company and themselves.*

They attribute the turnaround at Pembroke to the introduction of a total quality process. Previously people didn't have the spirit of participation needed. They were too used to being told what to do. Nothing more was expected of them. Total quality management can succeed only if everyone's mind is attuned and their contribution not only welcomed, but expected.

Texaco's top management declare that:

> *The customer is demanding better service, and the company needs to be in a position to provide it. The total quality process also generates productivity and quality improvements that contribute directly to the company's bottom line . . . and personal rewards . . . a pride which drives Texaco forward.*

17. *Quality with ICL*

This chapter describes ICL – Britain's major indigenous computer company, which has gone down the Crosby route on quality.

ICL employs approximately 27,000 people and operates in over 70 countries world-wide. The combined turnover of the group in 1990 was over four billion US dollars. The Ashton plant was opened in 1979 as the centre of ICL's mainframe production. Since then it has expanded and makes the complete ICL product range from personal computers to mainframes.

A MODERN FACTORY

The Ashton plant is a modern factory, using productive methods such as 'just-in-time' and 'flexible manufacturing'. 'Just-in-time' means that the material or components from the previous operation arrive just in time for the next operation. It is an example of a close customer/supplier chain. This makes each person in the chain responsible for supplying high-quality, defect-free products. It means that bottlenecks no longer build up because the material arrives too soon and in too great a quantity. Flexible manufacturing means that fewer people are dedicated to a single product. It also means that the production schedule can be changed at very short notice to cater for fluctuating customer demands.

All this is necessary to respond rapidly to customer requirements in the competitive information technology industry.

The factory has been so successful that in 1989 it was voted one of the best British factories in terms of quality, productivity, cost and customer satisfaction. This was followed in 1990 with a British quality award. However the company makes the point that the success of this factory can be understood only in the context of a company-wide programme launched in 1986, which has changed the face of the whole organisation.

QUALITY IN ICL

ICL recognised that if it was to survive in the 1980s and beyond, the quality and reliability of the product range must be second to none. This could not be achieved piecemeal; the whole company had to have a common understanding and a common goal.

A completely new quality management structure was introduced, led and monitored from the top by a steering committee of board members. A new post of director, quality was created and Joe Goasdoué was recruited to direct the programme.

Over the next four years a dramatic change occurred. Everyone in ICL went through a training programme so that everybody in the organisation, from operator to managing director now speak and understand a common language of quality. This is based on a policy which states:

> *We will provide competitive systems products and services which fully meet our internal and external customers' requirements first time, on time and every time.*

Supporting this, ICL defines four principles or rules of quality, based on the Crosby four absolutes:

- Quality is defined as conformance to requirements - not goodness.
- The system for quality is prevention - not appraisal.
- The performance standard is zero defects - not 'That's close enough'.
- The measurement of quality is the price of nonconformance - not indexes.

ZERO DEFECTS

ICL took the approach that zero defects was to be the objective, whether it took weeks, months or years. It meant measuring where you were, being clear about where you wanted to get to, and consistently reviewing the performance of the products to identify areas for improvement.

Zero defects in terms of ICL's approach means not producing anything which the customer would view as not conforming to requirements. Chris Hodgkinson of ICL makes the point that zero defects should not be confused with absolute perfection. This is sometimes misunderstood by people who think of it as an idealistic impossibility. Philip Crosby makes a distinction between defects and errors. He sees a defect as something which is wrong from the customers' point of view, which will be objected to when delivery is taken. Errors may be made, but are identified and corrected.

ICL follow Philip Crosby's approach quite closely and therefore you will hear in everyday conversation within the company, reference to the price of nonconformance. If you don't conform to the agreed specification which your customer, internal or external expects, there will be a cost associated with it. Everybody takes responsibility in a zero defects programme for doing their work right first time. 'Right' being conformance to customers' requirements.

Philip Crosby goes in for quite a lot of razzamatazz, as noted earlier, and this is part of the secret of his success. You might expect this to be alien to the ICL culture, but at Ashton alone, three zero defects days have been held so far. All staff freely sign a zero defects board which pledges their commitment to the goal of zero defects.

CHECKING YOUR OWN WORK

In the sixties ICL, like most of British industry, employed people to inspect other people's work. This meant that if anything was wrong by defined standards, delivery to the external customer would be prevented.

Inspection by people other than the person who produces the

component takes away responsibility for quality from where it really lies, that is with the person doing the job. You would often hear the phrase: 'It's not my fault, he let it go!'

The days of separate inspectors have long since gone in ICL. Now everyone is responsible for getting it right first time and checking their own work. Operators self-inspect so that errors are corrected at each stage of manufacture. ICL operators also have the power and ability to identify and suggest improvements to the process or procedures which affect the way they do the job. This new-found freedom means that employees find their job much more interesting and their pride in their work has been restored.

CONTINUOUS IMPROVEMENT

There are a number of ways in which staff can suggest improvements in the way the job is done. All staff have access to an Error Cause Removal system (ECR). When a person isn't able to solve the problem immediately, either alone or with the help of the supervisor, an ECR is raised. This identifies the problem and sends it up the line for resolution. The ECR stays open and is reviewed by the management team until it is resolved to the individual's satisfaction. This gives the individual operator a mechanism for alerting management to the need to make changes to the system and for contributing ideas to management. (For discussion of the variations which are systemic and require management attention as distinct from those which operators can handle themselves, see chapter 3.)

If the ECR is outside the scope of the division then an inter-divisional Corrective Action Request (CAR) can be raised. This is logged on a corporate computer system and again not removed until the problem is resolved. This contributes to a complete check on the total price of nonconformance.

At Ashton there are over 40 quality circles in operation. A group of people from the same department meet weekly for one hour to discuss and identify problems or introduce better ways of working.

Process improvement teams and corrective action teams also

operate across all layers of staff. They have a common aim, that of identifying ways to improve customer satisfaction.

At the end of 1990 over 60 per cent of Ashton workers were involved directly in quality improvement teams, the total of ECRs raised reached over 500 and 28 CARs had been raised on other ICL divisions.

INVESTING IN PEOPLE

Everyone in ICL is a 'member of staff'. The word staff was chosen quite deliberately, for in ICL there is no white collar/blue collar divide. There is no reserved car parking space, everyone eats in the same restaurants, no one clocks on or off, everyone works the same number of hours, and gets paid monthly.

ICL publicly recognises its people as one of its most important assets. The company invests time, effort and resources in developing them to their highest potential. Everyone in ICL has clear objectives set each year. These are reviewed every quarter. How you perform against these agreed objectives decides the level of your pay rise the following year. Some quality gurus are opposed to this approach: there is a need for some in-depth research into the detail of what actually happens in companies adopting it. There is also an annual appraisal which identifies the individual's ambitions and training requirements for the next year.

Also on an annual basis staff opinion is sought by a confidential survey. Management acts on the information to improve all aspects of the working environment.

TRAINING FOR QUALITY

The fundamental of this total quality approach is a well trained staff. Some 24,000 ICL people have received quality training which started with the chairman and managing director. At Ashton alone this amounts to over 16,500 hours in total.

The surprising fact connected with this training is that it was given by line managers and not by the training or quality departments. Line managers were first sent on a quality training course. They then coached their own staff in quality theory and practice. This cascaded learning approach has worked very well and has generated a real sense of ownership at grass roots level in the company.

The training courses were initially bought in from Crosby but since 1986 ICL has developed its own range of quality courses, for which in 1988 it received the training industry's highest accolade, a national training award.

THE QUALITY CHAIN

Jim Baglin, a production manager at Ashton, says that quality is a state of mind which now permeates the whole staff. He also identifies the customer/supplier chain as a significant help in the progress of the company. Everybody has a customer within the company who is waiting for the results of his or her activity. Thus the stores are suppliers to various sections who are their customers. If what is supplied is not of the correct quality, then the internal customer communicates with the supplier directly. The faulty item is not put to one side for another person to resolve. This reduces manufacturing time, reduces inventory and instils a sense of ownership of the problem at the lowest level in the organisation.

It also ensures that quality is attended to at each stage of the process by the people who find the errors rather than by end of line inspectors, where the task of providing a defect-free product to the customer would be much more difficult.

There is a readiness by management and other staff alike to halt the production process at any stage when the quality is not right. This goes against 'keep everything moving', which has been traditional in the manufacturing sector. The staff soon became aware that zero defects really meant that no product must leave the factory until it was right. This has extended to closing down production on more than one occasion in order to trace a fault.

Another prominent factor of the work being done at ICL is that labour costs have come down. In the early eighties materials cost about 50 per cent, and the other 50 per cent was down to labour and overheads. Currently the top of the range product cost is around 93 per cent materials and only seven per cent labour and overhead. This highlights the essential nature of 'just-in-time', flexible manufacturing and quality to the survival and prosperity of the manufacturing division of ICL.

Alastair Kelly, director of manufacturing, says that as more and more of the product costs move towards materials, then the investment in materials has to be kept to a minimum, because that's where most of the cost is. The product has to move through the factory as quickly as possible to reach the end customer. However, in spite of this there are no shortcuts on quality, as this would be counter-productive.

SUPPLIER RELATIONSHIPS

The quality emphasis involves other external companies in the chain. The chain is only as strong as its weakest link. Quality vendors have to deliver the right material just in time so that there are no inventory costs due to holding excessive stocks in the stores at Ashton.

ICL has a very clear policy towards sourcing components from other European companies wherever possible: the figure is currently over 60 per cent. The number of suppliers has been progressively reducing over a number of years. This means that ICL works very closely with its vendors sharing future strategy and new product information way in advance of what would have been considered a few years ago. Having established a mutual relationship based on trust and understanding, ICL are able to save time and money by not inspecting or 'shipping to stock' the vendors' product. It can be used in production right away; currently some 80 per cent of parts go through this system.

ICL operates what it terms a vendor accreditation programme; membership of the programme is based on business and quality credentials including Electronic Data Interchange (EDI) of essential information, for example, orders and production schedules. The suppliers are also expected to gain accreditation to BS5750 or ISO9000 or at least have clear plans to achieve it within a defined timescale. ICL operates similar schemes for its authorised traders.

The general manager of one of ICL's suppliers, Jarrobs Ltd of

Alsager, Stoke on Trent, tells how it took over two years to get the ISO9000 accolade. ISO9000 accreditation does not guarantee quality, of course, but it's a step in the right direction.

BS5750/ISO9000

ICL considers BS5750 registration to be a major element in its quality strategy in all areas of the company in the UK. In fact ICL is proud to be the first company to receive a corporate registration to the standard from the British Standards Institute in 1991 and plans to seek equivalent registration for all its subsidiaries world-wide.

RECOGNITION

Another part in ICL's quality jigsaw is recognition. All employees are encouraged to improve quality. Any member of staff who is seen to be doing a quality job can be recommended for a quality award. The cross-company scheme has three levels – bronze, silver and gold. At the highest level the gold winners, together with a guest of their choice, are taken away by the company for an all expenses-paid weekend where 22-carat solid gold medals are presented by the ICL chairman and managing director. All winners' names are included in the Excellence scheme roll of honour which together with quality stories, appear in the company magazine.

QUALITY CUTS COSTS

At Ashton, Alastair Kelly was the plant director during the time the quality programme was initiated. He was the driving force behind the plant's move to total quality. In 1980 the company was running at a loss and could not compete with Far Eastern suppliers either on quality or price. It had to get a competitive edge and quality was seen as the way. Alastair says that the ICL manufacturing division does not have the absolute right to manufacture ICL's products. If as an internal customer it cannot compete with external competition then the division will not survive. However, that day has not yet arrived. In the first five years of the programme ICL calculates it eliminated £163 million from the price of nonconformance (the cost of not getting it right first time). This supports the view that quality does not increase costs overall. Rather the reverse.

At Ashton the manufacturing cycle time is now down from 50 days to 12, inventory turns (the number of times stock is rotated) is up to 12.2 from 3.2 in 1985, goods in process time is down from 40 hours in 1985 to 0.5 hours now. At the same time operator efficiency and quality have improved dramatically.

QUALITY THE ICL WAY

ICL stresses that only by visible and total commitment by management will a quality programme succeed. The rules apply in bad times as well as good. You cannot expect an instant return on the investment. Quality improvement may take many years, but at the end of the day it is a matter of business survival.

What ICL has discovered is that there is no simple way to implement a quality programme, no single tool or off-the-shelf product will suffice. ICL aims to search out best practice tools and techniques and implement them to produce constant improvements in the quality of their products and services. Above all it considers that generating a new attitude throughout the company is fundamental to success.

18. Cameos on Quality – A Prison in London Japan in Plymouth Germany in Cardiff

This chapter shares a few glimpses of other organisations where quality and learning to improve performance are key principles of action. There is a prison at the leading edge of continuous improvement involving prisoners and staff in creating a better environment. There is a German company which has settled down in South Wales and a Japanese one in Plymouth.

QUALITY AT HOLLOWAY PRISON

You would not normally think of a prison as a place where quality and learning are key concerns of the management and of many of the inmates. So often the press reports what is wrong with our prisons that there is little coverage of valiant attempts being made to provide custodial services of a quality which will contribute to reformation; to ensure that the stay of the inmates is at least civilised; where the loss of liberty is seen as sufficient penalty.

Fresh Start
Quality in British prisons is defined by a programme of working called 'A Fresh Start: the new improvements.' It aims to bring about fundamental changes in all aspects of the prison service, from staff

employment conditions to the care regime for inmates.

Each prison governor has a contract with the prison service. Corporate aims and objectives are drawn up for each prison based on the statement of intent exhibited at the prison entrances.

> *Her Majesty's Prison Service serves the public by keeping in custody those committed by the courts. Our duty is to look after them with humanity and to help them lead law-abiding and useful lives in custody and after release.*

The governor has drawn up a statement of functions specific to Holloway Prison.

> *Through treating everyone as an INDIVIDUAL*
> *by encouraging good RELATIONSHIPS*
> *and providing constructive ACTIVITY*
> *to achieve the BEST CUSTODY AND CARE of prisoners.*

Clear guidelines are given for all the action necessary to turn these aspirations into reality, with details of how to make cells habitable.

Teamwork

Quality is as much a concern at Holloway prison as any other organisation, so is teamworking. The staff used to work as one big group with a daily allocation of individual jobs. People often had different jobs each day, responsible for different inmates. There was little continuity. When staff shortages arose, officers were often moved around from inmate activities, inmates were locked up for longer periods.

Now teams are organised around the main functions such as residential, visits, medical and admissions. Small self-monitoring groups work in continuity with each other and inmates. They pull together as a team when there are staff shortages.

They have changed shift times to fit in with work, education and prisoners' leisure pursuits and to avoid excess locking-up time. The inconvenience is outweighed by a better mood created in the prison.

Stable and continuous relations with prisoners are considered vital. There is a sense of sharing and belonging, which spreads beyond the actual teams to the inmates as well. There is a clear sense of having a line manager and a definite area of activity.

The quality of relationships with inmates

The prison officers are able to build up constructive relationships with inmates. Rapport is created. Whatever the prisoners have done they are people with interests, feelings and emotions who one day will rejoin free society. This approach fits the language of total quality. It goes beyond 'conformance to requirements or specifications' and approaches the definition of quality as 'fitness for use'.

Unfortunately the quality falls down when it comes to aftercare. The trust and familiarity that has established a tolerable human existence is withdrawn. For good reasons prison officers are prohibited from maintaining relationships with prisoners after release, yet they are the ones who have built trust and have often become the mainstay of the prisoner's life. In prison inmates have someone who will listen and have time for them. Once released they often feel isolated and forgotten by those who did care.

Some of the officers are concerned to find a way round this problem. They are loking for improved pre-release courses which will ensure that the prisoners have the skills to cope after they leave the prison.

Investing in people

A feature of quality companies in the commercial and industrial world is that they are, in the words of the government training award scheme, 'investors in people'. In the prison service every effort is made to motivate staff by investing in them, showing them that they are valued and respected, and that they are worth the investment of proper training and development, crucial to any quality programme.

In Holloway this philosophy is extended to the inmates. There is a major spending budget to provide them with adequate facilities. This is summed up by the comment of the previous hairdressing trainer, who transformed the drab training salon into a proper professional one 'If you want success you have to provide the right surroundings and resources.' This preoccupation with sound conditions for all does not mean that there have never been any problems. There was a period when there were strikes due to a breakdown in communication, which ironically came about partly because everyone was so busy setting up 'Fresh Start'. The shift system has been improved so that it is easier to get home leave, particularly important where officers work away from home.

Occupational health training is given to all staff and every effort has been made to ensure that the environment of a prison does not make the officers neglectful of their own health in such matters as diet and exercise.

Empowerment

The governor is seen around by staff and inmates and hierarchical status does not prevent any member of staff from going to him to talk about a matter of concern. He engenders a sense of trust and responsibility in the staff.

There are issues that need addressing. Of twelve governor grades at Holloway only one is a woman, yet it is a women's prison. Furthermore the change which has been brought about would have been more easily established if there had been more preparation. The change to teamworking requires a move beyond the purely functional skills to the interpersonal ones, which don't just grow automatically. A workforce prepared for changes can move forward more quickly.

The lesson has been learned; training in management and leadership skills has been introduced. Anyone made up to even a temporary senior role does not carry it out without preparation. The Holloway Training Department is working with Pentonville Prison to develop suitable courses. Feedback from staff on these is being sought and listened to.

Just as in the business world companies have feedback arrangements and suggestion schemes in order to generate participation, so in the prison. Suggestions are encouraged, even those from the inmates.

Arrangements also exist for part-time day-release courses to be attended by the prisoners. This helps them to establish links with the outside community which they will ultimately rejoin. In a six-month period 3,500 day releases were carried out, with only 14 run-aways. The inmates themselves help to control the situation; they assert peer pressure on their fellows, because they don't want withdrawal of privilege. The governor's attitude is: 'If it won't hurt give it to them.'

Everyone needs responsibility

This is difficult enough in quality commercial establishments. How much more difficult with prisoners. From the moment of arrival the tradition has been to take away all freedom to decide anything, from time of going to bed to time of rising. They are stripped of all decision-making rights and are taken over by the system. The attempt is being made to give as much responsibility as possible to the inmates. One officer told Corinne Seymour: 'We pass responsibility right down the line to the inmates' toes and right back up the line again.' Holloway Officers take this spirit with them when they move on to other prisons. Thus the new approach may spread. It is recognised that there is a long way to go. Money has to be spent on proper facilities. The demeaning task of slopping out, for example, has to be removed. There will then be a chance that a measure of respect from others will generate self-respect in the inmates, with good results when they are released.

It may seem strange to have a section on a prison in a book on total quality, but it shows that the nature of the product or service is not the point. It is a matter of ensuring that all action produces the result aimed at 'fitness for use'. If the prison experience could be of such a quality that fewer inmates returned, then the ultimate customers would be benefited, by fewer crimes and a safer society. In fact Deming's definition of quality as delighting the customer would apply.

JAPAN IN PLYMOUTH

British and Japanese cultures have been married in Plymouth by the formation and successful running of Toshiba Consumer Products (TCP), primarily manufacturing television sets. The synergy which has been created has developed a more effective organisation than one element alone could have produced.

Throughout the late 1970s there was a joint venture between the Rank Organisation and Toshiba, in which the 'jointness' was less apparent than under the new single banner. TCP was born as a totally new entity in early 1981 and so has a ten-year track record to look back upon. Three hundred of the 2,600 workforce, under new terms and conditions, were employed from the old joint venture which had faltered badly. Many of the former management team were re-employed, including the managing director. The aim was to operate Japanese policies, systems and procedures through a British workforce.

The whole design process comes from Japan, though local computerised design capabilities are now being developed. The production technology is Japanese and the company will remain linked with Toshiba's world-wide product planning.

Financial matters are mainly controlled from Japan. There is no autonomy here. Production costs and forecasts are tightly monitored and controlled. Human resource management is influenced by the Japanese philosophy of valuing people and investing in them. However there is no attempt to be prescriptive about the details. Cultural differences are recognised and there is freedom to adapt to the needs and outlook of a British workforce, so long as the people principles of the quality movement are observed. These require that workers should be encouraged to be 'thinking workers' and contribute to the continuous improvement of everything that is undertaken.

TCP's objectives
The company proclaims six major objectives and follows them in practice:

- Product quality (this is the prime consideration).
- Investment in employees (who create the quality).
- Fostering sound employee and trade union relationships.
- Working closely with suppliers (a key to quality).
- Close relationships with the local community.
- Support of the total corporate objectives and policies.

The overriding mission is to 'generate the highest levels of profit, in a consistent manner, without deviating from the high principles of Toshiba'. The high principles refer largely to the commitment that goes with quality. The word consistent is significant, because it is the essence of quality. If a company consistently delivers what it promises then the consumer has confidence and may even find delight! Customers need to know where they stand.

Further statements of objectives include the following:

To develop within TCP an industrial culture in which all members of the company:

- *willingly maximise their personal contribution;*
- *can identify with the objectives of the company;*
- *can develop and grow in personal terms;*
- *feel a joint loyalty to Toshiba as the parent company and to TCP as a UK operation.*

The language used might appear 'corny' in an old-style context. The British are happy to have extravagant loyalties to sporting teams, but similar language about working relationships are thought 'over the top'. The quality movement seeks to reverse this, and no country has been more successful than Japan in creating it in countries outside their own.

These objectives are built into the thinking of all employees; all policies and practices are geared to facilitate this. The company is sales driven and if outlets need more televisions, then more televisions must be produced, but without sacrificing quality. So high is the level of commitment that it is not an uncommon sight to see non-production staff on the factory floor assisting with production, and submitting to the instructions of operators. This contributes to an overall team spirit and enables new friendships and understanding to emerge.

Teamworking and communication

The impetus behind the success of the whole operation comes from the team concept. This link with the open-style management ensures a feeling of belonging to a great venture. When Corinne Seymour visited Toshiba, one team member said: 'We're a part of a family,' and it rang true. Commitment to quality means the sense of ownership and participative style. This is why so many of the Deming 14 points of quality contain people elements. Open-style management is based on clear communication. There is a structured approach to this.

- Every morning there is a five-minute meeting to discuss the previous day's performance and today's changes and targets.
- There is a monthly production meeting which discusses the effectiveness of feedback and the impact on production targets.
- Every six months the managing director addresses the whole company on performance and future plans.
- Briefing notes on all main meetings are prepared and circulated to all staff.

'MPs' on the Advisory Board

Staff also share in decision making through the company's joint Advisory Board. This meets every month under the chairmanship of the managing director, to discuss the operations, to advise on policy and planning and to reach decisions on collective issues. It is a forum for open discussion, listening to arguments and reaching consensus. It works on a constituency basis with elected representatives (as it were MPs) attending the meetings. The union could have

10 of these 14 seats, but it has never taken them up, leaving them to the elected representatives, who then have a free hand to express their views without a party whip. All are equally able to place items on the agenda. Emphasis is being placed on feedback mechanisms to the constituencies.

Many of the representatives have gained skills on the Advisory Board which have been useful in enhancing their promotion prospects, and they have been able to move up through the company. As the personnel director says:

> 'It is interesting to see them grow in confidence and become more rounded in their attitudes and approaches. They are exposed to another bit of the learning experience.'

The representatives receive some initial guidance on procedures and processes and their learning by doing is supported by volunteer observers who are able to coach them in how to contribute more effectively.

Open surroundings

Alongside an open management style there is an open physical ambience. It is felt that closed doors foster suspicion and rumours; so the whole complex is on an open plan basis. Even the managing director sits out in the open and can be approached by anybody. This has drawbacks when space is required for quiet thought. There are places to go to for this, but it often happens anyway after hours. A case of the Japanese penchant for long hours unobtrusively finding a way in without edict. The few Japanese who work at the plant are, however, usually the last to go home and a midnight lock-up is not unusual.

One workforce

We have already met this in the earlier chapters. The concept of single status is essential to uphold the ideology of the valued worker. Simpler things like the provision of blue coats for all staff help. Many do wear them, although there is no compulsion. Tabards are also available for warmer weather.

207

Company cars are about the only difference between managers' and other employees' reward packages. Managers are not paid overtime either. Basic hours are 39 for everyone, but actual weekly hours vary according to seasonal demands.

There are few grades of staff and layers of management. This aids effective teamwork, with direct team leadership and responsibility for team members. Team results are published on quality, output and efficiency. The Japanese practice of visual images has not taken off among these British workers, so you won't see pink swans pinned on people in TCP.

Quality groups

Quality circles have not been universally successful. They tend to wane when a key member moves elsewhere. There is however the EQuIP group at TCP. This stands for 'Excellent Quality Improves Profitability.' The 'u' stands for 'you', to stress that the attitude of each individual makes a major contribution to quality. The findings of the group are presented to the rest of the company and ultimately in Japan.

The contribution of all the staff to improvement and beneficial change is taken seriously and everyone is encouraged to give feedback on what happens in their own job. Their views are valued and as far as possible acted upon, and certainly always acknowledged.

As one team leader put it:

'Each extra set out of the door will bring in extra profit to enable the business to grow; therefore we need to improve all the time. I am part of this.'

Soldering on

No, that is not a mispelling, I mean soldering.

Soldering is a key activity in the manufacture of television sets; so considerable investment is made in training and development in this skill. There are different grades of solderers, dependent on training and demonstrated competence. Every year two people from Plymouth and all other plants world-wide attend intensive training in Japan. They then come back and train people in their plants to a fixed time and procedure. They have to train 80 people in a two-year period. Others are then selected to attend the trainers' course. Those who train the trainers have themselves completed 800 hours training.

Competitions are held in soldering. A world-wide Soldering Olympic-style gathering is held to compete in all aspects of the art of soldering. This may appear incredible to the lay person, but it is taken extremely seriously by those participating and their plants. This approach has bestowed a high status on a key activity in the production of the television set. It is the reverse of Taylorism, which led to the belittlement of supposedly mundane activities.

Growing staff

Career progression through the various grades is facilitated in the company. All vacancies are advertised internally and internal candidates are preferred. People are encouraged to attend a wide range of training courses, inside and outside the company. For an accredited course the company will pay if the first year is successful.

All staff have an annual performance review which identifies improvement needs and supportive training. Training is continual and much of it is through the job itself. This too is characteristic of companies which go for total quality. So much of the learning is in the doing and the off-the-job components are rigorously linked to what goes on in the job. Team membership of itself creates training opportunity. Interpersonal skills and the art of communication and feedback are crucial.

The majority of the production staff in Toshiba are female. Women receive equal opportunity to move up through the company. There are a number of female engineers and a female production manager is already in post.

In the late 1980s TCP launched their sales drive into continental Europe. The manufacturing base grew tremendously and in 1990, 500 staff were recruited. As the company is sales driven, speed in recruitment and the related training and rapid absorption of the quality philosophy was essential. In fact turnover, overtime and absenteeism have grown because of the numbers recruited and the time lag in their grasping the quality approach.

What is a Toshiba supervisor?

All these difficulties are key areas of the concern for the supervisor, superintendent or team leader. In every work area charts clearly display to the teams the records of timekeeping and attendance. Peer pressure is thus stimulated, as absence affects the working and the pressures on the teams. They have an 88 per cent attendance rate, which though good for Britain has to be compared with 98 per cent in Japan! Absence tends to increase when the six floating days off have been used up toward the end of the holiday year. We mention things like this so that no one gets the idea that perfection resides in a quality firm like Toshiba. There is room for continuous improvement and supervisors and all staff are on the look-out for it all the time.

Many of the problems of attendance and timekeeping have genuine causes and superintendents are not quite sure whether they are supervisors as the term used to be envisaged, or whether they are really counsellors. Certainly the team leader role is much more concerned with people management and growth under the regimes we have been considering.

One supervisor says:

'The majority of my time is spent listening and trying to sort out my team's problems. Who else can they go to who knows them and will listen?'

The supervisor is not complaining. The company is there 'to provide the best possible working day for each person to enable them to give the best possible return'. It is thus not simply a matter of being nice to people but of creating personal conditions conducive to productivity.

No longer do supervisors or team leaders see the work of counselling and of helping people to sort out problems of any kind that are affecting their work as the job of the Personnel Department. Personnel cannot know all the people or have the time to help them, though some of the supervisors would welcome more training in areas such as counselling.

People whose needs are being considered and met are going to be happier. They will return this by commitment to the company.

The British senior production manager is totally committed to the way he has learned essentially from the Japanese owners.

'It is so simple', he says, 'a good day's work is expected of employees and together we prosper.'

This remark is not just a one-off from one individual. There is a spirit of enjoyment about the plant and a belief in the product. Staff take pride in their work and are continually striving to be the best. They feel valued and they are part of a 'we' culture, not an 'us and them' one.

GERMANY IN SOUTH WALES

Now we turn from Japanese companies and look at a German one which has settled in South Wales, near Cardiff. It is yet another illustration that the total quality approach is not peculiar to one locality or nation. It is a culture which can find root anywhere if properly introduced.

Bosch is over 100 years old. It employs 170,000 people in 130 countries. It is a private company with 93 per cent of the ownership held by a charity foundation for the support of medical and scientific projects and those for international understanding. The remaining seven per cent is with the Bosch family. There is therefore freedom from continual pressure to achieve higher short-term profits for shareholders or the need to worry about fending off takeovers.

Long-term investment and progress is the main concern. Research and development, capital investment and training are high among priorities. Solid growth and continual steady improvement are guiding lights.

Setting standards in total quality
That slogan is printed on all Bosch literature and documentation in Cardiff. It is not just a bland statement, but an attitude that impresses

you the moment you enter the new buildings. There is an air of excitement about the quality they are creating and aim to enhance. The ambience reflects this.

The Cardiff plant is a greenfield site, which is being established and nurtured largely by the efforts of Martin Wibberley, director of human resources. I first met him at a conference of the Institute of Personnel Management in the UK, where he stated that the total quality movement was the great opportunity for personnel specialists to use their skills in a way that was central to the business. He is certainly practising what he preached.

'Of all things the best'

This is another Bosch resolution, enshrined in the statement of corporate values.

1. Commitment to total quality.
2. High priority to training and development, to achieve continuous improvement in quality, productivity and individual skills.
3. Meeting responsibilities to customers, employees, the local community and suppliers.
4. To establish single status among all employees to the maximum possible extent.
5. To create an organisational climate which encourages open communication, minimises hierarchy, invites involvement and partnership, and creates enjoyment.
6. To focus on the individual.
7. To be a responsive organisation – through flexibility and teamworking.
8. To maintain a long-term commitment to Wales.

These objectives are not unique, but they have a flavour which is evident in all the best total quality companies. Although there are many task-orientated techniques, the essence of total quality lies in the people areas of communication, teamwork, reduced hierarchy, collegiality, partnership, commitment, personal responsibility, learning all the time and continuous improvement. Personal integrity lies at the root of many of these objectives and characteristics. After all that is what quality is about.

A learning climate

The Cardiff site was a greenfield one. The first six months after its inception were spent in training, developing and preparing the workforce. This ranged from the two-week induction programme through organizational and behavioural training to four to six months in Germany for technical training. This was not a one-time event but will be a continual cycle of investment in the workers. As Martin Wibberley told Corinne Seymour: 'Training is absolutely critical: it is the motor to achieving total quality.' The employees who receive training feel valued; it often contrasts with their previous work experience. As a cleaner put it, speaking of the induction programme: 'It was the best fortnight I ever had; no one has treated me like this before. I feel involved; I'm part of things.' The training has been thorough. For those who went to Germany there was a language and preparation course at a local college. A tutor was flown to Stuttgart with a video camera to gather materials for the course, which not only teaches the language, but familiarises the trainees with the area, the plant and city, so that their learning has a more relevant ring.

Organisation and status

There are five levels of employee grade; team member, team leader, group leader, department manager and director. And that's it. Single status terms apply to all employees in relation to pensions, eating places and everything except overtime. The most senior do not receive overtime payment. Manufacturing staff wear a uniform which they have chosen and other staff have a jacket of the same style provided for when they enter the manufacturing area.

The idea is to diminish distinctions and create a sense of unity, and there as elsewhere it seems to work. It is further supported by the banning of certain words from the company vocabulary. 'Semi-skilled' and 'unskilled' are out as descriptions of workers. Martin Wibberley feels that there is nothing more demotivating to a worker than to be called unskilled. All workers have some skills that can be nurtured. Organisations need all their workers to believe that they have skills to offer.

Union relationships follow a non-confrontational approach. There is a single union which works in partnership with Bosch and all the employees to develop and implement corporate values which they can own. After much discussion with a number of trade unions an agreement was reached with EETPU. The two most innovative elements in the agreement were:

- Total interdepartmental and interpersonal flexibility.
- Performance-driven pay for all.

Flexible teams

All contracts of employment reflect the flexible approach. The wording appoints people as 'working initially' in whatever job they start with. It implies continuous learning and changes of activity to meet personal and company needs. Everyone is expected to do anything they think they can do and or learn to do.

This means that manufacturing teams operate as integrated flexible teams. There is flexibility between manufacturing and technical skills and workshops are run to enable people to achieve this ability. Everyone is able to attend four modules over a period of six months (run twice to ensure accessibility to everyone). Credits are awarded at the end of each module so that employees can drop out for a time and then rejoin later. And it is all in their own time. There is no guarantee of promotion, but there is eligibility for promotion. Those who show exceptional ability are placed on the fast track for attendance on full-time courses of study. These are to be linked with accreditation through National Vocational Qualifications (NVQ).

Encouraging the learning habit

Currently the emphasis is on the functional, technical and behavioural training essential to the working of the plant. Later it is hoped to recognise that any learning from training and education helps to develop workers in the learning habit, with obvious benefit to worker and firm. However one step at a time.

Every six months there is a training and development review for all staff. This is completely separate from a performance review linked to salary, which is held six months later. Thus, twice a year at least, attention is focused on employees as individuals, on how they are doing and where they are going.

Before the development reviews the employees complete a summary of their concerns. Then a joint form is completed during the discussion. The review covers what needs to be learned and the changes taking place which will require new skills and career directions. An action plan is then completed.

Improvement

This is a key concept, both in relationship to individual work and the methods and processes by which the job is carried out. Better absentee and timekeeping levels are constantly sought by making the information available and then by peer pressure.

More significantly performance is reviewed against the extent to which people are improvement-orientated. The unions found this difficult at first, but now people are beginning to realise that they are responsible for thinking about their jobs and seeking to develop better ways of doing them.

'We want thinking workers, who continually strive to improve performance.'

So said Martin Wibberley, adding: 'After all no one knows better than the person doing the job.'

To elicit this knowledge from the thinking worker the techniques used are: problem solving through brainstorming, fishbone diagrams, Pareto charts, variation graphs and histograms. The aim is to get to the stage where quality is no longer inspected at the end of the line. As one team leader put it: 'We have to move to building quality in at the beginning of the line.'

In addition to the daily continuous search for improvement as the work is done, there are also off-line meetings to solve problems. Off-line but not off-job, because it is everyone's job to have ideas.

In the open plan meeting areas it is usual to see teams working through problems with a real enthusiasm to share ideas.

The team leaders are crucial to the success of these processes. They are trained to lead by total involvement with their teams, to coach and guide rather than merely to direct and order.

Other communication methods are employed; for example a Plant Council, with elected delegates, both union and non-union members, who are given training to enable them to contribute effectively. The delegates ask questions, gain information and inform the pre-decision discussions. The minutes of these meetings are circulated to all teams.

As in many companies who pursue the quality route there are daily meetings of the teams. At Bosch these last about fifteen minutes. Five minutes on the previous day's work, problems and today's targets; five minutes' feedback from the organisation and the Plant Council delegate and five minutes' hand-over from the previous team.

A multinational plant

At the time of writing there are 28 German members of staff although it is intended that in the end there will be only a handful. There will be a Welsh workforce operating a German company. The commitment to Wales is strong. The German staff have fitted in well, once they got used to the prevailing use of first names and other informalities.

There are Japanese ideas, German organisation, Welsh enthusiasm and a spirit which believes that anything is possible. There is also a ripple effect on other organisations.

19. *Learning from the Case Studies*

We have been looking at ten organisations doing things to secure a quality approach to business. It may be that none of the companies we reviewed would be called total quality companies or organisations by purists. Also, we have to recognise that how you set about ensuring quality in your organisation is determined by the situation.

However, if you pull together all the main ideas emerging from the companies we have reviewed, the key themes of total quality are all there, even though if we spent a few weeks in them we should doubtless find inconsistencies and non-quality examples. Principles are in action which could transform business.

CUSTOMER FOCUS

In all the companies described, there is a distinct focus on the customer as the purpose of whatever anybody does. This fits in with the quality concept which is all about either conforming to the requirements of a customer, producing something fit for the use of, or delighting the customer. Customers define quality.

In order to ensure that customers were getting the quality they required, a number of the companies we looked at had very clear links with their customers to ensure feedback on customer satisfaction. Beyond customer satisfaction and customer delight, they sought feedback on what customers might want in future. Some of this feedback was secured by customer surveys. We also had the case of Braintree District Council who, if they did not welcome complaints, certainly were very ready to learn from them.

We have seen the word 'customer' redefined to mean anybody who receives the result of your work. We have been introduced to the concept of the supplier/customer chain working its way right from the initial suppliers of raw material and components, through a factory or service operation to the outside world, ultimately landing in the homes of end users. This customer chain idea is extremely important and links together the people of an organisation into a system which is interlinked and interdependent. This is better than working in their own little fortresses interested only in maximising their own advantage. In the end this is self-defeating, because disadvantage to the organisation will ultimately mean disadvantage to the individual.

Quality Defined

Our studies also produced a number of definitions of quality. These came out incidentally from many of the people interviewed. There was 'consistency of product or service'. Somebody else said that quality was doing what you say you'll do. The leisure centre manager in Braintree said quality was making people happy. Somebody else called it a way of life. There was a warning about not providing gold plated taps when brass ones would do. In other words, quality is not a term that you use to describe mere superiority or excellence. Something can be too good for the requirement. Thus, somebody who wants a Metro or Ford Fiesta will regard those cars as quality products if they conform to specifications, if they do all that they say they will, and give thousands of miles of trouble-free driving. To somebody looking at that price range, quality does not mean a Rolls Royce or a Cadillac.

Quality tools

Our case studies also showed how companies made use of techniques to support the attitude of mind which the word quality expresses. Stanbridge Precision Turned Parts was an outstanding example of this, because it had to have the techniques to demonstrate to Ford that it was worthy to fly the Q1 flag.

We have seen self-inspection replace inspectors looking at the goods after defects have already been built into them. We saw the responsibility for inspection restored to the people doing the job to ensure that what they do is correct.

We have seen shop floor workers involved in using problem-solving tools in order to enhance the quality of the work they were doing. At Stanbridge again we saw the computer system presenting graphs of statistical process control so that operators could look at visual display units and see any variations in the process.

The 'right first time' philosophy was adhered to in some of our examples, and the measuring of progress was significant. Others gave examples of working closely to share information with suppliers to ensure that there was a chain of quality from the suppliers' input, through the transformation process, to good quality output.

TRAINING FOR QUALITY

All our cases were deeply concerned to ensure a well-trained workforce from the newest apprentice to the chief executive. We saw Rothmans with their particular concern to ensure that their team leaders, or group managers, went through what they called a team leader cadre process, whereby a reservoir of team leaders was ready to move in and lead teams along the path of self-management.

We saw companies providing special training areas, whether this was for a purpose of learning how to use machines or to retire for an hour or two to work on a distance learning package. We saw flipcharts everywhere in working areas so that the workers could draw what they were discussing and clarify it visually. We came across the phrase 'total employee development' and we coined the phrase 'learning through the job' as the most significant way in which people learn. We preferred this term to 'learning on the job', because the preposition 'through' has a purposeful ring. Learning on the job may be accidental, and may suffer if not presented properly.

Phrases like 'releasing people's potential' and 'readiness to learn' and 'organisations exist to grow people' were frequent.

COMMUNICATING AND QUALITY

We found that all companies which went in for any degree of quality management were companies where there was a lot of talking going on. In fact we heard that in their early days, Rothmans plants were called talk shops. But when the talking finished, the action showed the resultant benefit. Thus it is the Japanese companies quite often take a long while before they are fully productive, but when the production starts to flow, it really flows.

In all the companies concentrating on quality that I visited, including some not in this book, boards displayed the results of the previous shift's activity and groups of workers would avidly consider them. No doubt with a degree of competition, not of the 'dog eat dog' type, but of the recognition that everybody's success was success for all the other teams as well. We saw how quality companies encourage networking, with people leaping across boundaries to learn from what others are doing. We saw shared vision from the top to the bottom, if terms like top and bottom were appropriate anyway. We saw respect for people. We talked to workers who obviously understood the key result areas for the company, and their own part in them. This enabled them to identify with company objectives.

We did see some companies in which quality circles existed, though often they were called improvement groups. They did not follow a rigid pattern. We realised that the early idea that Japan was offering the rest of the world, the concept of quality circles, was only the tip of the iceberg. Total quality goes well beyond quality circles. We noticed that in companies that concentrated on quality, answering the telephone clearly and promptly was a factor. When you consider that telephone answering is often the first contact with a company, it is worth spending money on training people to answer the phone in an effective manner. They are key ambassadors to the outside world for the health and quality of their company.

In the companies we visited we also met recognition that praise was worth giving and that people do not live by money alone. If they don't have it, they are dissatisfied, but if they do have it, and are never appreciated, they are still dissatisfied.

NEVER-ENDING IMPROVEMENT

We repeatedly met the word 'improvement', usually in tandem with the word 'continuous'. Quality means never being satisfied. When you have done everything to satisfy customers in their present frame of mind, there is always the opportunity to offer new satisfactions. These give a competitive edge over the company that has not discovered them. Total quality means being committed to a better way.

It includes knowing what your competitors are doing so that you can do it more effectively. However the Deming School suggests that it's much better to get on with doing what you are doing in a way that will delight any customer and let your competitors get on with whatever they're doing. If you do it right, you need not worry about them. There is something to be said for that.

The never-ending improvement approach encapsulated in the Japanese word *kaizen* is a responsive one. It welcomes change. It is ready with suggestions for new ways of doing things, and it is flexible.

Never-ending improvement was not part of Taylor's vocabulary as far as the workers were concerned. Improvement was the job of the management. In contrast total quality requires thinking workers, who recognise that even in little things they can make a big difference.

PARTICIPATION

If you have a thinking workforce who can make contributions to the progress of change; who can demonstrate daily that they are committed to improvement, then the things we have seen in our case studies are to be expected. We saw workers meeting suppliers along with their managers; the workers planning their own work. We saw less referring upward because people had the intelligence and the information to make the decisions that lay within their own competence. We saw self-monitoring going on, and people honestly recognising difficulties because the old 'management by blame' was out. We saw empowered workers with some control over their own destinies at work.

Linking with this were common conditions of service or single status where the old dividing lines between management and workers were disappearing – shared restaurants, common pension rights and private health insurance.

We also saw how the voice of the unions was consolidated so that the confrontational approach was being written out of the contract and a co-operative approach beginning.

TEAMWORKING

Of course in every company we visited teamworking was the high road to success. Groups of people, largely in charge of their own work, led by somebody who empowered them, created openness and trust. Whole task working was evident. Also people could operate on a multi-skilled basis where each could stand in for others.

In these teams there was no elitism, jobs were enriched, barriers were got rid of, knowledge and information were shared and there was a spirit of collegiality, with everybody listening to each other. All these qualities are essential to autonomous work groups with commitment to what they are doing.

LEADERS FOR QUALITY

We saw that managers became leaders in quality companies, with the manager as coach, counsellor and enabler. Colin O'Neill at Rothmans said this was all a manager had to do – but what an all. In the leadership style of the quality movement, hierarchies mattered little and example mattered much.

THE QUALITY MINDSET

All in all, the examples we have seen in the preceding chapters showed quality as an attitude of mind. The quality mindset is a learning one. It creates learning cultures where people can hardly distinguish between working and learning. They work as they learn, and they learn as they work, and this is fundamental to continuous improvement. Organisations exist to grow people who can do an ever better job.

The quality mindset enables people to have pride in their work. It believes in people's ability to deliver, it generates enjoyment of work, harmony of relationships and loyalty to a cause. It's a good environment for living and working, and it spans every activity – from the most complex engineering activities to the simple things like picking up rubbish and keeping the work environment tidy.

THE TOTAL THEME

This chapter has pulled together from our case study chapters some of the key issues illustrated by the visits we paid to organisations. All the themes that you will read about in treatises on total quality came out of the practical action of thinking workers seeking continuous improvement in organisations that might be described as learning organisations.

20. Total Transformation

Deming's fourteenth point in the 1986 version really sums up the whole theme of total quality and therefore of this book

> *Put everybody in the company to work to accomplish the transformation. The transformation is everybody's job.*

As I came to the end of a fairly intensive period of writing, it occurred to me that it isn't only about transforming individual companies and other organisations. It is about transforming society; it's a new philosophy of life, about working together. It operates successfully in a competitive environment, where market forces prevail, yet it encourages co-operation rather than confrontation. Even in the sharp battleground of competitive forces, it sees the benefit of collaboration over 'dog eat dog', recognising that if the whole market expands, then everyone is better off, rather than concentrating doggedly on market share.

TRANSFORMATION OF SOCIETY

However a little reader scepticism is in order at this point. The object of this penultimate chapter is to allay it by demonstrating 'a more excellent way' – giving customers what they want, rewarding lives for workpeople, self-directed teams in place of autocratic direction, pride in workmanship instead of unthinking obedience, learning in place of blaming, enjoyment in place of fear, profit instead of loss – for all the stakeholders, from shareholders to shop floor workers.

The total quality movement really is a revolution. It is about transforming working life, business achievement and customer delight. It must contribute to the transformation of the whole of society as it takes root and is therefore a subject that goes beyond technicalities of how to ensure products and services conform to requirements, important though that is. Never-ending improvement in the workplace, in the goods and services upon which the life of the community is based must contribute to the common good as well as to the individual benefit.

In this chapter I shall not try to restrain my enthusiasm, unfashionable though this might be in an age noted for cynicism. If Roger Harrison can talk about 'love in the workplace' and Deming about the 'joy of work' perhaps I may be forgiven for heeding the old song to 'spread a little happiness as you go by'.

A QUALITY JOURNEY ROUND BRITAIN

Quality is not a series of techniques or ways of working. It is a mindset, a way of thinking. This has been abundantly clear from everything we have considered. In the case studies in the second part of this book we saw organisations at work with a new zest as a result of adopting this mindset.

There was a little company like Stanbridge Precision Turned Parts winning the much coveted Ford Q1 award, with the prime minister's private parliamentary secretary unfurling the Q1 flag in the warm July sunshine. We sampled the vast amount of detailed work and statistical awareness that went into this achievement. We savoured Bob Knox's optimism and admired the way in which he could take on 10 per cent extra staff as an investment in the midst of a recession.

We visited Braintree in Essex and were infected by the quiet and resolute enthusiasm of Charles Daybell and his team as they served their customers – the inhabitants of a large rural area surrounding three substantial country towns. We shall not forget our visit to the Riverside centre, where the manager promised the 'complete leisure experience' and the refuse collector felt that quality standard BS5750 'didn't go far enough'. And all this was in the public sector!

At IBC Vehicles we saw how Bedford commercial vehicles had been saved from extinction by a union-supported move to teamworking and free communication, which won the enthusiastic support of professionals like the late Tony Jackson and training specialist Phil Steele, who had been brought up in the old regime.

The lovely coastline of north-east England attracted us at Seaham Harbour Docks, as did a company where the managing director, David Clifford, could talk to us while his team negotiated the annual wage round and a the professional falconer kept the seagulls from ruining quality storage.

There was Rothmans in County Durham with self-directed teams at work on machines surrounding their 'bungalows', sharing management responsibility with well-trained team leaders, even joining in discussions with external suppliers. We listened to Colin O'Neill describing the job of a manager as solely to coach, counsel and facilitate the efforts of the team.

We visited Holloway prison where the governor was empowering officers and inmates to find meaning in teamwork. Staff, without relaxing discipline, seemed to regard their job as a service supplied to society.

Then there was Toshiba where we saw how the Japanese approach to quality succeeds just as well in Britain as in Japan. It is not a question of a particular national culture; it is human to want to experience togetherness in pursuit of a shared objective. That way both company and individual prosper.

We saw Germany at work in Wales at the Bosch plant and caught some of Martin Wibberley's enthusiasm as he told of his banned words 'unskilled' and 'semi skilled' – just not applicable to any of the employees. Partnership, yet individual focuses were paradoxically emphasised at Bosch. The word 'enjoyment' of work came up again.

Pictures in the videos accompanying this book tell more than mere words of the quality approach of Texaco in Pembroke, particularly in the successful maintenance shutdown, illustrating the quality concern with prevention.

We went to north-west England and heard how the Ashton-under-Lyne plant had played a major part in the ICL turnaround, because of its conversion to the total quality approach. They went for zero defects, which to them meant not producing anything to which the customer would object. We also saw the quality chain of suppliers and customers, internal and external well established at Ashton and throughout ICL.

All in all it was a pretty impressive tour. I don't think it is extreme to say that it creates optimism for the future of Britain, particularly as we had time to explore only a small sample of what there is.

QUALITY MINDSET

We have seen quality in action as a route to excellence. We have pieced together the different aspects of quality emphasised by the varied range of organisations. It is indeed a matter of a mindset, a philosophy of life, as Deming would have it.

At the beginning of this book we listened to the wisdom of the gurus, Deming, Juran and Crosby. We can learn much from them. Their apparent differences of perspective are much smaller than the vast areas of their agreement. Inevitably one tends to respond to some aspects of their teaching more than others. I could not disguise the fact that I was especially attracted to the overall approach of Dr Deming. However, this was not to disparage the contribution of the others and a number of colleagues whose work is mentioned in chapter 21.

Deming's 14 points, in their various versions, gave me a means of holding the quality mindset in *my* mind and therefore afforded some structure to my writing.

I suppose a real breakthrough for me came in the attempt to write chapter 3 on an unpromising subject like 'Variations'. I came to understand how a statistician like Deming had arrived at a humanistic philosophy through an apparently mechanistic branch of science.

If random variation is a function of a process, once special causes have been dealt with, then the situation is stable and it is futile and demotivating to pressure people to do better, to blame the shop floor worker for poor quality. Further improvement can come only from improving the system and that is the responsibility of the management, guided and advised by the people closest to the action, the operators themselves. Nonetheless management have the authority to create the framework in which the rest of the staff operate.

Once these responsibilities are clear, then everything else in the 14 points is obvious: driving out fear, creating harmonious teams, restoring pride to work, liberating people's talents and uniting everyone under the banner of delighting the customer, who at the end of the chain pays the wage bill. If you are supposed to have an angle when you write a book, this for me was it.

The values that have grown for me during my professional life all chime in with the quality mindset. The combination of business discipline with caring about people come together. I found myself responding to the view that quotas and goals, over which one has little control, do little to inspire achievement. When linked with individual rating schemes they can be divisive and alienating, preventing the full growth of the self-directed work team.

More than ever I realised that what we want in business life, and indeed in life as a whole, is leadership which will enable us to do our own thing in concert with others, rather than to bow to the edicts of people called bosses, who can take away our freedom and order us to do what they say, without explanation or inspiration. In the quality movement I saw how these ideals could be and are being realised, without making business soft. Rather the reverse by insisting on high standards and high levels of personal responsibility.

COMPETITION AND CO-OPERATION

In particular on the broader front I want to pick out the issue of the possibility of collaborative competition. I do this with help from Rafael Aguayo's book, *Dr Deming: the man who taught the Japanese about Quality*. He expands the idea from the individual company to the wider business world, without proposing that market forces should be disregarded.

One of the contentious areas of Deming's teaching is his insistence on getting close to single sourcing as a realistic aim. He is not suggesting that you could move in one leap to having only one supplier for a particular ingredient of your needs. But it is certain that where firms have entered into close alliance with their suppliers, so that there is a family-like bond created. It has worked well again and again, to the business benefit of both parties.

The supplier has security of custom and can innovate and invest in order to meet the customer needs. The firm is assured of consistent supply of material of uniform and dependable quality. If difficulties arise they can work together as a team to overcome them. When new products are developed by the firm, the supplier is involved at an early stage working to ensure that both can benefit.

So is there wider scope for the co-operative approach, without getting dragged into the uneconomic ways of central planning or the equally user-unfriendly ways of monopoly trading. Aguayo is concerned at the loose way in which we use the word competition in our language. It is used to describe almost anything we do.

When a company develops and offers a product, we say that company is competing in the market place. Is there an alternative way of looking at it? Yes. A company can offer a product, and sales of that product may not detract from the sales of other companies. A product can expand the market without negatively impacting on sales of its 'competitors'.

Aguayo reframes the idea of market share. If the market expands by the activity of several competitors, (for example, people increasingly having second and third cars in a family), each company may have a smaller share of a larger cake. Why should they grumble at this? Aren't they all doing better? The firms are earning a good return and there are more satisfied customers.

The companies still compete and are thus stimulated to follow the route of continual improvement, but if one company triumphed over all the others, where would the competition and incentive to pursue continuous improvement be?

Rather than a headlong drive to increasing market share infinitely why not concentrate on quality, exceeding the customer's expectations, so that the market expands and there is more wealth for all? Looking for the niche, the something that your firm can provide uniquely is better than trying to grab market share by duplicating effort and trying to drive competitors out of business. Challenge them with superior products and the whole public benefits from your innovation and theirs as they fight back.

The quality mindset is about co-operation to please a customer. Deming suggests that we concentrate on this without always looking over our shoulder, seeing the competitor as an enemy. (I take it he would not object to our learning all we could about what is happening out there in the competitive world by competitor benchmarking, though not to the extent of taking our attention away from our own unique and ever better contributions.)

As well as ensuring consistent quality of input, single or near single sourcing reduces waste to the community as a whole without creating a conspiracy to keep prices artificially high. There is a place for sharing unused resources; more firms survive in the market place and then there is more constructive competition which will drive quality up.

The message is getting through to the business world as a whole, with the growth of joint ventures in specific areas, joint research activities, partial mergers and a whole range of organisational devices, which get the best of both co-operation and competition.

Aguayo proposes 'competing with' as superior to 'competing against'. This kind of competition can help everyone to improve. This approach is a wider way of applying Deming's 'drive out fear'. Many of the less acceptable activities of competition spring from fear – fear of losing, which often leads to desperate attempts to score, even to the extent, in some well known cases, of cheating.

Commenting on the futility of companies putting in their mission statement that they want to be first in some area, Aguayo comments:

A company's focus should be the customer. It should be looking to constantly improve its products, its people, its systems. It should be striving to improve the standard of living of society by meeting the needs of the customer. It shouldn't put its head in the sand and ignore what others are doing, but its focus isn't on beating the other guy. It should be open to any new ideas wherever they come from, including other companies, the customer or its own employees. Naturally if it's forever improving and other companies are not, in time it may offer such superior goods or services that some companies, its 'competitors', may find they can't 'compete' and may be forced out of business. But it would be a mistake to say it is 'competing against' anyone.

Perhaps this is the biggest lesson I have personally learned from studying the total quality movement. The widest implication of the quest for quality is that the spirit which substitutes internal collaboration for confrontation also substitutes win/win for win/lose in the outside world and in doing so often wins over those who practice only win/lose.

The Japanese share the secret of their success quite widely, confident in the knowledge that by the time we get where they are now, they will have moved on and still be ahead.

TOTAL PARTNERSHIP

While writing this chapter my optimism received a further spur when I heard Bill Jordan of the Amalgamated Engineering Union (AEU) speaking on the BBC programme *The Financial World Tonight*. He was describing a meeting of the National Economic Development Council which he had attended that day (8 January 1992). He, as a union representative, had put forward, in partnership with a British manager, a paper to the Council urging firms to invest in new Japanese-style production, following the lead set by Nissan and Rover.

Bill Jordan was delighted by the positive response his proposals met and the interest shown in the detail of his paper, which got the support of the three parties in the council – the CBI (Confederation of British Industry), TUC (Trade Union Congress) and the government. The paper had laid the emphasis on the need for partnership to apply these methods to achieve sustained growth for British Industry. Jordan said:

'My anxiety is that unless this revolution that's taking place is understood, unless these techniques are aggressively adopted by British

management, then our influence in engineering and in manufacturing will continue to decline. We don't think that's necessary; we think we have here at home now in Britain companies that are showing the way. What we need to do is to spread this doctrine wider, much faster; it can be done . . . and we're going to make sure that it is.'

This book aims to make a small contribution to the spread of this 'doctrine', as Jordan said, 'not through gimmicks, not looking for grand solutions, but through partnership in a particularly important job'. The meeting showed signs of a growing realisation that the total quality movement and other related changes do amount to a revolution in the way we do business and has to be taken seriously.

THE LEARNING ORGANISATION

Another quotation from Aguayo introduces another key lesson of the quality approach:

'Isn't trying to win necessary to achieve excellence? NO! Try keeping up with someone who loves what he or she does. What we need to cultivate is love of learning, love of work, love of playing. Love of what you're doing is what leads to mastery and excellence.'

To me this is one of the most significant statements in the whole of the now growing quality literature. Love of learning is implicit in continuous improvement, in self-directed work teams and in the whole idea of trying to exceed the expectations of the customer.

There is a growing literature on 'the learning organisation'. Writing this book and summing up what I have learned over the past three years from total quality companies has made it clear to me that the total quality company is the archetypical learning organisation. Everything is geared to learning to do everything better.

In a paper I gave at Ashridge in January 1991 at the AMED/AMRG conference I said:

'When people are looking for a better way and finding it they are learning. When they are all doing it together, then you have a learning organisation. The slogan of the learning organisation is "learning together to do it better".'

I didn't know as much about total quality then as I do now, but I wouldn't change a word of it to describe a total quality company.

THE SYSTEMS APPROACH

A learning organisation is not necessarily a company which does a lot of training, though it will probably do a lot, largely 'through the job'. The whole organisation grows organically into a network of mutual understanding. Individuals still learn, but the whole learns through the interweaving of the parts.

As Peter Senge shows in his book *The Fifth Discipline*, the concept of the learning organisation is based on systems thinking. This is implicit in total quality, where everything that goes on in a company in the search for pleasing the customer is dependent on everything else. Every action is taken in the light of the whole, which was the thought behind Deming's point which urges us to break down barriers.

A key factor in any system is feedback. It is also prominent in the quality approach to business as we have seen in almost every chapter of this book. Everything from team meetings to process control charts is about feedback.

ORGANISATIONAL LEARNING

The learning which takes place is more than the sum of the individual learning. Something is added in synergistic interrelationships. Individuals think and talk and act. Organisations as such can't. It's the people in them who do. Peter Senge writes:

Organisations learn only through individuals who learn. Individual learning does not guarantee organisational learning. But without it no organisational learning occurs.

Dialogue is the hallmark of the learning organisation. The word dialogue in its original Greek form expressed the idea of 'meaning passing between people in the sense of a stream that flows between two banks'. In dialogue a group accesses a larger 'pool of common meaning' than can be accessed personally.

This is surely an appropriate analogy when we are talking about reflection. The team structure which has been so prominent in our consideration of the quality approach depends on dialogue. Some of the most important moments in the day may be when little seems to be happening. Thinking time is not idle time. Dialogue is not idle chatter. Total quality recognises this in its regular team meetings. Witness the early morning meeting at Nissan.

The chain of supplier and customer concept is implicit in the learning organisation. Everyone has to learn about the requirements of the next in line. This means dialogue with them as well as one's own team. One could could say that the sides of a learning organisation are elastic as they encompass neighbouring organisations involved in mutual transactions. Suppliers learn from customers and customers learn from suppliers.

OUR BUSINESS IS LEARNING

These ideas are well expressed in a Club of Rome report called 'No limits to learning' (Botkin *et al* 1979). A distinction is made between 'maintenance learning' and 'innovative learning'. Maintenance learning is shock learning – reacting to the unexpected, to crises, as in the special causes situation we discuss in chapter 3. Innovative learning is the planned attempt to learn and implement new things, as exemplified in continuous improvement. It implies an attitude 'characterised by co-operation, dialogue and empathy' according to these writers.

Pedler, Boydell and Burgoyne (1991) define the learning company, as they call it, as:

An organisation which facilitates the learning of all its members AND continuously transforms itself.

The purpose of learning is continuous transformation.

John Akers, former CEO of IBM, put the significance of learning very potently when he said of his company:

'Our business is learning, and we sell the by-products of that learning'.

That is exactly what any total quality company is doing. Whatever your job in a company, when you are working on your own and when you are working with others, the whole purpose is to learn and to put the learning into practice. There is no other purpose to work. As Bob Garratt has put it 'learning is the key developable and tradeable commodity'.

And what Peter Senge says of the learning organisation is true of all the concepts we have been considering in this book

As lifelong learners you never arrive . . . You can never say 'We are a learning organisation,' any more than you can say 'I am an enlightened person'.

Quality, too, like the learning organisation is a journey. In being so described it partakes of the very quality which makes us human.

Human beings are not static; being alive is all about development and change. Right from birth human beings are set on the path of change or development. There is a seven-year cycle of total physical change. From infancy to old age, every microsecond yields new learning to mind and spirit. Human beings can never say that they have arrived and that what they are now is what they will ever be. Perhaps we should stop calling ourselves human beings and speak instead of 'human becomings'. Life is a journey and we are always on the move; we are each of us 'learning organisms' and together can form ourselves into learning organisations. Continuous improvement is based on continuous learning and that is what quality is all about.

21. Come into my Study: an Invitation

NOT JUST A BIBLIOGRAPHY

It is normal at the end of a book which discusses issues which people may want to study further to supply an appendix listing books and articles which may help them. I will go beyond this and tell you a little about each book so that you have some idea of its usefulness for your particular needs.

I decided it was worth a chapter in its own right, though one which may well be referred to rather than read straight through.

I have not made a distinction between those books which I have specifically quoted and those which I have absorbed ideas from. In the text I mention a number of names and their works can be tracked down by reference to this list. Where it has been important to link a quotation with an author who is represented in this chapter by more than one book I have included a date at the appropriate point in the text. If only one book is listed here then that's the source of the reference. I didn't want to litter the text with reference signals.

So much for the mechanics of this chapter, which tested my word processing skills more than most. I hope you will actually find it not only useful, but also enjoyable as your eye runs down the brief descriptions and that you will feel it is not just a list. I hope it will lead you on to many new areas and ideas which will benefit your business life and indeed your whole life. The two cannot be separated.

WHAT'S ON MY BOOKSHELF

We will dive straight in. There is just one difference from my bookshelf. My shelves are not in alphabetical order. So what follows is a suggestion to me for some *kaizen* in my study. Physician heal thyself!

Aguayo R. (1990) *Dr Deming: the man who taught the Japanese about Quality*, London: Mercury Books.

> *One of the best books about total qualty as a management philosophy. It's in my top five. The principles of variation (my chapter 3) are clearly explained. The Deming 14 points are expanded. A key concept is co-operation all along the supplier/customer chain and even to the point of a non-confrontational approach to competitors. Total quality is about collaboration.*

Atkinson P. E. (1990) *Creating Culture Change: the key to successful total quality management*, Bedford: IFS.

> *A valuable handbook with lots of practical bullet points; emphasises that TQ is not something that can be created by a accreditation system; it has to be owned by everyone in the organisation. Practical ways of ensuring this.*

Botkin J. W., Elmandjra M. and Malitza M. (1979) *No Limits to Learning*, Oxford: Pergamon Press.

> *A report to the Club of Rome. Distiguishes between maintenance learning, to keep the status quo; and innovative learning to move into the future.*

British Deming Association (1989–1991) *Deming's 14 Points for Management and other pamphlets*, Salisbury: British Deming Association.

> *About a dozen pamphlets of 20 pages each, mainly written by Henry Neave, covering most of the issues in the 14 points. Very good on*

operational definitions where words are used in a specific way, clear on statistical process control and challenging on the rating type of appraisal. The Association also stocks technical literature on statistical process control, most of them written or co-authored by Donald J. Wheeler.

Byham W. C. and Cox J. (1988) *ZAPP! the Lightning of Empowerment*, London: Business Books.

A fun novel with a very serious purpose: people as individuals and in teams are given responsibility and respect with powerful effect on the way everything is done and benefit to the bottom line.

Carlisle J. A. and Parker R. C. (1989) *Beyond Negotiation: Redeeming Customer-Supplier Relationships*, Chichester: John Wiley & Sons.

Shows how to get customer/supplier relationships out of the adversarial mode, so that both benefit by a joint effort to provide the final consumer with products or services which will contribute to a high quality of life.

Carlzon J. (1987) *Moments of Truth*, Cambridge, Mass: Ballinger.

The president of Scandinavian Airlines tells the story of a turnaround based on inverting the hierarchical pyramid and giving responsibility to the people who face the public daily, with the top acting as support.

Collard R. (1989) *Total Quality: success through people*, Wimbledon: Institute of Personnel Management.

A wonderfully concise summary, which covers all the main TQ issues, from the views of the gurus to how to train teams in statistical process control (SPC) and problem solving. Quality as a people development matter.

Cox D. L. (1991) *Exploiting Change: By GABB & by GIBB*, Lichfield: WS14 0LD. Published by the author

A lively story of the turnaround at Ind Coope Burton Brewery, based

on self-directed teams and breaking down internal barriers. I have used his team diagram in chapter 7.

Crosby P. B. (1979) *Quality is Free*, New York: New American Library.

Many lively anecdotes and mini novels to back a clear expression of the basic TQ principles. ZD days and the tendency to sloganise may not suit all companies, and may not be appropriate where the problems are systemic. Crosby has a lot of successes and for many he is the introduction to the new philosophy, by his practical and down-to-earth approach.

Crosby P. B. (1984) *Quality Without Tears: the art of hassle-free management*, Maidenhead: McGraw-Hill.

Plenty of Crosby stories, but a very clear exposition of his four absolutes and 14 steps for implementation.

Crosby P. B. (1988) *The Eternally Successful Organisation*, Maidenhead: McGraw-Hill.

Another Crosby special which gets over the principles of quality by telling stories which are true to life.

Cullen J. and Hollingum J. (1987) *Implementing Total Quality*, London: IFS.

Sponsored by Coopers and Lybrand, this goes into detail about some of the statistical issues in a very clear way, while still linking in with overall philosophy. Is in favour of single source purchasing for each purchased product line, for better service and better price.

Dale B. G. and Plunkett J. J. (Ed.) (1990) *Managing Quality*, London: Philip Allan.

Twenty-four articles by various authors, combining case studies and guidelines for implementation. Less of the people approach, but a good account of some of the techniques which people use, including some I have only alluded to such as quality function deployment and quality costing.

Davis S. (1988) *2001 Management*, London: Simon and Schuster.

Future trends. Customers will get what they want at any place, at any time, with minimum physical matter and with the ecomomies of mass customisation. 'We are managing the consequences of events that haven't happened yet.' The book is called 'Future Perfect' in the States.

Deming W. E. (1986) *Out of the Crisis*, Cambridge: Cambridge University Press.

One of two or three classics. Written in a discursive way, yet very easy to find what you want. Loads of good little stories to illustrate every point. Hammers home his 14 points, his operational definitions theme and the principles of variation. It's a must.

Fiegenbaum A. V. (1983 3rd ed.) *Total Quality Control*, Maidenhead: McGraw-Hill

A classic by one of the group to which Shewhart, Deming and Juran belonged. Considered a 'bible' by many. To stick with him you have to want the facts and not an upbeat message.

Fisher R. and Ury W. (1991) *Getting to Yes*, London: Business Books.

A classic on negotiating in a way that will ensure that both sides win. It takes the line that the participants are neither friends nor enemies, but joint problem solvers. Separate the people from the problem. Focus on interests, not positions, and invent options for mutual gain.

Fraser-Robinson J. and Mosscrop P. (1991) *Total Quality Marketing*, London: Kogan Page.

The slogan on the last page sums it up. 'The customer is a holy cow; you don't milk a holy cow; you worship it.' 'Customer relationships, not individual sales or transactions, will become the unity of marketing currency.' Not much overt quality teaching, but an appeal to get rid of the mentality that was too preoccupied with 'closing the sale'.

Garratt B. (1987) *The Learning Organisation*, London: Fontana.

Succinct presentation from a top management perspective of what needs to be done to ensure that a whole organisation learns and not just individuals.

Garvin D. A. (1988) *Managing Quality: the strategic and competitive edge*, London: Collier Macmillan.

Harvard teacher challenges the failure of USA to live up to the quality mythology by a comparison between Japanese and American firms, particularly in the air conditioning industry. Continuous improvement is superior to acceptable quality levels (AQL) and stable internal standards in winning customers.

Groocock J. M. (1986) *The Chain of Quality*, Chichester: John Wiley & Sons.

One of the books which emphasises the internal/external chain at the root of customer satisfaction.

Hakes C. (Ed.) (1991) *Total Quality Improvement: the key to business improvement*, London: Chapman & Hall

A PERA International executive briefing. It's probably the quickest way for a newcomer to get to grips with the theme. Six key concepts, six management elements; six stages to launch it are the basis of the first main part with good diagrams. Then there is a 100 page 'dictionary' of all the main quality issues: B is for BS5750; C is for Cause and effect diagram; C is for Crosby; P is for Pareto analysis and so on. Finally some brief case studies. Another one of my top five.

Halpin J. F. (1961) *Zero Defects*, London: McGraw-Hill.

The classic which influenced Crosby. It expresses many of the TQ ideas of worker responsibility. It defines ZD as a constant, conscious desire to do any job right first time. People sign pledges to strive for this and a lot of promotional activities are proposed. However the concept of variation is not addressed, though people are given opportunity to make suggestions up the line.

Harrison R. (1987) *Organization Culture and Quality of Service: a Strategy for Releasing Love in the Workplace*, London: Association for Management Education and Development. AMED.

A consultant puts his career on the line by talking about love; tough love perhaps, but lifts the quality issues on to the highest ethical level.

Harrington H. J. (1987) *The Improvement Process*, Milwaukee: Quality Press.

A quality executive with IBM, he describes their quality revolution. Quality grows out of management style and not just a series of techniques or worker motivation. He gives a step by step detailed guide to implementing quality improvement.

Hasegawa K. (1986) *Japanese Style Management*, New York: Kodansha International.

Read this to understand the relationship of Japanese culture to management methods. A frank insider's view.

Hatakeyama Y. (1981) *Manager Revolution*, Cambridge Mass: Productivity Press.

The President of the Japanese Management Association talks of two aspects to managing; occupational and human. Within the first, like Botkin et al he sees maintenance and structural innovation. He addresses ability to influence higher management, enthusiasm for work, the joy of achievement, getting away from the role of judge, work as development and development by entrusting.

Hayes R. H., Wheelwright S. C. and Clark K. B. (1988) *Dynamic Manufacturing: creating the learning organization*, London: Collier Macmillan.

'People are the means by which control is achieved, not the thing to be controlled.' Everybody should be included in the learning process, because important insights arise at every level. Everyone in manfacturing thinking about their work and responding to feedback will ensure quality products. 'Learning is the bottom line.'

Heskett J. L., Sasser, Jr. W. E. and Hart C. W. L. (1990) *Service Breakthroughs*, Oxford: Maxwell Macmillan International.

Helps understanding the costs involved in poor quality service, well beyond rework, warranties and system audit. Deals with recovery of the customer when things go wrong. The service concept is defined in terms of results achieved for the customer rather than the services performed.

Hutchins D. (1990) *In Pursuit of Quality*, London: Pitman.

An update of the earlier Quality Circles Handbook puts quality circles and the responsibility of all employees in the context of total quality and culture change.

Imai Masaaki (1986) *Kaizen: the key to Japan's competitive success*, New York: Random House.

The standard text on continuous improvement as the umbrella under which all the quality concepts can be viewed. Emphasis on doing little things better, with specific examples. System improvement, not error correction is the true Kaizen area. Innovation is the larger scale, long term change.

243

Ishikawa K. (1985) *What is Total Quality Control?*, London: Prentice Hall.

One of the Japanes gurus surveys the whole quality scene and stresses that people have more ability than they are given credit for, and want to do a good job if given the chance. The approaches and tools of enablement are described and the two kinds of variation recognised.

Juran J. M. (1964) *Managerial Breakthrough*, Maidenhead: McGraw-Hill

The classic which saw the role of management as decisive, dynamic movement to higher levels of performance, not just controlling to maintain the status quo. Good changes must be developed as well as bad ones prevented.

Juran J. M. *et al* (Ed.) (1988) *Juran's Quality Control Handbook*, Maidenhead: McGraw-Hill.

It's all there in great detail – 1,000 pages of it. A lot of statistics and essentially a reference book.

Juran J. M. (1989) *Juran on Leadership for Quality*, London: Collier Macmillan

Detailed, but easy to find your way around. The Juran trilogy made clear: quality planning; quality control; and quality improvement.

Lessem R. (1991) *Total Quality Learning*, Oxford: Blackwell

Transforming the substance of business by a synthesis of quality and learning so as to innovate. Lessem starts from a set of beliefs about the inner dynamics of being human and how these can interact in tough thinking and tender feeling.

Likert R. (1961) *New Patterns of Management*, Maidenhead: McGraw-Hill.

Classic motivational text. Introduces the ideas of interlocking teams with representatives of one contributing to another.

Macdonald J. and Piggott J. (1990) *Global Quality: the new management culture*, London: Mercury Books.

Valuable survey of the whole quality scene; all the gurus are there, the cultural context and the techniques and attitudes necessary for success. Thorough without being too technical.

Mann N. (1989) *The Keys to Excellence*, London: Mercury.

Very readable story of how Deming's thinking developed, with a good summary of the 14 points as a new way to manage business.

Mead G. H. (1962) *Mind, Self and Society*, Chicago: University of Chicago Press.

Founder of symbolic interactionism, which describes how, through the use of symbols like words, we are constantly recreated in our interactions with other people. Very relevant in teamwork and learning organisation thinking. ⁻

Neave H. (1990) *The Deming Dimension*, Knoxville: SPC Press.

This is another one of my top five. It deals with statistical issues so simply and conversationally, yet keeps them in the context of management. Urging people to do their best without the tools and systems needed is fruitless. Joy in work and win/win for everyone are other themes.

Oakland J. S. (1989) *Total Quality Management*, London: Butterworth Heinemann.

A thorough 'how to do it' handbook, covers most of the practical ground with less of the philosophy and context than some. Good for those who want facts rather than inspiration. Strong on simple statistics.

Pedler M., Burgoyne J. and Boydell T. (1991) *The Learning Company*, Maidenhead: McGraw-Hill.

First fifty pages give an excellent survey of what a learning organisation looks like. The rest of the book reflects on this and gives examples.

Popplewell B. and Wildsmith A. (1988) *Becoming the Best: how to gain company-wide commitment to total quality*, Aldershot: Gower.

A novel which I couldn't put down. The TQ truths gradually dawn on everyone in this company. Plenty of memorable discoveries, like 'everybody who is doing the job is the expert'; 'everybody is a supplier and a customer'; 'there's always a better way'.

Price F. (1990) *Right Every Time*, Aldershot: Gower.

An entertaining presentation of Deming's 14 points with interesting examples. Deals with the cultural climate in which quality tools are put to work. Not just 'how to do', but 'how to understand what you are doing'.

Robson M. (1982) *Quality Circles: a practical guide*, Aldershot: Gower.

Concentrates on how to run and gain benefit from quality circles.

Rosander A. C. (1989) *The Quest for Quality in Services*, Milwaukee: American Society for Quality Control.

A quality veteran applies it all to the services area. Distinguishes it from manufacturing and while believing in market research accepts subjective judgments of customer reaction. He applies the variation categories to services. Plenty of checklists, case studies. A valuable 570 pages.

Scherkenbach W. W. (1986) *The Deming Route to Quality and Productivity*, London: Mercury.

A concise and accurate exposition of the 14 points with the statistical aspect simplified.

Scherkenbach W. W. (1991) *Deming's Road to Continual Improvement*, Knoxville: SPC Press.

Sets about turning the theory of what Deming calls profound knowledge into practical methodology. Detailed techniques made simple, with plenty of examples.

Scholtes P. R. (1988) *The Team Handbook: how to use teams to improve quality*, Madison: Joiner Associates Inc.

A splendid spiral bound guide with details, methods and techniques for running successful self-directed teams. Any company based on teamwork should issue one to the team leaders and no quality circles should be without one.

Schonberger R. J. (1982) *Japanese Manufacturing Techniques*, London: Collier Macmillan.

Links quality with just-in-time and the range of innovations that have been adopted in Japan over the last decade or two. The link with flexible mass production is particularly close. It needs thinking people.

Schonberger R. J. (1990) *Building a Chain of Customers*, London: Business Books.

As the blurb says of the supplier/customer chain he 'shows how the universal adoption of this simple yet fundamental principle can replace destructive inter-personal and inter-departmental wrangling with a powerful and profitable synergy'. Every part of a company is united into being a cohesive learning organisation.

Senge P. M. (1992 UK) *The Fifth Discipline*, London: Business Books.

Will be an all time classic on the learning organisation. The whole company is seen as a system in which everything and everybody is interdependent and learns by feedback and communication how to achieve continuous improvement. It is one of the simplest expositions of systems thinking extant. Neither Deming, Juran nor Crosby is mentioned! But he's playing on the same field from another angle.

Shetty Y. K. and Buehler V. M. (Ed.) (1985) *Productivity and Quality Through People*, London: Quorum Books

Over 30 case studies covering the activity of companies in the quality and continuous improvement field.

Shewhart W. (1931) *Economic Control of Quality of Manufactured Products*, New York: Van Nostrand

By the man from whom Deming learnt. The real founder of statistical process control. You'll probably have to go to a national library to get sight of a copy.

Taylor F. W. (1915) *The Principles of Scientific Management*, New York: Harper and Row.

It lasted about as long as the Russian Revolution and like that its effects still linger on in many places.

Thompson K. (1990) *The Employee Revolution*, London: Pitman

If we are to have an internal chain of suppliers and customers, then internal marketing is a reasonable concept. Thompson warns about misconceptions on employees as if they are a homogeneous body who can be ordered about and who should respect authority, instead of being seen as individuals with a lot of talent to offer.

Townsend P. L. and Gebhardt J. E. (1986) *Commit to Quality*, Chichester: John Wiley & Sons.

Prefers the self-directed work team 'quality team' to the quality circle. Quality is everybody's business. Adding value and measuring it. Focus is on the service industry.

Trevor M. (1988) *Toshiba's New British Company*, London: Policy Studies Institute.

The full story of one of the companies reported on in chapter 18.

Walton M. (1990) *Deming Management at Work*, London: Mercury.

Story of six successful companies which followed the Deming route. A good chapter on performance appraisals and how to do better without them.

Webb I. (1991) *Quest for Quality*, London: Industrial Society.

An examination of Ford, Marks and Spencer, Nimbus Records and the National Trust and others as quality enterprises.

Weisbord M. R. (1987) *Productive Workplaces*, London: Jossey Bass.

Included here because he gives one of the best outlines of the founders of the participative approach to employment, with details of people like Kurt Lewin, seen as the founder of the learning organisation concept. A lot about Frederick Taylor too. Weisbord speaks from practical experience of scrapping productivity targets and going for quality.

Wellins R. S., Byham W. C. and Wilson J. M. (1991) *Empowered Teams*, Oxford: Jossey Bass.

About the clearest book on teams that from the start have been designed to be self-directed and to consist of all the people doing a particular job as a group. Its recipe is detailed and capable of specific application.

Whitley R. (1991) *The Customer Driven Company*, London: Business Books.

A handbook on the management of product and service quality, which emphasises their interdependence; the tangibles and the intangibles must be addressed as one issue. Referred to by Christopher Lorenz in the Financial Times, *10 January 1992.*

Wickens P. (1987) *The Road to Nissan*, London: Macmillan.

The story of how Japan came to County Durham and built up the most successful automobile plant in the UK, by following the total quality, people matter and countinuous improvement routes. One of the companies in the Ashridge research.

Wille E. (1990) *People Development and Improved Business Performance*, Berkhamsted: Ashridge Management Research Group.

The full summary of the Ashridge research for the Employment Department out of which most of the case studies in this book arose.

Wille E. and Hodgson P. (1991) *Making Change Work*, London: Mercury Books.

Thinking about change in general business terms was a useful preparation for writing this book, which has a more precise focus.

Womack J. P., Jones D. T. and Roos D. (1990) *The Machine that Changed the World*, Oxford: Maxwell Macmillan.

Based on in-depth study of the auto industry, lean production emerges as the way to mass customisation instead of mass production. It requires the total quality approach for its success.

Appendix A

INVESTORS IN PEOPLE – NATIONAL STANDARD FOR EFFECTIVE INVESTMENT IN PEOPLE

An Investor in People makes a public commitment from the top to develop all employees to achieve its business objectives.

- Every employer should have a written but flexible plan which sets out business goals and targets, considers how employees will contribute to achieving the plan and specifies how development needs in particular will be assessed and met.
- Management should develop and communicate to all employees a vision of where the organisation is going and the contribution employees will make to its success, involving employee representatives as appropriate.

An Investor in People regularly reviews the training and development needs of all employees.

- The resources for training and developing employees should be clearly identified in the business plan.
- Managers should be responsible for regularly agreeing training and development needs with each employee in the context of business objectives, setting targets and standards linked, where appropriate, to the achievement of National Vocational Qualifications (or relevant units) and, in Scotland, Scottish Vocational Qualifications.

An Investor in People takes action to train and develop individuals on recruitment and throughout their employment.

- Action should focus on the training needs of all new recruits and continually developing and improving the skills of existing employees.
- All employees should be encouraged to contribute to identifying and meeting their own job-related development needs.

An Investor in People evaluates the investment in training and development to assess achievements and improve future effectiveness.

- The investment, the competence and commitment of employees, and the use made of skills learned should be reviewed at all levels against business goals and targets.
- The effectiveness of training and development should be reviewed at the top level and lead to renewed commitment and target setting.

Promulgated by UK Employment Department

INDEX

GREEN & GOLDEN MOMENTS

Bob Harlan
and the Green Bay Packers

Bob Harlan
with
Dale Hofmann

KCI SPORTS

CREDITS

Copyright© 2007 Bob Harlan & Dale Hofmann

ISBN: 0-9758769-8-8
ISBN 13: 978-09758769-8-5

This book is available in quantity at special discounts for your group or organization. For further information, contact:

KCI Sports Publishing
3340 Whiting Avenue
Suite 5
Stevens Point, WI 54481
(217) 766-3390
Fax: (715) 344-2668

Publisher: Peter J. Clark
Managing Editor: Molly Voorheis
Photo Editor: Kristofor Hanson
Cover Design: Nicky Mansur
Book Layout and Design: Nicky Mansur
Sales & Marketing: Wayne Wiza, Joey Anderson
Media & Promotions: Ted Kerske

Front Cover Photos: courtesy of Mike Roemer and Nicky Mansur

Insert Photos & Backcover Photos: courtesy of the Bob Harlan family, the Milwaukee *Journal-Sentinel*, AP/Getty Images, Jim Biever Photography, Mike Roemer Photography, the Green Bay Packers, Marquette University Sports Information Office, Harmann Studios and the Green Bay *Press-Gazette*.

Printed and bound by Worzalla Publishing, Stevens Point, WI

DEDICATION

I dedicate this book to my wife, Madeline,
who truly is – using football terminology – the
ultimate triple threat. She is a marvelous wife,
a thoughtful and considerate mother and a
loving, caring grandmother.

. . . .

To our sons, Kevin, Bryan and Mike.
How very blessed your mother and I have been.
Thank you for making us so proud.

I love you all.

ACKNOWLEDGEMENTS

I would like to thank all of my fellow employees with the Green Bay Packers, the St. Louis Cardinals and Marquette University; all the players and coaches who have created so many great memories through the years; Ron Wolf and Mike Holmgren, who combined their tremendous talents to take the Packers back to the top of the National Football League as world champions; the dedicated members of the Packers Executive Committee and Board of Directors, who are totally devoted to keeping Green Bay a viable part of the NFL; Packers fans and shareholders, who have such a boundless passion for this storied franchise; and, finally, all the wonderful friends Madeline and I have been so fortunate to have in Green Bay and across the state of Wisconsin.

FOREWORD

I had no preconceived notions before I met Bob Harlan for the first time. I didn't know him at all. I was in town to interview for the Packers general manager's job in 1987, and he took me from the airport to a Denny's restaurant in Green Bay. I don't remember exactly how long we talked that night, but when I left the place, it was as if I'd discovered a long lost friend.

If I could pattern myself after a person from a personality standpoint, it would be Bob. He has what I call the three H's. He's honest, he's honorable and he's humble.

When I came to work for the Packers, he promised me that I would have complete authority to run the team, and he never backed off on that promise. I always abided by his wish to let him know what I was doing, but that never got in the way. In a business where you have to make split-second decisions, you need that. At least I needed it, and I'm convinced that that helped us. He's always been a man of his word, and believe me, that's rare.

I can just imagine the flak he caught after the first or second meeting we had with the Executive Committee when I started talking about trading a first-round draft choice for this quarterback from Atlanta. I told them No. 4 would be the dominant player in Green Bay Packers history, and of course that came to be. But I'm sure when I left the room, most of them were asking Bob, "What's the matter with this cuckoo?" But he went with it, and it worked out pretty well.

The thing that shines through with Bob is his sincerity. I know there are three very important things in his life – his family, the Green Bay Packers and his religion. I'm not sure what order those go in, but that always comes through. When you sit and talk with him, you know there won't be any BS. He lays out what he wants, how he wants it and what's expected of you. And then he lets you do it. That's remarkable.

We had some success, and that made it a little easier for him, but then he had a great deal to do with that. He's the guy who led the way.

-Ron Wolf
General Manager
Green Bay Packers 1991-2001

FOREWORD

Not many guys have played for one team as long as I have, and I might not have either if that team hadn't been the Green Bay Packers. The Packers have been a second family for me for 16 years, and the head of that family for as long as I've been here has been Bob Harlan. I think the franchise is really going to miss him. I know I am.

People thought Ron Wolf was crazy when he traded a first-round draft choice for this wild kid from Mississippi, but Ron took the heat, and Bob backed him up every step of the way. That wasn't always easy to do in the early years. A lot of owners wouldn't have been that patient, but Bob's the best at finding the right people and then getting out of their way and letting them do their jobs.

He hired Ron, and Ron hired Mike Holmgren, and those guys turned things around for the Packers. But I don't believe there would have been one Super Bowl for us, let alone two, if Bob hadn't made sure that we got everything we needed to win.

The players here know that they'll have the best of everything, and that includes the best place in the whole league to play. Bob gets credit for that. He's the reason we have a new Lambeau Field.

Everybody knows he's good at what he does, but everybody might not know how much he cares about people. I've had some rough times off the field in my years here, and he's always made sure that I knew he and the whole organization were there for me and my family. Some people just say that, but with Bob you know he means it with all of his heart.

And of course he loves the Green Bay Packers to death, just like I do. I don't know where we would have been without him.

-Brett Favre
Green Bay Packers
Quarterback

CONTENTS

GREEN BAY PACKERS
FOUNDATION

A percentage of the proceeds from this book will benefit the Green Bay Packers Foundation, which was created to assure continued contributions from the Packers organization to charity. The Foundation distributes funds to a variety of activities and programs across the state of Wisconsin that benefit education, civic affairs, health services, human services and youth-related events.

INTRODUCTION

I never quite understood why Bob Harlan worked so hard. As president of the Green Bay Packers, he had his dream job, heading up the company with the most loyal customers in one of the most lucrative businesses in the world. It seemed to me that he'd have to go out of his way to mess up something like that.

Win or lose, the Packers could count on filling Lambeau Field and cashing in on the National Football League's immensely profitable television contract while Green Bay could hang out with the biggest, most prestigious cities in America. If ever there was a chief executive who could have kicked it into cruise control, it was Bob Harlan.

But you could tell it never occurred to him to look at things that way. And because he didn't, the Green Bay Packers became an elite franchise again after spending the better part of two decades as an NFL afterthought. In the 18 years that he was in charge, the team went to the playoffs ten times, played in two Super Bowls, won one of them and lived through only three losing seasons.

Nobody in the league had a better record during Harlan's administration, but after his first 12 or 13 years, lots of teams were making more money than the Packers were. So he threw himself at that problem and almost single-handedly convinced the voters of Brown County to go along with a stadium renovation that might very well have saved the franchise. Cruise control? He held the pedal to the floor for eight frantic months that almost ruined his health.

He did it because he doesn't understand any other way. If you know Harlan even a little bit, you know two important things about him. He has a love and a reverence for Green Bay's professional football franchise that's almost religious, and he takes absolutely nothing for granted. Not the Packers' place at the NFL table, not the power and perks of his office and certainly not the people who make all of that possible.

Every professional franchise could treat its customers the way Harlan treats the Packers' fans, but hardly any of them do. It's not just that he answers his phone. He spends hours just trying to put himself in their place, so he can figure out what it takes to keep them happy. Maybe that's one reason why he understands fans. Another reason might be that he's always been one, from the time he left Des Moines until today.

When you combine Harlan's brand of dedication with effort and undeniable smarts, something good usually happens. And plenty of good things have happened to the organization since he took charge. It's pretty clear to most people that he was exactly the leader the Packers needed to find their way back to the top. It's just not clear to Harlan. He simply calls himself "a caretaker."

That could come across as false modesty with anybody else, but there's nothing false about this man. In my 40 years in the newspaper business, I have dealt with exactly four people who would absolutely astound me if I found out they'd ever lied to me. That's not to say that everyone else I dealt with was dishonest, just that there were only four whose integrity was so far beyond question that I never considered the possibility that they wouldn't be telling the truth. Bob Harlan always topped that list.

And so when I was asked to help him tell his life story, it took me about a second to say yes. I knew that he not only would have some great stories to tell, but that the readers could believe everything he said.

I've learned a lot about his family in the time we've spent together working on this book, and I've decided that the Harlan household was a warm place for growing up. I'm told the Harlans have kind of a family tradition. Whenever something really good happens to one of them, they call it "a golden moment." Bob's wife, Madeline, expanded on that a little when the Packers named the plaza outside Lambeau Field after her husband. She called that "a green and golden moment."

Bob Harlan has had a lot of those, and it's been fun for me to share them. I think it will be for you, too.

— Dale Hofmann

CHAPTER ONE

Lambeau Showdown — Saving the Franchise

The letter in the newspaper had a big headline over it that said, "Vote No, Fire Harlan," and that's when my wife told me to stop reading the letters. They got nastier and nastier as we got closer to the referendum for renovating Lambeau Field, and this was the one that finally set her off. She said, "Okay, that's it. You don't read any more letters."

So I kept reading the news stories, but I quit reading the letters. Ethics had flown out the window, and they just ripped us every way they could. I guess I understood that that was just politics, but sure I took it personally. What it was doing to Madeline bothered me, and I knew it bothered my boys.

Nobody likes to be attacked, but we had told the voters three things. We said this project was going to keep the franchise a viable part of the National Football League for the foreseeable future, that it was going to help us field a competitive football team, and that it was going to bring visitors to Brown County and Green Bay from literally around the world. Today I can go up to any voter on the street and look him right in the eye and say it's doing exactly what we said it would do.

If you had asked me 10 years earlier if we would have to renovate Lambeau Field, I would have said absolutely not. It was the best stadium in the National Football League. We'd added private boxes and club seats, and we were making a couple of million dollars a year. We thought we were fine. We weren't very competitive, unfortunately, but we were making money, and I thought the stadium would be fine. I never would have guessed we would have to go through something this enormous to keep the franchise alive.

I was probably naïve. I was naïve about politics in Wisconsin, and I found myself naïve about politics in Brown County. Before I got into the project, other owners who had built new stadiums told me, "It's a nightmare." And it was, but you can't imagine how bad a nightmare it is until you live through it. People kept saying to me, "Bob, you're the only one who can win this for us. It's got to be your credibility and your integrity, because you've been here for a long time."

And I kept thinking, "Well, if we lose it I'm also the guy who's going to lose it for the franchise." That weighed on me a great deal.

Madeline told me there were a lot of days when she was about ready to go to the office and drag me home. I remember giving a speech to a group in June when we'd been on this for six full months. A lawyer I knew who had come to hear me went home and told his wife, "I was just at a place where Bob Harlan spoke, and that man is going to have a heart attack."

I'd been going to league meetings for years, and we never talked about stadiums. Then all at once Camden Yards opened up in Baltimore in 1992, and people started seeing what a retro stadium like that could do. Baseball teams started building them, and the next thing you knew basketball got into it, and football got into it. Every time a team in the NFL moved into a new stadium, it jumped ahead of the Packers in revenue, and so in the mid-nineties we started looking at what we could do to Lambeau Field.

We started out with a very minor project. It was still going to cost $75 million, but it was more along the lines of a stadium club that wouldn't really do much to keep the team alive. While we were in the planning stages for that project a couple of other teams moved into new stadiums, and by the time we got to 1999 we were getting panicky.

I had two bank presidents on my seven-man Executive Committee, John Underwood and Pete Platten, and they both said that at the rate we were going, dropping in rankings and losing revenue, by the year 2004 we were going to be in a lot of trouble. We would go through whatever we had in reserves and be in a very terrible situation. So we got serious.

The main goal was to have the stadium open as much as we could. I knew that if we were open for just two preseason games and eight regular season games, there was no way we could continue to exist, even in a stadium like Lambeau Field, which I thought was ideal. We just couldn't keep up with everybody else in the league.

We were ninth in revenue when we won the Super Bowl in 1997, and we had dropped to 20th by the time we got into this project. I honestly believe that if we had not done the stadium, we would be sitting at 30, 31 or 32 today. We would be at the bottom of the league and have nothing to look forward to. We couldn't say, "Let's try this revenue source or that revenue source." We had no other sources.

People would say, "Well, you're never going to move," and I'd say, "No we're not. That's not the threat. But if we're going to compete, if we're going to be a player in this league, we can't stay in a stadium that's open ten days a year. It simply cannot be done."

So we called in Ellerbe Becket, the architectural firm that had designed the Notre Dame stadium, because we knew they could take an older stadium and totally redevelop it. They'd also done new stadiums, like the baseball park in Arizona. Then we hired the Hammes Company out of Madison to be the project manager.

I had made it a point whenever the team was in a city that had a new baseball park to get up early on Sunday morning and walk around that ballpark. I couldn't get in, obviously, but I could walk around the outside and get ideas about different things I saw in concourses that I liked. I did it in Baltimore, Cleveland, Arlington, Texas, and Denver, and I really fell in love with the retro look. I thought it was perfect for those cities, and it was even better for Green Bay. With the history we have here and the longevity we have here, the retro look would be just outstanding.

We flew to South Bend to take a tour of Notre Dame, and I was very impressed with that, and then we went to Conseco Field House in Indianapolis, which was the one retro arena in the NBA.

So when Ellerbe Becket came to me and said, "What are you looking for?" I really knew what I wanted. I told them I wanted a red brick building with green wrought-iron gates, and I wanted it to look like a warehouse. I told them I wanted everything in the building to look like the 1950's. I wanted the pipes to show, I wanted glass elevators, I wanted the concession stands to look like they might have looked in the 1940's or 50's, and I wanted black and white pictures all over the place, like they'd been hanging there for years.

The people from Hammes came up with the idea of the atrium. Then we started talking about restaurant ideas and the pro shop, and we talked to the Board of Directors of the Packers Hall of Fame about moving here, and that was a great asset for us. The longer we put the pieces together, the more encouraged I became that it really was going to be a huge success. I say that because we're one of the few historic stadiums left in this country. If you take away Wrigley Field, Fenway Park, Yankee Stadium and Lambeau Field, there really isn't much left that has historic significance. All the great ballparks have been torn down and replaced by parking lots.

The tax people who were opposed to us kept saying we were out looking for land where we could build new, and that just wasn't true. We didn't do that once. We never explored any other possibility after we knew the original bowl could be saved. When we started talking about what would eventually cost $295 million, we brought in engineers, and I asked them whether this bowl that was built in 1957 in this climate could hold up for another 30 to 35 years. They gave it every test possible and came back to us and said, "Absolutely."

The key was to save the intimacy and the tradition, and now we knew we could do that. I looked at what a new stadium would cost just because I knew we had to make that comparison for the fans. We found that the cost to buy land, do the infrastructure work and build a new stadium would be an estimated $450 million.

Here's something that really frightened fans. They'd call me and suggest, "Why don't we just tear down the stadium and buy some land where we can have 22,000 parking places and put backs on the seats and make us more comfortable?" And I'd say, "You know, we could do that, but just let me tell you something. We currently seat 56,000 people in the bowl. To build a new stadium with the building codes, the ADA and all the things that go into a stadium today, 20,000 people who are currently sitting in the bowl would have to move to an upper deck." When I said that, the fans said, let's keep what we have.

The figure that was put on the project from the very first was $295 million, and when we unveiled the plans in January of 2000, that's exactly what it cost. The thing that makes me happiest about it in the long run was we finished it on time and on budget, and maybe most important, we played through construction.

In one of the first meetings I had with Ellerbe Becket, they asked me if we could take the team out of town for one year so they could just keep working straight through. I gave them three reasons why we couldn't. First of all, it wouldn't be fair to our football team to take it on the road for 16 weeks. That's a disaster. Secondly, it wouldn't be fair to the fans. The only place we could possibly have gone was Madison, and we couldn't take the fans across the state for a full year. The third reason was the businesses in this little community budget those 10 weekends tremendously. What it does for restaurants and stores and hotels and motels is huge. So not once did we consider shutting down.

Did we run into problems? Sure we did. For example, in 2002, the last year of construction, we were terribly short of restrooms in the north end zone. I'd come to work on Monday morning, and my phone would be lit up with messages from people saying they were all over the north end zone on Sunday and they couldn't find a restroom. I think we rented every portable toilet in the state and put them in the north end zone, but we still didn't have enough.

We'd initially been talking about something that was going to cost $75 million, so to watch the cost rise to $295 million frightened me. We started talking to our lobbyist about how we were going to fund this. We talked about a number of things, including a tax on liquor and cigarettes, but our guys who knew a lot more about politics than any of us did, suggested we go to Brown County with a half-cent sales tax. This was coming right on the heels of the Brewers building Miller Park, which taxed five counties.

I guess I really didn't know how much the word 'tax' would bother people. It was enormous. The state fiscal bureau came out and said the tax would cost the average citizen in Brown County 13 cents a day or $47 a year, which is basically a Friday night fish fry for most of these folks. But you would have thought we were asking for $10,000 a person. They were very upset about it.

The first thing we had to do was go to Madison and meet with Governor Tommy Thompson and state legislators to build support for a bill that would provide Brown County voters with the opportunity to approve the sales tax through a referendum. We made 15 trips to Madison, and all of them were vitally important because they gave reluctant officials a chance to talk with us face-to-face on their turf. Our lobbyist would give us a list of who we were going to be visiting with, and he'd tell us, "So and so likes you, so and so doesn't," and so we kind of knew what we were facing when we went into every office. We would go in and tell them the history of the franchise, what was going on with the league and what we were tying to do.

We caught a lot of backlash because of Miller Park, but we'd point out that we were different from Miller Park. For one thing, we wanted to go to a referendum. We didn't intend to jam this down anyone's throat.

We wanted to leave the final say up to the voters, and we were willing to answer all of the tough questions at any time. In the end, I think that's why we won in Madison.

Our key lobbyist was John Matthews, who used to be Governor Tommy Thompson's right hand man. Thank God we had him. He knew everybody in the capitol. Everybody. He knew exactly how they would feel when we walked in the door. He would tell me, "Expect this from this person, expect that from that person." He'd give me a little background on the people. Like if I knew someone was building a new house, I could ask him how it was going. John was very good and very thorough.

Governor Tommy Thompson tried to help us whenever he could, and State Representative John Gard battled for us from Day One. I really think he changed some people's minds who were going to vote against us.

Our lobbyist kept assuring us that we were going to be all right in Madison, but I was worried. Every time he got frightened I'd hear from him. One time I was at a league meeting in Florida, and he called me from Madison and said, "You've got to get on a plane and get back here right away." I was there with my wife, and we flew to Detroit together, and then she flew to Green Bay and I flew to Madison. There were a lot of those phone calls. They'd call me on a Tuesday night, and I'd have to be in Madison at 8 o'clock Wednesday morning.

There were so many times both in Madison and in Brown County when I'd drive home at night and think, "We're not going to win this thing, and then what do we do?" We had no Plan B. Whatever we did, we knew we had to do it well enough that it would sustain us for a very long period of time.

We faced a lot of negativity, and a lot of it was because we were coming on the heels of another ballpark. But we made the 15 trips, and we won, and that was the key thing. We started in Madison in January of 2000, and we left in the spring and came home to Brown County.

I thought the worst was behind us, and that's when I found out how naïve I was.

We met with the people from the Green Bay City Council and the Brown County Board, bringing them up to my office individually or in very small groups and talking to them about what we wanted to do. We basically came right out and said this is what's going to save the franchise. Some of them were very good, and some of them pretty much let us know they didn't think it was needed. They told us we had enough money to do this on our own and we didn't need to be going to the public for tax money.

We polled the public almost every week, and every single poll came out almost dead even. There was no chance at all for us to get really excited about our chances. We found out our main opponents were elderly males, and our lobbyist said he had no idea why that was. When we started the project we worried that women would be against us, and so we made it a point to invite women's groups to the stadium and sit down and visit with them. We let the women on our staff kind of entertain them and make sure they were in our corner, and we did extremely well with them.

One time we went down to talk to the retired men's club at the Brown County library, and there were probably 300 men at the meeting. There was one woman in the entire audience, and she was very much against us. She was writing letters to the Green Bay *Press-Gazette* constantly. She stood up in the middle of this meeting's question-and-answer session and said, "Do you want to explain to everybody in this room why you're trying to buy 180 acres of vacation property in Door County, Wisconsin, for your staff and your Board of Directors?"

I asked her, "Where did you hear this, ma'am?" and she said, "My friend who is sitting right here next to me heard it. He talks to the man who owns the property, and the man up there says you call him every day, and that money is no object." When I told that story to my wife, she said, "It's got to be another Harlan, because money is always an issue with you."

So I said to the woman, "Why don't we get this gentleman on the phone and let him tell that story to the 300 people sitting here?" She said the man wasn't talking, and so I said, "Then I will invite you and that gentleman to come to my office any day you choose and have him make that accusation to my face. But please bring your attorney, because I'm going to have mine there." I never heard from her again.

We faced that kind of opposition. People would write letters making accusations about all the money the Packers had stowed away that we would never tell them about. One letter said we had this marble table in our boardroom that cost thousands of dollars, and it asked how we could have that kind of furniture and then come ask for tax dollars. That wasn't true at all. It was ridiculous. The *Press-Gazette* would devote page after page to letters, and you saw a lot of the names over and over. The negativity was really surprising.

We went through a lot of meetings with the City Council and the Brown County Board, and then as we got closer to the election, we had a town hall meeting at St. Norbert College that was live on TV. I had an uneasy feeling about how this was going to go. The polls weren't indicating that things were going well, and I didn't feel they were going well, even at that session.

I started going to paper mills around the area talking to people. John Gard would meet me at the office to take me to a plant at one location in the morning, and then we'd go to another one at 3:30 in the afternoon when a shift was letting out. On those days, we'd start at 5 o'clock in the morning, and I'd get home at around 6:30 or 7:00 at night.

When we went to the paper mills, I would just stand there meeting people and saying, "I sure hope you vote for Lambeau Field." Some people would wish us well and say they hoped it worked out, but some people would walk right by me as if I wasn't there. They wouldn't even acknowledge that I was holding out my hand. Others would just say, "Don't talk to me. I'm against it."

One afternoon I had the CEO of the company standing with me, and he was thinking this would be easy. As long as he was standing next to me, his employees would be friendly to me. Well, I was out there about five minutes when a woman came by and I put my hand out to her. She turned on me and said, "Don't you dare touch me. You people are crazy."

When she walked away, the CEO was shocked. I told him, "Don't worry about it. I see it every day." After that very same session, though, I went back to my office and got a call from a gentleman who said, "You don't know me, but I walked by you today. I was going to vote no, but since you took the time to stand out there, I'm going to vote yes."

Anytime my phone rang, I answered it. A local businessman called me one day and told me he couldn't believe I was still answering the phone with all the garbage that was going on. But I told him if I could talk to a voter who's upset and win a vote, I was going to do it. If somebody would call me and leave a nasty message I'd call him back and ask him just to let me tell my side of the story. Sometimes we hung up doing much better than we had before. Other times, people had made up their minds and didn't want to change, and that was fine. But I tried to return everybody's call. That had been my pattern for all these years, and I thought, why change now?

During the referendum I also had an emotional event taking place in my personal life. In late December 1999, my mother, who lived in Des Moines, Iowa, had a severe stroke that left her partially paralyzed. She couldn't speak, and she didn't know me. We would fight these battles with the Legislature during the week, and then Madeline and I would jump into the car on Friday night and make the eight-hour drive to Des Moines. We would return to Green Bay on Sunday night.

I didn't have any brothers or sisters, and my father had passed away years earlier, so I felt it was mandatory that I spend as much time as possible with my mother. She had a feeding tube, and her parish priest told me we didn't have to resort to artificial means to keep her alive. He said, "You know, Bob, you don't have to keep that tube." And I told him, "I know that, Father, but I can't starve my own mother. I want to keep the tube." My mom lived in a nursing home for the next eight months. She had a second stroke and passed away on August 8, just one month before the referendum.

The vote was September 12, and the polls in the last week showed we were deadlocked at 47% for the project and 47% against. The team was playing at Buffalo that Sunday, but my lobbyist said I would have to stay home so they could take me around all day on Saturday to see people. They picked me up at 6 in the morning and took me to 12 places in town where they were serving breakfast. I'd go from table to table, and I could tell when I was 10 feet away from a table whether the people were for or against us. Sometimes they'd wave and say they were happy to see me, and sometimes they'd just turn around and not have anything to do with me.

After we were through with the restaurants they had me stand in front of Sam's Club for an hour, and then I stood in front of Wal-Mart for an hour. I wound up the day in De Pere going door to door. I went to 30 or 40 houses, and some people would see us coming and wouldn't answer their doorbells. Others were happy to talk. It went back and forth. Some good, some bad.

The night before the vote I was just full of question marks. I thought our chances were about 50-50. I didn't sleep very well that night, and the next night was even worse. The polls closed at 6 o'clock, and Madeline and I just sat at home till about 7. Somebody from the office called and said, "The polls look great from the outlying districts," and that made me feel really good. Unfortunately, whoever was reading the polls was reading them wrong. He called back 10 minutes later and told us it didn't look good at all.

I needed a change of scenery, so we drove to the stadium. Madeline was as upset as I was, and I don't think either of us said a word on the way over. When we got there, everybody was just staring at the TV, watching the returns in the public relations library area. Finally at about 8 o'clock or so, it started swinging a little bit in our favor. And by 8:30 or 9, we knew we had won, 53% to 47%.

People say timing is everything, and that was never more true than it was in this case. In fact, if we had waited a year to put the measure before the voters it almost certainly would have doomed the renovation. The referendum passed on September 12, 2000, and if we had delayed it, the vote would have come on September 11, 2001, one of the most tragic dates in our nation's history.

And that could very well have happened. We were under a lot of pressure during the debate in Madison to put off the legislation until after the November, 2000 Presidential election. But we fought that every step of the way, because it would have cost us at least a year in preparing for the future in a new Lambeau Field. One delay could have led to another, and the fate of the franchise would have been changed dramatically. I kept telling people God must have told us to get it done when we did.

The timing was also crucial in controlling the cost of the project. The Hammes Company's Bob Dunn has told me that the same renovation would cost $600 million today.

Once we knew we'd won, we went down to the Stadium View Bar where the victory party had been planned. When we walked in the door, people were already going wild. Everybody was yelling, "Thank you, Bob. Thank you, Bob." They were coming up and hugging me. We had a great time, but the party broke up before midnight. Most of us were so exhausted that going home and going to bed sounded awfully good.

Once we started construction, I would leave work at night and drive around the parking lot and take a circle around the entire stadium. Sometimes I'd stop on the east side of the stadium and just look at this brick wall being built and think, "Who would have ever guessed this in little Green Bay?"

I got a lot of pleasure out of the fact that a number of NFL teams made special trips to Green Bay to tour the redeveloped Lambeau Field once the project was done. The Kansas City Chiefs have been here a couple of times, as have the Miami Dolphins and the New York Giants. Dallas owner Jerry Jones requested a special tour when the Cowboys visited Green Bay a couple of years ago, and other owners have asked for quick pre-game tours of specific areas like the weight room, locker room or club seats.

The late Bob Tisch, who was a part owner of the New York Giants, took a tour of the stadium and told me that he'd gone home and told his architect, "You give me in New York what they have in Green Bay, Wisconsin, and I will be totally delighted." That pleased me to know that New York envied what we have in Green Bay. When the Pittsburgh Steelers visited Green Bay in 2005, their owner, Dan Rooney, stood next to me in the press box, looked out at the full stadium and said, "This is real football. This is a remarkable stadium." I consider that a great comment coming from a person I deeply respect.

Even the politicians wanted to see the stadium. Vice President Dick Cheney requested a tour when he visited Green Bay a couple of years ago as did Senator Ted Kennedy when he was in town for a political event. President George Bush was in Green Bay late in the summer of 2006. He didn't have time for a visit, but he instructed the pilot of Air Force One to fly low over the stadium so he could see it before he headed back to Washington.

The Kansas City Chiefs' owner, Lamar Hunt, came to Green Bay the first year we were in the redeveloped Lambeau Field, and he sent me a letter that I will always treasure. Lamar lived in Dallas, and he brought several of his Dallas friends to Green Bay just to witness the game-day atmosphere. They visited the tailgate parties in the parking lot prior to the game, and then they took a tour of the stadium. When he returned home, Lamar sent me a hand-written letter telling me how much his friends enjoyed seeing our stadium. Lamar closed his letter by writing, "You have made the NFL proud. I am honored to be in the same league as the Green Bay Packers."

I wouldn't ever want to fight that battle again, though. Nobody should ever try to build two stadiums in one lifetime. It's just too much.

When I went to my doctor a year later for my annual physical, he told me he couldn't believe how much better I looked, even though I was a year older. I didn't think I looked as bad as people told me I did. I was tired, and eating wasn't good because of the worrying, but I can't say that I felt that bad. I guess it was wearing on me more than I let on.

So many different people had told me that I was the guy who had to sell this project that I had to believe them. They'd say it's going to be your credibility that wins it for us, and I kept fearing, "Well then, what if we lose?" We could see how we were falling in revenue, and I couldn't be more honest when I say we had to have this stadium to save the franchise.

I'd been here since 1971, and I'd been president since 1989, and I kept hearing the same thing over and over. It was all up to me. You can't help but feel the pressure of that. In my wildest imagination, I never would have thought I'd wind up in that position.

CHAPTER TWO

Under the Fence and
On To Marquette

I guess you could say my claim to fame is I've never paid for a ticket to a Green Bay Packers game.

I hadn't paid much attention to pro football until I enrolled at Marquette University, but a fellow who lived down the hall from me there was from Green Bay, and we talked about the Packers a lot. When they'd play at County Stadium we would hitchhike or walk or take a bus down Wisconsin Avenue to the game. Out in the corner of left field there was a hole under the fence that was just big enough to crawl under. They had wooden bleachers then, and the place was so deserted that we could get up into those bleachers and walk almost to where the line of scrimmage was.

There weren't a lot of ushers around because there weren't a lot of people to deal with. At the time the team was drawing crowds of about 16, 17, 18 thousand. We never came close to getting caught.

I went to Green Bay only once. I was a sophomore, and a group of us came up to see the Chicago Cardinals play the Packers at old City Stadium, and we got in there free, too. We just got in the middle of a bunch of people and kept walking through the gate.

The Packers were never very good then. My freshman year they were 4-8, and then they were 6-6 and 4-8 and 3-9. But that was my first taste of pro football, and I really developed an interest in it. If the Packers were on the road we'd listen to them on the radio, and when they were at home the same group of guys would head out to the stadium. One of them was Leo Scherer, who's on the Packers Board of Directors now. Leo was with me a lot when we crawled under that fence, and we developed a lifelong friendship.

I always had a great interest in sports when I was growing up in Des Moines, Iowa. My dad bought us season tickets to the Des Moines

Bruins, who were a Triple A farm club of the Chicago Cubs. I grew up a baseball fan, because when you think about it, the 40's and 50's really belonged to baseball. I would listen to the Cubs a lot, and I could pick up KMOX out of St. Louis and listen to the Cardinals at night.

We also had season tickets to Drake University basketball. They played in a little fieldhouse that had been built in the 20's and only seated 5,000, but it was a great atmosphere. Drake was in the Missouri Valley Conference, which at that time was a terrific basketball conference. It had Bradley, which was a national power every year, and Eddie Hickey at St. Louis, and Henry Iba at Oklahoma A&M.

God bless my mother. My dad traveled a great deal, so she took me to the games. I remember cold winter nights when we'd walk four or five blocks to the fieldhouse and four or five blocks back to the car. She was a real trouper. Once I got my homework done she always saw to it that I got to the basketball games, and that meant a lot to me.

My father started out very low in the trucking business and rose through the ranks until he eventually bought the company he worked for. He was just a clerk in the office, but he was a hard charger, and he wound up becoming president and owner. He sold the company in the fall of 1971 and retired when he was only 56. But he had a massive heart attack in February of 1972 and passed away. He never got a chance to enjoy retirement. I am proud to say that I get my work ethic from both my mother and my father. They were motivated, high-energy people.

My mother was born in Minnesota, and my father was born in Osceola, Iowa, a little farm town. They came to Des Moines and built our house in 1939, and my mother lived in that house until she passed away in 2000. When I was a little kid I would spend two weeks every summer with my grandparents in Osceola. I always timed my visits for when the threshers were going from farm to farm. I would get on a pony and carry water to the threshers out in the field. It was a big treat for me.

My mom was a huge influence in my life. She and I were extremely close, and a lot of that was due to the fact that my father had to travel so much. I was her focus. But I wouldn't say I was pampered. She was very strict, and she kept a watchful eye on me. She'd leave the bathroom light on next to her bedroom when I was out, and I would have to come home and turn out that light to let her know I was home. There was never much doubt about me breaking curfew.

I played a lot of Little League baseball when I was a kid, and I tried football and basketball at school. But the sport I played most was golf. A lot of times I'd caddy 18 holes in the morning at the Des Moines Golf and Country Club and then play 18 holes in the afternoon. I was a mid-seventies player, and I was on the high school golf team for three years. I reached the semifinals of the city junior tournament one year, but then I stopped playing for the next 15 years or so because I went away to college, and then I got married and had a family right away.

I was a 17-year-old high school senior, and Madeline was a 15-year-old sophomore when we met for the first time on a double date. As the night went along, I kept thinking, "I like his date better than mine." So I called her a couple of weeks later, and we had our first date on July 23, 1954. We went to see the movie *Three Coins in the Fountain* at the Ingersoll Theatre. I remember it vividly. I have to, because she does.

She had two brothers and a sister, and she went to St. Joseph's Academy, an all-girls Catholic school. She lived way over on the south side of town when we started to date, but within two months her family moved five blocks away from where we lived. I always claimed they did that because Madeline didn't want to take a chance of losing me. She denies that's true, but I still maintain that the family was desperate to hang on to me.

When I went away to Marquette, she had two more years of high school, and then she got out of school and went to Drake University and Mercy Hospital where she got her RN. We wrote back and forth for five years, but the only time I would see her would be when I was home for Thanksgiving, Christmas and Easter vacations and during the summer. But we dated continually through those five years.

My mom always told me she felt better when I was on a date than when I was out with the boys. It wasn't that we had a wild bunch. I mean the 50's were pretty calm when you think about it, but those were great times, and I have fond memories of them. But I can't say I would recommend all of my high school antics to everybody following me.

From the time I was a sophomore in high school I really felt I wanted to be a sports writer and work for the Des Moines *Register*. I went to Dowling High School where I was an average student, but I did get an award for my work on the student newspaper. I worked on the paper for three years and became sports editor my senior year.

I wanted to major in journalism when I went to college, and I really wanted to go to either Iowa or Iowa State. They both were very strong in journalism, but my mother was deeply religious and said, "You're going to a Catholic school."

I had an English teacher in high school who told me Marquette was very, very good in journalism, and so without ever having been to Milwaukee, I applied and was accepted. I didn't see Marquette until I went to enroll in the fall of 1954. My mother really wouldn't let me look seriously at Iowa or Iowa State. Being the only child, all the focus was on me, and it was going to be a Catholic school or nothing. So my choice was Marquette, and it turned out to be a great choice for me.

I worked for the Marquette *Tribune* for four years and became the sports editor my senior year. I also took a part-time job with the Milwaukee *Journal* where I kind of fibbed to a gentleman. During my sophomore year I applied for a job covering high school sports, and one of the questions I was asked was whether I had a car. I didn't, but I told him I did, and I got the job.

I stood on a lot of street corners waiting for buses to go to high school games, and then I'd come back to the *Journal* to write the story before taking a bus back to the dorm. I learned firsthand that journalists don't get a lot of space in the paper. I remember the very first high school football game I ever covered. I must have written a page of copy, and I couldn't wait to see the paper the next day. Well, I had about an inch in there.

I'd start at 3 or 4 in the afternoon and get home about midnight, which was a long time to get an inch or two in the paper. I mean I used to stand on those corners in February or March when the weather was miserable, and I'd think, "You've got to be out of your mind to do this." I'm still glad I did it for one year, but I wouldn't recommend anyone doing it longer than that.

I got more involved with the Marquette *Tribune* my junior and senior years, and then I'd come home from school during the summer and work at the Des Moines *Register*, basically answering phones and giving out information like baseball scores. They also put out an afternoon paper called the Des Moines *Tribune* at that time. It would come out on a Saturday night, and they let me sit on the copy desk and write copy and headlines. I really enjoyed that. I don't regret any of those experiences. I thought at the time that you should do whatever you can do and learn whatever you can learn because it's all going to pay off as you go along.

One of the highlights of my years at Marquette came during the 1957 World Series. Several of us went out to the stadium the night Henry Aaron hit a home run in the eleventh inning to lead the Milwaukee Braves to the pennant. We went down on Wisconsin Avenue and celebrated.

When the Braves played the Yankees in the World Series, a bunch of us from the journalism school got jobs at County Stadium. My job was to stand in the photo deck along the first base line. Every couple of innings the photographers would give me their film, and I'd put it in a bucket and lower it on a rope down to the concourse where somebody would pick it up and take it into a darkroom and develop it. I got to see the games for free, and I loved it. So I didn't pay for Braves tickets, either. I was too cheap.

I was a B student at Marquette. I loved the journalism courses, but there were some others that I didn't care for so much. I enrolled in the ROTC program and graduated as a second lieutenant, and that was not easy for me because it was engineering and I'd never been great in math. But I got through it in four years and went into the service for six months. I spent some of that time in Fort Belvoir, Virginia, but most of it in Fort Leonard Wood, Missouri.

When I was about ready to get out of the service in the spring of 1959, I started looking for a job. I called Jerry O'Sullivan, the dean of the journalism school at Marquette, and he helped me get a job with United Press International in Milwaukee. I worked there for six months, and that's when I met Vince Lombardi.

Ray Doherty, my boss at UPI, invited me to go to a Packers pre-season game at County Stadium with him and told me I didn't have to work. The assignments were already out, and he said I could just go with him and see the game. So I sat in the press box and just watched, but the person who had been assigned to the Packers locker room got sick that afternoon. When he called in to say he couldn't make it, Ray said to me, "I hate to bring you here as a guest and then put you to work, but we need someone for the Packers locker room."

It was Lombardi's very first game as the Packers' coach, and they were playing the Bears. The Bears won, 19-16, and I took my pad and pen and went down to the locker room. I was 22 years old and dumb, and Vince Lombardi didn't mean a lot to me at that point. He was just an assistant coach coming from the New York Giants. So I went to his press conference and went through all the questions, but when he was done I had a few more.

I never would have done this two years later when he became the power he became, but I went up to him and said, "Coach, could I ask you a couple more questions?" We sat down together, and he answered all my questions. He just couldn't have been nicer. I wrote the story and actually got a byline on page one of the Milwaukee *Sentinel* the next morning.

It was my first byline, and I was overwhelmed. I was just thrilled to death, and later when Lombardi became what he became I was even more thrilled. I always wished I had a clearer memory of that interview. All I remember is the two of us sitting together, me asking questions and him answering them. He couldn't have been better to me.

I was working at UPI when Madeline and I got married. I found a little one-bedroom apartment on Prospect Avenue right near Lake Michigan and lived in it by myself for five months before we were married in August. The apartment was so small that when you opened the front door you walked right by the kitchen. You had to get in and out of the bed from the end because it touched both bedroom walls. The apartment was on the third floor, and we were sitting right on the water with no garage. In the winter I'd park my car so it was facing away from the wind. I'd go out every night at 10 o'clock and start it and run it a while because I was scared to death I would go out there in the morning to go to work and it wouldn't start.

Once my mom and dad saw the place we didn't last there very long. They came to visit us after we'd been married a couple of months, and they were shocked. My dad said, "This is a firetrap. We've got to get you out of here." So we started looking for a house.

Madeline was pregnant with Kevin when we moved to Wauwatosa and bought a house on Lefeber Avenue for $22,000. Kevin and Bryan were both born there. I remember one Sunday in the early 90's when Madeline and I were leaving Milwaukee, and we decided to drive by our old house. We were sitting out in front in the car and reminiscing about this room and that room, and a gentleman came to the door and asked if he could help us. I apologized, explaining that we had lived there years ago, and he asked, "Are you Bob Harlan?"

I told him I was, and he asked us if we wanted to come in. So we did. Madeline went up to the little room that served as the nursery where we had Bryan and Kevin, and she got all teary. It brought back a lot of great memories.

Kevin was born in June of 1960, nine months and three weeks after we got married. So you can imagine what our two little Catholic mothers were thinking, just praying the baby didn't come early. Fortunately he held off.

We have pictures of ourselves with Kevin out in our front yard. It was one of the great jokes of the neighborhood because we'd take him out on Sunday mornings and run him up and down the sidewalk so that he would nap during the Packers game. People would look at me and say, "The Packers game must be pretty close," and I'd say, "Yeah, but I've got an hour," and we'd just run his little legs off and put him to bed so we'd get to watch the Packers game. Bryan was born in 1962, named after Bryan Bartlett Starr, and as soon as he was walking, we had both boys running up and down the sidewalk every Sunday.

Madeline graduated from nursing school a week before we were married, and shortly thereafter she was pregnant, so all of her nurse training went into raising three boys. She had the degree and everything, but she stayed home and raised the boys.

Madeline has been with me every step of the way. She's been a great, great partner. You know the old saying about your wife being your best friend? Well, I value her opinion and her caring, commonsense approach to things, and she really is my best friend.

I spent six months with UPI, and I learned a lot in that time about being accurate and concise. It wasn't a job I wanted to do forever, but I thought it would certainly help prepare me for going into the newspaper business later on.

Then one day I got a call from Ted Carpenter, who ran the news bureau at Marquette when I was a student there. He told me that Jim King had resigned as sports information director to become the public relations director at the Marquette medical school. I had become very close to both Ted and Jim because as sports editor at the Marquette *Tribune* I was talking to them all the time. So when Jim resigned, Ted called me to ask if I'd be interested in the SID job.

I'd never given any thought to that at all, but I thought, "Why not go and do it and see what it's like?" Once I got there, I loved it. I enjoyed dealing with the athletes and coaches and the athletic director, and I liked doing the media guides. I'd go out and make some appearances on behalf of Marquette, and it became very appealing to me.

I really kind of decided after being there for a couple of years that maybe I didn't want to go into the newspaper business after all. Maybe I could be happy doing this. I remember Madeline and I were at a Packers game at County Stadium when I told her, "You know, I would really like to become good enough in this field that maybe someday I could become the public relations director of the Packers." That was kind of my goal at that point.

When I left Marquette after six years, I was making $7,000. We had two children, so we were eating a lot of pizzas.

Eddie Hickey was the basketball coach when I got to Marquette, and he was tough to work for. He would go after me if he could. I was always nervous around him because of the way he acted. I was 23, so I wasn't much older than the players. In fact I grew to be very, very close to four of our starters: Ron Glaser, Bob Hornak, Dave Erickson and Dick Nixon. To this day Ron and I visit on the phone several times a year.

It was a tumultuous time. We dropped football after the 1960 season, so all I really had was basketball, and the only guy I worked for was Eddie Hickey. Eddie had come in after a great career at St. Louis, and he'd taken over as head coach in the spring of my senior year. When I came back a year later, he was coming off his best year. He'd gone 23-6 and made it to the NCAA tournament.

But we weren't real good in the years I was with him. We were 13-12 the first year and then 16-11 and 15-11. But then we went 20-9 with his second-best team. That was when Hornak, Glaser, Nixon and Erickson were seniors, and they'd been starters for three years. But after that, Hickey's recruiting dropped off tremendously. I think too many kids got the message that he was a tough guy to play for, and they just wouldn't come to play at Marquette. In his last year he went 5-21 and lost 15 games in a row. He was fired in March, and Al McGuire got there in the spring of 1964.

I was with Al for one year at Marquette, and it was one of the most remarkable years of my life.

CHAPTER THREE

Al and Me

I was sitting in my Lambeau Field office one day when the girl at the switchboard called and said, "Al McGuire is here to see you." I hadn't talked to Al since he'd won the NCAA title in 1977, and this was at least three years later. I said, "Great. Send him up."

So he came upstairs, and his hair was flying, and he had on these dark glasses, a T-shirt, a pair of tattered Levis and tennis shoes with no socks. And he said, "I thought you might want to buy me a cup of coffee and let me make a few phone calls." I told him to sit down, and I'd get the coffee.

When I asked him what he was in town for, he told me he had ridden up from Milwaukee on his motorcycle and he was giving a speech. "Dressed like that?" I said. "Oh, no, no," he said, "I've got a suit. It's on the back of my cycle."

Then he finished his coffee and made all of his phone calls. Interestingly enough, every phone call he made was long distance. We went downstairs when he was done, and he said, "You've got to point me downtown and show me where I'm supposed to go." He had this suit rolled up and tied with a rope on the back of the motorcycle. I mean it looked god-awful.

I said, "Al, where are you going to change?" He told me he'd use the restroom at the restaurant to change and shave. "I'll be fine, Bob," he said. "It's been wonderful to be with you." And then he hopped on his motorcycle and took off through the parking lot.

I stood there thinking, "I wonder if people have any idea who this man is?"

That was Al. Everything was off the wall, and I guess that's one of the reasons you love the guy so much. He was such a unique individual. I only worked for him for one year at Marquette, and I would have loved to have been around him for a couple more as he really started to achieve success. His era turned out to be the greatest in the history of

Marquette basketball, and I can remember sitting with him when he told me how he was going to build that era. To see it actually happen probably gave me as much pleasure as it did Al.

The first time I met him was in April of 1964. I got a call from a member of the Marquette staff working for the president of the university, and he told me to come down to the campus immediately and set up a press conference because they had a new coach.

The rumor going around Milwaukee on all the radio stations was that Frank McGuire, who had coached Al at St. John's and then had been successful at both North Carolina and South Carolina, was going to be the new coach. In reality, someone from Marquette had called Frank and asked him for some advice on how to set up a basketball program – what we needed to do for recruiting, what we needed for facilities and so forth – and while this person was talking to him he did ask if Frank was interested in the job. Frank said he wasn't, but that he would recommend Al McGuire.

I'd been listening to the radio driving downtown, and I walked into the room at the president's office and started looking all over for Frank McGuire. He wasn't there, but this tall, young, dark, good-looking guy comes over to me, shakes my hand and in a very soft voice says, "Hi, I'm Al McGuire." I don't think he knew who I was. I had to say I was the sports information director at the university. And that's how we met.

He was only 35 years old, coming from Belmont Abbey, and the Marquette job had come down to Al and Hank Raymonds, who had been an assistant to Eddie Hickey. I've always admired the way Hank handled that, because he really was the heir apparent. He'd worked for Eddie for a number of years, and he'd played for him at St. Louis. Eddie was not easy to work for, but Hank did a marvelous job and gave him everything he had. But he accepted Al right away.

I remember one of the first things Al did was go out and look at a couple of houses in Brookfield. He saw one he liked, and he gave Hank a signed blank check and told him to go buy the house for him, and he'd be back in Milwaukee in a couple of weeks. Hank was really startled. "I hardly know the man," he said, "and he's given me a signed blank check." But they turned out to be great, great friends.

I kind of became Al's traveling companion. We just got along so well right from the start. We would go to places together when he gave speeches, and I felt more like a friend of his than an employee. Eddie

Hickey kind of tried to intimidate everybody, but Al never did. I could go to him with any kind of an idea. It might be a thought about a speaking appearance or something we should do at the Arena, and he went along with almost anything. He was a delight to work for.

We could sit and talk about anything, and in some of those long car rides we did. He would talk about growing up in the bar in New York and people he knew in New York, and basketball would just never come up.

He used to tell me when we were driving around the state, "Bob, you ought to quit this job and tend bar for one year and drive a cab in New York for one year and then come back to Marquette and work." I reminded him that I had a wife and two babies at home, but he still thought that was a great way to learn about life.

I was in his office one day early on when he asked me who the mayor of Milwaukee was. I told him it was Henry Meier, and he started thumbing through his phone book. He picked out the name of an individual in town he wanted to talk to, and he called the man's office. When the secretary answered and asked who was calling, Al said he was Mayor Meier. She put the call through immediately, and the guy came on and said, "Good morning, Mr. Mayor."

Al told him, "You know, this isn't really Mayor Meier, it's Al McGuire. But if I had said I was Al McGuire, you wouldn't have taken the call, and I need to talk to you. I need some help with recruiting. You have a private plane, and I may need to use it some time."

He used the Mayor Meier thing over and over and got away with it. It never hurt him, and I never heard the mayor complain about it, either, though I don't know if he knew about it.

Al and I would go to his speeches together, and he would see somebody in the room and ask me who he was and what his position was. If it was a prominent guy and someone Al thought could help him down the line, I'd say "That's Joe So and So," and Al would go over right away and say, "Joe, it's great to meet you. I'm Al McGuire." The guy loved it. The coach knew him by his first name. Al would play that tremendously.

But he was just brutal with names. There would be times when we were at these events, and he'd ask me someone's name, and then five minutes later, he'd ask, "What's that guy's name again?" And then he'd forget it right away. He didn't know half his players' names, so he'd refer to them by their numbers. He'd say, "Bob, No. 11 is driving me crazy." I'd

say, "You mean so and so?" and he'd say, "Yeah him," and then two minutes later he'd say, "I've got to do something about No. 11. This can't go
on."

I remember walking up to the Eagles Club in Milwaukee with Al
shortly after he'd been named coach. He was going to give a speech to
the M Club, which was a group of men who had been football players at
Marquette. This was 1964, and we had dropped football in 1960, so
these gentlemen were still upset, and they were also holding out hope
that football would be brought back.

So Al started his speech and told everybody that he was an all-state
quarterback in high school and that his favorite sport had always been
football. He said he just loved the sport, and he didn't want to get away
from it, but he finally chose basketball because he thought the injury situation wouldn't be as severe, and he might have a better chance of getting to the pros.

We're walking back to the campus afterward, and I said, "Al, I've been
running around this state with you for months, and that's the first time
I've ever heard about your football career." Al said, "I've never played
football in my life, but that's not what these people want to hear. Those
are football people, and they want to talk about football. Remember this:
Always tell people what they want to hear."

I did find out later that he had played a little bit of high school football, though he wasn't very good. But Al knew what that crowd wanted
to hear, and he endeared himself to them by telling them about his love
for football.

He always wanted to know what kind of crowd he was playing to and
what he should expect from the group. And he always wanted to know if
there was a big Marquette booster that he needed to talk to, or if there
was a prominent businessman from town who he needed to get to know.
I would try to point those people out and bring him over to talk to them.
Al could win them over in a minute because of his warmth.

He never really prepared anything for his speeches, which amazed me,
too. He just walked in and talked off the cuff and gave a very entertaining speech. I think a lot of times people enjoyed those talks because they
didn't have a subject. He just roamed from here to there, but that was
typical Al.

He used to say, "I don't know if I'm a coach or not. I feel more like a
master of ceremonies. I can kind of create a party and keep it going." I

think that's exactly the approach he took. If he thought that he had to get the officials wound up, he would start working on the officials. But he'd tell the kids, "Leave the officials alone. I'll handle the officials, and I'll handle the opposing coaches. You stay out of it." He was always willing to be the guy who got the technical fouls or got into trouble.

He said, "Nothing beats game day." He loved to compete on game day, but I think the preliminary work almost bored him.

Hank was the guy who did the X's and O's and the travel. He was the heavy lifter with everything. I'd go to practice a couple of nights a week, and a lot of times Al would just be sitting on a bench over at the side. Practice was something that had to be done, and it was almost like he really didn't care to get overly involved with it. But Hank would be out there working and working and working. They were the perfect duo because Hank would do anything for him, and Al was comfortable delegating anything to Hank because he knew it would be taken care of. He never gave it another worry.

There were so many games when tip-off might be at 8 o'clock, and at 10 minutes to 8 nobody had seen Al. He hadn't shown up in the building. I remember Hank and I talking and saying, "Do you think he's going to be here?" And finally about two minutes to game time, he'd come in, drop his coat in the locker room and walk out looking like a million dollars.

He'd never say where he'd been, and I think if we'd asked him, he wouldn't have told us. Hank and I would talk about it, but we didn't want the media to know we were worried about this. It went on all the time.

I don't think he had any idea when he took the job that Marquette's material was down as low as it was. It shocked him a little bit considering the reputation of the school. He finished 8-18 when I was there, and that was the only losing season he had in 13 years at Marquette. But the thing I enjoyed so much about Al was that everybody just adored the man, even though he was having a very, very bad season. He had a great way of warming up to people.

There were some good signs in that season. He beat Wisconsin twice, and St. John's came to town ranked in the top ten in the country, and he beat them badly. To beat Wisconsin twice when he won only eight games was an enormous accomplishment, and the Marquette fans loved him for it.

But he did get frustrated. I remember the third game of the season when we went on the road to play a very good Minnesota team. They were ranked like sixth in the country at the time. They beat us, 78-59, and we were never in the ball game. We were back in the Minneapolis airport after the game, and Al and I were sitting together, and he was looking at the box score. "You know," he said, "you get material like this with a three-cent postcard. We've got to go out and get better material."

Al really didn't like to recruit much. Hank did most of that, but Al was a great closer who could go in at the last minute. Al knew when to walk in and make an appearance, and that appearance only became more important as his stature grew. He was so comfortable going into New York after African American players. It was like, "I know if I go after this kid, I'm going to get him." He grew up around a rough crowd, and I don't think he was intimidated by anything.

He told me his philosophy was if he got one blue chipper a year – or one thoroughbred as he liked to call them – after he'd been there five or six years, his teams were going to be dynamite. The one senior could have his year of glory, and by the time he'd been there five years he'd have five pretty good ball players.

Ironically in his sixth year, which was 1969-'70, he went 26-3, turned down a bid to the NCAA because he didn't like the region he was assigned to and went into Madison Square Garden and won the National Invitation Tournament. So he did exactly what he told me he was going to do in 1964, and it worked out.

When I left Marquette, Al couldn't have been nicer about it. I had been there for six years, and all we had was basketball because football had been dropped, so I'd kind of decided that I wanted to try something else. Merle Harmon was announcing the Marquette basketball games as well as the Milwaukee Braves and the New York Jets in those days, and we were driving to Chicago to play either Loyola or DePaul when I remember asking him to drop my name if he ever heard of anything in the pros.

Merle and I had a great relationship, and it was only a few weeks later that the Braves went into St. Louis to play the Cardinals. The Cardinals were preparing for their 1966 move into the new Busch Memorial Stadium, and they were adding some staff and new departments. Merle mentioned my name to Dick Wagner, the Cardinals' assistant general manager.

Dick called me and wanted to meet me in Chicago for an interview, and so I drove down to Chicago on a Saturday morning where we met at a hotel and had a great meeting. By the time I arrived back home I had had a call from Dick asking me to fly into St. Louis on Tuesday morning to meet with Bob Howsam, the Cardinals' general manager. So I did, and I was hired as the Cardinals' director of community relations and the speakers bureau.

I hadn't told Al about this at all, because I didn't know what it was going to lead to. I could have been one of 40 interviews. In fact I don't think I mentioned it to anybody except Ted Carpenter, who was my boss at Marquette. When I came back to Milwaukee I went in to tell Al about it, and he was delighted for me. I was 29 years old, and I think he thought this wasn't a bad time to make a move.

The next thing I knew, he'd set up a luncheon for me with the athletic department at a hotel up on Wisconsin Avenue, and then he and his wife, Pat, had a going away party at their house for Madeline and myself.

I didn't have much contact with Al after I left, although I followed his teams all the time. But in 1974 the University of Kansas was looking for an athletic director and somebody had put in my name as a candidate. I didn't even know if I was interested, but I called Al and asked if he'd write a recommendation letter for me. Well, he wrote this letter about how I was a "blue chipper" and a "thoroughbred" and all of that. I mean it was one complimentary phrase after another, but it was all from Al's vocabulary, and I don't know if the people at Kansas understood a thing he said.

It was like he was riding in a car when he wrote it on an envelope and gave it to somebody and asked them to type it up and send it to me. I finally withdrew from the Kansas situation, but I loved that letter. I kept it for years. In fact, I may still have it.

The very first National Football League meeting I ever went to was in the spring of 1977. It was in Phoenix, and Madeline and I got into town early on Saturday afternoon and listened to Marquette's semifinal game in the NCAA tournament in our car on the way from the airport to the hotel. They won on a last second shot. Then on Monday night the NFL had a great big event planned.

They put up two huge TV screens in the room. One of them had the Academy Awards and the other had the Marquette-North Carolina NCAA final. I may have been the only one in the room who was rooting for Marquette. I got such a kick out of seeing what happened that night and remembering those first days when we were so down, and now Al had reached the ultimate.

I wish I'd had many more years to work with him, because I enjoyed him that much. I think the time I spent with him helped me in how I relate to people. He was a great example, and I treasure that time to this day.

CHAPTER FOUR
Cardinal Virtues

I was a nervous wreck. I'd been hired in the fall of 1965 as the St. Louis Cardinals director of community relations and the speakers bureau, and on my first day on the job my boss, Dick Wagner, came to me and said, "Call Red."

I thought, "Call Red? Oh my God!"

I mean I had watched Red Schoendienst star for the Milwaukee Braves when they won the World Series in 1957. I had watched him star for the Cardinals. He was like a god to me. I'd grown up in Des Moines, Iowa, listening to Harry Caray doing Cardinals games. I used to tell people about Vinegar Bend Mizell, which I thought had to be the coolest name ever, and here was Dick saying, "Call Red. We need to get him involved in something for us."

So I called the house, and his wife Mary answered and got Red on the phone. I was so nervous I think I called him Mr. Schoendienst, but he couldn't have been more pleasant. I don't even remember what I was asking him to do, but he agreed to do it, and he said he was going to be in his office the next day and he'd like me to come by so I could meet him. He wound up being the manager for all the years I was in St. Louis. It was a great start to what turned out to be a very, very nice relationship.

About three years ago when we had a National Football League meeting in Florida, I visited the Cardinals spring training site in Jupiter, and when I looked into the training room, the first guy I saw was Red Schoendienst. He came out and gave me a great big hug.

I was in St. Louis at a wonderful time. It is a great baseball city, and the comparisons between the Cardinals franchise and the Packers franchise are phenomenal. There's a tremendous similarity in their tradition and in their fan base, and I say to people, "How lucky can I be to have worked for these two organizations?"

It did take me a little time to get comfortable with the Cardinals.

Going to the pros, dealing with pro athletes, finding out what they were like and who you could go to and who you couldn't was a brand new experience for me. I didn't have the chance to go to spring training where I could have met these guys and been around them. I just had to do it from the office. But in a short period of time I started to enjoy doing what I was doing and being around the fans.

I also got a nice raise. It wasn't enormous, but it was nice for someone with two young children. We were only in St. Louis a few years before Michael was born in 1969, so all at once we had three young boys to raise.

The move to St. Louis went smoothly. My dad was running his trucking company, and he had a terminal in St. Louis, so he knew the city very well. The gentleman who ran the terminal for him was a huge Cardinals fan who had known me since I was a kid, and he helped us find a place to live.

We chose a neighborhood that was practically being built as we got there, and almost everybody was our age with young families. We lived on the corner with a big side yard that we marked out as a baseball diamond. Kids came over every night to play, and we liked that.

When I joined the Cardinals they were adding some people and some new departments as they prepared to move into the new Busch Memorial Stadium. Basically my job was to make speaking appearances, and I got my feet wet in a hurry. I think I spoke 10 or 15 times the first week I was there, and I went out about 250 times a year. I'm not sure Dick Wagner had that in mind for me in the beginning. I don't know if we knew how popular this was going to be. My phone rang off the hook.

During the off-season I would book eight or nine players for appearances, mostly in the state of Missouri but sometimes a little further out in areas where we had farm clubs. The Cardinals fan base reminds me so much of the Green Bay Packers fan base. People were spread around in several states, and they loved their Cardinals.

It wasn't always easy to get players to speak. You had to be careful who you selected. I tried to pick people like Dal Maxvill and Joe Hoerner. Dal was our shortstop, and Joe was a left-handed relief pitcher, and they were both outstanding at events like that. Lou Brock was very good. He lived in St. Louis, and he was to St. Louis fans what Brett Favre is to Packers fans today. Lou was a warm guy, and fans loved him.

I tried to book players about four times a month, so I didn't overdo it.

I kind of went back to the same players every year because I knew they were reliable and popular with the fans. I didn't have many problems with players, although I did have some interesting situations myself.

I remember one night when I went to East St. Louis to speak to a group. Normally these groups would have a cocktail hour from 6 to 7 o'clock, and then we'd sit down and have dinner at 7. I used to time it so I would get there right at 7, have dinner, give my speech and go home. They must have had a really long cocktail party in East St. Louis that night, because I had just gotten seated at the head table when a guy over on the right-hand side of the room stood up and took a roll out of the roll basket and threw it across the room at another guy. And that guy stood up and threw a roll back at him.

I was sitting next to the master of ceremonies, and I said to him, "Am I supposed to give a serious talk to this group?" And he said, "Oh, they'll eat their dinner and calm down," but I decided I'd better just have a question and answer session, because if I stood up and tried to give these people a 10- or 15-minute speech, I'd lose them. I mean there were guys putting little pads of butter on their knives and shooting them across the room. They had 200 or 300 people there, and the cocktail party had gone way too long.

Another time a guy called me and asked if I'd come and give a speech. I started taking down the details that I needed to set up the appearance and I asked him how many people would be there. He said, "Just me." I said, "You're going to be there alone, and you want me to give a speech?" He said, "Yeah. Just me." I suggested that we just talk on the phone, and that's what we did.

And then there was the time I gave a speech to a group of men in a department store. They had a room reserved upstairs, and they had set up a table and chairs and a podium. But there was a restroom right next to the podium. As the people in the store got off work they would get their coats, use the restroom and leave. And then the people who were coming in to work would drop off their coats and use the same rest-room. I was talking over those flushes the whole time.

In the wintertime, we had what we called the "Cardinal Caravan." We would get on a bus a couple of days a week and maybe go to Springfield, Illinois, for a Rotary Club luncheon and then get back on the bus and have a dinner that night in Peoria. We would always take one of our two announcers, Harry Caray or Jack Buck, and we tried to take two or three players every time. They were great events that drew crowds of around 1,000 people everywhere we went.

Harry and Jack could not have been better. People listened to them every day or every night on the radio, and to have Harry Caray or Jack Buck come into their town was huge. They were idols, and I knew both of them would be dynamite when they got up to the microphone.

Harry was a wild and fun guy. He loved life, he loved to party, and he caused me more concern on the caravans than any of the players because I knew the players would be on the bus in the morning and ready to go. I was never sure Harry would be there. I noticed he would sleep a lot on the bus, but when it was show time he was ready to perform, and he never let me down.

Lou Brock was someone I could count on. When he would come to the ballpark in the afternoon he might stop and see me before he went down for batting practice. It was that kind of relationship. It wasn't me begging him. I wasn't that close to all of the players, but I was close to Lou.

A guy I got a big kick out of when I was doing the job was Ernie Banks. Every time the Chicago Cubs came to town, Ernie would walk from office to office saying hello to everybody, saying how great it was to be at Busch Stadium, and "Let's play two." He had a warmth and a love for the game that you really appreciated, and I wouldn't be surprised if he did that in every town he went to.

Hosting the All-Star Game in the new stadium was the highlight of my first year in St. Louis. That was July, and it was 103 degrees on the day of the game. I remember Madeline and I had seats about five rows behind home plate, and we couldn't sit still long enough or drink enough water to be comfortable. The home plate umpire was miserable. He'd come over to a photo area behind the plate after every half inning and douse himself with water. The National League won the game, 2-1, in 10 innings, and the thing that made it so much fun for St. Louis was that Tim McCarver, our catcher, scored the winning run.

Bob Howsam left as general manager after the '66 season, and both he and Dick Wagner went to the Cincinnati Reds. They offered me a chance to go with them, but we loved St. Louis, I loved the Cardinals, and we had just moved the family and were getting settled. I thought, "No, I'm not going to do that again," and so we turned down that opportunity. I was delighted I did because 1967 was a great year for St. Louis baseball.

Our general manager was Stan Musial. We moved into first place in mid-June, stayed there for the rest of the year and went 101-60 and won the pennant by 10½ games. The most interesting part of the year was that on July 15 Bob Gibson got hit by a line drive off the bat of Roberto Clemente and broke his right leg. Gibby didn't come back and pitch until September 7, and yet when we went into the World Series against the Boston Red Sox, he pitched three complete-game victories, including Game 7 at Fenway Park.

We got on the charter plane after the seventh game to go back to St. Louis, and the champagne was flowing, the wives were there, and everybody was walking around and having a great time. But Gibby was over in a seat next to the window sound asleep. I think the man had given every ounce that he had in him, and he slept the entire way home.

I did the speakers bureau job for two years, and then Jim Toomey, our public relations director, was promoted to assistant general manager under Bing Devine, who had just replaced Musial. I went to Jim and told him that if he was going to be looking for candidates to succeed him I'd like to apply. He said he'd been expecting me to do that, and he promised to mention my name to Bing. Shortly thereafter I was promoted, and I worked as public relations director for the next three years.

The hardest players for me to work with in that time were Gibson and Curt Flood. Bob was tough. I didn't really deal with him when I was with community relations, but obviously I had to ask him to do some things when I became public relations director. I had a relationship with him where he and I could kind of go back and forth at each other, and at times he was really good, though I had to be careful to pick my spots for approaching him. But no one ever admired a competitor more than I admired Bob Gibson. Until I came to Green Bay and watched Brett Favre, Gibby was the best competitor I ever saw in my life. He was unmatched.

Curt didn't want to deal with public relations, and consequently I kind of stayed away from him and let the media handle him themselves. He was the kind of player who would show up at the ballpark every day at maybe 2 o'clock for an 8 o'clock game. He was always there. If he had been more cooperative it could have been a lot easier for us, but that wasn't Curt's way, and I kind of knew that. So I just didn't go to him unless I absolutely had to.

One player who I was extremely concerned about was Roger Maris.

When we acquired Roger I knew what he had gone through with the home run record in 1961, and I'd heard about the relationship he'd had with the New York media. I thought, "This is not going to be easy." But he couldn't have been better. I never approached him and asked him to do anything that he didn't agree to do.

I got a totally different feel for what kind of man he was once I met him personally. You always heard that he was moody and standoffish, but he wasn't either of those things in St. Louis. He was a very private person, and I just think the pressure he went through in breaking Babe Ruth's record was tremendous. Some people really didn't want him to break that record. Maybe it would have been more popular if Mickey Mantle had done it, but it was Roger and not everyone liked that. When he came to St. Louis he was obviously in the declining years of his career, but he was a wonderful person, and I enjoyed him tremendously.

We won the pennant again in 1968, and this time we played the Detroit Tigers in the World Series. *Sports Illustrated* came to St. Louis as we were getting ready for the Series, and they wanted me to get the starting lineup together and pose everybody in front of their lockers in street clothes. Red was in his uniform, and the players were wearing whatever they wanted. The picture ran on the cover of the magazine, and the headline read, "The highest-paid team in baseball history."

It featured nine players, including Gibson as the pitcher, and Red as the manager, and the combined salaries of those ten people was $607,000. The highest-paid player on the team was Gibson at $85,000, with Orlando Cepeda next at $80,000. It shows you how much times have changed.

We took a three games-to-one lead on the Tigers in that Series and then lost the next three games, including two at Busch Stadium, which was almost unheard of. Denny McLain was the pitcher we feared the most because he had been a 31-game winner that year, but Mickey Lolich was the one who did us in.

Gibson won Games 1 and 4, and he came back in Game 7. We had a scoreless game in the seventh inning at Busch Stadium when a fly ball was hit to center field. Flood was in center, and he took one step in and realized he had misjudged the ball. When he tried to go back, he slipped and fell, the ball dropped in, and the Tigers went on to win, 4-1.

Thirty years later when I was with the Packers and we sat in San Diego and watched that Super Bowl game slip away from us, it brought back such memories of watching Game 7 get away from the Cardinals at Busch Stadium. It was phenomenal how similar the feeling was. We were stunned in St. Louis. We thought we had that Series won. And then for us to go into San Diego and lose that Super Bowl 30 years later was a nightmare.

I was the Cardinals' public relations director in 1968, 1969 and 1970, and those were wonderful times for baseball in St. Louis. It was a great experience for me, but it was very hard on my family. Kevin was 9 and Bryan was 7 when Michael was born, and Madeline was basically raising the boys herself.

I'd be at the ballpark every day for home games, and most of those were at night, so I'd get home about midnight and then leave for the stadium again at 8 o'clock the next morning. I'd take my suitcase with me before the last game of a homestand and then hop on a bus for the airport afterwards. Then I'd be gone for eight or nine days.

I remember when I could come home for dinner in those days. Madeline would light the candles, fix a special meal, and the boys would be all dressed up and looking nice because Daddy was going to be home.

It was a great job for a single person, but it wasn't fair to Madeline, and it wasn't fair to my kids. If we had any kind of situation with the boys when I was on the road, Madeline would have to call, and I'd get either Kevin or Bryan on the phone and tell them they couldn't do this or that and they had to listen to their mother. It was no way to raise a family. A lot of baseball marriages fail, and I began to realize the job was simply something I could not do any longer.

On the positive side, however, I was able to take my family to spring training for a week each year. Madeline also brought the boys to as many home games as possible. They would sit behind home plate and always wave to me in the press box. And when we were home for a weekend series, I would take one of the boys with me to the stadium on Saturday and then take the other one on Sunday. They would help me with my statistics and pre-game notes, and they had an opportunity to be around the players. But I still felt like I needed a change.

Bing Devine had taken over as general manager in 1968, and I was ready to go to him and ask if there was some other area of the operation that I could work in, because I couldn't keep doing this to my family. Madeline was very good about it. I give her all the credit in the world, but I knew what it was doing to her, and I knew I had to be around my boys more. My parents kept telling me the same thing.

But I never got a chance to go to Bing. I was in spring training in St. Petersburg in 1971 shortly after Dan Devine had taken over as coach and general manager in Green Bay when Bing called me. He had gotten a call from Dan Devine, whom he was not related to but whom he knew very well, and Dan had told him he needed someone to help him with some contracts and paperwork.

I never knew Dan when I was in Missouri, but he would show up in our press box once in a while, and he was very close to Bob Broeg, who was the sports editor of the St. Louis *Post-Dispatch*. He was a god in the state because of the great job he'd done with the University of Missouri football program, kind of like Barry Alvarez is in Wisconsin now.

I was 34 years old at the time, and Bing was kind enough to tell me the Packers were looking for someone. He knew I'd been a big Packers fan when I was at Marquette, and he thought it would be a step up for me in my career and in my salary, so he offered to mention my name. I said I wasn't looking to leave the Cardinals, but Green Bay was special and I would appreciate the opportunity to see what they had to offer. So he gave Dan a call, and Dan flew down to St. Petersburg where I had dinner with him and Bob Broeg.

The Cardinals opened their season with a day game in Chicago that year, and then the next day was an open date. So on the open date Madeline flew up from St. Louis to Chicago, and then we flew to Green Bay together to be interviewed. When we got on the little plane to Green Bay, who should be sitting there but Bart Starr? Obviously, I didn't speak to him. I mean I wasn't going to approach Bart Starr, but it made me feel pretty special to be on that plane with him.

We flew into Green Bay and spent the day with Dan, and he offered me the job. It was just that quick.

You know how you hear about people taking out a pen and pad when they have a decision to make and listing all of the reasons why in one column and all of the reasons why not in the other? Well Madeline and I actually did that when we got on the plane after Dan made the offer. The funny thing was that the weather in Florida had been marvelous during spring training, and it was marvelous in St. Louis, too, but when we got into Green Bay snow was still piled up on the streets. It wasn't pretty snow, either. It was dirty and gray. Yet when we got off the plane in St. Louis, our list of reasons to come to Green Bay was overwhelming compared to our reasons to stay in St. Louis. And the No. 1 reason was family.

We owe a lot to Bing Devine. He didn't have to pick up that phone for me at all. At that same spring training where I ran into Red Schoendienst three years ago, I ran into Bing, and the first thing he said to me was, "I got you that job in Green Bay." And I told him I'd never forget him. It meant the world to me.

The first reporter I talked to in Green Bay after I took the job was Lee Remmel, who was working for the Green Bay *Press-Gazette*, and his first question to me was, "What does a baseball guy know about football?"

I told him, "We'll find out."

CHAPTER FIVE

Devine Guidance

an Devine was renting a duplex in Green Bay when Madeline and I came to town for our visit, and I could tell right away that he was a great one-on-one guy. He was so low-key and down to earth. He fixed us a couple of sandwiches, and we sat right down at the kitchen table and talked. We'd started with him early in the morning, so this was after a full day.

I told Madeline that I could see why the man was a great college recruiter. He could come to a house and sit down with the mother or father, and they'd think, "This man is going to take care of my son for the next four years." I wasn't surprised when he left us and had success at Notre Dame. I think he belonged on the level where he could coach the college kids. He was very effective with that age group.

I'll always appreciate the fact that he gave me a chance to come to the Packers. He was very kind to me. He really was, but things just slipped away from him in Green Bay. I was amazed at the turmoil and confusion going on in this organization when he was here. It was a tumultuous time, and it just got worse and worse.

I think it was partly because the Executive Committee was divided when Dan was hired, and then he started making moves the Committee never approved. That was a horrible mistake. The vote on his hiring was 5-2. Tony Canadeo and Dick Bourguignon both wanted Joe Paterno, and they thought they had a chance to get him. So they didn't vote for Dan, and I always had the feeling that Dan knew that, and he believed he had to get their support. That didn't work out very well.

Dan took the job on January 14 of 1971, and I started on June 1. Some of the people on his coaching staff, like Dave Hanner and Red Cochran, were veterans, but he brought in a lot of people that he knew very well, too. Hank Kuhlmann, Burt Gustafson and Rollie Dotsch were extremely close to him, and so there was kind of a division on the staff. It was not a real comfortable time because some of the older coaches had a tough time buying everything Dan wanted to do.

I remember one of the first things he did was show a Missouri high-light film to the team, and I heard a lot of grumblings in the locker room about that. It really upset the veteran coaches because they were the ones who had trouble accepting some of Dan's methods. He was in trouble with those guys right away.

I was new on the staff, and I didn't want to get in the middle of that debate. I mean Dan Devine hired me. I thought it was best that I just delve into my work, and fortunately Dan threw a lot of things at me in a hurry and gave me a chance to be very busy.

Dan had me start out negotiating contracts. I didn't deal with the top people. Pat Peppler was here at the time, and Pat would negotiate the top draft choices and the veteran players. Dan had me take the lower draft choices and the back-up players just to get me started. My family didn't move from St. Louis until the middle of August because we were build-ing a house in Green Bay, so I stayed in a downtown hotel and worked late in the office every night. I had nothing else to do.

I'd never negotiated contracts in my life, and so I'd go back through the files and see what kind of clauses were being given to people. I kind of put together a book to educate myself. I spent night after night going through the contracts of the sixties, the Kramers, the Thurstons and the Hornungs, people like that. The thing that amazed me was how low the numbers were. A guy would come off an all-pro year, and he might get a $2,500 raise. That shocked me.

We had a very small front office at that time. Basically it was Chuck Lane, Tom Miller and me. Dan also had me doing most of the mail that came to him and helping him with speaking requests. I was trying to get more involved with the public relations department, the ticket depart-ment and even the stadium crew. I was doing a little bit of everything.

I remember helping Al Treml in the film department. I'd take Polaroids at some games and give them to the coaches so they could study them on the sidelines. There were also times when the ground crew needed to take the tarp off the field or put it on for practice, and if they were short staffed, I'd go down and put on some sweats and help roll the tarp. I wanted to be accepted. I knew there was turmoil on the staff, and I felt if I could show that I was there to pitch in, it would be a plus for me.

Dan broke his leg in his very first game as the Packers coach in 1971, and he was taken off the field in an ambulance. We were playing the Giants in Green Bay, and the Giants won the game, 42-40. Dan got hit on the sidelines, and I left the stadium after the game to see him at the hospital. He was really in pain. He was very stoic, but he was miserable, and he spent most of the year in a cast and on crutches.

Many nights I would take him home in the back of my car where he could stretch out and be more comfortable. It was a tough way to start a career. No doubt it made things more difficult. Still we went out and won the next two games, so that was kind of encouraging for him.

We had a great year his second season. Bart Starr was the quarterbacks coach that year, and that was really the thing that eventually was going to elevate him to the head coaching position. The team played very well, and we clinched the division championship on the next-to-last weekend at Minnesota. We beat the Vikings, 23-7, and that was huge for us. When I went into that locker room after the game, people were so excited because of what we'd done. My first reaction was, "Hey, this isn't going to be too bad. We're going to win here pretty fast."

We were 10-4, and we went to the NFC division playoff game against the Washington Redskins, but we got beat, 16-3. Our backfield at that time was John Brockington, who was having some phenomenal years, and MacArthur Lane. John had been Rookie of the Year in 1971, and we'd picked up Mac, who was both a good runner and a wonderful blocker, from the St. Louis Cardinals. We basically just ran the ball that day against the Redskins, and we couldn't get any momentum on offense. We got beat pretty badly.

But Dan was Coach of the Year, and things seemed like they were going to be much better. I felt very optimistic after that year. The only thing was, there were some comments from people who didn't feel he deserved Coach of the Year honors. The comments weren't coming just from fans, but also staff members. That was too bad because this was one of the best years we'd had in a long time, and we had won the division. People were giving a lot of the credit for that to Bart.

Again, I kept trying to avoid the controversy. I thought, "You know, the man has been in the league two years, and he's won the division. That's not bad."

But then in 1973 we started going the other way. We finished 5-7-2 and were third in the division. We started the season with Scott Hunter at quarterback, and then we went to Jim Del Gaizo, and then we went back to Hunter, and we finished with Jerry Tagge. That hurt us a great deal. There's no doubt that 1973 was when things started to unravel. When we won the division in '72 Hunter was the quarterback every single game. But we changed constantly in '73 and lost our leadership and our continuity. It's tough to win that way.

The division among the coaches was getting deeper. I knew it was going on, but I couldn't get involved. I took the approach that I was just going to do everything that I was supposed to do, keep my mouth shut and see how it turned out. But it was getting rougher every year, and in 1974 it was really going downhill.

We started the year with Tagge at quarterback for six games, and then we went to Jack Concannon for two games, and that's when Dan traded first-, second- and third-round draft choices in 1975 and first- and third-round choices in 1976 to the Los Angeles Rams for John Hadl, a 34-year-old veteran quarterback.

I was sitting in my office after the trade was announced when Tony Canadeo walked through my door, and his face was beet red. He was just livid. He said the Executive Committee had known nothing about this, and he asked if I had known anything about it. I said I hadn't heard a thing. I could see the whole thing coming apart right there. I don't think there was a soul in the organization who knew about the deal other than Dan. Somebody said to me later that he did it because he was desperate. It was a huge mistake on his part, and I knew how the Executive Committee was going to feel.

His responsibility was to go to them with any personnel move of that magnitude. That's what the Executive Committee is there for, to oversee and approve the organization's operations. You certainly don't make a player move like that without their approval. Tony Canadeo and Dick Bourguignon were strong, strong people, and they had a deep love for this franchise, and it just tore them apart. Tony and I became very dear friends, and I'll never forget him standing in my doorway that day.

The trade really set the fans off, too. I was taking those phone calls in those days, and people were very upset. They were telling me, "The guy was old, he was finished, and what were we doing giving away our future for a guy who was on his last legs?"

I don't subscribe to the theory, though, that the fans were so angry that one of them shot Dan's dog. The question was whether the dog was killed because the guy didn't like Dan Devine or because it was bothering the guy's animals. The story I kept hearing was the dog was out roaming the neighborhood, and people would ask Dan to keep it tied up. But he didn't, and somebody came and shot him. I don't think it was done because Dan was coach of the Green Bay Packers.

The Hadl trade set us back for who knows how long. The fact that the Executive Committee wasn't consulted had those folks extremely upset, and the feelings on the coaching staff had gotten worse. If Dan had had more success after that '72 season, he might have been able to replace the coaches who weren't on the same page with him, but I don't think he would have been comfortable doing that under the circumstances. I just don't think he felt he could do it. All of these things were building up in '74 when we weren't playing very good football anyway.

He had some really strained relationships with the players at that point. It was terrible. There was a group that was with Dan and a group that wasn't. I'd say the split was probably worse than half and half, and many of the players who were against him were our team leaders. It was a very unhappy organization.

I had a couple of other situations that caused me trouble. We had acquired Ted Hendricks in a trade, and he came to us with a contract. But Dan took the option year out of the contract, so once Ted finished playing that year he was free to do whatever he wanted to do. Normally with the option year the player had to take a 10% pay cut, and it gave you a great chance to negotiate a new deal and add some years to the contract. But we didn't have the option year to deal with, and Ted and his agent put us up against the wall. They threw some ridiculous numbers at us, and we just couldn't get the guy signed. Ted had been a great player for us, but this gave him a chance to go out on the market and get what he wanted, and he left.

The other situation was with MacArthur Lane. His agent was in town one day, and I wasn't getting anywhere with him on a new contract. We finally reached an impasse, and I told him I didn't know where to go at that point. I'd just have to get back to him. And he said, "What about the scouting contract?"

I said, "What are you talking about?" And he told me MacArthur had a contract to do part-time scouting after his playing days were over. It was a 10-year deal for $15,000 a year, and nobody in the organization knew anything about it. I asked him if he had a copy of the contract, and he said he sure did. He was at the Midway Motor Lodge a couple of blocks from Lambeau Field, and so I drove down there and he met me in the parking lot and showed me the contract that Dan had signed with Mac. I went back to the office and called Fred Trowbridge, who was our counsel at the time, and asked him if he was aware of this scouting contract. He said he had no idea what I was talking about. So that upset the Executive Committee, too.

Dan never told me why he took out that option clause in Hendricks' contract or why he signed the scouting deal with Lane, but I do know he needed as much support among the players as he could find. He hadn't told me about Hendricks' clause, and nobody in the organization had known about Lane becoming a scout after he retired. Bill Tobin, our scouting director, had no interest in Mac scouting for us.

Even in the middle of the season, though, I thought Dan might get through this thing. We weren't an awful ball club. We were hanging pretty close to .500, and then we won three games in a row, and I thought, "Boy, if we can do anything in the last three games we've got a shot." If we could have won two of them we would have made the playoffs. So even though we had turmoil on the team, it was not that horrible. But then in the last three weeks, we sank.

All three games were on the road. We lost at Philadelphia, 36-14, and we lost to San Francisco, 7-6, and then we went to Atlanta to finish the season. That's when I started hearing rumors that the team was going to boycott the trip.

There were rumors going around the office that the players weren't going to show up at the airport. I just couldn't fathom anything like that happening, but I heard it from various staff members, and I was obviously very nervous about it. I never talked to Dan about it, and I don't know if he was even aware of it. I just remember when I got to the airport and saw the players walking in, it was a great relief. I always wondered if somebody had made up that story because we were having a tough year, but it turned out to be just a rumor.

So now we're in Atlanta the night before the game, and there's a story going around the hotel that Jack Noel of our equipment staff has just gone to the post office with a letter from Dan addressed to Father Edmund Joyce, the right-hand man to Father Theodore Hesburgh, the president of Notre Dame. Jack Buck was doing our game the next day for national television, and Jack had been very close to Dan because of their ties in Missouri. I happened to run into Jack, and he told me he'd heard that rumor, and he wanted to know what I knew about it. I told him I'd heard the story, but I found it hard to believe. I don't recall if Jack ever used that on the air, but I heard later that the letter was Dan's acceptance of the head coaching job at Notre Dame. He was obviously on his way out when we went to Atlanta.

The day of the game was miserable. There was fog, there was rain, it was cold, the crowd was just a little over 10,000, and it looked like less than that because the people didn't even want to sit in the stands. They were standing up under the cover by the concession stands. The season was over for both teams, and it was like a preseason scrimmage. It was just eerie.

We lost the game, 10-3, which left us with a 6-8 record, third in the division again. Some people said the team tanked, but I can't honestly say I believe that. It was just a miserable ball game.

After the game I thought I'd seen the last of Dan Devine. I still didn't know whether the Notre Dame letter was true or not, but I just felt this thing was so shattered that something had to happen.

The game was on December 15, and he resigned on December 16 and was hired immediately at Notre Dame. It didn't take him long to leave the building. It wasn't a surprise to me that he was gone, but it was a shock to me that he could walk out the door and take the Notre Dame job the next day. You talk about somebody landing on his feet. I mean Dan really landed on his feet. He had a great knack for that. By 1977 he had produced a national championship for Notre Dame.

I was very concerned when Dan left because of the fact that he had been the one who had hired me. Interestingly enough, right after he left, Bing Devine called me and was ready to come to my rescue again. He told me Hollywood Park Racetrack in Los Angeles was looking for a general manager. He didn't know what my situation was going to be in Green Bay, but if I wanted to go out there for an interview the woman who was running the track would love to meet me.

So I flew out to Los Angeles early in the morning and met with the people from the racetrack and then flew back that night. I really had made up my mind on the way home that I was going to say no. The job was never offered, but I knew I didn't want to raise my family there. It would have been awfully difficult with three young boys. I thought, "I'll find something. Something will happen," and I withdrew my name in the morning.

There wasn't much of a time period to worry about it. Dan left on December 16, and Bart Starr was hired on December 24. Dominic Olejniczak, our team president at the time, told me that the fans really selected this coach, that they almost demanded that he be hired. That was a great description of the situation because the fans couldn't wait for Bart to take over.

I was delighted when he came in, but I had no idea of my status with him. He and I had obviously been friends when he was coaching here, and he was one of the first individuals I'd met when I came to Green Bay. But I didn't know what his plans were for the front office.

I was sitting with Madeline and my mother in Green Bay on December 24, and Bart called the house and offered to have me stay on his staff. He was hired that afternoon, and he called me at home that night. It certainly made my Christmas a lot happier. My mother was so happy when I got the phone call. She was very nervous. My dad had only been dead a couple of years, and she was feeling alone anyway. And it really helped her to know that her son still had a job.

Bart told me he'd like to give me more responsibility. He wanted me to do all of the player contracts and the assistant coaches' contracts. When we finished the conversation I told him that I was extremely relieved, and then I said, "Bart, it's an honor to work for you."

And he said, "Bob, you won't be working for me. You'll be working with me."

CHAPTER SIX

A Falling Starr

The atmosphere in the organization changed tremendously once Bart Starr arrived. It was almost a feeling of relief because everyone really believed he was the right person for the job. It was a new time, a fresh start. That normally happens with a new coach, but I think it was special this time because of who he was.

The people in our building were as excited as the fans on the street, and the fans had insisted that Bart be the coach. If someone else had been named coach, they would have stormed the building.

Bart faced two major obstacles when he took over. First of all, he had limited coaching experience. He probably got the job too early. He should have been an assistant coach longer and had a chance to grow a little bit rather than just taking over the franchise. He left Dan Devine's staff after the 1972 season because he really wasn't comfortable with his situation. I don't know that he felt he was being used the way he wanted to be used to make the contributions he felt he could make. Consequently, he stepped away from the job after only one year.

Secondly, the Hadl trade had left him dry at the draft table. He was already coaching a team that wasn't very talented, and yet he didn't have a chance to build it up quickly through the draft. That set him back a great deal.

But Bart was always positive. There was never any attacking anyone about what had gone on before, no "woe is me." He never took that approach to anything.

Although he wasn't connected to the team in Devine's last two years, he knew exactly what was going on and how badly the staff was split. I think he got a good feel for it when he was here in 1972. He continued to live in Green Bay while he did some TV work, and he still talked to people in the organization.

I can tell you that of all the coaches I've watched here through 36 years, I don't know of anybody who worked any harder or any longer than Bart Starr. He was so proud to be coming back to this franchise and taking over as the coach, and he was probably devoting 20 hours a day to coaching. That included holidays. He was just going to do everything possible to get this franchise up to where it had been in the Lombardi years.

But things just never fell into place. It's a shame that they didn't, but they just never did. One year we were dead last in the league in defense, but we still finished 8-8. We had a great offense with Lynn Dickey, Paul Coffman, James Lofton and John Jefferson, but the defense struggled all season. We never got the whole picture together to put us in a position to be a winning team.

There was much more disappointment than there was celebration for Bart during his nine years as head coach. He wanted so badly to succeed, and I've never seen a coach here who had the love affair with the organization that he had. It just didn't work out, and I think that bothered him terribly. He covered it up a lot better than most people could have.

When he was hired, we sat down in his office right after the Christmas holidays, and I started talking contracts with him because I wanted to get his philosophy. One thing I really appreciated about him was he never allowed an agent to go to him behind my back. That was happening on a regular basis with Dan, and if an agent knows he can go to someone else, you've lost all of your effectiveness. Bart understood that.

I had an agent one time who was quoted in a newspaper headline as saying, "I can't deal with Harlan anymore." I know for a fact that he called Bart, and Bart told him, "No, the only person you do deal with is Bob." Within a couple of days I had the player signed. That taught me a great lesson once I became president. I made sure that the people who were doing contracts knew an agent would never be able to affect the negotiations by going to me.

Bart's first draft pick was a guard out of Southern Cal named Bill Bain, who we took in the second round. He was the first top draft choice I had ever negotiated with, and his agent was Howard Slusher, who had a reputation for being extremely difficult. Howard had had a lot of players hold out, and I was very nervous because I thought the last thing I needed was to have Bart's first draft choice not show up when we went to training camp.

The first time I phoned Howard, he gave me his ideas on playing clauses. There must have been five pages of them, and by the time I'd finished writing them down I was sweating like crazy. I thought, "How am I ever going to get this kid signed with that kind of agent?" But we got it done, and in the long run I actually wound up having a pretty good relationship with Howard Slusher.

I always tried to be fair and up front with agents because I knew I was only going to get a contract signed if the agent agreed to it. You're going to face that same agent down the road some time, so you don't want to start out with a miserable relationship.

I truly believed that worked with Howard because other clubs would call me and say you're never going to get your guy signed with Slusher. But we did. Bain didn't turn out to be a great player, but I was always relieved that he was there at camp because he was Bart's first guy.

Bart's first game was in Milwaukee, and we got beat, 30-16, by the Detroit Lions. It was not a good performance. I think we got a couple of punts blocked that day, and reality set in. We had this head coach who wanted nothing more in the world than to see the franchise succeed, and his staff was working so hard, but we were not very good. We just didn't have a lot of talent.

We lost our first four games but then we beat the Cowboys, 19-17, in Dallas. I don't know that I've ever seen Bart any happier than he was after that victory. He and his son Bart were hugging in the locker room, and the whole team was so excited that you would have thought we'd clinched a playoff berth. There was the relief that the losing streak was finished, and there was just happiness for Bart overall. After the Ice Bowl and all of his other experiences against the Cowboys as a player, to have that be his first victory was probably very special for him. And then we went out and lost the next four games.

Bart always said the right thing after losses. He never got to the point where he was throwing obscenities around. He never talked down to people, and he would never criticize one player in front of the rest of the team. He tried to talk about the positive things, how we were going to get better if we kept working hard.

One of the reservations people had about him before he took the job was that he might be too nice to be a head coach, but I don't think that was the case. I never got the impression that there wasn't great respect for him as a person and as a coach. And because of that, the players listened to him and worked for him.

It was so different from what I'd seen during the Devine years. Of course every locker room has dissension, particularly when the losing goes on and on. A lot of times, the assistant coaches would try to take care of those situations.

In April of 1976 we traded John Hadl and defensive back Ken Ellis to Houston for Lynn Dickey, and that gave Bart a chance to get his own quarterback and kind of start his program without Hadl. Lynn really was the quarterback for most of the years after that, but still we couldn't find a way to be successful. We went 8-7-1 in 1978, and we got to the playoffs when we went 5-3-1 in a strike-shortened season in 1982, but those were Bart's only winning seasons in nine years.

In his first few years there was always one change on the coaching staff every season. The first year he was here he had his assistants dress up in suits and ties and posed them for a beautiful picture that we hung in the board room. We did that every year, and then at the end of the year a coach would be let go, and we'd have to get the group together so we could take another shot. I used to kid Bart about it. I told him he was killing my photo budget.

The toughest change came in 1979 when Bart fired defensive coordinator Dave Hanner. He just wasn't pleased with what Dave was doing, and he replaced him with John Meyer, who had been our linebackers coach. It was a major change because Dave had been a huge part of this organization as a player and coach for such a long time. When he found out that he'd been fired, he came to my house and wanted to talk about it. He was so upset he actually sat on my living room couch and cried. It was very sad. He was assistant head coach at the time, and Bart just felt he had to make a change in an extremely important position. I think he was getting very concerned about the future.

Bart's first full draft came in 1977 when we got Mike Butler and Ezra Johnson in the first round and Greg Koch in the second. It was a good draft, but I was having trouble getting Butler and Johnson signed. All of the coaches kept telling me, "Don't worry about it. Don't worry about it." Until we went to training camp and they still weren't signed. Then the coaches were coming to my door every day saying, "Why aren't these guys here?" I was worried because I thought Butler and Johnson could really help turn the club around and I had to get them into camp. We did get them signed within a couple of days, but those were tough negotiations.

There was pretty good confidence in the organization after we went 8-7-1 in the '78 season. We'd had some good drafts, and there was no doubt that the roster was getting better. But I'd heard something very disturbing in those first losing seasons. It was after we'd dropped a game at Detroit, and I happened to be on the team bus going to the airport. Dickey was sitting right behind me, and I heard him say to the person next to him, "You know, this is just awful. I'm not sure I'm the right quarterback for this team."

To hear your leader say something like that is pretty tough. That was a bad sign. I wasn't sure how bad it was, but I thought it was very significant, and even after we'd had that good season I wondered how many other players had that same frustration. Then in 1979 we fell all the way to 5-11. It just seemed like we couldn't get the offense and the defense together at the same time.

The organization suffered a major embarrassment during the preseason in 1980 when Ezra Johnson was spotted eating a hot dog on the bench while the game was going on. Everybody jumped on the story, not only locally but nationally. I didn't actually see the incident, but I heard about it the next day. The story was that a fan had offered the hot dog to him, and he'd gotten up and taken it and eaten it on the bench.

I heard from a lot of fans asking how anyone could do that. They wanted to know where the discipline was on our ball club. Bart was very upset, and Johnson was fined $1,000 and required to make an apology to the whole team. But Fred vonAppen, our defensive line coach, didn't think the punishment was severe enough, and he resigned. I just remember wondering, what in the world are these players thinking, and where is their concentration?

I could see Bart's stress increasing. The longer I worked for him the better friends we became. We would go to league meetings in March every year, and Madeline and I and Bart and his wife Cherry would go out to dinner. We just became closer as time went along. I don't want to say we socialized a lot, but if we were at an event where the organization was involved, we would be at their table and have a good time with them. Cherry was the perfect partner for Bart. She was so upbeat.

But I knew the pressures he felt when we just couldn't get over the hump, and those pressures grew tremendously. Even when we started adding some better material, we couldn't find a way to win. Bart definitely aged. In the pictures of his initial press conference, he almost looked like the young quarterback he used to be, but he looked much different when he left the organization. Still, there was never a time when he just leaned back in his chair and said, "This is driving me crazy."

Sure the job wore on him, but losing wears on everybody. It wears on every single person in the building because that's your life, and the most important thing you do happens on Sunday afternoon when the whole world is there to grade you for three hours. If it doesn't go well, eventually certain people are going to turn on you.

Bart's frustration was always more likely to come out when he was dealing with people outside of the organization. His relationship with the press deteriorated as time went along because of the years of losing and obviously because the press was becoming more critical. Overall he got along with the media very well most of the time, but there were some exceptions.

We brought Duane Thomas into town one time to work him out, and some members of the media saw him in the locker room. There was a feeling within the organization that we needed to keep it quiet that Duane was here, and when the reporters questioned Bart about it, he got very upset. The two times I saw him get really angry were when that happened and when Dave Begel of the Milwaukee *Journal* ran a diagram in the paper of a special play that Bart had put in for our next opponent. Bart had closed the practice, and Begel had pulled his car up to the fence that was surrounding the field and stood on the roof of the car to watch. That was probably as upset as I've ever seen Bart, and I'm not sure he ever spoke to Begel again.

He understood that as a coach he was going to get criticized. That came with the territory. But after a while, the frustration of losing and having some members of the media turning on him more than they should have had to hurt him. He never told me it did, but you could look at him and read it in his face.

Nobody likes to be criticized, but Bart might have been extra sensitive to it because he had been such a hero here as a player. The criticism cut through to him more than it would have to a toughened coach who had not had that glory as a player.

Bart really was a private person. There were times when being in the spotlight was almost awkward for him, but he handled it so well that you would never know he was uncomfortable. I thought he went overboard in his relationship with the fans. He always had time for everybody. People could stop him in a hotel lobby, and Bart would always take the time to smile and talk to them. His parents had taught him to be a Southern gentleman, and that's what he was.

There was a change in the Packers president's chair in 1982 when Dominic Olejniczak retired and Judge Robert Parins replaced him and became the first fulltime president of the organization. The seven men who had preceded Judge Parins all had other jobs in town, and they spent more time in those than they did in the Packers office. For example, Dominic was very involved in real estate. But the game was becoming more complex, and we needed someone here fulltime.

Both Dominic and Judge Parins took the approach that they were going to give Bart every possible opportunity to win. I was going to Executive Committee meetings then, and I never heard much grumbling. Everybody wanted to see Bart succeed and get us back to where this franchise should have been. That's why he was given the nine years.

I never heard any rumblings until Bart's last couple of years. You might get fans who would write letters or say something, but nothing from inside our building. It certainly helped to go to the playoffs in '82, but I kept hearing from the fans, "Yeah, but that was a strike year." And it was, but that wasn't our fault. We still finished 5-3-1 and won a playoff game. Then we went to Dallas and played a very good game, but we didn't win it. Things started to get noisier after that.

I don't think Bart was wired into that, though. He was so focused on his football team and on his job that a lot of distractions just went around him. People have said over and over again that he was a much better coach the year he was let go than he'd ever been earlier, and I think that's true. The interesting thing is that if he had won his last game in Chicago in 1983 he might have stayed on as the Packers' coach.

A victory in Chicago would have put us in the playoffs. We had to win that game and New Orleans had to lose that Sunday for us to make it, and the Saints did lose earlier in the day. We had that sitting there for us, and we had the lead when the Bears marched down the field and won, 23-21, on a field goal in the final seconds. Bob Thomas kicked the field goal, and I mean to tell you that ball was wobbling through the air like a knuckleball, but it still went through.

That was such a devastating loss. I never saw Bart more discouraged. I don't think he had any idea that his job was in jeopardy at that point.

His disappointment was simply that we were right on the verge of getting to the playoffs, and we didn't do it. Detroit won the division at 9-7, and we were 8-8. We were that close to getting to the playoffs. As the Bears kept moving you got more and more nervous. Thomas' field goal was not something you would take a film of and show to anybody, but it was good and it killed us.

We had a plane delay for some reason after the game, and there was just a deathly silence as we waited in the airport. I knew Judge Parins was upset, but we all felt terrible, and Bart was as upset as any of us.

I found out later that during the delay the judge had talked to the members of the Executive Committee who were on the trip and told them he was ready to make a change in the head coaching position. They all agreed with the decision. The next morning the judge called the Committee members who didn't travel with us to Chicago, and he received their approval.

The judge came into my office at around 8 o'clock that morning and said, "I have just talked to Bart, and I've let him and his staff go." It was a very brief conversation. He'd gone into Bart's office and told him of his decision, and then when he was coming back down the hallway, he leaned into my office and told me what he'd done.

I can't say that I was astounded. I knew things were getting tougher, but I kept thinking if we got through the season and into the playoffs, Bart would have a great chance to continue, but it just didn't happen. The judge might have had other things that piled up in the meantime and finally just decided to make a move. Maybe the biggest issue was the fact that it had been nine years, and that sealed it. Maybe the calendar hurt Bart more than anything.

I think Bart was surprised. He said when it was all over, "I was becoming a better coach, and we were ready to go and do something." I don't know if that was true or not. We didn't improve on the field, because we had the same 8-8 record in 1984 and 1985 under Forrest Gregg.

Bart had a meeting with the staff that day before he left the building, and he just thanked everybody. It was funeral like. He was typical Bart Starr, but it was very, very emotional. I wouldn't say he was close to tears, but it was tough to listen to him. What he'd wanted so badly just didn't happen.

It was a tough thing for the judge. He had something he felt he had to do, and he did it. I have never discussed it with Bart, and I never really talked to the judge too much about it, either. I would face the same kind of thing in a few years with Tom Braatz. It is never an easy decision, and it wasn't easy for the judge.

We had a Board meeting the day that Bart was released, and when the judge stood up at the podium the Board gave him a standing ovation. They were applauding him for taking a strong stand.

Later the judge showed me a drawer in his desk with all the mail he'd gotten after he'd fired Bart, telling him how upset people were. The thing I get such pleasure out of now is that when Bart does come back and he's introduced, people still love and respect him. I think all of those people who were angry in the 80's when he was coaching have disappeared. It is almost like those years had never happened.

I can't imagine another coach in the country going through nine years of what Bart had here and still having the adulation that he has. Nobody else in the world that I can think of would have made it through that time.

CHAPTER SEVEN

Crime and Punishment — the Gregg Years

I t took only 10 minutes for the Cincinnati Bengals to give the Packers permission to talk to Forrest Gregg. When Judge Parins called them, Paul Brown called back almost immediately, which surprised everyone. We didn't expect it to be that easy.

Forrest had been Coach of the Year when he was with the Cleveland Browns in 1976, and he'd taken the Bengals to the Super Bowl in 1981, so we thought it would be much tougher to get him. I never found out why it wasn't. Mike Brown, Paul's son, always talked fondly of Forrest and his days in Cincinnati, but I don't know if Paul was that close to him or not. The father was in charge at the time, and that could have had something to do with it.

Bart left on December 19, 1983, and Forrest was hired on December 24. That made two coaches in a row who'd been named on Christmas Eve. Maybe we were trying to wish everyone happy holidays.

Forrest signed a five-year contract very quickly, and Judge Parins gave him full power to run the football operation. We had the press conference, and he took over.

People in the office were sad when Bart left, but Forrest was another Vince Lombardi hero coming home, and so he was very welcome. He'd left here with a great reputation. Lombardi had referred to him as the finest football player he had ever coached, and it looked like a coup when he came here.

But his four years as coach were an era of turmoil both on and off the field. It was a different kind of turmoil than Dan Devine had experienced. This was almost 100%. People who had been around the organization when Forrest was a player and were still around when he became coach were very surprised that things got away from him the way they did. When he left, we were at an all-time public relations low.

There weren't a lot of times when Forrest was really happy, to be quite honest about it. A couple of years after his regime was over, I asked a player what it was like. He said Forest was stern, vocal and at times intimidating. He told me it was negative motivation, and it was a negative time in Packerland. I think that described it very well.

Forrest went 8-8 in his first year, and it was an odd season because we started out 1-7 and finished 7-1. We were second in the division, and things didn't look too bad. But then he went 8-8 in his second year when the Chicago Bears were 15-1 and won the Super Bowl, and from that point on it really went downhill.

I didn't know Forrest until he came to Green Bay to coach, but we had a very good relationship early on. The first time I met him was when he came in for his press conference, and he was very pleasant. In fact, there were times when my wife and I went out to dinner with Forrest and his wife, Barbara. We'd go out on a Friday night before a home game and have a wonderful time.

I'd watched his career when I was working in Milwaukee and going to school at Marquette, and I'd admired him for what he'd done as a coach and as a player. I thought the judge had done a great job in getting him. But a couple of difficult situations tarnished things.

Judge Parins called me in one time, and when I got to his office Forrest was sitting there. The judge said Forrest had a couple of requests. One was that we drop family photo day, and the other was that we move training camp out of Green Bay.

I said I could understand dropping family photo day because it had really gotten to be a negative public relations event. People were pushing each other around and almost fighting to get in line for the players. It wasn't at all what we intended, and I said we could find a different way to get autographs for the fans.

But I said moving training camp out of town would be a horrible mistake. Businesses planned for those weeks, and people loved the fact that training camp was right at Lambeau Field where they could come to watch. So the judge said, "Okay, that's what we're going to do. We'll drop family photo day, but we won't move training camp."

Well, Forrest didn't appreciate that. I can understand why he didn't like the decision, but I truly felt that moving training camp would be terrible, terrible public relations.

The other situation where we differed came up in 1987, Walter

Payton's final year with the Chicago Bears. Payton had meant a lot to the National Football League both on and off the field, and when he announced that this was going to be his final year, the home team in every city where the Bears played that season honored him. I went to Judge Parins and said we needed to pay tribute to Walter Payton when he came to Green Bay. I suggested we give him a couple of gifts and have him go out to the middle of the field to be introduced and receive a round of applause. The judge was in total agreement, but Forrest didn't like it, probably because Payton was a Chicago Bear.

He came to me and said, "I don't want to do this." And I said, "Forrest, we're going to look very bad if everybody else is doing it and we don't. This needs to be done." He said, "Okay, but let me know what he's going to get before we do anything."

So we worked up a list of gifts, and Walter received them, and it went over very well. He got a wonderful round of applause from the people at Lambeau Field, as he should have. But the dinners with Forrest and his wife kind of stopped after that. Our relationship really cooled.

The happiest I ever saw Forrest was after the 1984 season. I think he really felt things were turning around when we finished so well, and he seemed at ease. The unhappiest I ever saw him was after the two games we played with the Bears the following year when William (the Refrigerator) Perry scored two touchdowns against us.

In Forrest's four years as coach we were penalized more than 100 times each year, and in 1987 we set a league record with 135 penalties. The most notable infractions came against Chicago. Forrest had a deep hatred for the Bears that I think went back to his playing days. Maybe the fact that Mike Ditka was playing for the Bears at the same time as he was playing for the Packers had something to do with it. The rivalry took on a whole new atmosphere when Forrest was coaching here.

In 1985 we played a Monday night game at Soldier Field, and the Bears had a goal line play where they took Perry, a defensive tackle, and put him in the backfield. He scored a touchdown, and that really set Forrest off. The Bears came into Lambeau Field two weeks later, and this time they threw a pass to Perry for a touchdown that added fuel to the fire.

I saw Forrest in the locker room after the Monday night game, and he was livid. And that wasn't just in the locker room. He let everyone in the building know how upset he was for the next couple of weeks. I think it bothered him even more that it happened on national television. He hated to lose to the Bears, and Ditka really added to the turmoil by having Perry score those touchdowns.

We had another incident that season when we played the Colts in Indianapolis and got beat, 37-10. It was an ugly game, and I was late coming down from the press box to the locker room. Normally the locker room is open 10 minutes after the game so the press can get in to talk to the players and coaches, but this time it was still closed after a good 15 or 20 minutes. Everybody was waiting outside the door, and you could hear a lot of noise inside. Finally when the doors opened I walked in behind the press, and some of the players who were standing there looked liked they'd witnessed a train wreck.

I found out later that our strength coach, Virgil Knight, had picked up a full can of soda and thrown it across the room at linebacker Mike Douglass. Fortunately it didn't hit anybody, but it was that close to total chaos in the locker room. Lee Remmel, our public relations director, had witnessed the whole thing, and he just walked over to me and shook his head without saying a word.

I knew then that Forrest had tremendous unhappiness in the locker room. I would hear it from the players, particularly in those last couple of years when he let a lot of veterans go. He had to know it, and his coaches had to know it, too.

We had a total change in our roster going into the 1986 season. Douglass was let go, and so were Paul Coffman, George Cumby, Greg Koch, and Mike Butler. Forrest didn't want to re-sign Lynn Dickey, and so we terminated him. Randy Wright started all 16 games at quarterback that season, and we were 4-12. It was a terrible, ugly year.

Al Stevens, our security officer, came to my office one day and told me that James Lofton had been charged with taking a woman into a stairwell at a bar in downtown Green Bay and sexually assaulting her. Al was also the one who told me that Mossy Cade, a cornerback who we'd gotten from San Diego in 1985 for a first- and a fifth-round draft choice, had been charged with assaulting a woman who turned out to be his aunt. Both of these incidents happened in the same season. The police came to Al first, and then he went to the judge and then he came to see me. It was like a nightmare that just wouldn't end.

There was a flood of letters, and the phone was ringing off the hook. People would ask, "What are you doing? Are you bringing a bunch of convicts to town?" It was an awful time because the organization was taking such a public relations hit, not just in the state but throughout the country.

Our slogan "Pack Attack" was going around Wisconsin in the early 70's, and when the Lofton and Cade cases came along, the Green Bay *Press-Gazette* said in an editorial that the Packers had given the slogan a whole new meaning. The fans were upset about that, and they were upset about all the penalties. Not just the fact that we were a penalized team but with the kind of penalties we were getting.

In a nationally televised game with Chicago, our defensive end, Charles Martin, turned Bears quarterback Jim McMahon upside down and slammed him to the ground. Martin had a towel hanging from his waist with some numbers on it, and the television announcer said it looked like a hit list. In another incident, safety Ken Stills hit Bears fullback Matt Suhey long after a play was finished. He just flew through the air and hit him. When they saw that, fans were writing in and saying, "What kind of people do you have here?" We were playing dirty football, and there was no need for it.

Suhey talked to me about it after another game at Soldier Field. The two locker rooms were right next to each other, and when he saw me coming out of ours he walked over and said, "Mr. Harlan, this stuff has got to stop." And I told him, "Matt, I know it does. It's embarrassing for our organization."

But if there was a reprimand from Forrest I never heard about it. I got the impression from other players that he was encouraging that behavior. The fact that it was intimidating, that it was "negative motivation"...I always felt that was a strange description. I don't know if that was what the players were being taught to do, but I do know we had a lot of penalties, and the ones with the Bears seemed to be more severe than the ones against other clubs. I thought that was the great Ditka battle.

Forrest had told his players, "You take care of the Bears. I'll take care of Ditka." He and Ditka never got into anything wild with each other, but I think they sent their message by the way they coached. It became very vehement on both sidelines.

The thing that upset me was that we kept bringing in these people who weren't football players. They were thugs. And that was the reputation we were getting across the country.

When the fans called, we had no excuse. We really had to make a move to let them know that we felt as badly about the situation as they did. We told them that we realized that this was very harmful to the organization, and we were going to deal with it. The whole thing had to be cleaned up, and we started cleaning it up by letting Lofton go.

Even though he was eventually acquitted, his reputation had gone downhill so quickly that the organization really didn't have much choice but to trade him. And so in April of 1987 we sent him to the Raiders for a third-round draft choice in 1987 and a fourth in '88.

All of us in the Packers organization have been pleased to see the way Lofton turned his life around after he left Green Bay. He went on to play for the Raiders, the Buffalo Bills, the Los Angeles Rams and the Philadelphia Eagles before he retired following the 1993 season. He was elected to the Packers Hall of Fame in 1999 and to the Pro Football Hall of Fame in 2003. He and his lovely wife Beverly and their three children live in San Diego where James is the Chargers' wide receivers coach. It is always nice to see the warm welcome he receives from Packers fans when he returns to Green Bay.

The 1987 season began with a players' strike. It was only a three-week strike, but it was enough to make Forrest more bitter. I'm not saying he was out on the picket line raising heck with everybody, but I don't think he was really ready to forgive the players when they came into training camp. It was a very, very difficult season. You could see it falling apart the same way you could see Dan Devine's last season falling apart. Things just got worse every week.

Brent Fullwood was our first-round draft choice, the fourth player taken overall, and he turned out to be a total bust. I kept hearing that he was having difficulty learning the playbook. It was scary hearing the stories about him. That was just another part of the picture.

We played only 15 games because of the strike and finished 5-9-1. Wright started seven games at quarterback, Alan Risher started three and Don Majkowski started five. So we were back to having a different quarterback every time you looked up. James was gone, and it just wasn't much of a ball club.

As things continued to deteriorate, most of the people in the office kind of backed away when they saw Forrest coming down the hall. He was a huge man, and he had an angry look on his face most of the time. He was not a happy camper during those times, and it showed.

Tom Braatz was hired in 1987 to work with him, and the key word there was "with." They shared the front office duties 50-50. Neither of them could overrule the other. I thought hiring Tom was a good idea, hoping he might bring some stability to that department. The judge had called Eddie LeBaron to ask if he'd be interested in the job, and LeBaron had said he wasn't, but he'd suggested that we call Tom. So the judge called Tom, and he accepted the position.

But the move wasn't real popular with Forrest. The judge had some headaches over that. It wasn't easy for Forrest to accept somebody else coming in, even though Tom made it as easy for him as possible. Tom was kind of laid back, definitely not the type to storm right in and take charge. Still the new configuration was difficult for Forrest to accept.

It was similar to the situation we had later with Mike Sherman and Ted Thompson. It can be tough for those people to live together. Forrest fought it for awhile before it happened, but the judge had made up his mind that he was going to do it, and he did it.

Things were in such disarray by the end of that season that the feeling in our building was that Forrest would not be brought back for another year. We had the off-field problems, the team was terrible, and Forrest had to know that his days were numbered. It all ended when Southern Methodist University made a phone call to him, and he jumped on it.

He got up early one morning in January and just drove out of town. I was in my office, and my window looked right out on the parking lot toward Lombardi Avenue. One of the coaches came to me and said, "Forrest Gregg is going to resign today and leave." I asked him how he knew that, and he said he'd heard it in the back hallway. Then I looked out my window, and there were Forrest and his wife driving away.

This was about 7:30 in the morning, and the next person to come in to see me was Dick Modzelewski, the defensive line coach and defensive coordinator. Dick had come with Forrest from Cincinnati and he had been on his staff at Cleveland, so he was a long-time coaching companion. Dick said Forrest was going to take another job, and he hadn't said good-bye to one person in that back hallway.

All of the coaches were upset that he hadn't called any kind of meeting. What he was doing was going to affect their families tremendously, but he had just left. Dick was crushed. He'd been with Forrest for a long time, and he felt that he was not only a colleague but a good friend.

This was on January 15, and the next time anyone saw Forrest was on TV that afternoon when he held a press conference at SMU. At the time the organization was very close to releasing him. I think he could see the end was near, and he made his escape before it happened. It was very reminiscent of the Dan Devine thing.

He'd told the judge he was leaving, got a couple of things out of his office and walked out. Modzelewski was shocked that he could just up and leave his staff high and dry like that.

The next time I heard from Forrest was in the fall of 1991 when I had fired Tom Braatz. I had already made contact with Ron Wolf and was ready to hire him when I got a call from Forrest. I thought, "My God, maybe he's calling to say good-bye after three years."

So Forrest got on the phone and said, "How are you?" And I said, "Good, Forrest, how are you?" And he said, "Fine, how's the family?" And I said, "Good, how's your family?" And he said, "Fine. I still love the Packers. All I'm doing is calling to say if you're still looking for a general manager, I think Ron Wolf would be a good choice."

I told him, "Well, then you will be pleased to know that I have already hired Ron. We haven't announced it yet, but we will in the next few days." And he said, "Sounds great. Good luck. Good-bye." And we hung up.

He and I haven't talked since then.

CHAPTER EIGHT

Guns and Roses —
Negotiating Contracts

Clarence Williams was a defensive end and a huge man. He stood 6-5 and weighed about 260 pounds, and he wasn't happy with what I was offering that day when he came to my office to negotiate his contract. Every time I put a number on the table he got a little angrier. Suddenly he stood up, and I thought, "My God, he's coming across the table at me."

I kept saying, "Clarence, sit down, we're just talking." But my office door was closed, and he was leaning forward with both hands on the desk, and I was wondering how loud I could scream. I thought, "This is it. This is how it's all going to end."

I did contracts for the Packers for 14 years. I started doing them exclusively in 1975 when Bart Starr took over, but that was the only time I ever thought I was going to be assaulted. Clarence and I eventually got the deal done, and we could joke about it later, but boy, he was mad that day.

When you do contracts, they're on your mind all the time. You know how much pressure the coaches are going to feel if training camp starts and they don't have everybody there, and that was my biggest concern. I could be on a golf course, and I'd be thinking, "If I do this, what's he going to do?" Or "If I offer that, will he counter with this?" I wanted to keep the coach out of it because I thought it was one thing he didn't need to be bothered with. If there was a chance we could lose somebody by not paying him, then I would go to the coach, but most of the time I knew where we needed to go, and I would just do it.

I think everybody who does contracts loses sleep over them. You might have 10 or 15 veterans going into their option years, and as soon as you get them all signed, you're looking at your roster to see who's coming up next year. It's almost like a recruiting class. It weighs on you because it's such a big obligation to the organization.

On draft day, as soon as we drafted somebody, we'd call the player with a form sheet. One of the questions on the sheet was, "Who is your agent?" I would always look over the shoulder of the person taking the notes, and I'd be either happy or sad depending on who the agent was because I'd know what was in store for me.

Players don't do their own deals anymore. That pretty much ended with the salary cap era, but I had a group in the 80's that felt quite comfortable negotiating for themselves. People like Larry McCarren, Greg Koch and Lynn Dickey. I know I was fair with them because they kept coming back. They knew me well enough that I don't think it ever crossed their minds that I would try to take advantage of them. Larry is one of my best friends today, and I have a great relationship with Lynn when he comes to town.

I can still remember the last contract we did with Lynn. It was in the $600,000 to $800,000 range, and I went to the Executive Committee with it because it just seemed like such an enormous figure. I got approval to do it, but I was a nervous wreck when Lynn and I were in my office signing the deal. I couldn't imagine that kind of money. But he was a veteran quarterback at the time, and that's where the market was.

If you're fair, you don't make a player live with a contract that's not up to date and isn't compatible with what's going on in the league and with what he's contributing to the team.

For example, a couple of weeks after the 1978 draft, Lew Carpenter, our receivers coach, came to me and said he was a little thin at tight end and he needed to have one more kid in training camp so that our starter, Rich McGeorge, wouldn't get run into the ground. Earlier in the spring we'd had one of our coaches go down to Kansas State to work out a linebacker, and while he was there, this young tight end kept asking if he could run for him and show him what he could do.

The coach had told me if we ever needed a player just for training camp, I might want to call this person and see if he was signed with anybody. His name was Paul Coffman, and the coach said he seemed like a decent kid. Just don't go overboard with him.

So I called the Kansas State athletic department, and ironically Paul was in the building at the time. He said he'd love to talk. I offered him a two-year deal with a $2,000 signing bonus and base salaries of $24,000 and $30,000, figuring this was somebody who would be in camp for two or three weeks. He agreed to it immediately, and we got the contracts in the mail that afternoon. They came back in a couple of days, and Paul Coffman was ours.

Well, Paul showed tremendous talent right from the start. Carpenter came into my office after a couple of practices and said the kid from Kansas State had something going for him. The next year Paul replaced McGeorge as a starter and led the team in receptions. He would become an All-Pro in 1984 and play in three Pro Bowls.

Once Paul became a starter, we amended his original contract and extended it an additional two years. I never upgraded a contract unless the player or agent would also agree to an extension. I didn't want to improve what we previously negotiated unless I got something in return. Paul and I had a lot of negotiating sessions through the years, and we always got it done, but he never let me forget that I gave him only a $2,000 signing bonus.

I always tried to get a feel for what the market was for every position, and I had to keep in mind that when I did one contract it affected every other contract on the ball club. I would never give a guaranteed contract. Dan Devine had given a guaranteed contract to John Brockington, and John became a different ball player after he signed it. He was not the effective star runner he'd been in his first three years.

If an agent argued, I'd say, "Listen, James Lofton doesn't have a guaranteed contract, and if he doesn't I'm not about to give one to your guy. I've got an all-pro here who doesn't have a guarantee, so please don't tell me that a young man just out of college deserves one."

There were certain agents that I was happier to negotiate with than others because I knew what to expect. Leigh Steinberg was a great example. He was not easy by any means, but he knew exactly how I would operate. The first year I stopped doing contracts was 1985, and our first draft choice that year was Kenny Ruettgers, an offensive tackle out of Southern Cal. Leigh was representing Kenny, and the negotiations between him and Chuck Hutchison, who had taken over the contracts for us, were moving slowly.

After several weeks, Leigh called me and asked if I would step in on Ruettgers. He said, "When Green Bay drafted Ken, I told him I knew exactly what to expect. We'll get an offer on draft day that will include clauses and Bob and I will get it done, and you'll be in camp in no time. But things aren't moving like that."

I told Leigh I understood his frustration, but when I was doing contracts I always appreciated the fact that no one could go around me, and I couldn't do that to Chuck, either. Leigh understood that, and we've remained very close friends through the years.

Some agents weren't quite as pleasant, but I kept one thing in mind: I have to have a businesslike relationship with this individual. I can't let things get confrontational to the point where we stop talking because this is the guy who finally has to agree to the numbers. And next year the same agent may have three of our draft choices. Why create animosity now with somebody I may be dealing with for the next 10 years?

In 1980 we took Bruce Clark, the defensive tackle out of Penn State, as the fourth choice in the draft because he was someone we felt could have a great impact on our team. Bruce had the same agent as Eddie Lee Ivery, the Georgia Tech running back who was our first choice the previous year. I called Bruce's agent on the day of the draft to make a proposal, and I followed up with phone calls in the following weeks and made a couple of changes in the numbers and the clauses.

We were working back and forth, but then just a few weeks after the draft I got a call from a member of the press who said, "Did you know that Bruce Clark is up in Canada signing a contract?" Well, nobody in the organization knew that.

I reached the agent the next morning and asked him, "Why in the world would you do this and not give us a chance to make a counter-offer and keep negotiating?" He told me the negotiations were going too slowly. I asked him how he could say that when the year before he'd had Ivery, and Eddie Lee didn't sign until July. The agent seemed very content with that, but here it was May, and Clark had already gone to Canada. But the agent just said he wanted the negotiations to move faster.

I had a difficult time believing that was the reason. We'd had some people hold out and not sign until close to the start of training camp, but we'd never had anybody just up and say, "I'm out of here" after a few weeks because the negotiations weren't moving the way they expected.

We finally found out from people at Penn State who knew Clark well that the real reason he went to Canada was that he refused to play nose tackle, and that was what we'd wanted him to play.

He didn't have a great career in Canada, and he didn't have a great NFL career when he came back here, but what he did was very detrimental to our organization and very disappointing to me because I know if I had had the normal amount of time that I would have gotten him signed. The agent could have told us that Clark didn't want to play nose tackle, but I think he just thought it was easier to get out of it by saying they didn't like the way the negotiations were going.

Four years later, we took Alphonso Carreker, a defensive end from Florida State, because we badly needed someone at that position. I was home watching a United States Football League game on television one Saturday night, and who shows up for a halftime interview on national TV but Carreker and his agent? They said they were down there negotiating with the USFL.

I got on the phone with the agent the next morning and really started moving negotiations along. I honestly overpaid to get Carrecker after what we'd gone through with our first-round draft choice in 1980. I thought there was no way in the world that we could repeat that, so we got it done and got him into camp.

When the contracts were signed, the agent said to me, "Tell me, were you concerned when you saw us on television with the USFL?" And I said, "Of course I was. It was a first-round draft choice, and I had to get him signed." And he said, "Bob, you have to understand something. I'm a hired gun, and my purpose is to get every penny out of you that I can get."

Two years later, this same agent was representing one of our players, and he called me to say he wanted to renegotiate the player's contract. I went to Forrest Gregg and told him our numbers were very fair, and I really didn't see a need to renegotiate his deal. Forrest said, "Then let's not do it. He's not contributing that much. Let's leave him where he is." So I called the agent back and told him that.

The agent said he was amazed that I'd act that way. And I said, "Well, now somebody else is holding the gun."

I really felt my best friend was the calendar in getting players signed. The draft would be in April, I would just beat my head against the wall in April, May and June, trying to get people signed. I was almost happy when it got to early July and we were going to camp because I knew things would start getting wrapped up. That happened almost every single year.

I did have agents who would tell me when we were all finished that their clients had told them just to get it done and get them into camp.

They wanted to be tougher than they were, but they were getting pressure from the other side.

In 1978 we took John Anderson, a linebacker out of Michigan, as our second choice in the first round, and I was having some trouble getting him signed. One day one of our coaches came to my office and told me that John's mother had a birthday coming up that weekend. So we called a florist and sent a dozen roses to John's mother for her birthday.

Well, the negotiations turned around almost immediately. Later Steinberg, who was John's agent, told me, "You killed me with those flowers, Bob. John's mom had told him, 'How can you not sign with these nice people?'"

The toughest negotiation I ever had may have been when we drafted Mike Butler and Ezra Johnson in the first round in 1977. Butler was represented by Donald Dell and David Falk, who were from the same firm in Washington, D.C. Donald really dealt in tennis, and David was very big in the National Basketball Association. In fact he still represents Michael Jordan. We had a very solid negotiation, but it was hard because neither of them had ever done a National Football League contract before.

The first time they came to meet with me, we must have sat in our board room for eight hours, and a lot of that time was spent with me explaining NFL contracts because they were so different from tennis and the NBA. It wasn't a case of me saying, "Well, you guys don't understand." I was just trying to explain where I was coming from.

I don't remember who Johnson's agent was, but he was waiting to see what Butler was going to get before he settled on his numbers. Until I got Butler signed, I wasn't going to get Johnson signed. David finally took over most of the negotiations, and we got it done, but we went to training camp without either player. It bothered me a lot to have two No. 1's and not have either of them at camp.

Someone else who came back to me with the same approach in 1980 was George Cumby, a linebacker from Oklahoma, who we took late in the first round. Cumby's agent was Dr. Jerry Argovitz, who became extra tough because he knew we were on the ropes after losing Bruce Clark. I think I overpaid on that one, too, but we simply couldn't afford to lose two No. 1 draft choices all at once.

I worried a little bit about Dr. Argovitz because he was a dentist and kind of new to the business. I would hear from other clubs that he was very difficult. Sometimes this really can be like pulling teeth.

For example, when we had a chance to sign John Jefferson in 1981, Howard Slusher was his agent. Howard and I had been through a couple of negotiations in the past, and I think our familiarity with each other helped us a little bit in that situation. The problem was that Howard was at a dentist's office when we were negotiating.

We were calling back and forth between my office and the dentist's waiting room, and the numbers were getting pretty high. I wanted someone on the Executive Committee to approve them, but I couldn't find Dominic Olejniczak, our president. Howard told me we had to get this done quickly because he didn't want to be doing it after he got into the chair. I finally reached Jerry Atkinson, another Executive Committee member, and told him I needed his permission to make the deal because the agent was very impatient. Jerry gave it to me, and I called Howard back before he got in the chair, and we agreed to the contract.

Howard had also represented Jefferson when he was coming out of college, and he was the only agent I can remember who ever called our football staff and told us not to draft his player. He said Jefferson did not want to come to Green Bay. I'd never heard that before, and we signed JJ three years later.

In all the time I did contracts I doubt that I did more than 50 face-to-face negotiations. I did practically all of it on the phone, but occasionally an agent would come to Green Bay, and I'd pick him up at the airport and we'd go to my office and talk. One of those agents was Irwin Weiner, who was also big in the NBA. I was driving Weiner to my office when he held up his hand, and he had a great big ring on his finger. He said, "See this?" I said, "Yeah." And he said, "They call me 'Goldfinger,'" and I thought, "Boy, this is going to be a rough one."

I would say that 95% of the agents I dealt with were very professional, and most of them were very good. But there were some out there who weren't, and a lot of those people disappeared in a hurry. I noticed that I rarely had a player who would come back with the same agent for a second contract. If I signed the player as a rookie, he would almost always have a different agent and a different horror story two or three years later.

I had one first-round draft choice who got a nice signing bonus and a lucrative contract, but his agent called me the following April and said his client needed an advance on the next year's salary to pay his income taxes. I asked the agent where in the world the money had gone, and he said the kid had just spent it. When I asked him if he was managing the player's money, he told me, "No, I just do the contracts."

I also remember one Christmas Eve when I was home opening gifts with my family when I got a call at 8 or 9 that night from a player who wanted to know if I could wire him an advance on his next year's salary. He said he needed the money so that he could buy his children shoes for Christmas. This was a veteran player who was making a big salary.

As time has gone along, more players have signed with firms that do everything. They have someone for contracts, someone for endorsements, someone for speaking engagements and someone for the taxes. They're pretty well-protected.

One of the key things you have to keep in mind when you're dealing with a player is the effect that can have on every other player. If you do something stupid with one guy, there are 52 other guys downstairs who will be knocking on your door the next day. It's common sense.

Holdouts can be a major problem. The Mike McKenzie situation a couple of years ago became a cancer. The thing that bothers you is that when a player holds out he becomes the major story every day. He gets to be a big distraction, and then if he decides to come back into camp, he's unhappy and he's a distraction in the locker room. You lose either way.

I saw McKenzie totally occupy Mike Sherman's mind. I'd be talking to Mike, and it was always "McKenzie this" or "McKenzie that." That took away from what Mike should have been doing, which was coaching the football team.

I think that's exactly why Ted Thompson and Mike McCarthy traded Javon Walker. They were not going to let Walker become the key story through May, June and July and then have a disgruntled player in their locker room. That doesn't do anybody any good, and it becomes a major headache for the organization.

I was very surprised by McKenzie. I thought he was a pretty good guy who liked it in Green Bay. Fortunately we haven't had a lot of that kind of thing over the years, but everybody faces it to a degree.

Another disruptive situation occurred in 1994 when Sterling Sharpe threatened not to play in our season opener against Minnesota because he was unhappy with his contract. Sterling was a great talent, but he was a different guy to be around. There were a lot of things he did off

the field that you weren't sure how you were going to handle. One time we were on a plane going to a game, and he came by my seat and asked if I was going to be in the office on Monday. I said I was, and he said he'd like to stop by and talk to me. I said okay, and he came in on Monday and talked and talked and talked. I kept waiting for the punch line. What was he there for?

But there was no punch line. We talked a little bit about football, a little bit about family, growing up, things like that, and then away he went. He just wanted to talk. It was probably the only conversation I had with him in all the years he was here, and to this day I still don't know what his purpose was. You just never knew where Sterling was coming from.

On the Saturday afternoon before the Minnesota game, Ron Wolf asked if I could get together in the draft room with Mike Holmgren and him to talk about Sharpe. I asked what the problem was, and he told me that Sterling was threatening not to play the next day. He said that Mike Reinfeldt, who was doing contracts for us then, had been on the telephone with Sharpe's agent all day, and they wanted to make sure I knew about it. The story was going to be in the newspapers and all over television if Sharpe went through with it.

So we went to the draft room, and I served as kind of a sounding board. Ron was livid, and Mike wasn't taking it any better. You're talking about two guys who are extremely competitive, and I understood them totally. I was angry, too, and very disappointed. I'd never heard of anything like that before. Obviously, the timing was terrible. You just couldn't believe this was truly going to happen.

Mike and Ron were willing to just let him sit. "Hey, we go and play, do the best we can and see what happens," Mike said to me. Ron felt the same way. I went home that night thinking that we would be facing Minnesota in our season opener without our star receiver, but it turned out that Sharpe did play. In fact, he caught a touchdown pass, and we beat the Vikings, 16-10.

It was a great relief for me when I stopped doing contracts in 1985. I mean it wasn't all bleak. I got a lot of satisfaction out of some of the ones we did, and I enjoyed the relationship with the players when they did their own. But Judge Parins kept giving me more and more responsibilities. He had me overseeing every department in the organization at that point. Tom Miller was going to retire in 1987, and the judge was trying to get me involved with more and more things before Tom left.

I was overseeing ticket sales and the public relations department, and once we opened the private boxes he wanted me to lease those. We were also getting ready to start a marketing department in 1988, which involved opening our first team store at Lambeau Field. I told the judge I was happy to take on more responsibility, but I wasn't going to be able to devote enough time to contracts if I had those extra duties. So he said, "Let's look for somebody."

I happened to mention it to Forrest Gregg, and Forrest knew Chuck Hutchison from when Chuck played guard for him the last year he coached in Cleveland. So Forrest called him, and Chuck replaced me as our contract negotiator.

I had all of the contracts in my files, and I put maybe 30 at a time in a cart and wheeled them into Chuck's office before he even got on the premises. I was probably smiling too much while I was doing it, but I wanted to make sure he didn't change his mind.

I wrote on the file, "Welcome, Chuck. Glad to have you here."

CHAPTER NINE
The Outsider from Iowa

I got home at about 7 o'clock after the Board of Directors meeting thinking Madeline would be there and we'd just have a quiet night together. I was a little early, and I guess nobody was expecting me. The first person I saw was Kevin's wife, Ann standing in the dining room holding our first grandchild, Abigail.

I said, "Ann, what are you doing here?" And that's when Madeline came around the corner, along with about 30 other people – my family, people from the front office and a lot of good friends. They had all come to celebrate my election as the Packers president.

It was a great surprise party and a great night. Madeline had planned the whole thing, and when it was over, I said to her, "What were you going to do if I wasn't elected?" She said, "Well, then we would have had a lot of food left over."

I was elected on June 5, 1989, and believe me, I never saw it coming. I had assumed I'd reached the top level as executive vice president, and that would be my title for the rest of the time I was with the Packers.

I've told Madeline many times just how lucky I've been. I've had the chance to work with Al McGuire. I've had the chance to work with the St. Louis Cardinals and their great tradition in baseball. I've had the chance to work with the Green Bay Packers and their great football tradition. And then to become president...I just never dreamed it would lead to anything of this height.

After all, I was a total outsider. I'd come from Iowa and worked my way up through the ranks, while the eight previous presidents had all come from Green Bay, had strong Green Bay backgrounds and had come off the Executive Committee. The first inkling I ever had that any of this might be possible came in the winter of 1989 when Judge Parins and I were flying home from a league meeting.

During the flight the judge started talking about the way the organization was set up, and he said, "I don't think we can continue to go to someone on the Executive Committee without football experience and ask him to run this organization. It's too complex. There are too many things to be dealt with. We need to find a football person to lead it."

I was shocked. I thought the organization would continue to do what it had always done, and probably John Fabry or Don Harden, who were on the Executive Committee, would be the two candidates who would make the most sense when the judge decided to retire. Don was the associate chancellor and acting athletic director at the University of Wisconsin-Green Bay, and he had a great background. The judge had put him on the Committee, and they were very close. Ironically, Don and I had talked earlier about how he might become president of the corporation someday.

I never had a clue from the judge or anyone else that they might move away from the Executive Committee and go to a football person. He and I met a lot during the week, and in all that time he'd never let on that he was thinking about this.

But I had been here 18 years, and so I told the judge that if that was what was going to happen, I would certainly have an interest. He told me he'd been sure I would, and he said he planned to put together a search committee from the Board of Directors and make it a formal procedure.

I went home and told Madeline that I was caught completely off guard by what he'd said, and she was as surprised as I was.

So the judge put together the search committee, and they began talking to people. I don't know exactly who they interviewed. The only outside candidates who I knew they had an interest in were Joe Bailey, who had been with the Dallas Cowboys and is now with the Miami Dolphins, and Eddie Jones, who was with the Dolphins for a long time and has since retired. Tom Olejniczak, the son of former Packers President Dominic Olejniczak, was definitely a candidate, and John Fabry was probably considered a candidate at that time. I felt privileged just to be a contender because it was so unexpected.

It was a very friendly process. There weren't any darts thrown at anybody by anybody else. I didn't campaign for the job. I didn't make any phone calls because I didn't want to get into that. I thought if I'm the person, fine, and if it's someone else I can certainly accept that. I hoped that if I wasn't the person, I could stay on as executive vice president.

I knew it was a major change for the organization. When it was rumored that I was a candidate, a letter ran in the newspaper asking how the Packers could hire an outsider. I thought, "Well, I guess I am an outsider, but I've been here 18 years, and I'm totally familiar with every single department in the organization."

The judge had put me in charge of all those departments, and I knew what their needs were and what their personalities were. I could go to all of the department heads and know what kind of problems they were having and what they might be confronted with in the future.

The search committee had me in for an interview in the old administration building, and they just kind of let me tell my story. I had gone to the Board meetings, so I knew everybody on the Board, and certainly I knew everybody on the Executive Committee. So I really wasn't surprised by anything.

The judge called me into his office after my interview and told me I'd done very well. He said the only question the Committee members had was whether I could make the tough decisions. I was a little surprised that they even brought that up.

I knew there would be tough decisions to make, and it was never my concern. I don't recall that question being put to me in the interview. Maybe it was in a roundabout way, but never directly.

I told Judge Parins, "Believe me, if that's their only concern, tell them not to worry." I could tell he was very glad to hear that. The judge was kind of a fighter himself, and it was almost like he was thinking, "Good. You show 'em."

The judge was extremely kind to me during the entire process. I've heard from Board members that he gave me his full support from day one, and I'm sure that's true. I thought, if I'm going to get this, it will be because of him giving me his support, and I appreciated that. We weren't social friends by any means, but we worked together very well.

One of the Committee's questions that I found very interesting came from Bob Gallagher, who at that time was president of Associated Bank in Green Bay. He asked me if I was elected and got hit by a truck the next day whether I had someone who could take my place. I thought that was very interesting planning, and I told him I really didn't, but I would make it a priority to get someone right away.

Two Committee members requested individual interviews with me. One of them was Bob Bush, who was president of Schreiber Foods in Green Bay. I went down to his office where he asked me questions for about an hour. When we were finished, he said he would give me his full support. That made me feel good because I didn't know Bob very well at the time, and he is a very powerful man in the city.

The other member who wanted to interview me one-on-one was Don Schneider, who was on the Executive Committee and was president of Schneider National Trucking Company in Green Bay. We talked a lot about my background, and I kind of jolted him when he asked me about my father. I told him my father had passed away in 1972, and he had also been president of a trucking company. Don knew my father's company, so we talked a little bit about that. He never really said that he'd give me his support, but I think we had a very good session.

The Committee also sent me down to Milwaukee to take a series of psychological tests. It's the closest I've ever come to being in analysis, and I hope it's the last time.

Madeline and I drove down and stayed at the Pfister Hotel, and I got up at 7 o'clock the next morning and met with two gentlemen who put me in a room and just drilled me with one question after another. The most interesting part was this math thing where they threw questions at me, and I had to solve problems without a pencil or paper.

One guy would come after me for a while, and then the other guy would come after me for a while, and there was no rest. It was just continual, one question after another. Then they sent the results back to the judge, who reported them to the Committee. I don't know how all of that affected my getting the job or not getting the job. I just remember that I didn't get back to the hotel until 2 o'clock, and I was physically and emotionally exhausted.

I was also fortunate that members of the media were very kind to me during the process. Once the judge came back to me after updating the media and said, "If it's up to the press, you're the man." I asked him what he meant, and he said that Cliff Christl of the Milwaukee *Journal* had just stood up at their meeting and said, "How can you consider anybody but Bob Harlan?"

In the 18 years I'd been with the Packers, I had good support from the press. I always tried to be available, and during all those years when I was doing contracts I tried to be honest with them about where we were in negotiations. Somebody would call me and say, "If I write this, am I wrong?" And I'd say, "Yeah, don't write that."

I remember the night that I was elected. The judge nominated me at the Board of Directors meeting, and Bob Bush, who was in the audience, said, "We'd like to hear from Bob." I went up to the microphone and told everyone how honored I was to be nominated, how I loved the organization, and how it was the thrill of a lifetime. I said we were going to succeed from top to bottom both on and off the field. I wasn't arrogant about it. I was just very confident that we were going to do well.

It was a big change for me, but I'd been here 18 years, and I knew the organization from top to bottom. From that standpoint I didn't have any questions whatsoever. There was a very nice financial change, too, and I think Madeline was happy about that. At least the department stores seemed pleased.

I called my mother from the surprise party, and she was very, very proud. The only problem was, every time I called her after that on a Monday morning following a loss, she'd say, "Bob, what am I going to tell the people in Des Moines?" I'd tell her, "Mom, first of all we have to decide how many people in Des Moines care." But she was always concerned about how she was going to defend her son.

I certainly opened myself up to more criticism after I took the job. I was pretty much under the radar when I was working for Judge Parins, and now all at once it was, "Harlan did this and Harlan did that." Some good, some bad. You have to get used to it. It was tougher on Madeline than it was on me, but I think she did very well with it. She was always there for me.

Naturally there were always people second guessing my decisions. I would get phone calls where the caller would just leave things on my voice mail and hang up. Or I'd get anonymous letters. If I got an envelope with no return address on it, I almost knew what I was going to read. I would open it up and people would rip me left and right and not have the courage to sign. After a while if I saw an envelope with no return address I would just dump it. I figured if a person didn't have the courage to sign it, I wouldn't take the time to read it.

But if people wrote and signed their letters, I'd go through information and get their phone number and call them back when they got home from work. All I ever asked was that people listen to my side of the story. I didn't want to do everything via letters because that didn't give me a chance to answer more questions or really make sure I was saying everything I wanted to say.

Of course the job came with longer hours and more weekends. I would come in on weekends and clean up things I couldn't get to during the week. I could come in on a Saturday or Sunday, work for a couple of hours each day and get a lot accomplished. Then I'd be ready to go again on Monday. All at once it was my show, and I knew my show had to change.

I got to the point where I couldn't stay and watch the fourth quarter of games, particularly on the road. I'd usually go down after the third quarter and walk the hallway outside the locker room. If I needed to, I could look inside and see the television. Or I could walk down by the players' tunnel and peek out on the field from there. That started when I became president, and I still do it today.

I realized that everything was going to land back on my desk, and I'd better do it right. We're in a very visible business, and it all boils down to those three hours on Sunday.

I really set a priority when I was elected that the first thing we were going to do was find a way to get better on Sunday afternoon. We were making money, and we had a nice stadium. We had started the private boxes and the club seats, and we were doing the things we needed to do as an organization. Our marketing department and the team store had started to take off. But I thought, we're here for football, and we have to get better in football.

When I was talking to the fans before I moved into the president's chair, I kept hearing the same things over and over. People would call me and say, "Who's making the football decisions? Is it the Board, is it the Executive Committee? Where is it coming from?"

And other people would call and say the trouble with the Packers is they don't care whether they win or lose. Whether they're 4-12 or 12-4 doesn't make any difference because they're sold out and they have a huge waiting list for tickets. The other thing I kept hearing was the good times were past. The Lombardi years were the last time the Packers were going to be a highlight in the National Football League. It was never going to happen again.

I thought we needed to find a way to get rid of all of those negative perceptions. I saw the great pride in this state during the 60's when Lombardi was here. That was a phenomenal story, and it had fallen in the 70's and 80's, not only on the field but off. My thought at that point was that I had to find the one football guy who could get rid of all those rumors that we didn't care. I needed somebody to come in and say, "Hey,

I'm taking this thing by the neck, and we're going to do it."

And I knew exactly who I wanted to hire.

I had met Ron Wolf in 1987 when he came to Green Bay to interview for the job that eventually went to Tom Braatz. One of my duties was to go to the airport and pick up the candidates for the position and bring them back to the judge. I didn't know Ron real well, but I did know his background, and I had seen him on scouting assignments.

He landed in Green Bay at about 9 o'clock, and the first thing he said when he got off the plane was that he hadn't had any dinner, and he wondered if we could go somewhere for a bite to eat. There wasn't much open on a Sunday night, but I took him to a Denny's restaurant that was just a few blocks south of Lambeau Field.

He and I sat there for three hours talking football. He wanted to know things like what the Board did, what the job of the Executive Committee was, what our facilities were like and what the town was like. I in turn got to ask him some questions. I asked him what it was like working for Al Davis for 25 years. I thought anyone who worked for Al that long had to have two great qualities. He had to be a very hard worker, and he had to have great football knowledge, or he wouldn't have lasted for 25 years.

I asked him about the years he was general manager in Tampa Bay and the problems he had with the Buccaneers ownership. We talked about how he set up his draft board, and we discussed how much time he spent on the road during the college football season. He had a solid plan for everything. He was very structured, and I was impressed by his organization and his great attention to detail.

I was very comfortable with him, and I thought he was comfortable with me. It was just the two of us sitting at a table, having a couple of hamburgers and talking. That was the night I decided that if this doesn't happen now – and this was before I had any idea that I would be the one making the decision – that I would certainly go back to the president and recommend that we take another look at Ron Wolf.

I took him to his hotel that night, and he got up in the morning and had the interview. Then I took him back to the airport. We didn't talk about the interview on the ride. I just told him a few things about the city. And then the very next day he withdrew his name from consideration. I never asked him why. I always felt he must have heard something he didn't want to hear. But those three hours at Denny's were very valuable to me.

When I became president, I'd made up my mind that if anything ever blew up, Ron would be the first one I would call. I had Braatz under contract then, and my big concern was that we were just treading water.

My first year as president we went 10-6, but four of those victories were by one point each. So 10-6 could very easily have been 6-10. But we were just delighted to have a winning season. People on the Board of Directors were so excited that we went out at the end of the year and extended Lindy Infante's contract.

I was extremely fortunate that within the next couple of years I had the chance to work with an exceptional Executive Committee. We had a good group when I got there, but two people were ready to retire.

Phil Hendrickson was leaving as the treasurer, and I asked John Underwood to succeed him. John had been a good friend since he'd come to Green Bay, and I had been on his board at the Firstar Bank. He was the bank's president, and he helped me tremendously with the numbers and with looking at the finances and the future of the Packers corporation.

When Tony Canadeo retired from the Committee, I wanted Jim Temp to take his place. I thought a former player would be very beneficial. I had pushed to get Jim on the Board of Directors before I was president, and I wanted him on the Executive Committee because of his football knowledge and the football thinking he could bring to the table.

John and Jim joined John Fabry, Don Schneider, Pete Platten and Don Harden, and that group of six worked together for 11 years, which is a tremendously long time. They were so valuable to me because they were not only great business associates, but they became very strong personal friends.

They went through some major things with me. They dealt with the move out of Milwaukee, the two Super Bowls, Ron Wolf's retirement, Mike Sherman taking over and the shareholder vote when we sold the stock. Most importantly, they were there for the referendum and the redevelopment of Lambeau Field. I will salute all of them for as long as I live.

I wanted people who I knew would bring talents to the Committee and with whom I had great comfort. You certainly want someone on there who you think is compatible with you and with the others. We didn't agree on everything all of the time, but we did extremely well.

For instance there was one individual who wasn't pleased with the way we hired Ron Wolf. He wanted to have a search firm recommend candidates. That's the way a lot of businesses do it, and it does make a great deal of sense. But I had heard that other clubs were interested in Ron, and I wanted to jump ahead of them and get him to Green Bay.

John Fabry stood up at the meeting and said, "Bob says if he's going to get Ron Wolf, he needs to go for it right now, and I think we need to give him our unanimous support." And they did.

I think it helped that my first year as president went so well. We were 10-6 with a very exciting team. We'd had so many down years that I think we kind of went, "Oh boy, this is it."

I remember my first day on the job very well. I had been asked the night before to come in early and call a Madison radio station to do an interview. So I got to the office at 6:45 in the morning thinking, "Boy, this is really going to be something. The big president of the Green Bay Packers is calling this radio station, and it's going to be great."

I called the number, and a woman answered. I said, "This is Bob Harlan calling." And she said, "Are you the guy with the apples?" I'll tell you what. I was deflated in about seven seconds.

I don't know if they were having a produce show that morning or what. I just said, "No, ma'am. I'm the president of the Green Bay Packers." And she said, "Okay, I'm going to put you on hold. We'll be right with you."

From that day on, I figured I can't be too important. I'm just the guy with the apples.

CHAPTER TEN

Worst to First and Back Again

I have never ridden on a bus as silent as the one we took to the airport after the last game of the 1991 season. We had beaten the Vikings, 27-7, that day, but we finished the year 4-12, and I think Lindy Infante and his wife Stephanie both knew it was over.

I was sitting in the front seat on the left side of the bus, and Lindy and Stephanie would normally be sitting in the front on the right side, but they hadn't gotten on yet. They were out in front with their backs to the bus, and it was obvious that Stephanie was crying. Then Lindy's shoulder started to shake.

I don't think anybody on that bus uttered a word all the way to the airport until we got on the plane. We flew to Green Bay, and as we were getting off the plane Ron Wolf asked me if I'd be willing to meet with him in my office that night.

I told him I'd go directly there, and he came in shortly afterward and asked if I would be all right with him making a coaching change. I said, "Ron, when I hired you, I said I was going to give you full authority over the football operation, and I'm not going to stop you on the first decision you want to make."

He went in the very next morning and let Lindy go. The game was on December 21, and he fired Lindy on December 22.

We had all felt so good after the 1989 season, when Lindy had taken us from last to first in his second year. We were ending the decade with a 10-6 record after having only three winning seasons in the 70's and 80's. There was real excitement in Green Bay for the first time in a long, long time, and we were all caught up in it.

I had members of the Board of Directors calling me and saying, "We've got to make sure we hang on to this coach. This is the guy." We wanted so desperately to produce a winner here, and we thought we had finally found the coach who was going to get us over the hump.

Don Majkowski had a great year at quarterback in '89, and Lindy was

Coach of the Year. His offense was basically a passing offense. He wanted to throw the ball, and Majkowski appeared to be the guy to do it. We were as excited as the fans were, and the fans loved what happened that year. And so we extended Lindy's contract for two more years through 1994.

But then in 1990 we fell back to last place in the division. We had gone from last to first and then back to last. We finished 6-10, and Majkowski wanted more money after his big year. He held out until just before the first game, and he wasn't really in great shape when he came to camp. Then he wound up hurting his shoulder and was never the same player again. He was finished after game 10.

It didn't take long before I started to think that 1989 may have just been a flash in the pan. And then when we started 1-6 in 1991 I made up my mind that we had to do something. That was when I hired Wolf to replace Tom Braatz, and he fired Infante less than a month later.

Lindy had three years left on his contract when we let him go, and in those three years I know he had other job opportunities. But he turned everything down. I'm sure he was bitter. I had breakfast with one general manager who said he had offered Lindy the offensive coordinator's job, and he told him he didn't even want to talk about it. The general manager said, "He's obviously made up his mind to get every penny out of you guys before he does anything."

The three years cost us $1.95 million, which isn't big money by today's standards, but I had no idea he was going to string it out like that. He was building his dream home in Jacksonville, Florida, where he would eventually retire, and he just spent those three years working on the house. Within days after he got his last check from us, he took another job. I understood. Everybody's bitter when they're fired.

The interesting thing was that Lindy wasn't even our first choice when we hired him. Judge Parins put Tom Braatz in charge of finding Forrest Gregg's replacement in 1988, and Tom came back with a recommendation for George Perles, who was then head coach at Michigan State.

Tom worked out a contract with Perles, and everything seemed to be in place when he, Judge Parins and Lee Remmel left to go to the Super Bowl. Before Lee went, he wrote a news release to announce that Perles was going to be the Packers' next head coach, and he left an open space after the first couple of paragraphs for me to fill in. I was going to call

Perles that day and get some quotes about how happy he was to be our head coach, insert them in the space and get the release out.

I called Perles at home in the morning, introduced myself and told him what I wanted to do. And he said, "Bob, I'm not going to be there." I was shocked. I asked him what he meant, and he said he wasn't going to make the move. I said, "George, are you alone? Who all knows this?"

He said he was there with Nick Vista, the sports information director at Michigan State. As it happened, Nick and I had known each other for a long, long time. He had been the assistant sports information director at Michigan State when I was at Marquette. I asked George to put Nick on the phone. When I asked Nick what had happened, he said the governor of Michigan had come to George's house and almost begged him to stay.

I told Nick that he had to give me some time. Our president and Tom Braatz were on an airplane going to the Super Bowl, and I had to catch them at the airport when they got off and let them know what was going on.

Tom and the judge called me when they landed, and they were as shocked as I was. Then I placed a call to the NFL headquarters at the Super Bowl to let Lee know. I got back to Vista, and we came up with a time to release the story that Perles was going to stay at Michigan State. Tom started his search for a coach then, and he hired Infante on February 3.

The judge pretty much put it into Tom's hands to come up with a successor to Forrest, and Infante and Perles were the only names I ever heard. Perles was at the top of the list, and when he turned down the job, Tom went after Lindy.

We went 4-12 and tied Detroit for last in the division in Lindy's first year when we had a lot of confusion at quarterback again. Randy Wright started the first five games, and then Majkowski started nine before he ran into injury problems that just got worse as he went along. We were a bad ball club, a terrible ball club.

But then in 1989 we tied Minnesota for first place in the division. We didn't go to the playoffs because the Vikings had a better division record, but we finished 10-6. That was the year we had so many comeback victories that people were calling us the "Cardiac Pack." We beat New Orleans, Chicago, Minnesota and Tampa Bay all by one point.

This was also the year we made Tony Mandarich the second player taken in the draft. The Dallas Cowboys took UCLA quarterback Troy Aikman with the first choice.

Mandarich seemed like a slam dunk choice. He was on the cover of *Sports Illustrated* prior to the draft, and he was supposedly going to become the best offensive lineman in the history of pro football. This was the perfect guy. The fans practically demanded that we take him. All the national writers who were predicting who everybody was going to take said he had to go early because he was going to be an outstanding offensive lineman in the league for years.

So we took him on draft day, and then we flew him into Green Bay so that he could meet with the press that evening. We were sitting in the draft room when he got here, and he was so huge that he almost had to come through the door sideways. We thought we could not have done any better.

If there were any steroid rumors then, I never heard them, but I do remember walking into the locker room one day when he was coming out of the shower. This was when we had already seen that things were not nearly what we'd hoped for. Tony had a towel wrapped around his waist, and I was amazed at how small he was in the chest and shoulders. He wasn't the same person who had walked into the draft room.

The funny thing about it was Detroit was sitting with the third draft choice, and their people told me afterward that they were just sick that they had to settle for Barry Sanders.

The 1989 season was also a big year for us off the field. We had looked around at what other teams were doing with their stadiums and decided that we had to develop a way to increase our local revenue. The best way to do that was through club seats and private boxes, and we had the perfect structure for it. We had the bowl, and it was easy to build on top of it.

We had built 72 private boxes in 1985, and we added 36 in 1990 along with 1,920 club seats in the south end zone. We were stunned at how fast the boxes went. We sold them faster than we could build them. Judge Parins put me in charge of leasing the boxes when we built the first ones, and I was on the phone constantly talking to people.

I'd meet them at the stadium and take them up to the area where the boxes would be so they could choose their location. Then we constructed a mock box in a building downtown, and they could look at that if they wanted to. It was an exciting and busy time for me.

But on the field we were treading water. One of the things that bothered me terribly was that in the 70's and 80's, when we were going through all of those struggles, every coach we had hired to try to rescue us had a lower winning percentage than the coach he'd replaced. Devine was .474, Starr was .410, Gregg was .405, and Infante would finish .375. We really needed something to give this organization a jolt.

I went to the NFL meetings in October of 1991 and had breakfast one day with George Young, the general manager of the New York Giants. George and I had been friends for years when we were both doing contracts, and we always exchanged a lot of phone calls and talked about different problems. We were early risers at league meetings, so we were usually down in the hotel lobby ready to open the coffee shop. I told George I was prepared to make a change at the top of our football operation, and I asked him if he knew of any second tier people around the league who were ready to make the jump from assistant general manager to general manager. I asked him if he wouldn't mind putting together a list for me, so that I might be able to call him sometime down the road. He said he'd be glad to do that.

Then I told him that the guy I really wanted was Ron Wolf. George was the first one who I'd ever told that to, and he said Wolf would be good, but he wasn't sure I could get him to leave the New York Jets. Plus, he thought Wolf might be on a couple of other clubs' lists. But I said I was going to go after him first and see how I did, and that's where we left it.

When Ron and I sat at Denny's that night four years before, one thing became very clear to me. He would never take a job as the head of our organization or any organization unless he was given full control. Everything he said indicated he wanted to be able to do whatever he needed to do in the football operation and not have somebody step on his toes. He had had a very bad experience with the ownership when he ran the Tampa Bay Buccaneers, and he was extremely cautious about that. So I thought, "I've got to find a way to give him full power if he's going to talk to us."

I planned to tell the Executive Committee at its November 20 meeting that I wanted to go after him and let Tom Braatz go. And that's what I did. I told the Committee that I knew my timing was strange. The normal procedure is to wait until January or February to hire someone, who then comes in and looks at the team on videotape. But I needed to move faster than that for two reasons.

I wanted Ron to be around this team, watch it practice, travel with it and see if something jumped out at him that told him why it wasn't having success. And, since George Young had mentioned that a couple of other clubs might have an interest in Wolf, I wanted to beat them to the punch.

I planned to sit down with Braatz in my office immediately after the Executive Committee meeting and tell him what I was going to do. The meeting was scheduled for Tuesday, and I had checked with our travel agent all day on the Monday before to make sure Tom was going to be in town. Every time I called the travel agent he said Tom wasn't going on the road to scout. But when I went home for dinner Monday night, the travel agent called me at about 5:30 and said Tom had just booked himself on a 6:30 flight to Indianapolis.

I couldn't let that change my plan. It was important that I talk to him on Tuesday because I needed to get the Jets' permission to talk to Wolf and get this thing rolling. They could have turned me down, and I had to find out where I stood with Ron. If I was in trouble there, I would have to go back to George Young and see what his thoughts were.

So the next morning I met with the Executive Committee, and they gave me their approval to go after Wolf and let Tom go. Then I had to get Tom's number in Indiana and do it over the phone, which is not the right way to do it at all. I would have much preferred to do it face-to-face, but I was in a position where I had to move quickly.

When I reached Tom I told him that I was going to have to bring him back off the road because we were making a change at the top of our football operation. It was a very brief conversation. He asked me why, and I said I just felt we needed to find somebody to take this thing over. I said we might find later on that I was wrong, but I just didn't think he was that person. We hung up then, and he flew back that night.

Then I called Steve Gutman, who was the Jets president at that time. Steve and I had always gotten along well, and I told him I knew this was an unusual time to do something like this, but I wanted to have somebody here with the team who could tell me what was wrong with it. Steve said he would go along with that, but it was up to Dick Steinberg, who was the Jets' general manager.

Dick was out scouting, but he called me that same afternoon and gave me permission to talk to Wolf. He wasn't fond of the timing, but he thought it was a marvelous step for Ron, and he didn't want to hold him back.

Next I called Ron. He was on the road scouting for the Jets, and it was the first time he and I had talked since that night at Denny's. I said I wanted to give him full authority over the football operation. It would be his team to run. There would be absolutely no interference, and we would make sure that he had everything he needed to succeed. I also told him that I didn't even have a second choice for the job. I intended to do everything I had to do to get him to say yes.

I had typed up his title and salaries for a five-year contract, along with the clauses that would go into each of those contracts and his responsibilities, and I offered to fax all of that to him right away.

Ron went down to a business office in the hotel where he was staying and called me with the fax number. That was Friday afternoon. He called me back at the office on Saturday morning and said he thought we had a deal.

I was thrilled. I had the guy I wanted, and I got him when I wanted to get him. Just one week after Tom Braatz left, Ron Wolf came to town for a press conference.

It was the first time in my life that I had ever fired anybody, and I can't imagine anybody in any business finding that easy to do. It bothers you a great deal. I had had a pretty good relationship with Tom. I was excited when the judge hired him because I thought he was a good choice. He had been at Atlanta for a long time, and he had a good reputation in the league.

I guess I just wanted someone with a little more fire, and that wasn't Tom's way. I'm not saying that as a negative. I wanted someone to give the organization a jolt, and I didn't think it was going to be Tom.

I didn't see Tom until a couple of days after he'd gotten back from Indianapolis. He was leaving his office, and it was a very cool conversation.

I remember when I was being considered for the presidency, there was some question about whether I could make the tough decisions. This was my first tough decision, but that really didn't occur to me at the time. In fact, right after I hired Ron, Bud Lea wrote a column in the Milwaukee *Sentinel* with a headline over it that read, "Harlan puts his neck on the line." I happened to see Bud the next day, and he said, "I imagine you're upset with me."

I said, "No, I'm really not. The way I look at it, I would put my neck on the line if I didn't do anything." My No. 1 priority the moment I became president was to make us better on the football field. So if I didn't do something, then my neck should be on the line.

We were in Atlanta on Wolf's first day on the job, and we lost to the Falcons, 35-31, which gave us a 3-10 record. The next day he went down on the practice field to watch the team. He walked into my office afterward and said, "You have a problem on your practice field. There's a country club atmosphere down there. Those guys are 3-10, and they're walking around like they're 10-3. We're going to change that." I knew that meant Lindy wasn't off to a good start with his boss.

After Wolf fired him, Lindy just kind of disappeared. I don't know if he had somebody clean out his office for him or not, but he was out of there in a heartbeat. The last time I was with him was on that quiet bus ride.

Lindy was a very nice man. He and Stephanie were wonderful people and great citizens. You truly wanted to see them succeed, but it just didn't happen. And the fans were starting to have that "Here we go again" attitude. They had been through this time and time again, and they were saying that something had to be done about it. I felt the same way.

And then Ron Wolf walked through the door and made the move on Infante. Basically we were going to be paying two head coaches for three years, but that never came up in my conversation with Ron. Believe me, I thought about it and I talked to the Executive Committee about it, but I didn't mention it to Ron.

My calls stopped pretty soon after that. People knew that Ron Wolf was making the football decisions for the organization, and they were saying, "Hey, they do want to win. They're willing to let a coach go with three years left on his contract. They're ready to make their move."

CHAPTER ELEVEN

"Hey, Bob"

We were in Atlanta the weekend after we hired Ron Wolf. He said he was going to finish a couple of scouting assignments for the Jets, and then he'd meet me at the game Sunday morning. I was in the press box about an hour before kickoff when Ron came up, sat in the seat next to mine, put his briefcase on the counter and said he was going to go down on the field and look at Atlanta's backup quarterback. He said he had a great arm coming out of college, and he wanted to see if it was as strong now.

The first thing I did was take the flip card and check Atlanta's backup quarterback. I thought his name was Fav-ray.

Ron went down to the field and came back 45 minutes later, sat down next to me and said, "Bob, we're going to make a trade for Brett Favre." That was his first day on the job.

Ron saw so many problems so quickly, and he wanted to move quickly. Hiring him in November, which seemed like such a strange time, turned out to pay huge dividends. I wasn't even sure at the time how much it was going to help us, but he decided immediately that we needed a quarterback, and we needed to change the way we practiced and ran our football operation.

I will always say the man who restored this franchise to elite status was Ron Wolf.

Once Ron told me, "When you hired me I was 53 years old, and I thought my chances had passed me. I didn't think I would get another chance to run a team." But we won the world championship, and Ron was the one who did it. He found the pieces that had to be put together.

If Ron's mind was made up to do something, he would show up at my door and say, "Hey, Bob," and right away I knew, "Here it comes. Something else is cooking."

In the nine years he was here I never said no to Ron Wolf. It wasn't that I didn't go to the Executive Committee with some of his ideas. I did, for instance, when he wanted to trade a No. 1 for Brett and when I realized it was going to cost in the area of $15 to $20 million to sign Reggie White. But he just had such sound reasons for every decision that he brought to me.

He would come to see me about everything. If he was going to release a player he would show up at my door that morning and tell me what he was going to do and why he was going to do it. He always made it a point to be sure I was totally informed before anything that happened in the organization would appear in the newspapers.

The interesting thing I found out about Ron through the years was that he could be with a person and decide very soon if he could or couldn't work with him. He was pretty quick to form his opinions. Mike Holmgren was a great example of that.

When we brought Mike into town for an interview, he and Ron went to lunch, and Ron came back that day and told me how comfortable he was with Mike. He said, "I can work with that man."

I think he had Mike in mind the whole time when he fired Lindy. I don't recall a lot of other names coming up. Mike had five or six clubs after him, and one thing that helped us in that situation was that his agent was Bob LaMonte, and the very first contract Bob ever did was in 1981 with a quarterback out of California named Rich Campbell. Rich was our first round draft choice and the sixth player selected. I negotiated that contract with Bob, and we had developed a very good relationship. After Mike took the job, Bob told me that he had told Mike, "I know the people in Green Bay. They will be fair with you. They'll let you do your job there." I think that was a factor.

And it was an enormous factor to have Ron Wolf. Mike knew that Ron would get him the players and let him coach them.

I was really excited when we hired Holmgren. I remember going to a league meeting at the time, and Charley Casserly, who was general manager of the Washington Redskins, stopping me in the hallway and saying, "How in the world did you ever get both Wolf and Holmgren?" I told him I hired Wolf, but I didn't get Holmgren. Wolf did that. And he said, "Well, they're dynamite."

Ron hired Mike on January 11, and he traded for Favre on February 10. The next big thing he did was to come to me and say, "You know, Bob, we have a nice indoor facility, but if we're going to keep our key players and if we're going to be attractive to other free agents, we have to have a better one."

When we looked into it, the cost of a new facility came to about $3 million, but I told the architect that he needed to sit down with the general manager, the head coach, the video staff, the trainers, the equipment staff and everyone else who was going to use the building and find out what they needed to be effective in it. The architect spent a couple of days talking to those folks, and that $3 million building cost me $4.67 million. I always kidded Ron about that. I told him, "I guess you guys got everything you wanted."

Ron's schedule was crazy. He would be in the office a little while on Monday morning, and then he would be on the road for the rest of the week. He'd come back on Friday night or Saturday morning and go immediately to his office to watch video of the team's practices that week.

I would sit with him at the game on Sunday, and then I wouldn't see him until the next Saturday when I was in the office and he might stop in and talk a little bit. He just pounded himself during the college football season. I always knew where I could find him when he was in town – on the practice field or in a dark room looking at video of either our team or some college players.

Practice mattered a great deal to Ron. He spent as much time on the practice field as anyone I've ever seen. He was always working.

People in the organization who didn't know him well may have tiptoed around him a little. They had a great deal of respect for him, because they could see what he had done in a short period of time, but they may have been concerned about how to approach him.

He would come to our Executive Committee meetings every month and give a report and use whatever language he wanted to use to describe a player who wasn't performing up to standards. His language could be pretty colorful, and the Executive Committee loved it.

Officials bothered him tremendously. Before the remodeling of Lambeau Field, we sat in the old press box on the second floor where we really weren't that high above the fans. When the windows were open and there was something Ron didn't like, he would lean out the window and start screaming, and I thought, "My Lord, people are hearing words they never knew existed." When we were playing at Lambeau Field, Ron felt every official's call should go our way.

But I used to tell Ron, "Now you've got to be more careful with the

Board. There are some women on it." And he could tone it down once he got to the Board. But I would look at the members' faces when he was talking, and I could tell some people were a little shocked at his candid description of players and officials.

He loved to give the needle to people, and he had a great relationship with the players. He and Brett were extremely close, and he and Reggie were very close. But he might let some players know, too, when he was unhappy.

He always made it a point, no matter how well the team was doing, to have some free agents parade through the locker room on Tuesdays. It was the players' day off, and they would be sitting around and kind of enjoying themselves, and all at once Ron would come walking through the room with a few free agents, and everyone would start thinking, "Geez, is my job in jeopardy?" That was part of his makeup. We were never going to get too content.

There was a fire in the man, and he wanted his coaches and his team to have it, too. He could be pretty ornery and angry for a long period of time if things weren't going well. He knew he could vent with me. On Saturdays or on Sunday morning when we sat together in the press box, I would shut up and let him talk, and when he was finished, we'd discuss it.

Ron was not great with criticism. He would have unique words to describe writers who second-guessed him, but I think the great majority of the media got a kick out of him. Fan reaction didn't bother him a great deal. If he was convinced in his mind that he was doing the right thing, he was going to do it.

He listened to his scouts, but he pretty much ran his own show. But if he was wrong he would admit it, and he would make a change in a hurry. If he made a mistake on a player, he would get him out of here.

I think he really enjoyed the draft. It was his time to show that all of those months of traveling to college campuses and sitting in that dark room looking at videos were going to be finalized. It was like show time for him.

He was very calm on draft day. There was no panic in the room. He could be a minute away from making a selection and still taking phone calls from clubs wanting to make deals. He'd listen to what the people had to say, tell them he'd think about it, hang up, look at the board and make his pick.

I admired the way he would give everybody a chance to be part of it. He wanted to get as much information as he could, so he would go from scout to scout and say, "What do you think? What do you think? What do you think?" But he was the one who had to build the ball club, and eventually it would come down to his desk. It was so obvious who was in control. But if his coach really wanted somebody, Ron would listen and there were times when there might be a debate about two people, and he would let the coach have his player.

And of course he was dynamite at getting players in the fifth round and later. There was just no quit in the man. He wasn't ever going to take the approach that we could do all our work in the first three rounds and then just sit back. He would tell the staff in that room, "Hey, everybody, pay attention. There are good players out there. Let's go get them."

As we got close to the actual time of the draft he would tell me about certain things. He came to me in 1997 and said he wanted to take Ross Verba out of Iowa in the first round. "All of the national media is calling me, and I'm mentioning everybody but Verba," he said. "I think we can sneak in on this."

One prediction after another was coming out in the media, and nobody was putting Verba in Green Bay. And then three or four days before the draft, Paul Zimmerman of *Sports Illustrated* had us taking Verba, and Ron went through the roof. "Where the hell did he come up with that idea?" He wanted to know. Zimmerman was the only one who got it right, and he was the only one who made Ron mad.

Ron just kept putting the pieces together. When he came to me and said he wanted to go after Reggie White, I thought, "My Lord, is this a game we can even be part of?" But he went out and got it done, and everybody was amazed. Even the people in our own organization.

Some of our public relations people were at a league meeting in Atlanta when we were ready to announce Reggie's signing, and we needed to get somebody back here right away for the press conference. I called one of them and told him we were ready to sign Reggie White, and he had to get back to town. The guy thought I was making it up. I said, "No. I mean it. Get back here."

Reggie was the most attractive free agent in the history of the league at the time, and I don't think there's been a more attractive one since. Getting him for Green Bay put Ron Wolf and Mike Holmgren right on top of the football world.

I was convinced that we had the best general manager in the National Football League, and that's why I extended Ron's contract twice. I knew that salaries were changing for general managers, and I wanted to make sure he was at the top of the league where he belonged. I didn't want anybody coming knocking on my door and fooling with him. We did it very easily. He had a personal friend who advised him and knew the numbers in the league, but he never did have an agent. It was always just the two of us.

I got a call one time from Jeff Lurie, the owner of the Philadelphia Eagles, asking for permission to talk to Ron, and I said, "Jeff, just yesterday I extended his contract. I've got him signed for the next six years, and I don't want anybody talking to him. I want to keep him in Green Bay."

Jeff was very good about it. He was the only one who ever really called me and asked, but I was always concerned about it because of the job Ron was doing for us. I knew he was highly respected in the league, but I never felt that he was anxious to leave. He had a great feel for this tradition. He thought there was a great dignity that went with being a member of the Green Bay Packers, and I know he still feels that way today.

Nothing made him as happy as winning the Super Bowl in 1997. I will always remember the day we defeated Carolina to win the NFC championship. Ron and I went down to the field together and walked to the north end zone to receive the trophy. When the game ended, the players just started jumping up and down and throwing their helmets like kids on a playground.

The public address announcer said, "Ladies and gentlemen, the Green Bay Packers are going to the Super Bowl." The music was, "We Are the Champions," and every place you looked in that stadium the people were crying and hugging and high-fiving.

I turned to Ron and said, "You know, I could cry." And he said, "So could I." It was such a touching moment because who deserved it more than these fans after their patience and their loyalty through the 70's and 80's? It is still my most memorable moment at Lambeau Field, and I'm sure Ron will tell you the same thing.

Then we went to New Orleans and won the whole thing. That was a huge accomplishment for Ron. When he and I and Mike got up on the stage where Commissioner Paul Tagliabue presented the trophy, it was an unbelievable feeling. You wish everybody in football could experience that just once.

Losing the Super Bowl the next year was just brutal for Ron. Getting that far and then losing the game is one of the toughest things to deal with. I had breakfast with him before we left for the game in San Diego, and I asked him what he thought of Denver. He said they were about like New England, and I thought that was a good sign. We were big favorites, and I'm still convinced we were the better team. But we lost that game, and all of us in the organization were heartbroken.

We always have a party after the Super Bowl, win or lose, and the one after we beat New England the year before was just outstanding. The one after the Denver game was like a wake. People were talking in whispers. It was the worst feeling you can have because you always wonder when you'll get back to a Super Bowl. I sat with Ron for a while that night, and he was very quiet. It was a short-lived party, and the next morning was still that way before we got on the buses for the airport.

In 1998 we went 11-5 and lost to San Francisco in the divisional play-off, and it was becoming clear that Mike Holmgren wanted to run his own team. He knew he could never have full power with Ron here, and the Seattle rumors were rampant for a long time. As much as I hated to lose Mike, I understood him taking the job there. Even when he left he said, "Bob, if I just wanted to be a coach for the rest of my life, this is the best coaching job in the league."

During the season Ron told me that if we were going to make a coaching change he was going to go after Ray Rhodes. That wasn't what I was expecting him to say, but he said we had lost some of our toughness. We needed to get tougher, and he thought Ray would bring that to the table.

We won three of our first four games under Ray in 1999, but then we started not playing well. This was when Ron was away all the time at college campuses, and he kept telling me, "I'm not planning to make a change. I'm not planning to make a change." I would say, "That's fine, whatever you want to do."

But when the college season ended, he had a chance to be on the practice field regularly. This was late November, early December, and after a few days he came in and said he was going to make a change. I asked him what prompted his decision, and he said Ray had lost the team. "This isn't the same team, and that's not the same practice I saw in

August," he said.

I always admired how he admitted a mistake. He would never let it linger. He came back from watching practice and just said, "Bob, I was wrong." He thought Ray would make us tougher, and when he realized that wasn't happening, he was ready to cut the ties.

I don't think he relished firing Ray at all, but once he made up his mind that something had to be done, he was ready to do it. I kind of knew when he walked into my office what he was coming to do.

We hired Mike Sherman, even though Mike wasn't on top of Ron's or my list. One of the names that was going around at that time was Marty Schottenheimer. But Mike came in on a Saturday and met with Ron, and Ron called me at home on Saturday afternoon, which was very unlike him. He rarely called me at home.

He told me he had just spent the day with Mike Sherman and Sherman had "blown the socks" off of him. He said it had been a great interview because Sherman had been so well-prepared. "If I had any guts," he said. "I would hire him right now." I told him to go ahead, but he said he was going to sleep on it.

The next day I was sitting in Mike Reinfeldt's office, and Ron came in and said it again. "If I had any guts, I'd hire Mike Sherman right now." And I said, "Why don't you go do it?" I think he was already going to do it, but he just had to convince himself by bouncing it off of me.

So he left, and 10 minutes later he came back and said it was done.

He and Sherman got along very well the one year they worked together. Mike proved to be very resilient. We were 5-7 before December, but Mike kept that team together and finished on a really positive note.

I was shocked when Ron came and talked to me in July before that 2000 season and said, "Bob, I think this is going to be my last year." It just came out of the clear blue. I told him I was very surprised, but he said, "I think I've hit the wall. When you hit the wall, you know it."

I think one of the main things that really drove him out of the game was what he called "the new football" brought on by free agency and the salary cap. He missed the old days when if he lost an offensive tackle he could go find one, sign him and move on. Now he said the first thing he had to do was go to his salary cap guy and find out how much money he had and what the tackle was going to cost him. He hated to think about the money rather than thinking about the talent of the player he wanted to go after.

He used to tell me he couldn't even enjoy practice any more because after every play he was scared to death that somebody wouldn't get up, and he was going to have to go out and get a replacement. It was very hard to build depth. Many, many times I heard him say how much he missed the old football and how he didn't like the new football.

When he came to my office that day and told me he had decided to retire I said I was really hoping that he would be here at least through the opening of the redeveloped Lambeau Field in 2003. I asked him if he was willing to at least keep thinking about it, and he said he would.

He said, "Let's keep it between the two of us," which I thought was a great sign. If he was willing to keep it between the two of us, he might be willing to change his mind. So I said that was fine, and I didn't go to anyone. Not anyone on our staff or anyone on the Executive Committee. I just kept it to myself with the hope that he would reconsider.

We went through the year, and I would sit with him every Sunday like I always did, and we never talked about it. I thought it was good when he never brought it up. The more time that passed, the more it meant that he was still thinking about it.

Then we won our last four games and finished 9-7 on a very positive note. After that last victory, I stood up and we shook hands like we always did after we won, and I said, "It's still your team, Ron, and it's still winning." Then he and his son Eliot walked downstairs and across Lambeau Field to the locker room. And I kept hoping that it wasn't for the last time.

But a couple of weeks later, he showed up at my door like he always did with a "Hey, Bob," and I knew what it was from the look on his face. He asked, "Do you remember what you and I talked about in July?" And I said, "Yeah," and he said, "I'm going to do it. I'm going to retire." And I knew that was it. I told him that I could never thank him enough for what he'd done for the organization and that I was so disappointed to see it end.

He had put everything at full throttle, and it just stayed there. He just gave and gave and gave, and he needed a change. He said, "I always wondered what it would be like to hit the wall. I've hit it, and I know it, and I hope you feel the same way when your time comes. I know it's time for me to go."

I knew I had to get the Executive Committee here right away. All of this time had gone by since July and I'd never said a word to anybody. I called all of the members, and four of the six were able to come. We sat down, and Ron said, "I'm here to tell you gentlemen that I'm going to retire." There was shock in the room. Jim Temp told me later that he thought I was calling them over to extend Ron's contract.

Ron told them his reasons, and we started talking with the Committee about his replacement. The longer we discussed the subject the more I thought the best direction for the organization was to give both jobs to Mike Sherman. That is not my favorite way to do things, and we talked about a 50-50 split with somebody, but in the end I said I was tempted to give both jobs to Mike. Ron just turned and looked at me and said, "That's the way to go."

Then he and I left the Executive Committee in that room, and we met with Mike Sherman. The first thing Mike said was, "I can't talk you into changing your mind?" But Ron told him he was firm, and so we offered both jobs to Mike.

I still prefer to hire a general manager and let him select his coach, but I had three major concerns. First, we had beaten our four division opponents in our last four games, had momentum and finished 9-7. Then Brett Favre had made the comment that this was the best team chemistry he had seen since he'd come to Green Bay. I thought that was pretty heavy coming from a player who had been on two Super Bowl teams, and I didn't want to disrupt that.

I was also worried that if I brought somebody in over Mike, they wouldn't get along. And I thought there would probably be a situation where the new person would want to bring in his own scouting staff, and he would get rid of a young scouting staff that we had in Green Bay that I thought was very capable.

So I believed that what was most beneficial for the corporation right then was to give both jobs to Mike. And we did it.

We did the whole thing in probably five hours from the time Ron came to me until we offered Mike both jobs. And then we had the press conference the next morning. We had to move fast because it was going to be such a shock that Ron Wolf was retiring, and I didn't want the story leaking out. This certainly wasn't done because it was the easy way out.

I'm usually more deliberate in these things, but you have to understand that I had had those six months to think about it. I kept holding out hope that Ron would change his mind. He wasn't that old. When he and Mike Holmgren and I were together, I thought I was going to be the first guy to leave the corporation. I was the oldest one there. As successful as these two fellows were, I figured they'd probably both still be here when I left.

This may sound unusual to say, but I would probably do the same thing again with Sherman. Obviously, I wasn't happy with the way it all turned out, but if I was confronted with the same decision today with the same three factors being considered, I would probably go that way.

Ron moved out of the office very shortly after he made his decision, and it was a very sad time for me personally. He was the one I had wanted for a long time, and when I got him he did exactly what I thought he would do. He got us to the Super Bowl faster than I felt we could ever get there. I mean after hardly sniffing the playoffs in the 70's and 80's and then having him take over going into the '92 season, becoming world champions in '96 was pretty remarkable.

For three years after he left I kept him as a consultant, and I really prayed down deep that he wouldn't go to another organization. I knew other people were looking at him. His name would keep coming up, and the national press would call me and say, "Hey, did you hear that Ron Wolf is talking to so and so?" I still had him under contract, but if he had wanted to go somewhere, we certainly would have let him. But I really hoped he would retire as a Green Bay Packer because of what he had done for this franchise.

He's very happy in retirement, and we still talk a lot. Every once in a while he'll pick up the phone from his home in Maryland and just call me and see how things are going. Or I'll call him. He knows he'll always be a very important part of the Packers family. We bring him back for a lot of special events. He'll come into my office now, and the first thing he does is come over and give me a big hug. We'll always be close.

His health is good, and I'm very happy for him and Edie. I'll be forever grateful to the man because he was the one who got us back at the top.

CHAPTER TWELVE

A Football Place for a Football Player

Reggie White was on a recruiting tour. Everyone was hiring bands and limousines, holding parades and blowing up balloons for him. Somebody actually bought his wife Sara a fur coat. We picked him up in a Jeep Wrangler and took him to Red Lobster.

It was a typical Green Bay visit, and we signed him. And I thought, "What a great day for the Green Bay Packers. We had Ron Wolf; we had Mike Holmgren; we had Brett Favre, and now we have Reggie White." The foundation was there to bring this franchise back among the elite in the National Football League, and that's when we took off.

Ron handled that whole situation so well. He came into my office one day and said, "We're going to try to get Reggie White in here to visit and see if we can't make him a Green Bay Packer." I wouldn't say he was real optimistic about it, but he was ready to give it a great shot.

He asked me if I was okay with it, and I said I certainly was, although I had my doubts about even getting him to visit. So I didn't go to the Executive Committee at that point. I just told Ron to do whatever he could do and to let me know if I could help him. And he started the process.

Reggie told me later that he had had absolutely no interest in Green Bay when he first heard from us. But he was in Detroit visiting the Lions, and he mentioned to his agent, Jimmy Sexton, that the Packers just kept calling all the time. I'm sure that was Ron. Reggie suggested that they fly over and talk to us just as a courtesy, and so they did.

When it was announced that Reggie was coming to town, there was an excitement in this building that I hadn't seen before. I'm sure it had the same impact in the locker room. The players had to be thrilled.

We went to the Executive Committee, and Ron told them that a four-year contract would cost $17 million. Those were enormous numbers.

Only John Elway and Dan Marino were making more at the time, but there was such a positive feeling in the room that the Committee would have done anything at that point to add Reggie to the franchise.

They told Ron if he could do it, he should do it. There was no debate at all. They were just proud that Ron was in a position where he might be able to get Reggie White.

Jerry Parins, our director of security, picked up Reggie and his agent at a small auxiliary terminal at the airport. They'd landed there in a private plane, which came as a disappointment to the members of the press who had been waiting for them in the main terminal thinking they had taken a commercial flight. Then Ron took Reggie out onto the field before they went to dinner at Red Lobster. It was like me taking Ron to Denny's in 1987. They chose Red Lobster because it was close to the stadium. And instead of us blowing up balloons and hiring bands, we had our football people talk football to a football player.

We have always tried to tell people, if you want to play in a great stadium where there's a great tradition in front of wonderful fans on a great field, it's all here. There are no distractions. It's just football. And that was the approach that Ron and Mike took. Ron told Reggie he could go anyplace and be a hero, but if he came to Green Bay he would be a legend. And that's exactly what he became.

Reggie must have been impressed. Jerry took him back to the airport, and as he was walking up the stairs to get on the plane, he turned to Sexton and said, "Don't be surprised if this is where we end up."

There wasn't much of a bidding war. We made an offer that I think Sexton was comfortable with, and I don't remember Ron changing the numbers a great deal. It was done in a matter of weeks. There was no doubt that Reggie had a lot of teams after him, but we just went in with a very strong proposal. I think he was so surprised at what he saw here. Ron always said if you can't walk onto Lambeau Field and look at the names on the bowl and think of this tradition and the way it grabs you, then you shouldn't be here.

When we got Reggie, it sent shock waves around the country. Remember, Ron and Mike had just gotten here, and this was on the heels of all those losing seasons in the 70's and 80's. He was such an established star, such an icon in the league, that when he walked in, it was like, "Look what we've got."

I met him for the first time when he came to town for the press conference, and two things hit me right away. I had never heard Reggie talk a lot, so the hoarseness of his voice surprised me. And the size. He was a huge human being dressed up in a suit, with this immaculate appearance. The first thing I said to him was that we were thrilled to have him here, and he said he was thrilled to be here.

He became the team leader the moment he walked into that locker room. We had a very bad defense at that time, but when Reggie came in and signed we jumped from 23rd in the league to second. When you look back at the change, you realize he was the catalyst.

He was a giant in the locker room because the players had such great respect for what he'd accomplished in his career. I think players elevated their play because they wanted to please Reggie. He set a wonderful example for everyone.

And he always reached out to the fans. He would come out of that tunnel on Sunday while everyone was applauding, and a lot of the players would just keep their heads down and go right out and start practicing. But Reggie might go around the edge of the stadium, high five some of the fans in the front row and turn and wave. He always let them know, "Hey, we know you're here, and we appreciate you." I think that's one of the reasons he was so popular.

He would take one day a week in training camp during two-a-days when the autograph seekers could be around from 5 in the morning till as late as 9 at night and just sign. Most of the time Reggie and Brett and a couple of other players would get in a car at the back of the stadium and be driven to the practice field. But one day a week Reggie would walk from the practice field to the locker room after the morning practices. It was a good haul through the parking lot, and I could watch him because I had an office window that looked out toward the practice field.

It was hard to imagine the number of people who were around him, and the thing I got a kick out of was that he never stopped. He just kept walking and signing, walking and signing. He took care of a lot of people that way, but if he had ever stopped, he'd still be standing out there today. People were almost climbing on him like he was a statue. When he got to the locker room, he would thank everybody and walk into the building.

My favorite Reggie moment came in the closing minutes of our Super Bowl victory over New England when I thought the man found strength that I'm not even sure he knew he had. We were so close to winning that game, and he just literally took it over. He was brushing offensive linemen aside like they were little kids. He got the three sacks, which is still the Super Bowl record, and he did it late when he just dominated the game. I thought it was like the Good Lord had given him extra power all at once to get what he longed for, and what he longed for was the Super Bowl championship.

The next morning when we were coming back from that game, we kept hearing that it was so foggy in Green Bay that we might not be able to fly in. We knew there were people lining the streets and people in the stadium waiting to welcome us home, and we weren't even sure we could get into the airport. That's when somebody went back to where Reggie was sitting in the plane and told him that this was probably a good time for him to ask God for help. A few minutes later the sky cleared up and we landed. After that, whenever Reggie said that God was around I never doubted him.

He was always saying, "God is going to help me with this," or "God is going to help me with that." I think everyone's heard the story of when he was trying to make up his mind where to play, and Mike Holmgren called him and said, "Reggie, this is God. You'd better come to Green Bay."

There was that famous week before our game in New Orleans in 1995 when it was almost like God had made him well while he was sitting at home. He had a torn left hamstring, and the doctors were saying that he would need surgery, that he was done for the season. But he showed up at practice on Thursday, the day after he was originally scheduled to have the operation. Three days later, he played against the Saints, and he was back in the starting lineup the next week.

The story was that he knocked on Holmgren's door the night before and told him that God had made him better. He worked out with our strength and conditioning coach that night at our indoor practice facility, and he was walking around just fine at practice the next day. I'm sure Reggie believed that God healed him, and I don't know how else to describe it. I can't explain it any better today than he could if he were still here.

Reggie was unpredictable in many ways. He was always looking for new ideas and different things to do. He was very involved with the Urban Hope Project, a program designed to increase jobs, home ownership and education in the central city in Green Bay. Pete Platten and

John Underwood from our Executive Committee were very involved in that, too, and I thought that was good because if anything had gone astray there they would have told Reggie about it right away and straightened it out.

There were some bumps for Reggie along the way. Let's be honest about that. When his Inner City Church in Knoxville, Tennessee, burned down in January of 1996, people from all over the state raised $250,000 to help rebuild it. But the church was never rebuilt, and I got calls and letters from people asking what he was doing and where the money had gone.

I would tell the people that from what I had heard, the church was going to be rebuilt. It might not happen right away, but it would happen. That's all that ever came back to me. I never brought that subject up with Reggie, but he did talk with Underwood and Platten about it. The feeling was it would be built, and that was where it was left. Then Reggie left, and it all kind of went away.

I don't know if he was in with some people he shouldn't have been in with or not. I don't have any firsthand knowledge of that. But if people were anti-Packer, that certainly gave them a lot of ammunition.

It was very controversial, as was the speech he gave to the State Legislature in Madison when he made some unpopular remarks about race relations and homosexuality in America. We were at the league meetings when that happened. Madeline and I were at dinner with the Wolfs and the Holmgrens, and when we came out of the restaurant, there was a reporter standing outside. He asked Mike if he had heard about Reggie's speech, and we all said we hadn't heard a word.

The reporter told us a little about what he'd said, and our quick reaction was that we didn't know enough to make a comment. It was a tough thing to comment on when Reggie was just giving his opinion. I don't know if Ron or Mike ever sat down with him to talk about it. I didn't, but I was surprised by it.

Still, I didn't get a great deal of feedback on that. People never wanted to find much fault with Reggie. I might get a letter here or there, but I never got a really rough reaction to anything he did. Most people would stick by him because they had such great affection for him. They may not have agreed with what he did or what he said, but they never came out and started a full-scale assault on him.

Shortly before he passed away, Reggie told somebody that the biggest mistake he ever made was not to stay in Green Bay after his playing days, and I remember thinking, "Boy, it really was." He could have been like Ray Nitschke, who was a hero here until the day he died because he wanted to stay and become a part of Green Bay. Fuzzy Thurston has done the same thing, and the fans appreciate that. There wasn't a thing that Reggie could have done in this state that wouldn't have been supported by the people. But he went to North Carolina instead where I would hear rumors that he wanted to do this or he wanted to do that. He seemed to be having difficulty getting settled in his life after football.

Reggie actually announced his retirement three times. The first time was before the beginning of the 1998 season. Ron Wolf came to me with that, and he hardly had the words out of his mouth before Reggie changed his mind. It was just that brief.

I think everybody knew he was closing in on the end of his career because of his age, but he used to tell Brett all the time, "Don't retire too early. Make sure you're ready. Give it your full go." Reggie was probably saying the same things to himself, and maybe one day he would feel it was time to go, and the next day he would feel it wasn't.

But his career was headed south, and Reggie had to know that. So when he did retire at the end of the '98 season, I wasn't shocked. I really thought it was too bad when he came back and tried to play the 2000 season in Carolina.

Maybe the correct phrase isn't "tried to play," but he wasn't the same. He had been such a giant in this game for so long, you hated to see it end like that. I had hoped that when he left Green Bay that would be it. His best days were obviously past.

I don't know if the money had anything to do with him going to Carolina or not. Reggie did like money. Absolutely. He did extremely well playing this game, but he did a lot for the National Football League, too. I don't know if it was money or the fact that he thought he might live down there, and if he played a year it would help with things after he retired. But he was absolutely right when he said that he should have stayed in Green Bay because there would have been opportunities for him in this state for the rest of his life. And he realized that at the end.

The last time Reggie ever came to my office was in September before he passed away. I knew he was going to be in the locker room that morning, so I asked a member of our staff to have him come up and see me. That was when I wanted to tell him about retiring his number.

I had been thinking about that for a couple of months. I bounced the idea off a few people, including Lee Remmel of our public relations department. Lee pointed out that Reggie was one of the greatest players ever to wear this uniform, and we won a Super Bowl with him. And then I went to the Executive Committee.

We had retired only four numbers in our history, and I looked at what we had. We had this great era with Curly Lambeau, and we have Tony Canadeo and Don Hutson from then. Then we had the great era with Vince Lombardi, and we had Ray Nitschke and Bart Starr from that time. And then the great era with Ron Wolf and Mike Holmgren, and we would have Reggie White and eventually Brett Favre. That's kind of the way I sold it to the Executive Committee. They gave me their approval in a heartbeat, and I made a plan to see Reggie in September when he came to town.

So I was sitting at my desk on a Saturday morning at about 9 o'clock, and there was a quick knock at my door. I looked up, and there was Reggie in a sweatsuit and tennis shoes. He was just a huge presence. We talked for a few minutes, and then I told him I wanted to retire his number the following season.

I suggested that some time during that day he should go out and just take a look at the four numbers up there in that north end zone and see who he was joining. "This franchise has as great a history and tradition as any franchise in the National Football League," I said, "and we've only retired four numbers." He appreciated that. "I like that, Bob," he said. "I like that."

We decided that he would go back and talk to his wife Sara and the kids, so they could pick a game that they would like to come to when our schedule came out for the next season. We probably visited for half an hour, and then he said he was going to go out and look at the numbers.

About two months later, Reggie called me about something else, and I asked if he was still planning on coming here to retire his number. "You bet your life I am," he said. "Don't worry, we're going to do it just like I said. We'll call you when the schedule comes out."

We never did settle on that date to retire his number.

I was driving to the office when I got the news of Reggie's death. I had gone to Mass at St. Agnes, which is only a little over a mile from the stadium, and I had a Milwaukee station on the car radio. They were talking about Reggie White, which I thought was strange. Why would they be doing that at this time of the day and this time of the year?

And then about halfway through that drive, the announcer said, "For you folks tuning in late, we want you to know that Reggie White passed away this morning at the age of 43."

You can imagine the shock. The first thing I did when I got to the office was call Madeline at home to tell her about it. Then members of the public relations staff started coming up and asking me if I would do some interviews. I spent the rest of the day talking about the impact Reggie White had on this organization and what he meant to the history of the franchise. I wound up staying all day at the office. I don't remember what I was coming in to do, but I know that I didn't do anything other than to talk about Reggie for the rest of that day.

Reggie was such an important part of the Packers family that we chartered a plane to his funeral in Charlotte, North Carolina. More than 40 current and former players, office staff members, directors and team officials made the trip, along with Coach Mike Sherman. Don Beebe, Edgar Bennett, William Henderson, Gilbert Brown, Mark Chmura, Rob Davis, Mike Flanagan, Ryan Longwell, Doug Pederson, Marco Rivera and Darren Sharper had all played with Reggie, and all of them were there to pay their respects. Brett Favre served as a pallbearer.

Several members of our group had a chance to visit with Sara and her children after the ceremony, although we had to fly back the same day because Mike had to get the team ready to play our final regular season game with the Chicago Bears. The family truly appreciated the fact that we had brought so many close friends to share that emotional day with them.

The players also honored Reggie by wearing a No. 92 decal, the number he wore during his six seasons in Green Bay, on their helmets for the Bears game and for the NFC wildcard playoff game against the Minnesota Vikings at Lambeau Field.

After Reggie's passing, I let a few months go by before I asked Sherry Schuldes to call Sara. Sherry is the manager of our Family Programs Department, and she knew Sara well. I had seen the two of them talking at the funeral, and I thought it would be better if the call came from her. I asked her just to call Sara and see if she would be okay with retiring Reggie's number at the first game the following season.

I said we'd love to have Sara and the children here, but if she didn't feel up to it I would understand. Sherry contacted Sara, and there may have been a little hesitation at first on her part. Not about the fact that we wanted to retire the number but whether she could handle coming back that soon. But she agreed to it finally and said she would be there, along with the children.

Our plan was to cover up Reggie's name on the facade and reveal it just before the start of the game. Ron came back for the unveiling, and he and I were to walk Sara out from the tunnel to the 50-yard-line where she would speak, and then we would do the unveiling.

Sara was great in the tunnel. We walked out to the 50, and she gave a very nice little speech, but then we showed about a 2-minute video highlight of Reggie's career. Ron and Sara and myself were staring up at the replay board, and all at once I could feel Sara shaking terribly.

I turned to her and said, "Are you okay?" She said, "I'll be fine, I'll be fine," but she was totally emotional, and I understood it. Here this whole stadium was looking at her husband whom she had just lost, and there was Reggie talking and Reggie singing and Reggie playing. She handled it extremely well until she got to that video, and that's when she went.

The video ended, and we had the unveiling, and then Ron and I walked her off the field and back to the tunnel. She cried all the way off the field and even after that when we met Sherry in the tunnel. I'm sure there were people in the stands who were crying, too.

But now Reggie's name is up there twice. Once for going into the Canton Hall of Fame and once for having his number retired. It's pretty special to be up there twice. He meant so much to this franchise. He restored it.

CHAPTER THIRTEEN
The Irrepressible Brett

I usually have to tell the young players to call me Bob. It's always "Mr. Harlan this" or "Mr. Harlan that" until I say, "Listen, I'm Bob to everybody. Please call me that," and eventually they get around to it. But I didn't have to tell Brett Favre.

The first time I was really around Brett was on a terribly hot Saturday in September of 1992 when the team was working out in the Tampa Bay stadium. I'd gone over to watch the practice, and I was standing down in the end zone where he was doing some jogging. He came running by me and said, "How you doing today, Bob?" This was his second game with the team, and I might have met him once. And I thought, "I'm going to enjoy this guy."

And I really have. Brett plays the game with the enthusiasm of a little boy on a sandlot. He just loves life, and I love to watch him play. In fact I think it's a privilege to watch him play because he is the greatest competitor I've ever seen.

Until Brett came to Green Bay I thought the greatest competitor I was ever going to see in my life was Bob Gibson. Gibson just challenged everybody time after time. He couldn't wait to get the ball and come back at you. But Brett plays the most demanding position in pro football, and there are some weeks when you walk through the locker room, and he can hardly get up and walk. But then it's Sunday, and he comes running through that tunnel, and he's that young kid again.

I'll watch Sports Center on a Monday, and I'll see one quarterback after another limping off the field or going off on a stretcher, and I'll hear how they'll be out two weeks or three weeks or four weeks. But not No. 4. There's some luck there, but mostly it's Brett Favre saying, "Hey, give me your best shot because I'm coming right back at you." I don't think he wants to give anybody the satisfaction of knowing that maybe that last hit stung a little bit.

If you don't get wrapped up in the enthusiasm that he brings to the stadium every Sunday you don't enjoy the game of pro football. A lot of pro athletes take their games for granted. Brett never has. And his head size has never changed. He's the same down-to-earth kid who showed up here in 1992.

The first time I heard anything about him at all was just prior to the draft when he was coming out of school in 1991. I've always made a point to stop in the draft room for an hour or so every afternoon in the last week or two before the draft just to hear what the scouts and coaches and the general manager are talking about. I was in there one day, and they were watching this young passer. His name didn't mean anything to me, but I remember everyone kept talking about what a strong arm he had.

But nobody was talking about him on draft day. Maybe he was long gone before we got to the point that we were looking for a quarterback. The next time I heard his name was when Ron Wolf came up to me in the press box in Atlanta on his first day on the job and said he was going to go down on the field and look at the Falcons' back-up quarterback. And then all at once, Brett Favre became a very important part of the Packers.

He had some mischief in him when he came here, and we knew that. I've always said you can't hide in this community, and no one of Brett's stature can hide anywhere. He was a fun-loving guy who got the most out of life, and he needed to be corralled once in a while.

We talked to Ron Wolf about that. Ron had a little mischief in him, too, and I think to a degree he liked the daredevil, gunslinger approach that Brett took to things. But he was concerned. He and Mike Holmgren talked to Brett about that. He needed to get it out of his system. But Ron would tell me, "We'll be all right with Brett. We'll be all right."

Those two had a wonderful relationship. I remember when Brett signed one of his contract extensions he and Ron were sitting at a table together to make the announcement, and Brett wrapped his arms around Ron and said, "I love this man." Both of them had a great deal of admiration for what the other had done for the franchise.

At the same time, I think Mike Holmgren was the perfect coach for Brett because if he didn't like what was going on on the field he would get right up in his face and tell him so. Not everyone would do that, which is why Brett will say to this day that Mike was the one who made him a good quarterback.

I happened to see Mike at a league meeting in Orlando in March of 2006, and he came over to me and asked, "Is your guy coming back this year?" I told him I thought he was, and Mike said, "You know, other than the Baltimore game when you guys got blown out on a Monday night, you were in every game last year. Somebody just had to grab Brett by the collar and say, 'Hey, do it this way. Don't do it that way.'"

I thought Mike was probably right, and he was the one guy who could have done that. But there were times when even he just threw up his hands and said the hell with it.

Mike's favorite story about Brett came from a game in Lambeau Field when it was snowing and everything was turning to ice. It was late in the game and we were out of timeouts when Mike brought Brett over to the sidelines and said, "Now listen. Here's what you're going to do. If there's nobody open, you've got to throw the ball away. Make sure you throw the ball away. Or get out of bounds. Whatever you do, don't get tackled on the field because we're out of timeouts. Brett, are you listening to me?"

He said Brett just kept staring and didn't say a word, and he said, "So you throw the ball away or you get out of bounds because we don't have any timeouts left. Now do you understand what I'm saying to you?" Mike said he was right up in Brett's face, and finally Brett looked at him and said, "Coach, you ought to see your moustache. It's all icy."

You just never knew what was coming next from the kid, but that's why the fans loved him. For three hours every Sunday he was as entertaining as any player in the National Football League, and he kept finding ways to win.

But I had my doubts in the beginning. Everyone remembers how he came off the bench in our third game against Cincinnati in 1992. We were losing, 23-17, with 1:07 left, and he threw a 42-yard laser to Sterling Sharpe in front of the Bengals' bench. Then on the next play he threw a 35-yard touchdown pass to Kitrick Taylor, and we won the game, 24-23.

It was a great victory, but we'd had so many flash in the pan guys. I wondered, was this going to be permanent or was it going to be one of those "Look what he did yesterday" situations, and then it's over? Brett started every game the rest of that season, and we finished 9-7 after going 4-12 the year before. We were starting to show signs of coming back, but I kept hoping it wasn't a repeat of Don Majkowski and 1989 when we had such high hopes and Majkowski looked to be a great quarterback.

We had spent years looking for the right quarterback after Bart Starr left. Lynn Dickey filled in nicely for a while, but there was nobody like Brett Favre. He came back and started every game the next year, and we went 9-7 again, and when we did the same thing the following year you could see we were on the verge of something special. We had had only four winning seasons in two decades, and now we had three in a row.

But it wasn't until after that second 9-7 season that I thought that Brett might be the guy. And after we'd gone 9-7 three years in a row I was sure he was. He was becoming consistent and exciting, and Wolf was surrounding him with better talent.

He was also very outspoken. I don't think that ever caused a problem, though. It was just Brett being Brett, and the people in the organization accepted that. He is always going to say what's on his mind, and you had better listen because he's usually right on.

When Sterling Sharpe threatened to hold out the day before our 1994 season opener with Minnesota, Brett made it clear what he thought about that. He believes when a guy signs a legal contract, he owes it to the organization to be there. He's very loyal to this franchise, and I appreciate that. He has hurt the feelings of some players who wished he'd be more on their side, but he says what's best for the franchise and not just what's best for Brett Favre.

At the same time, he came right out and said the league had made a mistake when it suspended Koren Robinson and ruled that he couldn't have any contact with the team. Brett believed that Koren should be able to come into the locker room and be with the people who could help him get better. The thing is Brett went through this with his problem in 1996, so he knew what he was talking about.

The first I heard of his difficulties with Vicodin that year was when Ron Wolf came into my office a couple of days before Brett held his press conference. Ron told me Brett had this problem, and he was going to disclose it publicly, and he wanted to know my feelings. My reaction was just concern – concern for Brett and his family and concern that he get better. That's all that went through my mind.

I told Ron I wanted to talk to Brett before he held his press conference, and Ron said he'd take care of it. So about 20 minutes before the press conference, Ron told me that Brett and Deanna were in the building, and I went to talk with them at the end of the hall on the administrative floor before they went downstairs.

Brett was very quiet. There wasn't a lot of expression on his face. I just told him, "I admire what you're doing today, and I want you to know that we're here for you as an organization, and we're here for you individually. If there's anything this corporation can ever do, just ask. We're here to help you, and things are going to work out." I told Deanna the same thing.

And he said, "I know that, Bob." I hugged Deanna, and then I went down to the press conference. He was very contemplative, but I wouldn't say tense. I just had the impression that he wanted to tell the story and move on.

I have a lot of admiration for the way he's handled the things he's gone through off the field. There have been so many trying times, and his family has bounced back from all of them. Deanna has been by his side for everything, and he ought to just worship her for the wonderful influence she's been on his life. She is a very sweet person, and she's the perfect partner for Brett.

They've had so many things to conquer. In one 14-month span from October of 2003 until the end of the 2004 season, Brett suffered a broken thumb, Deanna's brother died in an accident, Deanna was diagnosed with cancer, Brett's father passed away suddenly, and Reggie White died. And then they had Hurricane Katrina the next year.

It was just awful. Brett admitted to Mike Sherman that he couldn't have a lot of fun because there were just so many things off the field. He said he wanted to come back and play so he could have some fun.

But he isn't one to say, "woe is me." The most emotional I've ever seen him was when we were in Oakland and his father passed away. Somebody called me in my room the night before the game and told me what had happened. I didn't see a lot of people, but the news just kind of made its way around the hotel.

I saw Brett and Deanna the next day in the lobby when we were getting ready to go to the game, and I told them how sorry I was. He was just typical Brett. "Thanks Bob, thanks Bob," that kind of thing. There was a very different atmosphere in the hotel as we got on the buses. It was a very quiet team, and you wondered how people would respond.

I was especially curious to see how the Oakland fans, who can be a little difficult, would react to the news. In a normal situation with nothing else going on, Brett would have been booed right out of the stadium because as much as those fans respected and feared him, they wanted to beat him. But when he was announced that night he got a wonderful, warm ovation from the Oakland fans, and I thought that was very touching. Not that Brett didn't deserve it. He had told people all day long that he was going to play because his dad would have wanted him to play. And he would have. Irv would have said, "You go play. I'm fine."

When Brett came out and got that ovation, it was kind of a tingly thing. And when he threw his first touchdown pass, you wanted to cry. You wanted so badly for the night to go well for him, and I don't think the Green Bay Packers receivers have ever had a better game as we won, 41-7. We had some incredible catches that night. If there were four defenders and one receiver, our receiver would come down with the ball. It was unbelievable. It was "Let's do this for Brett."

There is that kind of love and admiration for Brett Favre in this organization. Reggie was something special, but Brett is the most popular player I've ever known here. He has that appeal about him, with his daring on the field and the way he's battled back from so many things and given everyone such a great show.

My favorite Brett Favre moment came at the Super Bowl against New England in New Orleans. I remember how nervous I was going into the game, just because we were there, and it was such a great thing for the franchise. On the Packers' second play of the game, Brett threw a 54-yard touchdown pass to Andre Rison, and then he took off his helmet and ran off the field like a kid running to his mom and dad in a Little League game. It was like, "Look what I did, Mom." Of all the great moments he's given me, I can still remember the thrill I felt just being ahead by one touchdown and then seeing his enthusiasm coming over to that sideline.

The little boy in him just jumps out at you every once in a while, and I think it appeals especially to women. When he does something, Madeline will say to me, "Did you see what my boy did today?" And I'll look at the newspaper and find it open to his picture. Madeline has been like that for years. I think women look at Brett and think, "He's just like my little boy." Even as he's getting gray, he has that little boy mischief in his eyes, and people like that.

People would do anything to make sure he stays a Green Bay Packer. In 2001 we signed him to a 10-year, $100 million contract extension that made him the highest-paid player in the NFL, and the negotiations were easy. Ron came in and told the Executive Committee what he wanted to do, and I never heard anybody say, "Wait a minute. Let's think about this." The feeling was always that he was worth it and we should get it done.

I can't imagine the Packers ever trading him. I gave a speech in downtown Green Bay recently, and there were about 500 people there from all over the state. I happened to mention that Mike McCarthy had said that as long as he is here Brett Favre would never be traded, and people stood up and applauded right in the middle of the speech.

His popularity has had a big effect on what happens to us on the road. I always get a kick out of watching the players get on the bus on a Saturday afternoon after we've flown into a town. They're wearing suits and ties and these great looking outfits, and then Brett gets on the bus wearing Levis and some kind of gray T-shirt that's not tucked in and an old red baseball cap that looks like it goes back to the 1930's Gas House Gang in St. Louis.

But when we get to the hotel, no matter what city we're in, the fans are standing around waiting to see the team and they're looking for one guy. It's, "Where's Brett? Where's Brett?" And when he finally gets off the bus, everyone applauds. Then you go to the stadium the next day and you see that No. 4 jersey everywhere.

That jersey is off the wall in sales. Brett accounted for a little over $1 million in merchandise sales last year in our team store at Lambeau Field, which just runs away and hides from everybody else's numbers. It's enormous.

He has a huge impact on this franchise in many ways. When I was thinking about hiring Ted Thompson to take over Mike Sherman's general manager's duties, I decided to bounce it off of Brett first. He actually knew that was going to happen before Mike did.

Brett was talking again about whether he would be coming back the next year, and I felt that because of his status with the organization and what he had contributed I wanted him to know what I was thinking about doing at the end of the season. So I saw him one day and asked him if he'd stop by my office.

He came in and sat on the couch and we visited for awhile, and then I said, "Brett, I don't even want to get into what you're thinking about doing this off-season or your plans for next season, but I do think I

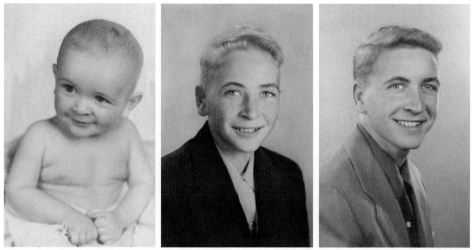

Whether I was eight months old or a fifth grader or a junior in high school, I had a good time growing up in Iowa.

I was a pretty decent golfer in my younger days. I played to about a 5 handicap throughout my high school years, and I enjoyed playing in this city junior tournament in Des Moines.

My father, Sy Harlan, rose from a very small position in a trucking company to become president and owner of the company. Unfortunately, he passed away much too early at age 56.

My mother Alice wasn't just my Mom, she was one of the best friends I've ever had. I was her only son, so she was strict, but she was always very, very good to me.

Madeline and I were married in Des Moines, Iowa, in 1959. I was 22 and Madeline was 20, but we still don't look like we're old enough to get married. On my left are my parents, Sy and Alice, and on the right are Madeline's parents, Mary Frances and George Kieler.

I learned a lot about public relations in the early 60s when I was the Sports Information Director at Marquette University. It could get pretty busy, but I loved the job.

The incomparable Al McGuire and his assistants, Hank Raymonds and Rick Majerus, led Marquette basketball into a golden era that culminated in the 1977 NCAA Championship. I've never had a more exciting year than the one I spent with Al, who was a great friend.

I would meet with Manager Red Schoendienst every morning when the St. Louis Cardinals trained in St. Petersburg, Florida, in 1969. I enjoyed my three years as the Cardinals' Public Relations Director, but the travel was hard on my family.

My boyhood hero Stan Musial couldn't have been happier than he was at the press conference where it was announced that he'd been elected to the Baseball Hall of Fame. Stan was the general manager of the Cardinals' 1967 championship team and as nice a man as you'll ever meet.

I watched from the press box when the Cardinals lost the 1968 World Series in seven games. It was a huge disappointment, but it was still a wonderful time to be with such a first class organization.

What 10-year-old wouldn't want to sit in a big league dugout? Taking my boys with me to spring training was one of the best things about working for the Cardinals. Kevin (shown here) would visit first, and then go home to make room for his brother Bryan.

Everything changed on this November day in 1991 when Ron Wolf became our general manager. Without Ron, we wouldn't have had Brett Favre, Mike Holmgren or Reggie White. He turned the franchise around.

I was delighted the day Reggie White joined the Packers as a free agent saying he thought we could win the Super Bowl. He knew what he was talking about.

My favorite foursome at the annual charity golf tournament in Door County will always include my sons (L-R) Kevin, Bryan and Mike. I got all of the boys involved in golf when they were young, and we still have a great time playing together.

It's going to be a sad day for the Green Bay Packers and for the National Football League when Brett Favre retires. He's the greatest competitor I've ever known, but his head size has never changed.

I am proud to say I've shared a locker with Brett Favre. This one happens to be in the staff locker room, and because I work out at home I've rarely used it. When Brett heard about that, he asked the equipment people if I'd mind letting him spend some quiet time there working on his beloved crossword puzzles. I was all for it, especially since I got to share a nameplate with him, too.

The most rewarding scene I've ever been part of at Lambeau Field took place on January 12, 1997 when we beat Carolina for the NFC championship. People all over the stadium were laughing, crying and hugging. Nobody wanted to go home.

Whenever I went to the Super Bowl, I would look at those huge blow-up team helmets the league always put on the field before the game. When it was time for us to have ours out there for Super Bowl XXXI, I knew I had to have my picture taken with it. Al Treml, our video director, took the shot on the morning of the game when I was too nervous to stay at the hotel.

The victory party after Super Bowl XXXI was a memorable one, and nobody deserved to enjoy it more than Mike Holmgren and Ron Wolf. Having them working together in Green Bay rescued the franchise.

Executive Committee members (from left) John Fabry, Peter Platten, Jim Temp, John Underwood and Don Harden savored our success at the 1997 Super Bowl celebration. They were part of an outstanding group that served together for 11 years.

I was in excellent company in May of 1997 when we visited President Bill Clinton at the White House. The best part was sharing the moment with Ron Wolf, Mike Holmgren, Brett Favre and Reggie White. They formed the foundation for our success.

When John Jones and I unveiled our plans to redevelop Lambeau Field to the press in January of 2000, it marked the beginning of an eight-month campaign that proved to be as difficult a time as this organization has ever faced.

The ground-breaking for the Lambeau Field redevelopment on May 19, 2001 was a team effort.

I met a lot of people while getting the message out on the referendum. There were some long days, but it was well worth it.

We celebrated the passing of the referendum at the Stadium View Bar near Lambeau Field on September 12, 2000. It was a great night for the Green Bay Packers.

Once the 1998 stock sale increased our shareholders from 1,900 to 111,000 we never knew how many people would come to our annual meeting. So we moved it to Lambeau Field.

The Executive Committee was kind enough to name the Lambeau Field plaza after me in the fall of 2003, and Kevin, Mike, Bryan and Madeline (L-R) turned the evening into a Green and Golden Moment.

The Inaugural Ball at the Lambeau Field Atrium may have been the only event that Brett Favre ever attended in a tuxedo. Brett, Deanna, Madeline and I joined in the festivities, which raised more than $500,000 for the St. Mary's Hospital Medical Center Endowment Fund in Green Bay.

Brett took time out for a quick photo with my grandson Robert and me during a practice at Lambeau in August 2006. Robert has the photo framed and hanging on his bedroom wall.

Ted Thompson was Ron Wolf's right-hand man in Green Bay. Then he went to Seattle with Mike Holmgren and built a Super Bowl team. Ted is a sound, dedicated general manager, and I've always been impressed with his work ethic.

Mike McCarthy and I shared a happy moment in the locker room at Detroit after he got his first victory as a head coach. He did an outstanding job last year of keeping the team together, and we won our last four games to finish with an 8-8 record.

We had just beaten the Minnesota Vikings in the last home game of 2006 when Ted Thompson invited me down to the locker room. After Mike McCarthy talked to the players, he asked me to step forward, and then the team presented me with a game ball. It was a great honor, and it meant a great deal to me.

Summers are special for us when we can share them with our grandchildren (L-R) Olivia, 14; Abigail, 18; Haley, 17; and King Robert, 11.

It was a special night when we visited Kevin's family in Kansas City, and watched the girls cheerlead at a basketball game. Shown here are Kevin's wife Ann, Haley, myself and Madeline, Robert, Olivia, Abigail and Kevin.

The Harlan Family gathered in Door County. Front (L-R) Abigail, Madeline, Robert, Olivia, myself and Haley. Back (L-R) Michael, daughter-in-law Ann, Kevin and Bryan.

Our place in Door County has been a great getaway for Madeline and me. We're looking forward to spending more time there.

should tell you that I'm planning on bringing in a general manager and taking some of the responsibilities away from Mike Sherman. And the person I'm going to go after is Ted Thompson."

He said he knew Ted very well, he liked him very much, and he was fine with that. I told him I didn't want to go into the reasons, but I just felt he should have that in mind when he went home and thought about his future. I said I wouldn't be talking to any other players about this, and in fact hardly anybody in the building knew about it at that point. He said he appreciated that, and we never talked about it again.

That's how highly I feel about Brett Favre. I wanted to make sure I wasn't off the wall on this, so I went to one member of the Executive Committee and told him I thought I should talk to Brett, and he agreed with me.

It's going to be a sad, sad day when he walks down the tunnel at Lambeau Field and disappears for the last time because you don't recover from losing a Brett Favre very quickly. I hope the team is strong enough overall that it can, but to lose his presence will be like losing a John Elway in Denver or a Dan Marino in Miami. Those men were icons in the game, and that's what Brett has meant to us.

People looked at me like I was goofy last year when I kept saying that I thought he was coming back. The only thing I could base that on was that he is such a competitor, and I felt he would come back as long as he felt he could throw the ball and lead this team and win games for us. I figured the longer he took to make a decision, the better it was for us.

Fans would call me and say, "What's he going to do? Ted Thompson doesn't want him back." I'd tell them that Ted Thompson does want him back. Ted met with Brett personally before Brett went home after the season, and they talked on the phone every single week. A lot of times Ted would come by and tell me Brett had called that day and he talked three minutes while Brett talked 45. The relationship between Ted and Brett is very good.

I can't tell you how many calls I got in January, February and March after the 2005 season from people from all over the country, and the majority of them were about what Brett was going to do. I was amazed. We were 4-12, our first losing season in 14 years, but they didn't want to talk about the 4-12. They wanted to find out about Brett.

I have a female fan who lives down near Milwaukee. Her name is Faye, and she calls me all the time. That winter she must have called two or three times a week to ask if Brett was coming back. If I wasn't there to take the call, she'd leave these long messages, and they were never about anything else but No. 4. I wonder how Faye is going to handle it when he leaves.

I can't see him ever being a detriment to the franchise. He's proud enough that he'll know when the time has come to leave, and I think he'll be very cautious about that. Deanna will be very cautious about it, too. Brett dearly loves to be with his two daughters, and that has weighed on his decisions a great deal. The family has encouraged him to come back, and that includes his daughters. He and his mother are very close as well. He always listens to his family.

He won't stay here after his playing days are finished. We'll bring him back here as often as we possibly can, and we're going to retire his number. But he's got to go home, and I totally understand that.

I tell people all the time that when he's gone, not only will the Green Bay Packers miss him, but the National Football League will miss him because of the color and the enthusiasm he brought to the game. We're all going to look back and say, "Boy, we saw Brett Favre play." He's one of the best ever, and people who want to criticize him now are going to miss him more than ever when he's gone.

CHAPTER FOURTEEN

First Steps to the Super Bowl

Everyone wanted Mike Holmgren after the 1991 season, and it was huge for the status of this organization that the Green Bay Packers were the ones who got him. It was like going out and getting Reggie White. Signing Mike to a guaranteed deal more than doubled our investment in the football operation because we already had Lindy Infante under contract for three more years, but that's when we sent the message to our fans that we really did want to be successful, and we were going to do whatever it took.

We knew we would have to be competitive right from the start if we wanted Mike to come here, and if there was any concern on the Executive Committee those gentlemen never relayed it to me. Ron Wolf had convinced the Committee that he could bring us success if we allowed him to run things his way, and his first major step was to hire Mike.

Having Ron was an enormous factor in convincing Holmgren to come to Green Bay instead of choosing another team. Mike wanted very much to get off to a good start in his first opportunity as a head coach, and he knew Ron could find the players so all he'd have to do was coach them.

It took him less than 15 minutes in their first meeting to convince Ron that they could work well together. He had everything Ron was looking for: the leadership, the toughness, the charisma and the compatibility. There was a kind of a cocky confidence to Mike that reminded Ron of Bill Walsh and what he had done coaching at San Francisco.

Now my job was to make sure that Ron and Mike had what they needed to win here. Mike told me once that he was always impressed by the fact that whenever he would come up and see me I'd end the conversation by asking him if he needed anything. "You always said that," he said, "and so I knew that I wouldn't have to beg for anything."

Recently *Sports Illustrated* polled 354 current and former players and asked them to name the classiest organization in the National Football

League. Players weren't allowed to vote for their own teams, and the Packers were voted No. 1. What that told me was that players on other teams were talking to players on the Packers, and the word was out that Green Bay was a quality place to go. And that's the approach we take.

We look out for player safety and comfort, and we do everything we can to help the coach and the general manager to be successful. I don't ever want a coach or general manager to leave here and say he didn't have a chance to succeed in Green Bay. Our focus has to be on football. We make our money on football, and we spend our money on football. That's all we think about here.

We got an idea of the respect Mike had around the league when he put together his first staff. Dick Jauron, Ray Rhodes, Jon Gruden, Steve Mariucci and Andy Reid were on that staff, and all of them became head coaches in the NFL. I'm sure they learned a lot from Mike about discipline and organization, just as Mike learned a lot when he worked for Walsh.

Mike told me one time that when the 49ers were on the road, Walsh's itinerary was planned almost to the minute. It would be like, "At 5:10 p.m. Coach Walsh will be seated at the table, and at 5:12 p.m., he will have his steak served medium rare." Mike wasn't that bad, but he didn't like glitches. People who planned our trips had to really be on their toes and prepared for anything. He was a very demanding guy. If he said something was supposed to happen at 8 o'clock, it had better happen at 8 o'clock.

He had an extremely short fuse. He could blow up on the sidelines in a heartbeat, and he could also get very upset if things off the field weren't happening right. I guess I was fortunate. He never showed that in my office.

Of course Ron had quite a temper, too, and I hope I dealt with both of them the right way. Never saying no to them probably helped me a great deal, but they always seemed to want to do things that I thought made a lot of sense.

Mike could be as engaging as anyone I've been around. He had this great, dry sense of humor that people just didn't think was in him because they never got a chance to see it. He could sit and tell stories and make fun of himself, and I could kid him about things when he stopped into the office to talk. He didn't just come around to ask for things. Sometimes he'd come in and tell me something, and we'd drift off into other conversations and have a great time.

You could have some good laughs with him, but you always knew that short fuse was there, and you would prefer not to be around when it went off. He wanted things done his way and only his way. Everybody knew that, including the coaches. It wasn't a fear thing with them so much as it was a respect thing.

On road trips I would sit across from Gruden on the plane, and he would work on his playbook for the entire trip. Then he'd work on it again for the entire trip home on Sunday. The guy just never stopped. Reid would come into work at 4 or 5 o'clock in the morning. I never thought Andy would be as successful as he's been as a head coach, but his work ethic was just outstanding. It was a very dedicated staff, and I always got the impression that they thought it was a real honor to work for Mike Holmgren.

Mike wasn't one of those coaches who had to be in the office before the sun came up and then leave long after it went down. If he had a meeting at 9 a.m., he didn't feel it was necessary to get in at 6 to prepare what he was going to do. A lot of that had to do with the fact that he was so organized and he knew what he was going to do anyway. We've had some coaches who spent a lot more time in the office than Mike, but they didn't get as much done.

And he was very definitely in charge on the field. Nobody knew that better than Brett Favre. You'd look down on the sideline many times, and Mike would be right in Favre's face.

We acquired Brett in February of 1992, and there was some controversy when he took over the starting job after coming off the bench to produce that famous come-from-behind victory against Cincinnati at Lambeau Field. He started against Pittsburgh the next week, and when we won, 17-3, his streak of consecutive starts had begun. It was the classic Lou Gehrig story. You never saw him on the bench again.

Nobody really knew what he could do before the Cincinnati game. Don Majkowski was still kind of a hero from what he had done in 1989, but when he got hurt Brett came in and threw this laser down the sideline for the touchdown that won the game. To this day Mike Brown, the Bengals owner, tells me when I see him, "We weren't concerned at all when you guys brought this kid off the bench, but then he threw that pass, and that started his career."

We'd started the season 0-2, losing to the Vikings, 23-20, in overtime and then getting crushed, 31-3, at Tampa Bay. The Tampa game was very depressing, but I remember getting a call from Ed Van Boxtel, who owned a local Ford dealership, and he said, "You're not letting that 31-3 game get you down, are you?" I said I wasn't, and he said, "Good, because as a fan I can already see things getting better. Just hang in there." It turned out he was right. We wound up winning six of our last seven games.

Brett passed for more than 3,000 yards and 18 touchdowns that season, and the most amazing thing to me was that his completion average was 64.1%. Believe it or not, that broke the team record that Bart Starr had set at 63.7% in 1968. It was hard to imagine a young kid coming in and doing that that quickly.

He was named as a reserve to the NFC Pro Bowl squad after the season, and Holmgren was delighted for him, even though he said, "He's way too young and I've been yelling at him way too much for him to do something like that." I thought it just showed how Mike could take a young, undisciplined quarterback and get him to do what he wanted him to do.

So we went 9-7 in 1992 and finished second to Minnesota in the division, and I thought we were really getting better. But I kept harking back to 1989 when we were so enthusiastic and then we fell right back down again. I had to see it a second year.

When we lost three of our first four games in 1993 it took some doing to convince me that we were going to be all right. But we lost two of them by a total of five points, and we just seemed to look better. And then we won three in a row, and I started to have some confidence that it wasn't 1989 all over again.

In the next-to-last game of the season LeRoy Butler ran an interception back for a touchdown, and we beat the Los Angeles Raiders, 28-0. As soon as LeRoy got to the south end zone, he started pointing into the stands. I didn't know what he was doing. I thought he might have had a relative or something up there. But he just kept running, and then he leaped into the stands. The fans loved it, and I did, too.

Then somebody started calling it the "Lambeau Leap," and that was perfect. Now in almost every game you tune in to, people are jumping into the stands. But nobody did it until LeRoy did.

The victory over the Raiders put us into the playoffs for the first time in a full season since 1972. It was just the second year of Wolf and

Holmgren, and we were doing things we hadn't done in more than 20 years.

We lost the next week to Detroit, but we got a rematch with the Lions in the Pontiac Silverdome in the wild card playoff game. We beat the Lions, 28-24, that day, and there were two plays that I'll never forget.

We were behind, 17-14, late in the third quarter, and the Lions were on our five-yard line when George Teague intercepted an Erik Kramer pass in the end zone and took it back 101 yards for a touchdown. I was sitting next to Wolf in the press box, and he kept pounding the table with every step the kid took. He was screaming, "Run! Run! Run!" at the top of his lungs, which you're not supposed to do in the press box. But George went down the sideline and scored that touchdown.

The other play was the one that won the game. There were 55 seconds left to play, and I was in the tunnel by the locker room, too nervous to stay in the press box. Our players were standing between me and the field, so all I could see was Brett running toward the sideline and throwing a 40-yard pass. His back was to me, and from where I stood it looked like a Hail Mary pass.

I was about 15 or 20 feet inside the tunnel when he let it go, and I ran all the way down to the edge of the field where I could see the replay board. And there standing all alone in the end zone with the ball was Sterling Sharpe!

When the play was over, Favre came running over to the sideline, and the first person he ran into was Bob Noel, our equipment guy. Bob hadn't seen Sterling catch the ball, and so he wrapped his arms around Brett and said, "That's okay, kid. We'll get them next time." And Brett said, "Hell, Bob, we just won the damn game."

I was so excited I didn't know where to go. Finally I headed for the locker room. It was then that I felt we were really on our way. We had finished our first two years under Mike with 9-7 records, putting together back-to-back winning seasons for the first time since 1967, and we had won our first playoff game since 1982.

We went to Dallas for the NFC divisional game the next week and lost, 27-17, but that game in Detroit was such a dramatic victory for us, and I remember thinking, "We've never done anything like this."

We did a couple of very important things in the spring and summer before we started the 1994 season. We announced in April that we were going to add 90 private boxes and a 57-seat auxiliary press box. We had built 72 boxes in 1985 and added 36 in 1990, so this brought the stadium total to 198. I was amazed to see the new boxes leased before we even started building them. I couldn't keep up with the number of people who wanted them.

Then in July we dedicated our indoor practice facility, the Don Hutson Center. I had a lot of fun with that. The Hutson Center is a beautiful building that covers two and a half acres and has two artificial turf fields. It's big enough to house two 747 jets, but our players and coaches always referred to it as "the barn." I thought if I'm going to pay $4.6 million for a building, I'm not going to call it a barn. Let's take advantage of our tradition and name it after Don Hutson.

Everyone I talked to who had followed this franchise for a long time told me that Don was the greatest player we had ever had. So I called him at his home in California to ask permission to use his name. His wife Julia answered the phone and said he wasn't there but was due back in about a half hour. I had never spoken to Don in my life, but I told her what I wanted to do and asked her to have him call me. He called back within the hour, and I said, "Don, it's really an honor to talk to you." And he said, "It's an honor to have that building named after me."

He and his wife and some other family members flew into Green Bay on the morning of the dedication. He spoke at the event, and I also had Mike Holmgren and Ron Wolf speak. It was such a pleasure to meet the gentleman, and "gentleman" was the best way to describe him. His wife told me that it was one of the nicest honors of his life, and that made me feel very good. Don passed away in June of 1997 at the age of 84. I was very glad that he knew about this honor, and that he was a part of it before he did pass away.

The 1994 season didn't start out well. We lost two of our first three games. Then we won three in a row in the middle of the season. Then we lost three in a row, and then we won three in a row to get into the playoffs. The three we lost were against Buffalo, Dallas and Detroit, and they were all on the road. Wolf just despised that.

He had a fit any time he saw three straight road games on our schedule. He could take anything else, but if you showed him that, he would turn beet red and start yelling. He really thought we were getting the short stick. There are so many things that go into scheduling, and I understand that the league office can't please all 32 teams all the time, but we would call them and say, "Please don't do that to us again."

But we survived it by beating the Bears in Green Bay, the Falcons in Milwaukee and the Buccaneers in Tampa Bay to close out the regular season. The Atlanta game was historic for a couple of reasons. It put us into the playoffs for the second year in a row, and it was the last one we ever played at County Stadium. Brett won it by diving into the end zone in the last second to beat the Falcons, 21-17.

We played Detroit again in the wild card round, only this time the game was in Green Bay, and we had to win it without Sharpe. Sterling had been telling our medical staff that he had numbness and tingling in his neck and a weakness in his limbs during the last two games against Atlanta and Tampa Bay. We had two neurosurgeons examine him, and they found two loose vertebrae that needed to be surgically fused. He was finished for the year. At that point we didn't know how serious the injury was. We just knew we wouldn't have him for the playoffs.

The Detroit game was played on New Year's Eve day, and we won it, 16-12, by holding Barry Sanders to a career low, negative-one yard in 13 carries. Sanders had led the league in rushing with 1,883 yards, but Fritz Shurmur's defense just shut him down.

It was very cold that day, and we always turned the heat on underneath the field in cold weather to make it soft enough that it wasn't mushy but cleats could be effective. I was sitting next to Ron at halftime, and he said to me, "Hey Bob, do you think we ought to turn off the heat for the second half? Look at what we're getting away with now. If we turn it off, we could really get him slipping and sliding."

I told him if we did the league office would be on our backs in a heartbeat. He just laughed, but I could see where he was coming from. As it was, we held the Lions to minus four yards rushing and a season-low 171 yards of total offense.

Unfortunately we went to Dallas for the NFC division playoff and got beat, 35-9. That was two years in a row that the Cowboys eliminated us.

We went to Dallas six times in Mike's first four years, and we lost all six of those games. A bunch of the Executive Committee wives made the trip for one of them, and that led to an interesting complication. They got locked in the stadium.

Different stadiums have different security policies, which can cause confusion for people who have to leave games late. I'm told that what happened to the wives has also happened to members of the media more than once.

The wives were sitting in a booth, and Don Harden stayed up there with them, so he could bring them down to the bus after the game. The buses don't normally leave the stadium until an hour or so after a game, and so Don and five of the wives, including Madeline, stayed upstairs for about 45 minutes. On their way down, they found out that the stadium had been closed up for the night. All of the gates and doors were locked. It was getting dark, and they couldn't find anyone to help them.

We were out in the tunnel by the locker room, with four buses waiting to leave, and nobody knew where they were. I was walking from one end of the tunnel to the other, and finally I saw Mike Holmgren coming out of the locker room. I went over to Mark Schiefelbein, who was doing the travel for us, and told him to send the first three buses to the airport, but to leave the fourth one and one policeman so I would have an escort.

Ron happened to be on that last bus, and he wasn't happy anyway after the loss. When he saw the other buses going, he screamed, "Why the hell aren't we moving?" Somebody on the bus said, "I don't know what's going on, but Bob's outside running back and forth looking for somebody."

Finally down the hill came Don and the five wives. Nobody even looked at me when they got to the tunnel. They just walked by. Madeline said, "I'm sorry," but nobody else said a word. We radioed ahead, and caught up to the other buses. By the time we got to the airport and loaded the equipment, we were fine, but it was a little panicky for awhile.

The wives only make a couple of trips each year, and I've always told Madeline to remind everyone that we are on a business trip. Everyone needs to follow the itinerary and not be disruptive. I certainly didn't want either Mike or Ron to know about our problem. Madeline told me she thought we would be able to laugh about the situation some day, but I have never found it to be very humorous, and Don absolutely refuses to discuss the evening.

In early '95 we found out how serious Sterling's neck injury was. He could hardly turn his neck, and when he did, he would almost have to turn his whole torso. His doctors had pretty much told him the dangers he was facing, and we released him on February 28. It was best for everybody, but we really missed him.

Sterling was the guy. There was absolutely no doubt about that. In 1993 he caught 112 passes, and Edgar Bennett was second on the team with 59. It was pretty obvious who Brett was throwing to. Even the next year when Sterling was cut short by a turf toe injury, he caught 94, and Bennett was second with 78.

Sterling was a phenomenal receiver. He was strong as a bull, and when he caught the ball he was going to get extra yardage. He was fast, and he was a good target. You can understand why Brett was looking for him. You knew if you threw the ball to him, he was going to catch it.

Ron got Keith Jackson and Mark Ingram during the off-season to try to beef up our receiving corps, and both of them came in late. Keith was 91 days late after being acquired in a trade with Miami, but Reggie White might have helped us with that. I always felt that when Reggie came here he set a great example for everybody. And then once we got to 1995 it was pretty obvious that this franchise had taken off, and that made us a lot more attractive to other players. They looked at Wolf and Holmgren and knew this was a very stable football organization.

We had an 11-5 record in 1995 that put us in first place in our division, and we could have been 12-4 if a backup quarterback named T.J. Rubley hadn't thrown an infamous interception at the Metrodome in Minneapolis. Rubley hadn't played a game in almost two years, and he was only in this one because Brett and Ty Detmer had both left with injuries.

The score was tied, 24-24, and we had a third down and a foot to go on the Vikings' 38 with a minute to play when Mike sent in a quarterback sneak. But Rubley called an audible, and he threw a pass across his body into traffic. Jeff Brady intercepted it for the Vikings, and Fuad Reveiz wound up kicking a game-winning field goal as time ran out.

That was as livid as I have ever seen Mike Holmgren. Mike had a very tough time tolerating stupid mistakes, and that pass may have topped his all-time list of stupid mistakes. Rubley had also checked out of Mike's play, which was all-time stupid mistake No. 2.

Wolf went through the roof, too, but then there were so many "through the roofs" with Ron that I had gotten used to them. I'll never forget another time when we were in Minnesota, and I was sitting in the press box with Ron on my right and a female reporter on my left. Something happened on the opening kickoff that Ron didn't like, and the language he used was right off the docks.

I was so nervous that the only thing I could think of to do was act like I was totally occupied by my flip card. Nobody has ever turned a flip card over more than I did that day, trying to pretend that I hadn't heard a word that Ron was saying so that I wouldn't have to apologize to the woman for his language. And it just went on and on through the whole first half. I don't know where she went at halftime, but she never came back. That was Ron. When he was unhappy, you just had to let him go.

We wrapped up our first division championship since 1972 by beating Pittsburgh on Christmas Eve of 1995. We were winning, 24-19, with 16 seconds left and the Steelers had a fourth and goal from our six. Neil O'Donnell, their quarterback, was in the shotgun, and he threw a pass to Yancey Thigpen, who somehow had gotten wide open in the left corner of the north end zone. The pass went right through his fingertips, bounced off his thigh pads and hit the ground. Thigpen just knelt on the turf and stared, and somebody said that was the earliest Christmas present the Green Bay Packers had ever received. There was nobody within 10 yards of him, and he just dropped the ball. It was like a gift from God, and I was thrilled to death.

Atlanta came into Lambeau Field for the wild card game the next week and we won, 37-20, setting up a trip to San Francisco and what some people called our biggest victory since the Ice Bowl.

We were 10-point underdogs when we went out there for the divisional playoff game. The 49ers were the defending Super Bowl champions, but we beat them, 27-17. Right off the bat, Craig Newsome picked up a fumble and ran it 31 yards for a touchdown. Then Favre threw touchdown passes to Jackson and Mark Chmura. It was early in the second quarter, and we were ahead, 21-0, and the crowd was taken totally out of the game.

When it was over, Ron said to me, "We had to do that to show people we're a real football team, and by God that's what we did today." And he was right. Nobody could say we weren't legitimate now.

Brett had been beat up all year, and still he won his first Most Valuable Player award. It was one of those seasons when you'd see him in the locker room in the middle of the week and he could hardly move, but he'd come out of that tunnel on Sunday and be ready to go. He was maturing every year, and thanks to Mike, he was a little more under control. He became the first Packer to win an MVP since Bart Starr in 1966.

Everything was happening faster than I ever thought it could. I remember my son Michael saying to me one day, "Dad, I'd love to see you get a Super Bowl ring. You have a World Series ring, and wouldn't it be something if you got a Super Bowl ring?" And I remember thinking,

"Boy, Mike, we've got a long way to go before that happens."

This was right after Ron and Mike got here, and while I never doubted them I wasn't sure how soon something like that could happen after all of those frustrating years in the 70's and 80's. Ironically, I got the World Series ring in 1967 and I got the Super Bowl ring in 1997, and I wear it to every game.

I'll never forget the way the 1995 season ended. We went to Dallas for the NFC championship game, and we lost, 38-27. That was three years in a row that the Cowboys had knocked us out, and I was so sick and tired of going into that Dallas press box and walking out of the stadium after a loss. I thought it had to be our turn to beat these guys.

Barry Switzer was the Cowboys' coach then, and he said after the game that he thought it was the best the Packers had ever played against them. I took that as a sign that we were getting better and better.

But what I remember most of all was walking from the locker room to the bus. I was all by myself, and Brett came up behind me and put his arm around my shoulder and said, "I'm tired of losing here, Bob, but we're getting closer and closer to these guys. We're going to start beating the Cowboys."

I thought that was a great competitor talking to me. And he was right.

CHAPTER FIFTEEN
Farewell to Milwaukee

If anyone had told me in 1989 when I became president of the Packers that I'd have to move the team out of Milwaukee, I wouldn't have believed it was possible. It was the hardest thing I've ever had to do.

Milwaukee was another home for me, and it was certainly another home for this franchise. I used to go to the games at County Stadium when I was a student at Marquette. The people in the stands and their parents and their grandparents had supported the team for more than 60 years. Not only supported it, but helped save it. I'm not sure the Green Bay Packers could have existed in the 20's, 30's, 40's and even the 50's if they didn't have Milwaukee to go to.

But for years our coaches and general managers had been talking about playing all of our games in Green Bay. Forrest Gregg had complained about the grind of taking the two-hour bus ride to Milwaukee and the two hours coming back, and Ron Wolf and Mike Holmgren kept telling me that Lambeau Field was such a great stadium, with all of its mystique and atmosphere, so why couldn't we be there more often?

Our coaches were always very concerned about the north end zone at County Stadium because it was right on top of that third base dugout by the wall. The locker rooms were very inadequate, too, because they were baseball locker rooms, and the coaches hated having both benches on one side of the field. In reality, County Stadium was a baseball park, and it had passed its time for housing two franchises.

The thing that bothered Holmgren and Wolf the most, though, was that there wasn't a better place in the league to play than Lambeau Field, and we were going away from it four times a year. They thought we took away our home field advantage by going to Milwaukee.

I pointed out to them that we played very well in Milwaukee. In fact we had a better overall record there than we did at Lambeau Field, but that didn't make a difference to them. Ron would say it was still a road game if we had to put our guys on a bus and take them down there on a Saturday. The players would try to have their wives or girl friends bring their cars down, and then they would drive home. The coaches let them do that, which meant that we never had many people on the bus ride home. County Stadium just wasn't what Mike and Ron wanted, and I think it was because of what they had at Lambeau Field.

So it was certainly something I'd heard a lot about internally, but I had avoided making a move because I didn't want to hurt Milwaukee. And we could have lived with all of those issues if it weren't for the economics.

I'd always thought it was a huge advantage in a small city like Green Bay that as we kept raising ticket prices people didn't have to buy the whole season ticket package. I think it helped a lot of people in Green Bay to maintain their tickets, and at the same time I didn't ever want to overlook the fact that Milwaukee had been very faithful to the Green Bay Packers.

But Green Bay had grown a great deal since I'd come to town in 1971, and we had spent millions of dollars on improvements to Lambeau Field. We started adding private boxes in 1985, and that number just kept increasing. In fact we had plans to build 90 additional boxes in January of 1995, which meant by the fall of that year we were going to have 198 of them. They were already filled, and we had a waiting list of over 50 names. At County Stadium all we got was a percentage of the tickets and a small percentage of the parking and concessions. The gap in revenue between the two stadiums was going to grow and grow as we went into the future.

Every time John Underwood, our treasurer, would make a report to the Executive Committee or the Board of Directors, he would tell them that we were leaving $2.5 million on the table by playing four games in Milwaukee. Considering inflation, he said the Packers would lose more than $12 million over a four-year period by not playing all of their games in Green Bay.

We just had so many more sources of revenue at Lambeau Field than we did at County Stadium that the financial numbers were overwhelming. And as I watched the eyes of the Executive Committee and Board of Directors getting bigger every time John talked, I knew I didn't have any choice but to come up with a plan.

But that plan had to have one major theme. We weren't going to leave

Milwaukee without taking the fans with us. We could abandon the stadium, but we could never abandon the fans.

So I decided to sit down and start working on this myself to see if I couldn't develop something that we could live with and our fans could live with. When the problem first started hitting me, I thought, "How in the world am I ever going to do this?" And I would just sit there putting different things on a piece of paper. I knew we had to move, but how could we do it and still be fair to the fans in both places? Finally one day I came up with five or six points that I thought had to be included in any plan, and I started calling people.

The first call I made was to the league office to find out if I needed to go to the rest of the ownership to get permission to leave Milwaukee. I was told that because of the short distance between Milwaukee and Green Bay it wouldn't be a problem. The league people said they really looked at the Green Bay Packers as a state team, and I told them we weren't going to leave anybody behind.

We were going to give every single Milwaukee ticket holder a chance to come to Lambeau Field and be with us, and that helped me tremendously with the league office. They gave me their support because they knew that was my requirement.

The second person I called was Bud Selig, who owned the Milwaukee Brewers at that time. Bud and I had been good friends since the 1960's when I was with the St. Louis Cardinals and he was going to Major League Baseball meetings trying to get a franchise back in Milwaukee. We formed our friendship in those days because of my background at Marquette.

I had been talking to Bud for nine years about a new stadium in Milwaukee that would take care of both the Brewers and the Packers. He was confident in those early days that one would be built, and I'm sure he wanted us to be part of it. Bud wanted to make it good for the Green Bay Packers. He truly did.

I also spent a lot of time with Gabe Paul, Jr., who was Bud's stadium manager, and I kept holding out hope that a stadium would come. It never occurred to me in those first years that we would ever have to think about leaving Milwaukee. But this was going on forever, and after nine years with no stadium on the horizon and us looking at an overwhelming financial situation, we had to start thinking about leaving. If there had been a new stadium, I'm sure we would have stayed, but the nine years wore us down.

When I called Bud, I asked him what it would do to him and his chances of getting a new stadium if we left Milwaukee. I almost felt there was a sigh of relief in his voice when he said, "You know, Bob, quite honestly it would help us from a couple of standpoints. If we had a baseball-only park it would cut our cost by $20 to $25 million, and we could build a stadium that was much cozier because we wouldn't have to make it big enough to put a football field on it. We could bring the seats in closer to the field."

He and I kind of came to the conclusion that the Packers leaving would make it easier for the Milwaukee County Stadium Commission to get the financing it needed to build a new stadium and keep baseball in Milwaukee. I told him I would get back to him after I talked to my Executive Committee, and I said, "Bud, this has to stay between us because I haven't talked to anyone about it except the league office."

So now I had approval from the league and I had cleared it with Bud that this would help the Brewers as well as us. That's when I starting working out my plan.

I decided to give Green Bay one extra regular season game because I felt I had to give something to the Green Bay fans there who were expecting to get all 10 games including exhibitions if we ever moved. I gave Milwaukee Games 2 and 6 because I wanted the league, not the Packers, to decide who played before the Milwaukee fans and who played before the Green Bay fans.

I thought it would be good to give Milwaukee a game early in the season when there's so much excitement and then a game late enough that the fans there didn't lose interest. We changed from the sixth to the fifth game in 1997 because a number of fans pointed out that the sixth game usually fell around Thanksgiving when they either had kids coming home from college or relatives coming in for the holiday.

One of the questions someone brought up to me was, what would we do if the opponent for Game 2 or Game 5 was the Chicago Bears? That actually happened in 1996, and it went by quietly.

I also planned to keep a preseason game in the Milwaukee package because I wanted to maintain our relationship with the Midwest Shriners. The people in the private boxes and club seats at Lambeau Field would get all 10 games because putting Milwaukee fans in the boxes would really cause confusion. And I decided the Green Bay season ticket holders would get all the playoff games.

I struggled with all of this, particularly the playoff games, but I knew I was going to be hearing from Green Bay ticket holders saying, "Bob, you mean to tell me I've been sitting in those seats for 30 years and now somebody else is going to have them for three games?" And I had to say yes to that.

The biggest complaint I got from Milwaukee fans when it was all said and done was that they used to have four games, and now they had only three. They wanted to know why we had taken a game away from them. And I would explain that Green Bay ticket holders thought they would have all 10 games, and they were losing three. That kind of helped both sides understand it.

My next thought was to go to our ticket office and get it on board. It was a two-person staff then, and I knew this was going to create a great deal more work for them. So I took the plan to Mark Wagner, our ticket manager, and Carol Edwin, his assistant, and Mark brought up a very valid point. He pointed out that we had a huge waiting list for tickets in Green Bay, and we could easily fill Lambeau Field for all 10 games.

There was no doubt that he was right, but I told Mark that wasn't the right way to do it. My bottom line was we weren't going to make the move until we knew we could bring the Milwaukee fans with us. And Mark understood. "We'll find a way to work it out," he said.

I didn't want to get involved in the political process in Milwaukee through all of this, so I decided not to deal with Mayor John Norquist or County Executive Tom Ament. I didn't know Ament at all, but I did know Norquist a little bit, and I know he was disappointed. He asked me one time after we'd made the move, "Why didn't we ever know that this was a possibility?" I told him we'd been waiting for nine years for a new stadium in Milwaukee, and it just hadn't happened. Reality had to set in eventually. I told him you can't run any business and keep watching money go out the door.

Interestingly enough, I attended various functions with Norquist after that happened, and it was very cordial. It wasn't like he would just turn around and ignore me. He'd come over and talk. He didn't seem resentful at all.

I knew, too, that our move would have a big commercial impact in Milwaukee, and I did call the Pfister Hotel to explain what we were going to do. We'd been staying there for years, and they loved having the

Green Bay Packers there. There was one year when Forrest Gregg moved the team to a hotel in Brookfield, but we went back to the Pfister in a hurry.

I called Rosemary Steinfest, the Pfister manager at the time, and told her we were going to make an announcement. I always told Rosemary that staying at her hotel was one of the delights of making the trip to Milwaukee. But we just had too many problems. I said I was sorry we were making the move. She didn't like losing us, but she had been a friend for a long time, and she was very good about it.

I went to the Executive Committee in October of 1994, and I think they were a little startled when I went through my whole plan. I really hadn't told anybody ahead of time that I wanted to do this, and the first big problem they had was the idea of leaving Milwaukee.

I told them that this was the toughest thing I had ever worked on, and I'd been working on it for three months. I didn't think it made any sense for a small-market team to lose $12 million over a four-year period. I also mentioned that we had spent $28 million in the previous 13 years on improvements to our stadium and our administration building, and we had another $8 million on the table for the addition of 90 private boxes in the north end zone.

I got the unanimous approval of the Committee, and it really wasn't a tough sell because I didn't just go in and say, "You know, I'm thinking about leaving Milwaukee." Instead I told them, "I think we have to leave Milwaukee, and here's why, and here's my plan to make it smooth." I remember Don Schneider said it was a great plan, and he thought people would buy it.

We had a Board of Directors meeting scheduled for October 12, and I told the Executive Committee that I'd like to go to the Board, not so much for its approval but just to let it know what we were going to do. Normally we would just make an announcement, and the Board would accept it because the Board had given the Executive Committee authority to make decisions like this. But I wanted to make sure everybody was with us on this.

We had the Board meeting scheduled for 3 o'clock in the afternoon, and we had a press conference set for 5. I went through my entire plan and said I was not really asking for a vote. But Gene Sladky, a member of the Board, stood up and said this was a major decision that was going to affect the entire state of Wisconsin, and he thought it was important that the Board give me its unanimous approval. And so we put a resolution on the table, and the members did approve it.

Then we had the press conference. I had kept all of this quiet as long as I could. I had started working on it in July, and I didn't call the league office until mid-September, so for more than two months it was just me working on it and deciding what to do. But the story started to leak the week of the announcement, and I don't know why it did. Stations televised the press conference live, and it was probably as high a profile issue as we've ever dealt with here.

The press conference was packed, and the rumor of what we were going to do was out there. I remember that Bud Lea of the Milwaukee *Sentinel* stopped by to see me that afternoon before I went to the press conference. I had been dealing with Bud for years, and he said, "Are you really going to leave Milwaukee?" And I told him, "Bud, I have to, but believe me I have a plan, and if people will just listen to us, it will be fine."

The headline in the *Sentinel* the next morning was "The Pack won't be back." I was always amazed that I didn't get more harsh letters and phone calls than I did.

I was pleased when 96% of the Milwaukee fans took the "Gold" ticket package at Lambeau Field. To identify the ticket packages we simply used Green for the Green Bay fans and Gold for the Milwaukee fans. People would tell me that it was much more fun to see a game at Lambeau Field than it was at County Stadium. County Stadium was a baseball park, and they loved coming up here. After awhile people told me they were making it a weekend event, coming up on Friday night or Saturday morning and staying until the game.

Some Milwaukee fans were disappointed that they didn't get more playoff tickets, but as time went by we were fortunate enough to make a lot of playoff appearances, and so more and more tickets were available for Milwaukee fans for those games.

To this day, I'll have people calling me about something else and in the course of the conversation they'll say, "By the way, I have the Gold package. Thank you for not forgetting Milwaukee. Thanks a lot for including us." And I always tell them the same thing. It was the right thing to do.

What could have been a public relations disaster for this franchise truly turned out to be a public relations plus. Wayne Larrivee, who is our radio play-by-play announcer now, told me one time that I should write a public relations book just on getting out of Milwaukee.

We were six games into the '94 season when we made the announcement. I thought we owed it to the fans to let them know as soon as possible what was going on, but I couldn't do it before the season started because my plan wasn't complete. I was still juggling numbers and moving things around at that point, and I wanted to be comfortable with it before I went to anybody.

We still had two games to play in Milwaukee when we had the press conference, and it didn't seem to affect the attendance at either game. We drew 54,995 for Detroit on November 6 and 54,885 for Atlanta on December 18.

Of course there were problems. Marv Fishman, who had been one of the founders of the Milwaukee Bucks, explored the possibility of bringing in a Canadian Football League franchise to play at County Stadium, and we didn't like to hear about somebody coming in so close to us. But I felt that down deep the history and tradition of this franchise would outweigh any kind of ball club that he brought into the city. I still feel that way today. Every game we have had here since 1960 has been a sell-out, so we're still going to be the show, and that's what's important. Nothing came of the CFL talk, and I had no plans to resist that.

Working out the Lambeau Field seat locations for the Milwaukee fans was a big problem, but then we had had problems at County Stadium, too. I remember one year the Brewers changed the seating configuration in left field, and Marge Paget, who ran our Milwaukee ticket office at that time, was calling me all of the time about the headaches she was having moving people. If they were moved two feet in another direction they would call and be very upset about it.

We did have a lot of that, but I knew in the beginning when I walked in on Mark and Carol and told them what I wanted to do that I was piling a huge workload on their desks. They worked it all out and did a tremendous job.

And then there was the traffic. I remember sitting in the booth with Ron Wolf before the first Gold game at Lambeau Field and looking at people coming off of Highway 43. It was bumper-to-bumper 20 minutes before game time.

But it was amazing how quickly the Milwaukee fans found alternate routes to get here and figured out where to go. They'd tell me they didn't even try to get into the stadium parking lot because they knew someone who would let them park in their front yard for 10 bucks. By the end of the first year you could see the change. They were savvy travelers. They solved it.

My biggest concern is still night games. When the league asks us whether we have any stadium requests I ask to have noon starting times scheduled for Games 2 and 5. But I haven't always done real well with that. Sometimes the league will help me, and sometimes it won't. When it won't, it will say it's in a rating period or the game is huge or something like that. Several times they've given me night games, and I do worry about that. I also worry about icy roads for that Game 5.

Still the pleasure of coming to Lambeau Field and seeing a football game there as opposed to watching one at County Stadium has proved to be a huge factor in our favor.

We played at County Stadium for the last time on December 18, and it was a memorable game. Brett Favre dived into the end zone in the last second to beat Atlanta, 21-17, and I only wish I'd been there to see the play. But Madeline and I were heading home on Highway 43 when that happened. We had left the stadium in the fourth quarter under police escort.

Two weeks before the game, both the Green Bay and the Milwaukee police came to me and said that they wanted to get Madeline and me out of the stadium before the game ended. I always sat in the press box at Milwaukee, and Madeline sat with the Board of Directors in the baseball press box behind home plate in the north end zone, and the police suggested that they come and get each of us midway through the final period and escort us to our car.

I hadn't given much thought to the idea that we were in any kind of physical danger, but they pointed out that all it would take would be one loony in the crowd who was upset that this was the last game in Milwaukee, and he might make up his mind to find me or my wife. I appreciated their concern, particularly for Madeline, because I had asked her if she wanted to stay home from this game. But she said, "If you're going, then I'm going."

We walked into the stadium together that day without any police protection. I kept my head down most of the time, and it was fine. In fact, I had some people say hello as I walked in. I was a little uncomfortable, but there were no threats at all.

Then with about seven minutes left in the game, I was sitting in the front row of the press box when I turned around and saw three policemen waiting to take me out of the stadium. I asked them if anyone was with Madeline, and they said someone had already gone to pick her up.

Fortunately it was an exciting game, and it was very quiet on the ramp as they led me down to the concourse. The three policemen were walking about five feet in front of me and we were halfway down the third ramp when all at once I heard somebody coming up behind me and running like crazy. I was just about to grab a policeman and tell him, "Here comes somebody" when I turned around and saw Mark Schiefelbein of our public relations staff. He was running down to the field because it was his job to get the stars of the games lined up for TV interviews if we won. The one loony turned out to be someone on our staff. Schief and I joke about that to this day.

Once he'd gone by, the police took me down to the lot where the Brewers players park during the summer. I met Madeline and they put us in the car and had us lock the doors and drive away. They were still standing there watching us as we drove up that little hill away from County Stadium.

We listened to the rest of the game on the radio, and we were 20 miles out of town by the time Brett scored. It killed me to walk away from that game, but the two of us cheered like crazy when Jim Irwin described him diving into the end zone. We were thrilled to death. When we got home that night we watched the highlights over and over.

I found out later that Mike Holmgren had climbed up on a snowbank after the game and blown kisses at the people as he said good bye to Milwaukee. Of course we were in Port Washington by then. It was a great gesture on his part, and the fans loved it.

As it turned out, none of my worst fears about making the move from Milwaukee were realized. If I had known that, I guess I could have saved myself a lot of grief. I tell people now that the two best business decisions made while I've been president have been renovating Lambeau Field and moving out of Milwaukee.

But we never could have done it if we hadn't taken the fans with us.

CHAPTER SIXTEEN

America's Real Team

I just wanted it to be over.

It was halftime at the Super Bowl, and we were ahead, 27-14, but all I could think about was how much I wanted the game to end right there. I was sitting by myself in the press box, and I didn't want to talk to anybody. I was so worried about a second-half disaster.

And the New England Patriots did come back and cut it to 27-21, but that didn't last long. Desmond Howard took the ensuing kickoff at the one-yard line and ran 99 yards for the touchdown, and that's when I finally started to relax. I thought, "We're actually going to win this thing."

Then Reggie White took the game over in the fourth quarter, and the Green Bay Packers were World Champions again.

I know every city appreciates a champion, but this was special. There was something extra about it because we had done it so much in the 60's. And then we had this forlorn feeling that it had passed us by forever. It was hard to imagine after living through the 70's and 80's that we could be this good again.

I truly realized how fortunate I was. I had gone through two World Series, and I knew what it felt like to win one, and I knew what it felt like to lose one. So to win a Super Bowl was such a great feeling, and I was thrilled that I had had an opportunity to be part of it.

Commissioner Paul Tagliabue came to town about three months after the game to talk to our Executive Committee, and he said that the Green Bay Packers winning the Super Bowl was the best thing to happen to professional sports in years. He said this was small town America, blue collar America, and it took everybody back to simpler times.

I thought he put it so well. I also got a kick out of him saying it because of what had happened with him immediately after the game.

With about five minutes to play, the security people had come to take Ron Wolf and me to the field. We got on the elevator, and the only other people on it were the commissioner and his wife. When we stepped on, Mrs. Tagliabue reached over and grabbed my arm and said, "Congratulations."

Since the game wasn't officially over, Paul really had a tough time with that. He pushed her hand away and told her, "No. No. Don't say anything." And down to the ground we went with no one saying another word.

I really do think the commissioner was pleased for our franchise, but I could see his point. He was responsible to all 32 teams, and he wasn't about to show any favoritism at that point. Still I really enjoyed Chan doing that.

Getting that championship trophy was an amazing feeling. It's something you always hope and pray for, but so many things have to fall into place for it to happen. You have to have some bounces go your way, and you can't be devastated by injuries.

We did have some key injuries, but Ron's ability to pick up players in the off-season was remarkable. All season long the people he got stepped forward when we needed them. This was a team that had been built very carefully, and it had so many strong parts. Ron just kept putting the pieces together, and Mike Holmgren just drove that team until it succeeded.

I've always thought that Ron's off-season in 1996 was his best. When you looked back at what happened during the year you thought, "Thank the Lord he got the players here that he did."

We had 11 unrestricted free agents in January, and Ron told me that his biggest priority in that group was to make sure we re-signed tight end Mark Chmura. He got that done on February 15, and then in the first week of March he signed Tampa Bay free agent Santana Dotson, who joined Reggie White, Sean Jones and Gilbert Brown to give us as solid a defensive line as we've ever had.

In April he signed receiver Don Beebe, who had been released by Carolina, and in June he made a trade with Seattle for safety Eugene Robinson. Then he re-signed Keith Jackson in early July, and a few days after that he got Howard.

It was an off-season that was filled not only with acquisitions but with a great deal of turmoil. In May Brett Favre announced that he was going to voluntarily enter the NFL substance abuse program to deal with his problem with Vicodin. It was a very emotional time for this organization, and I thought what Brett said at the press conference was very interesting. He told everyone, "My main objective is to get better for myself and for my family and to help this football team. I want to return to the level where I was before and to play in the Super Bowl." And ironically, he was on the verge of doing just that.

This was a very difficult time for Brett for a lot of reasons. During training camp, one of his best friends was killed. He was riding in a car driven by Brett's brother Scott in Mississippi, and Scott was found to be driving under the influence. A month later, his sister Brandi was involved in a drive-by shooting.

Brett was obviously concerned about all that had happened, but I think he handles these things the way he handles it when he's hit hard on the field. He's always going to get up and walk back to the huddle and be fine. That's the competitor in him. He's going to beat everything, including the team on the field or his problems off of it.

I was most concerned about the Vicodin situation because he had been so quiet that day when I talked to him in the hallway before the press conference. You just had to worry, "Can he beat this? And if he does, what's he going to be like once the season gets here?"

Brett made his announcement in May, which didn't leave us a lot of time before the start of training camp. Ron kept trying to convince me that everything was going to be all right, but you had to wonder if Brett was going to come back as the same person that he was before. Fortunately he did.

When the NFL released its 1996 regular season schedule in April it showed that the Packers had become an elite team. We had a club record four prime time appearances scheduled on national television. Three of our games were on ABC Monday Night Football, including two at Lambeau Field, which marked the first time in the history of the team that we were playing two Monday night games at home in one season.

We hadn't played host to a Monday night game since 1986, and the last time we'd had three Monday night games was 1983. We were back where I had always hoped Ron and Mike would put us.

As we got close to the start of training camp, Brett came back and discussed his six weeks in the substance abuse program at the Menninger Clinic in Topeka, Kansas. He was very blunt about it. He said he'd let things get out of hand. "If I'd never played football I wouldn't have taken the pain medication," he said, "but eventually it became a problem as the injuries kept piling up. All of a sudden I just started taking pills, and there was a snowball effect. Right now I no longer have a dependency on Vicodin or any other pain medication. I feel good about the year, and mentally I'm ready to go."

He was very upbeat compared to the somber press conference we'd had in May. The whole room was upbeat. Everyone felt the problem was behind us, and I thought that gave us a wonderful start to training camp.

Ron said he really felt good about what we had going into the season, and Ron is not prone to saying things like that. He told me, "I don't know if our record is going to be any better than it was last year, but I do know we're a better team than we were last year." This was as positive as any team I'd ever been around.

We opened the season in Tampa Bay, and everybody wanted to see what Brett was going to be like. He proved that he was not only back but he was going to be better than ever. We won, 34-3, and he completed 20 of 27 passes for 247 yards and four touchdowns with no interceptions.

What really jumped out at everybody, though, was how much our defense had improved. We had four interceptions and recovered two fumbles that day, and the year before we didn't get our sixth turnover until our seventh game. Reggie was becoming more dominant than ever, and Gilbert was stepping in as a really strong contributor when earlier there had been some questions about him. Philadelphia came to Lambeau Field the next week for the first Monday night game in Green Bay in 10 years, and we got four more turnovers to take a 30-7 halftime lead in a 39-13 victory. Brett was spectacular again, completing 17 of 31 passes for 261 yards and three touchdowns.

We beat San Diego, 42-10, at home the next week to go 3-0, but then we went to the Minnesota Metrodome where we'd had so many problems in the past. The star of that game was the Vikings' defense. They handled us, 30-21, getting four turnovers and seven sacks. The sacks were a big concern because we had a problem at left tackle.

Ken Ruettgers, who had been so solid there for 12 years, just couldn't come back from the knee surgery he'd had in March. He was on the physically unable to perform list for the first six weeks of the season, and we put John Michels, our first-round draft choice, in his spot. Kenny came back for the Dallas game, but then he hung it up. His knee just hurt too much for him to keep playing.

I don't know that anyone thought John would have to step in and play as much as he did. We wound up replacing him in the lineup in the last week of the regular season with veteran Bruce Wilkerson, another player Ron had signed as a free agent. The sad thing was a great deal of time had been devoted to taking Michels. I remember Ron saying we had spent a lot of time studying him before we drafted him. But he was only with us for two seasons.

We bounced back quickly from the Minnesota game by winning, 31-10, at Seattle, and the turnovers kept coming. Dotson recovered a fumble, and Robinson, White, Craig Newsome and Doug Evans all had interceptions. Then we went to Chicago and beat the Bears, 37-6, when Brett had another big night with 246 yards passing and four touchdowns. The team was so consistent. We weren't having any big letdowns.

We played our second Monday night game at Lambeau Field before a record crowd of 60,716 and beat San Francisco, 23-20, in a very dramatic game that Chris Jacke won for us. He kicked a 31-yard field goal with 8 seconds to play to send the game into overtime, and then he kicked a 53-yarder 3 minutes and 41 seconds into the overtime to give us the victory.

But we suffered a huge loss in that game when wide receiver Robert Brooks tore up his right knee on our first offensive play and was lost for the season. Here was where one of Ron's off-season finds really came through as Don Beebe caught 11 passes for 220 yards. Our fans hardly knew Beebe, but he had a career best that night.

We lost Antonio Freeman in the next game at Tampa Bay with a broken bone in his arm. Brett was held without a touchdown pass for the first time in 18 games, but the defense continued to dominate. Evans and Robinson both had interceptions, and Reggie blocked a punt for the first time in his career. We won the game, 13-7, and when it was over Tony Dungy, the Buccaneers coach, said the Packers had the best defensive team he had seen in the last six or seven years.

We were missing our top two receivers now, but our back-ups really came through. Beebe replaced Brooks, and Terry Mickens, who had missed the first eight games with a severe ankle injury, took over for Freeman. Mickens caught seven passes for 52 yards and two touchdowns, and Beebe had four catches for 106 yards and a 65-yard touchdown late in the third quarter as we beat Detroit, 28-18, at Lambeau.

It was then that we hit the only roadblock we had all year as once again we played three road games in a row. That was Ron's big bugaboo, and he had a fit about it. "They did it to us before, and they've done it to us again," he said.

Ron would always call Dick Maxwell in the league office to complain whenever we were scheduled for three in a row on the road. He and Maxwell were good friends, and after Ron retired I would see Dick in the press box and ask him if he got any phone calls from Wolf anymore. "None at all," Dick would tell me.

We lost the first two road games to Kansas City and Dallas, and we were afraid we were headed for a major slump when we played a terrible first half at St. Louis.

Injuries continued to plague our receivers when Chmura suffered a torn arch in his left foot in the first quarter of a 27-20 loss to the Chiefs. He was expected to miss four to six weeks, and I couldn't help wondering why this kept happening at one position. Especially when we were relying so much on our outstanding quarterback and talking about how we wanted to surround him with weapons.

You hear coaches say that losing players is part of the game, and when it happens other people have to step up. That's why you pay those other people. Our back-ups were responding about as well as back-ups possibly could, but then we lost, 21-6, at Dallas, and our wide receivers caught just seven passes for 51 yards. That's when Ron claimed Andre Rison off waivers.

Andre had been released by Jacksonville, and he came with a disruptive reputation. I'm not sure Ron would have taken him if we had done better in Dallas. That reputation certainly wasn't something he or Mike turned their backs on. Whether it was a draft choice or a free agent or someone claimed on waivers, they always talked about whether the guy had baggage. The biggest concern was, in this little town where do you hide somebody? And of course you don't. At the same time, they were willing to give players a chance.

Rison was at the very twilight of his career when we brought him in, and Ron told me, "We'll talk to him. If he doesn't work out, he's out of here." He said it wouldn't be long term in any case. We basically rented Andre for the rest of the season.

I'm sure Ron and Mike did sit down with Andre and talk to him about what was expected of him. Those are two pretty stern guys, and if you get them in your face telling you that they're going to give you a great opportunity but at the same time they expect you to behave yourself and do your job, you listen.

Andre didn't cause us any problems at all. You can talk to Andre Rison to this day, and he raves about his stay in Green Bay.

The Dallas game ended on a controversial note when Barry Switzer, the Cowboys coach, called time out in the final 30 seconds of a game they were leading, 18-6, so that he could send in his place-kicker. Chris Boniol needed one more field goal to give him an NFL record seven in seven tries that day, and Switzer had decided to give him a chance to set the record. He made the kick, but when Reggie saw him call the time out, he ran across the field toward the Cowboys' bench and pointed his finger and shouted at Switzer. I could tell he was very upset.

I wouldn't say there was bad blood between the Cowboys and us. The basic problem with Dallas was we had been going there for so many years, and they just kept beating us. They had won six games in a row against us, and all of them had been in Dallas. People kept saying to me, "What's going on that we just keep playing there all the time? Are they ever going to come to Green Bay?"

We went to St. Louis the next week to play a nationally televised game on ESPN, and we found ourselves trailing, 9-3, at halftime. It was the one time I had serious doubts about our season. We had stumbled twice, and we just weren't getting anything done. What's more, we had the Bears and Denver coming up. You just didn't want the slide to keep going.

And then on the second play of the third quarter, Evans intercepted a pass and returned it 32 yards for a touchdown to give us the lead for the first time. Brett came back and threw two touchdown passes, and we won the game, 24-9. Doug's interception was exactly what we needed. I think everyone believed we were going to be all right after that play. We were 9-3, and we had a three-game lead over Minnesota in the division.

Desmond Howard started to do great things for us in the Bears game the next week when he returned a punt for 75 yards and a touchdown and we won, 28-17. It was our sixth victory in a row over Chicago, which was something that hadn't happened since 1930.

Denver came to town the next week, and the Broncos were red hot. They were 12-1 with a nine-game winning streak, and this was supposed to be the marquee game in the league. But it didn't turn out that way. John Elway, Denver's All-Pro quarterback, didn't play because of a hamstring injury, and we won, 41-6.

Three days earlier, Philadelphia had lost to Indianapolis, putting us in the playoffs for the fourth season in a row. We also won our second straight division title, marking the first time in 29 years that we'd done that back-to-back. These were huge steps for this organization, and we didn't lose another game for the rest of the season.

We finished up by beating Detroit, 31-3, when Howard returned five punts for 167 yards, and whipping the Vikings, 38-10, at Lambeau Field in a game where we scored 28 unanswered points. Jeff Brady, the Minnesota linebacker who had played for us for one season in 1992, created a fuss when he said the week before the game that he was going to go "head hunting" in Green Bay. It didn't make any difference. We were playing so well that we didn't need any extra fuel from Brady.

The Wednesday after the Denver game we extended Reggie's contract for five years. He could have become an unrestricted free agent in February, and we didn't want that. The next day Reggie, Brett and LeRoy Butler were named NFC starters for the Pro Bowl and Keith Jackson was picked as a back-up. Then Brett was named the NFL's Most Valuable Player for the second year in a row.

San Francisco came to town on January 4 for the NFC divisional play-off game, and the weather was horrible. It was 34 degrees with a 20 mile per hour wind and a 9 degree wind chill factor, and there was a steady downpour all day. But we had a record crowd of 60,787, and it was announced that we had only three no-shows.

I have some doubts about that no-show count, but I can tell you the fans stuck with us to the very end. Nobody left the stadium because people were so hungry for playoff football in Green Bay. This hadn't happened in a long time, and they didn't know when it was going to happen again.

Two minutes into the game Howard returned a punt 71 yards for a touchdown, and shortly after that he took one back 46 yards to set up Brett's touchdown pass to Rison that put us ahead, 14-0. We won, 35-14, and it was a monumental day for this franchise.

Fifteen minutes after the game, a league official came to me and said we would have to completely re-sod the field for the conference championship game the next week. The grass had been torn up so badly in the rain that he didn't even have to go down and look at it.

The league sent Chip Toma, its field and turf consultant, to Green

Bay on Monday, and 28 trucks started delivering 85,000 cubic feet of sod from a Maryland farm on Tuesday. We had at least 50 people working on the field all week, and they had the job done Thursday night. The league insisted that we do it, and the league paid for it. Meanwhile, we made good use of the field that had been replaced. We sold it one piece at a time.

We cut up the sod in five-inch by five-inch squares, put the squares in little boxes and sold them for $10 a box. We sold 25,000 of those boxes, with all of the proceeds going to charity. A lot of people could hardly wait to get their own little piece of Lambeau Field history. The sale was supposed to start at 9 o'clock, and when I drove to work a little after 7 that morning, there were already cars parked on the street waiting to get in.

I have never seen Wisconsin go so crazy over the Packers. I wasn't in this part of the state during the Lombardi years, but I'm not even sure those teams captured the people the way this one did. People just loved the fact that we were back on top.

I heard from so many businessmen who said the Packers had brought pride back to our town. Our own team store did a magnificent business with souvenirs and licensed products. Every place you went you saw "Titletown Again." It really was resurrected.

The weather for the conference championship game with Carolina was even worse than it was for the San Francisco game, but we still had 60,216 people there. It was 3 degrees with a minus-17 wind chill, and the team got off to a bad start. Brett turned the ball over twice, and Carolina got 10 quick points.

But then we went 71 yards in 15 plays to take a 14-10 lead in the second quarter, and we went on to win, 30-13. Except for the Ice Bowl, this was the most memorable game Green Bay had ever seen.

As Ron and I stood in the end zone waiting to receive the trophy from George Halas' daughter, Virginia McCaskey, who owns the Chicago Bears, we saw fans everywhere jumping up and down like they were half crazy. My son Michael was there with friends, and he told me that he saw people all around him crying. In fact he said he was crying.

You can't imagine how emotional it was unless you were standing down there looking at it. As cold as it was, people just didn't want to leave. They stayed and stayed and stayed, cherishing the moment.

We accepted the trophy, and that's when I said, "This is America's real team." To be honest about it, that wasn't totally spontaneous. I had felt that way all along, and I thought about it for a while before I went out there. And then I decided, "By gosh, I'm going to say it."

I don't think I've ever been as emotional as I was after the Carolina game. I went into the locker room, and six or seven people started interviewing me. Jessie Garcia from Channel 4 in Milwaukee asked me how I felt standing in that north end zone, and as I described the excitement in the stands I discovered that the longer I talked the more emotional I got. Finally I couldn't talk at all. That had never happened to me before.

And then came the Super Bowl.

We talked to clubs that had been through Super Bowls to get an idea of what we as an organization had to do to prepare for it, and they all told us that tickets would be our biggest concern. They also told us to be sure to get things done before we got to New Orleans.

You have two weeks between the conference championship games and the Super Bowl, and you have to get your game plan together and be ready to go in that first week because the second one is a circus. There are so many obligations and so many things you have to do with the media then. Once you get to the site, it's just a lot of trying to keep everybody happy.

There's no question that tickets are a hassle. I always have a huge Super Bowl list anyway, and it was obviously extra large in '96. Some of the ticket requests I got were from people I thought were dead. We got 10,000 tickets from the league at $275 apiece, and we held a lottery for both the Green and Gold package season ticket holders. Each winner got two tickets.

We tried to get that done as quickly as we could because we also had to handle travel arrangements for more than 500 people and try to make sure that every family was comfortable. It's a big responsibility, and the biggest problem is you're fighting for time.

We had a huge staff working from early in the morning until late at night trying to coordinate everything and keep everybody happy, and they were handling some disgruntled people at times. Everybody wanted it to be smooth, and I thought it went pretty darn well.

On the Sunday before the game, we chartered a DC-10 for the team and most of our front office. There were close to 100 people on that flight because we had to set up an actual office in our hotel in New Orleans for the week before the game. Then on Thursday we chartered a

747 for our Board members and emeritus directors and their families and the rest of our party, including the families of the coaches, players and front office staff. There were more than 400 people on that flight. We wanted to make sure that anyone on our staff who wanted to go had the chance.

Every day we were in New Orleans presented new problems, but you figured as soon as you got to the game, those problems would go away. By Tuesday or Wednesday of that second week, I'm sure the team was thinking, "Let's get on with it. Let's play the game." And I was feeling the same way.

Super Bowl XXXI brought together the two highest-scoring teams in the NFL, and we jumped on the New England Patriots in a hurry, taking a 10-0 lead in the first six minutes. Rison caught a 54-yard touchdown pass from Brett on just the second play from scrimmage, and two plays later Evans made a terrific interception right along the sidelines to set up a 37-yard field goal by Jacke. We had three more scoring drives in the first half, giving us that 27-14 lead and making me wish the game was over as I sat in the press box.

When the game finally ended and we had won, 35-21, Ron and I went down to the field and stood in the end zone. There were fans yelling at Ron and celebrating with him, and he was waving back to them. It was a moment of great satisfaction for him, and it should have been.

At the awards ceremony, I said, "The Lombardi Trophy is going where it belongs. It's going home to Green Bay, Wisconsin." I said it because I believed it. We are America's team. We're owned by our fans, and we have a soft spot in the heart of anyone who loves football.

Afterwards Ron and I went into the locker room, which can best be described as pandemonium. There was just such total happiness. The coaches were going around shaking the hands of all the players and thanking them, and there was media everywhere. It was not only very happy, it was very crowded.

A lot of electronic media was lined up out on the field to do more interviews, and by this time the stadium was empty and most of the lights were turned off. After I made a series of stops with the radio and TV people, I walked back to the hotel with Kevin and Bryan.

Madeline had already gone back with the front office bus, and Mike was with some friends, but Kevin and Bryan had stayed in the stadium a little bit and waited for me. The three of us walked back right down the middle of the street because I guess we thought we owned New Orleans at that point.

The street was pretty empty until we got to a big bus full of people standing and celebrating. It turned out that they were from Appleton, and as we began walking by they started screaming. So we went over and talked to them. As I recall, Kevin and Bryan were smoking cigars, and I might have been smoking one myself for all I know. We posed for a lot of pictures and had a great time with those people.

The game had been over for more than an hour before we got back to the hotel and went up to the floor where our team party was being held. It was just jammed with players, coaches and families, and as I walked in, Madeline spotted me and came running over.

The party was wonderful. It was a $200,000 affair that we were going to have, win or lose, and it was packed. It also lasted a very long time. We left at around 2:30, and the boys may have stayed longer than that. I think there were still some people there at 4 in the morning. I just know it was a quiet plane ride home as people tried to recover.

The reception we got when we returned home was just unbelievable. The wind chill was a minus-10 degrees that day, but people just stood outside in the streets and waited for us. Thousands more waited in the stadium for who knows how long because it took us three hours to get our bus parade through town, and they had been in the stadium for a couple of hours before we got back.

At least the people in the streets could move around a little bit and try to keep active while they waited for us. Every inch of the way we went on that bus tour there were people waving and holding up signs. People talk about ticker tape parades, but there was never anything warmer than the welcome we got on that cold day.

It was dark when we got to the stadium, and the lights were on. A lot of our people were numb because they had been in open buses. They had to have the buses open so that the people could feel that they were a part of everything.

I was fine because I was in a closed bus with the Executive Committee, but Mike Holmgren told me he had no feeling in his feet. Mike wasn't a very happy camper. Our marketing department had planned that parade coming home, and Mike was not pleased with the marketing people at that point. I felt sorry for him. He was really miserable.

I think somebody gave him a policeman's jacket to wear in the locker room. The buses went around to the back of the stadium, and then we came through the visitors' locker room and down through the visitors' tunnel to the stadium. The roar of approval and the love that was shown in the stadium when the coaches and players came out on to the field was something I'll never forget.

The final celebration of the season took place in May when we were invited to the White House, and that caused some controversy. Four of our players weren't there, and one of them had his picture taken wearing a Chicago Bears jersey.

Chmura declined to make the trip for political reasons. He just didn't like Bill Clinton. Back-up quarterback Jim McMahon was the man with the Bears jersey. McMahon had been the Bears quarterback when they won the Super Bowl in 1985, but their White House visit had been canceled by the Challenger space shuttle tragedy. He wanted a picture of himself as a Bear at the White House for his family and for his scrapbook. So he wore the jersey under his shirt, and just as they were getting ready to take the picture he took the shirt off really fast. You had to know Jim. Everything he did was off the wall.

The other players who weren't there were Jacke, Rison and Howard, all of whom had left the team by the time the picture was taken. Rison had been released, while Howard had signed with Oakland as a free agent, and Wolf hadn't offered a contract to Jacke, who was an unrestricted free agent. Mike and Ron had decided not to invite any of the three, and it was strictly their call. I'd always felt very strongly about letting the coach and general manager run their football team, and so I continued to let them run their football team.

While Rison, Howard and Jacke were gone the following season, most of our players were back, and I believe to this day that that was a team that probably should have won two and maybe three Super Bowls. I really thought 1996 was just the beginning. Ted Thompson and I still talk about that now. You look back and you're upset with yourself because it's so tough to get there and you don't know how hard it's going to be to get back.

I guess you can make a case like that for a lot of teams. I think, for instance, that everybody in 1985 thought the Chicago Bears would win it for years and years, but they never got back to the Super Bowl. Different things go wrong.

Still, we had Brett in the prime of his career, and we had a very solid defense that didn't have a lot of age on it. The pieces were there.

CHAPTER SEVENTEEN
The One That Got Away

There's nothing like being a world champion. It's a high that doesn't end in a hurry, which was why 1265 Lombardi Avenue was a great address for a long time after we won Super Bowl XXXI. There was a huge sense of pride among the people in our building.

We had a wonderful time working on the Super Bowl ring. I basically asked Ron Wolf and Mike Holmgren to do it, and then we showed the design to the Executive Committee. We wanted very few people in the organization to know what the rings would look like beforehand. We presented 165 of them at a dinner at the Oneida Golf and Country Club where everyone received a box and opened it at the same time. It was a great thrill to be able to reward everyone for their hard work. You might never experience something like that again.

But it was very different the next year when I went back to Mike and Ron and asked them to help design an NFC championship ring. Ron didn't want much to do with that. "It's a ring for a loser," he said. "It's something you get because you lost the Super Bowl. I'll never wear it." And he was absolutely right. That just shows the monumental difference between winning and losing the Super Bowl.

In many ways, 1997 was a great season, but we let the game we should have won slip away from us . I always felt after this team won its first world championship that it was good enough to win another one and maybe even two more. It was a wonderful team, and it was a shame we didn't get it done against Denver the next year because I still think we were the better club. It was the most disappointing loss I've had since I've been with the Packers.

I remember sitting across from Don Beebe, our veteran wide receiver, on a bus that was going from the stadium to the airport after a pre-season game that year, and he said to me, "This is an awesome team. It's the best I've ever been a part of. I wouldn't be surprised if we went undefeated."

Don had been to four Super Bowls with Buffalo, and he wasn't making a big announcement. It was just a private conversation, but he said that none of those Buffalo teams was as good as this one. I couldn't disagree with him. I thought we were really going to dominate.

You always worry about the players' attitude coming back from a championship season, but I thought Ron and Mike did a good job of keeping them on an even keel. We had more guys than usual getting radio shows and things like that, but they came back in a very good frame of mind. I don't think there was any overconfidence.

We had a couple of monumental signings during the off-season. In April we extended Ron's contract through 2002. He was the best general manager in the National Football League, and I wanted to make sure we were paying him that way. I also wanted him to have a long term contract, so that if other clubs called about him I could say he was signed for six years. I didn't need someone coming in here and destroying us. We had a great partnership with Mike and Ron, and I didn't want it to end.

And then on July 25 we signed Brett to a seven-year deal that made him the highest-paid player in the NFL, surpassing the contract that Drew Bledsoe had signed with New England two years earlier. I think it mattered to Brett to have the best contract in the league, and with the kind of football he was playing, Ron was pleased to work with him on that. He appreciated everything that Brett had done for us.

So we had locked up two of the key people for the future of the organization, and I was delighted. It involved a pretty extensive expenditure, but it was money well spent. No one in this organization frowns on spending money to improve our facilities or our team. That's what we're here for.

Ron wasn't very active in acquiring players during the off-season because the team was young and it had been so cohesive the year before. His main goal was to re-sign nose tackle Gilbert Brown and linebacker Wayne Simmons, and when he did that we had 10 of the 11 starters back from a defense that had led the league in both fewest yards and fewest points allowed. The only defensive starter who left was end Sean Jones. Ron let him go in the off-season.

Jacksonville had targeted Gilbert as the No. 1 person they wanted to go after in free agency, and they offered him a longer, more lucrative contract than we did. But Gilbert said he wanted to stay a Packer. He appreciated the fact that we had picked him up after Minnesota had waived him in 1993, and he was having a great experience in Green Bay.

Gilbert was very popular with the fans. They loved that grave digger thing he did after he'd made a big play. I remember going through town on the buses after the Super Bowl victory when everybody was screaming and waving signs for Brett and Reggie. As we went by this one old house close to the downtown area, there was an older man standing on his front porch next to a big old couch holding a piece of cardboard in his hands. He had "Way to go, Gilbert" written on the cardboard, and he wasn't smiling or anything. He was just holding up that sign.

We did lose Desmond as a free agent to Oakland in March when the Raiders promised him that he could be a wide receiver. We were using Desmond only as a return man. And we let Andre Rison and Chris Jacke go, but having that outstanding defense back made everybody optimistic going into the year.

We suffered one severe injury in the pre-season when Edgar Bennett tore the Achilles tendon in his left leg early in the first game and was lost for the year. We still had Dorsey Levens, but that took away a lot of our depth at running back. Edgar and Dorsey had been such mainstays for us in the Super Bowl year. Still, we had a 5-0 pre-season record, and that was the first time since 1967 that we had gone unbeaten and untied in the pre-season.

We opened the regular season by beating the Bears, 38-24, at Lambeau Field, but we had another serious injury when Craig Newsome tore a knee ligament on the first play from scrimmage and was out for the year. And then any talk of going undefeated ended the next week at Philadelphia when the Eagles beat us, 10-9. It marked the first time in 85 regular season and playoff games that we hadn't scored a touchdown in a game.

But we won our next two games, beating Miami, 23-18, and Minnesota, 38-32, at home. LeRoy Butler intercepted two passes and Brett threw five touchdowns passes against the Vikings, which gave him 156 in his career, breaking Bart Starr's club record of 152. The Vikings made a big comeback in the second half of that game, and I remember Brett saying that we were going to have a target on our backs every time we went out on the field. "It's going to be like this all year long," he said, "so let's get used to it."

Brett threw three interceptions the next week at the Pontiac

Silverdome where the Lions beat us, 26-15, but then we went on a five-game winning streak. It started against Tampa Bay when 295-pound defensive end Gabe Wilkins returned an interception 77 yards for a touchdown in a game that we won, 21-16.

We faced the Bears again at Soldier Field the next week and won, 24-23, when their coach, Dave Wannstedt, made an interesting decision. The Bears had scored a touchdown with just under two minutes to play, and Wannstedt decided to go for two on the conversion. But Erik Kramer's pass fell incomplete, and we ran out the clock to improve our record to 5-2. We had traded Wayne Simmons to Kansas City the week before, but we got two interceptions from linebackers anyway. Brian Williams and Bernardo Harris each had one pick.

We kept the winning streak going by knocking off New England, 28-10, in a Super Bowl rematch at Foxboro Stadium when Brett threw for three touchdowns and the defense produced four turnovers. And then we won two home games, beating Detroit, 20-10, and St. Louis, 17-7. The two victories at Lambeau Field gave us 21 straight at home, breaking the franchise record set between 1929 and 1932.

A couple of important things happened off the field in November, starting with the signing of Butler to a five-year contract extension before the Rams game. Ron said that LeRoy was one player we simply couldn't afford to lose in free agency, and he didn't want it to come to that.

Then on November 13 we held a special meeting of the Packers shareholders, which was very unusual for us. Normally we meet just once a year in the summertime. We asked the shareholders to approve issuing additional stock for the first time since 1950. We planned to offer shares at $200 per share. The shareholders agreed, and within 24 hours of the announcement our designated national clearinghouse got 55,000 telephone calls asking about the sale. When we closed it in March we had raised $24 million for the redevelopment of Lambeau Field.

The next Sunday we played Indianapolis and got quite a surprise. The Colts were coached by Lindy Infante, and they were 0-10 at the time. I think if Lindy could have won only one game all year, he would have picked that one. As it turned out, he won three. I hadn't talked to Lindy since he'd left Green Bay, and I don't think anyone else in the organization had, either. There was a lot of talk in the office that week that nobody was going to lose every game, and we were just praying that when the Colts broke their losing streak it wouldn't be against us.

But it was. They were a 13-point underdog, and they were averaging 15.4 points a game. But they beat us, 41-38, on a last-second field goal as Lindy's offense rolled up 467 yards. It was probably the major blip in our whole season. Dallas was next.

It had been years since I'd seen as much anticipation for a regular season game in Green Bay as there was for when the Cowboys came to town. People couldn't wait to get them here because of what we'd gone through over the last four years. We'd lost seven in a row to them in that time, and every game was in Dallas. To get the Cowboys here was enormous. The people were wild, and it didn't hurt that we had the University of Wisconsin band here, too.

The game was tied, 10-10, at halftime, but then we scored 35 points in the second half and won, 45-17. We had touchdown drives of 69, 73, 61 and 88 yards in that second half, and Brett wound up with four touchdown passes, while Dorsey ran for 190 yards. Beating Dallas that day did two things for us. It started another five-game winning streak that would run to the end of the regular season, and it helped wipe out some of those memories of the last four years with the Cowboys.

We went to Minnesota the following Monday where we won, 27-11, clinching a playoff berth and giving Mike his first victory in six tries at the Metrodome. The week before the game got pretty hectic when a Minneapolis broadcaster faked a radio scene in which a woman was supposed to have been caught in Brett's hotel room. It was such a sad thing. The fans were hooting and hollering and holding up signs when Brett came out on to the field, and all because some guy was trying to create havoc and confusion. I mean we guard the players' floor like we're Brinks. If you step off the elevator there, you're going to be stopped and questioned immediately. The radio guy was fired, and I don't think anyone was bothered very much by the whole thing. Brett's only concern was for his family.

People love to spread rumors. It reminded me of another time when a fan called after Brett had had a tough game and said he'd seen him at the Oneida Casino at 4 a.m. the night before. I called Jerry Parins, our director of security, and he told me that Brett had been so sick with the flu that night that he couldn't even eat at the team meal or leave his hotel room.

We had 30,000 fans in Tampa the next week when we beat the

Buccaneers, 17-6, and it bothered the Tampa Bay people tremendously that we had taken over their stadium like that. You went in, and it was all green and gold. I can understand the Tampa Bay organization being upset, except that it was putting revenue in their pockets. They were embarrassed, and we'd be embarrassed, too, if a team took over Lambeau Field.

Our fans travel extremely well. A lot of them have told me it's easier to get tickets for a Packers game at Tampa or Chicago or Detroit than it is to get one for Lambeau Field. That's why they go on the road. Most places love to have them, but Tampa Bay did something later with its ticket package to block the Packers fans, even though we were filling up their seats. They loved the revenue part of that, but they didn't like the fact that it was Packers fans providing it.

We finished the regular season with victories over Carolina and Buffalo, giving us a 13-3 record for the second straight year. During the week of the Carolina game we found out that Brett, Reggie, LeRoy and Dorsey had all been named as starters on the NFC Pro Bowl team, while Mark Chmura was chosen as a reserve and Travis Jervey was elected the NFC special teamer. That was the first time the Packers had sent as many as six players to the Pro Bowl since the AFC and the NFC started playing each other in 1971.

We played just well enough to win the divisional playoff game against Tampa Bay. We had three turnovers, seven penalties and five dropped passes, but we still beat the Buccaneers, 21-7, when our defense held Trent Dilfer to 11 completions in 36 attempts and intercepted him twice. From there it was on to San Francisco for the conference championship game.

The weather changed everything that day. Both teams went into the game with 14-3 records, and both of them were very hot. The morning started with a light rain, and we had a full fledged downpour late in the first half. I remember standing in the end zone to receive the trophy afterwards, and by the time I got to the locker room my raincoat felt like it weighed 400 pounds.

We jumped ahead, 3-0, early in the second quarter, but then the 49ers drove to our 28-yard line. That's when Eugene Robinson intercepted a Steve Young pass and returned it 58 yards. Brett threw a 27-yard touchdown pass to Antonio Freeman two plays later to give us a 10-0 lead, and we just stuck to the running game the rest of the day as the rain got worse. We wanted to eat up the clock and get out of there. Dorsey finished with 114 yards on 27 carries, and San Francisco had only 33 yards rushing as we won, 23-10.

It was still pouring when Ron and I went out onto the field for the trophy presentation, and that was just spooky. There was nobody in the stands. Everybody had gone home. It was a real contrast from the previous year when we were at Lambeau Field and nobody wanted to go home.

There was a lot of talk this time of the network moving the presentation inside because the weather was so bad. But they decided to do it outside anyway, and the rain was just dripping off of me as I stood there. It was still an emotional scene, though, because of what we had accomplished. You always get a big thrill out of winning the conference championship because you know where you're headed.

Some of that thrill was taken away from me, though, because our fans weren't there to appreciate it. I guarantee if that had been in Green Bay, pouring rain or what have you, our fans would have stayed for it. I kept thinking, "This should be at Lambeau Field."

Two weeks later, we sent two planes to the Super Bowl, just as we had the year before, but this time the arrangements were much easier. We had been through this before, and our staff was much more comfortable with it.

After we got to San Diego we ran into a major distraction at Mike's first meeting with the media. A rumor was going around that he would be leaving us the following year to go to Seattle, where he could be both coach and general manager, and that rumor dominated the press conference.

I'd like to know who stirred all of that up because I think it changed Mike's demeanor as we went down the home stretch of the season. He went into kind of a defensive personality, and there's no doubt that the rumors caused problems.

In late November, Bob Whitsitt, the president of the Seattle Seahawks, had called me, and we talked about various things, as I did a lot of times with different owners or general managers. At some point Whitsitt started talking about personnel directors. He mentioned Ron Wolf a couple of times, and finally I said to him, "Bob, what are you looking for? What do you really have in mind?"

The Seahawks had been playing around the .500 mark over the last few years, and he said he was just thinking about a general manager. So we discussed a few candidates. He never asked for permission to talk to Ron. He just kind of used Ron as an example of someone who had taken a franchise and truly turned it around.

Then later in the season, the Seahawks owner, Paul Allen, mentioned Mike Holmgren's name in a press conference – again in the sense of someone who had done a remarkable job. Well, somewhere along the line Mike got the idea that when Whitsitt had called me he was looking for permission to talk to him about both jobs in Seattle.

So I had a meeting with Ron and Mike in the board room of our administration building, and I explained the telephone call from Whitsitt. I said, "Mike, there are two things you need to know. First of all, your name was never brought up. I can guarantee you that. And secondly, if the Seahawks had asked permission to talk to you, I would have had them go to Ron Wolf. They would come to me if they wanted to talk to Ron Wolf, but they would go to Ron if they wanted to talk about you."

And I said, "That never happened. Your name was never mentioned." I really didn't know who gave Mike the idea that the Seahawks had asked permission to talk to him, but I think he had a very difficult time believing that I had never been asked.

He kept asking questions about it. "Are you sure he didn't?" He'd say, and I said, "There are two points. You weren't mentioned, and secondly if he'd mentioned you at all I would have said you have to call Ron to get permission to do that. I won't get into that. That's Ron's decision. That's football."

In my mind, someone was telling Mike that the Seahawks were very interested in him. Maybe the thing that stirred him up was Paul Allen mentioning his name, although I think Allen may even have mentioned some other names as well. But that's when I said to Mike, "Let's you and Ron and I sit down and talk about this."

Subsequently, we had a league meeting before the end of the season, and when Whitsitt came into the room I made it a point to go over to him and say, "Bob, let me tell you how I remember our telephone conversation and see if you agree with me." So I went through it, recalling that we had talked about a lot of different things and that he had mentioned Ron Wolf and the great job he'd done here, and that he might be looking for a general manager.

He said, "Yeah, all of that is right." So I asked him, "Where would Mike Holmgren ever get the idea that we were talking about him?" Bob said, "I have absolutely no idea," and I believed him.

I didn't fault Mike for wanting to improve himself. Everybody wants to improve themselves, but the point was it didn't happen then. His name was never brought up in that conversation. I think Mike understands that today because he eventually got what he wanted anyway, but it did bother him. And it did create a little tension that the organization didn't need going down the stretch.

Ironically, in August, before the regular season, the Village of Ashwaubenon had renamed a street near the stadium Holmgren Way. The village had a nice ceremony for him, and Mike felt very honored by that. I did talk later to some politicians, though, who told me they probably should have waited until they found out if Mike was going to stay around a little longer.

I never held it against Mike when he left, and I think he still has a warm spot in his heart for Green Bay. I know he was very concerned about us when we were going through the stadium referendum. He came up to me at a league meeting after we had started construction and said, "Now you're not going to ruin Lambeau Field, are you?" And I told him not to worry. I said the outside would be vastly different from what he remembered, but once he got inside and came out of that tunnel he would know he was at Lambeau Field.

He came to town a couple of years ago to present Edgar Bennett when Edgar was installed in our Hall of Fame, and during his speech he looked down at me and said, "Bob, you're right. You did make it better."

There was also some talk before the Super Bowl about our offensive coordinator, Sherman Lewis, and his chances of leaving us for a head coaching job. But I wouldn't say that was any kind of a problem at all. You know you're going to hear that when a team goes to the Super Bowl two years in a row. People are always talking about the next hot assistant, and Sherm was kind of falling into that position at that point.

Our losing the game probably hurt his chances, and another thing that hurt him was that clubs weren't allowed at that time to talk to people who are coaching in the Super Bowl until after the game. Often teams anxious to fill a vacancy don't want to wait that long.

One thing that made the atmosphere very different for us at this Super Bowl was that we weren't the sentimental favorites anymore. I went down to the fitness room at our hotel to work out on the treadmill every morning that week, and the television in the room was always on ESPN where people were talking about the great feeling they had for John Elway.

The year before it was all about the feeling for little Green Bay and Brett Favre and Reggie White. It was just strange to see how the sentiment had switched over to Elway because of what he had meant to the league and to his franchise and how he was nearing the end of his career.

The Broncos were the sentimental favorites, but they were still 12-point underdogs, and I felt confident going into the game because of something Ron had told me at breakfast on the Sunday morning when we left for San Diego. I asked him what he thought of Denver, and he told me the Broncos were a carbon copy of New England the year before. We had beaten the Patriots and played so well against them that I thought we had a great chance.

When the game started and we went 76 yards in eight plays on our very first drive, I thought this might be the same kind of thing. We scored right away on a pass to Antonio Freeman, just as we had started out the year before with a touchdown pass to Andre Rison. But the Broncos came back right away this time to tie it at 7-7. And then we had an interception and lost a fumble, and they capitalized on both of them to take a 17-7 lead.

We closed it to 17-14 at halftime when Brett threw a touchdown pass to Chmura, but I remember thinking as I watched our players come out of the locker room for the third quarter that there wasn't a lot of spirit on the team. Everyone was just kind of walking out there instead of running out. I was sitting with Ron and Mike Reinfeldt in the press box, and I mentioned that to them, and they agreed with me. We didn't talk about it much, but it didn't seem to any of us that there was much spark there.

The game was tied, 17-17, in the third quarter, and it was tied, 24-24, in the fourth, and then Terrell Davis scored on a one-yard run with 1:47 left to play, and for the first time I felt a little bit of panic. We were in trouble, and we were running out of time.

As Denver was going on that final drive I had a lot of the same thoughts that I had had in 1968 when I was with the Cardinals and we were losing the last game of the World Series. I could feel the game slipping away then, and I had the same feeling this time. The clock was getting away from us, and we weren't going to get it done. It's an awful feeling.

I didn't know until later that Mike had told our players to let Davis score that last touchdown because he wanted to be sure we had enough time to get the ball and come back. Ron didn't know it either. The hole just opened up, and boom! Davis ran in. We all just thought we had blown the assignment, and we felt a little helpless.

We did move very quickly when we got the ball back. There was still 1:04 to play when we got a first down at the Denver 35, and then we picked up four yards to the 31, But the game ended with three incomplete passes, and that was it.

When it was over, I just sat there staring at the field and watching everyone walk off. It was such a terrible loss, and I was feeling it. In fact, Reinfeldt looked over at me and said, "Are you all right?" I told him I was fine, and then we just walked downstairs.

You had to give the Broncos credit. We truly couldn't stop Terrell Davis for some reason. And Elway was Elway. He played a phenomenal game. I remember on one play he was running with the ball, and he leaped over somebody, almost like a linebacker. He seemed to be driven the way Reggie had been driven in that fourth quarter the year before for us. They played an exceptional game, and they deserved to win. But as I watched the Broncos going up on that stage to get the trophy, I kept thinking that was us last year, and it should be us today.

I made a point after the game to have a league official take me over to Denver's locker room so that I could congratulate Pat Bowlen, the Broncos owner. Bob Kraft, the Patriots owner, had been very cordial to me the year before when we'd won, and I just thought I should do the same for Pat. If you've been beaten, you admit it and congratulate those who have beaten you.

Pat was holding up the trophy and his back was to me when I walked into his locker room. He was shocked when he turned around and saw me. I congratulated him on a great game, and he said thank you very much, and I just turned and left.

Our locker room was dead after the game, and the party back at the hotel was just as bad. People would come in and get a plate of food and talk almost in whispers. They just ate and went to their rooms. They wanted to go home and get it over with. It was the same way the next morning when we had a breakfast at the hotel before we got on the buses for the airport.

It got worse when we got to the San Diego airport. The buses were supposed to take us right to our plane, but they took a wrong turn when they got to the tarmac. Finally somebody on the bus said, "Hey, you missed our plane," and we had to turn back.

That was bad enough, but as we headed back, we passed the Denver buses going the other way. As soon as the Broncos players recognized us, they jumped up and started waving to us from the windows and giving us the Mile High salute that their fans loved so much. Mike and Ron were irate. It just added to a bad trip.

The Chamber of Commerce had arranged a welcome home party for the team for the Tuesday after we got home, and it was nice to see 25,000 people show up at the stadium that day. They were very good about it and very warm about it, but it was so different from the year before when we had paraded through the city and then come back to a full stadium. This was more of a forced appearance, and it was hard even to get Mike and Ron to walk out of that tunnel and talk to the people.

That was when Mike promised that we would be back to the Super Bowl. I believed him. We were still a young team and very much intact, and I think most of the world looked at us that way. I thought we were still going to be very, very strong the next year.

CHAPTER EIGHTEEN

Taking Stock

I started getting calls and letters from people who wanted to buy stock in the Green Bay Packers in the early 90's as we became more and more successful on the field. It was almost like a new generation of fans had discovered our story.

Brett Favre was obviously very popular nationally, and we had made a lot of trips to the playoffs and won a Super Bowl. As this was happening, announcers and writers kept talking about the fact that the Packers were owned by the fans. That prompted people to start writing and calling me to ask if we were ever going to have another stock sale so that they could buy some for their children and grandchildren.

I'd explain to them that there are no dividends and no benefits, and they'd say, "Oh, I know, but I'd just love to say that I'm an owner of a professional football team."

They understood, but people in other cities had a hard time believing it. The ones I got a kick out of talking to were the ones in cities that were losing teams and wanted to be like the Packers. When the old Browns were getting ready to leave Cleveland, for instance, I kept hearing from politicians, businessmen and fans there who couldn't understand how our little town could fill up its stadium every week and we could be successful here while they had a huge stadium in a much bigger city and couldn't make it.

"We'd like to set ourselves up the way you're set up," they'd say. And then I'd proceed to tell them that we're owned by 111,000 shareholders who receive no dividends and can't make any money on their investment. The people would say, "What? Give me that again."

When I explained it, they'd tell me, "We can't do that," and I'd say, "No, you can't."

But we can, because we're grandfathered back to the very beginning of the corporation. There have been four stock sales in the history of the Packers, the first in 1923 when local merchants met at the Elks Club and saved the team from bankruptcy by selling 1,000 shares at $5 apiece. Twelve years later, the corporation was in receivership and a second drive raised $15,000. And then in 1950, shares sold at $25 apiece generated another $118,000. Those numbers sound so small in today's world, but they saved the team.

The fourth sale started late in 1997 and ended in March of 1998, and I've always thought it was prompted by the fact that the Packers had become dominant on the football field again. We'd reached the top, and it became a big story.

Being owned by the fans makes us unique. I'll talk to total strangers around the country, who will tell me they're huge Packers fans. When I ask them why, they say it's because we're owned by the people. I had one fan tell me, "If you're an American, you've got to root for the Packers." That's what I think the stock has done for us.

Sometimes people will tell me they love the fact that the team is owned by the City of Green Bay, and I'll say, "No, we're really not. We're owned by stockholders." Then I'll go through the history, and they just love the story.

The big concern we had in the 90's was maintaining our facilities. In the previous 12 years we had spent $50 million improving the stadium and our administrative offices and building the Don Hutson Center. Ted Eisenreich, our stadium manager, had a great maintenance program every year, and with a 40-year old stadium in our climate, we needed a great maintenance program.

But maintenance was getting expensive, and as I kept getting these calls and letters about the stock, I thought if we could do a sale at a reasonable price, it would help us a great deal with our facilities. My intent was either to remodel Lambeau Field or to put the money into a new stadium. The sale helped us in many ways, although we would have had to do the renovation even if we hadn't had the sale.

I went to the Executive Committee in September of 1997 and told the members about the calls and letters I'd been getting and said it might be a good idea to have a stock sale. I wasn't getting those calls in the 70's and 80's, but I thought this made sense because so many people wanted it.

The most important thing we had to talk about was how to price the stock. We didn't want to price it so high that we took the little guy out of it. We wanted the blue collar fan to be able to say, "Hey, I can afford to be an owner of a team." We decided to try $200 and see how we did.

Then I called Roger Goodell, the NFL's chief operating officer, and asked him who could let me know how we stood legally. He suggested Frank Hawkins, one of the league attorneys. Frank saved us a lot of problems. He not only found out that we could sell stock, but he guided us through some complex legalities. He was very careful about it. He even went through old newspaper articles when he was making sure that we were grandfathered.

We had a two-day league meeting in Washington in October, and the Finance Committee asked me to make an appearance at the end of the first day. I did, and I got a surprisingly negative reaction.

I explained the background of our stock sale and how the money would be used for facilities, but I kept getting questions that were more negative than positive. As I was getting grilled I would kind of look over at Tom Benson, the New Orleans Saints owner and the chairman of the committee, hoping he would bail me out. But it didn't happen. I went to bed that night very concerned because I knew if the Finance Committee didn't approve the plan, the rest of the league was going to be extremely doubtful about it.

I went to breakfast at the hotel restaurant the next morning, and there was Benson sitting at a table across the room. When he saw me, he came over and said, "The problem yesterday, Bob, was that several of the owners are worried that you're going to use the money from the sale for personnel, and that would give you an unfair advantage."

I understood his point. Other NFL owners can't do what we do today. They're allowed to sell interest in their teams, but only if they give some value to the stock and get approval from the other owners. They can't just be selling a piece of paper, which was why Frank Hawkins had been so cautious about making sure we were grandfathered. The other owners' concern was how we were going to use the money.

Tom told me that Commissioner Paul Tagliabue had decided to put me on the agenda that day. I think he'd called the commissioner and told him what had happened, and Paul must have told Tom to get hold of me and let me know that he wanted me to talk to all of the owners. It just so happened that Tom and I are both early risers, so when he saw me at the restaurant he came over and talked to me.

I went to the meeting that day and basically said to the entire league what I had said to the Finance Committee. I said, "First of all, there's not a team in this room that needs its partners as much as the Green Bay Packers do. If we didn't have the revenue sharing and the other things that make this league so solid, we wouldn't exist and I wouldn't be standing here today. This money is going to be set aside strictly for the stadium. If there is any concern about that, we'll set up a separate account and let the commissioner and the league office know where every penny of the stock sale goes."

After I'd finished the presentation, Dan Rooney, the Pittsburgh Steelers owner, got up and said, "The Green Bay Packers are very important to this league, and I think this is a time when we can all give them some help. I think we should give them our unanimous approval."

And they did, which really surprised me after what had happened the day before. I don't know if the commissioner had talked to some of those owners or what, but we did get unanimous approval. And so we moved forward.

We had a special meeting of our shareholders on November 13 and told them that we wanted authorization to sell up to one million shares for $200 apiece. We had only 1,940 shareholders at that time, and we planned to split all of the existing shares 1,000-1 so that we didn't take away any of their power. All of the shareholders would have voting rights, but there would be no dividends, the stock could not appreciate, and no one would be allowed to own more than 200,000 shares so that no shareholder could assume control of the club. We got approval very easily.

We had another room set up where we announced the sale to the public and told people they could call a special toll-free number immediately to get information on buying the stock. It was amazing how quickly things took off.

Within 24 hours our designated clearinghouse got 55,000 phone calls, and in the first 11 days, we sold $7.8 million worth of stock. That was roughly one-third of the eventual total of $24 million. Paid orders were coming in at the rate of 3,500 shares or $700,000 a day in the first couple of weeks of December as the fans used the stock as holiday gifts. Wisconsin people bought more than half of the shares, but we sold at least some to citizens of all 50 states plus Guam and the Virgin Islands.

We didn't market the stock at all. We didn't have to. We just made the announcement, and people started picking up the phone right away. We turned it over to our lawyers, who put out this common stock offering document, and away we went.

I never dreamed we'd reach $24 million. In fact, if people had told me when we started that we'd go over $20 million, I would have told them they were insane. I was thinking we might make $10 million or $11 million, and I wouldn't have been embarrassed by that at all. But what really got me was that $7.8 million right away. I was very curious to see how long that surge would last.

After we got past the holidays and into late February and early March, sales went way down. It was as if everyone who really wanted a share got in at the beginning and said, "I'm interested. Here's my check." Then it died just as quickly, which told us it was time to close the sale. We ended it on March 16, 1998, with 120,010 shares being sold in 17 weeks. It did exactly what we had hoped it would do. We made a lot of friends, and we were able to set some money aside to help us with our facilities.

Our new shareholders tend to be younger and more aggressive than the shareholders we used to have. They tell us if they're unhappy. As we discovered after we went 4-12 in 2005, if things aren't going well, they want to know what's being done to heal the wounds. They were very, very concerned, for instance, about the relationship between Brett Favre and Ted Thompson.

I got calls asking whether Ted really wanted Brett to come back, and that's when I told them that Brett and Ted had sat down and had a meeting before Brett left town, and that they talked on the phone every week. They were fine with that, but in years past they might never have called.

But they'll call now. They'll start out by saying, "Bob, I'm a fan and a shareholder." And I'll say, "I'm just like you. I own one share of stock. Let's talk." And so we do.

It's true, too. I own one share. You have to own one to be on the Board of Directors, so when I became president in 1989 I paid my $25 and bought my share.

If people want to transfer their stock, they have to come back to the team to do it. Someone can't just walk up to his next-door neighbor and say, "Hey, I've got a share of Packer stock. Give me $500, and it's yours." We approve stock transfers almost every month at our Executive Committee meetings, but we don't get many people just selling it back.

One of the interesting things that came out of that 1997 shareholders' meeting was a change in the beneficiary in the unlikely event that the corporation were ever dissolved. When the corporation was formed in 1923, the original articles said that the net proceeds of any sale would go to the Sullivan-Wallen American Legion Post in Green Bay in order to build "a proper soldiers' memorial." Those were the words they used.

A shareholder at the '97 meeting stood up and said, "I don't think it's ever going to happen that the Green Bay Packers don't exist, but I do think we've gone beyond the point of building a memorial. I'd like to propose that if anything happens to the team in the future, the money would go to the Green Bay Packers Foundation so that it could be used for charity work throughout the state." He made a lot of sense, and the idea was passed unanimously.

As we were getting ready for our next shareholders' meeting in July of 1998, we had absolutely no idea of how many people would be there. We had always held the meetings at the Midway Motor Lodge, which was certainly adequate when I joined the organization, because we'd have only 200 or 300 people show up in those days.

But suddenly we had a lot more shareholders, so we moved the meeting to Lambeau Field. Each shareholder was permitted to bring a guest, and 18,707 people came. Once they got there, they found out that the meeting really was a meeting. They got a football report from Ron Wolf and a treasurer's report, and they learned about all of the business aspects of the Green Bay Packers. But you could tell what they had really come for was to see Lambeau Field. The next year attendance dropped to 7,064.

But then a couple of years ago we held the annual meeting at the Resch Center and had to turn people away. The crowds began to increase because we started trying to give the shareholders something special to do after the meeting. One year we took them inside the Don Hutson Center, and another year they were able to walk down the tunnel and around the entire playing surface at Lambeau Field. Once when only the rookies were in training camp we held a special practice open just to shareholders. And in 2006 we let them tour the football facilities and the locker room. I don't know that we can ever go back to the Resch Center now. It would be too small.

I suppose the one detriment to being owned by our fans is that we don't have that one deep-pockets owner who might help us a great deal. On the other hand, we're able to operate the ball club the way we think it should be operated. Obviously, a shareholder could stand up at a meeting and raise a major question about something we're doing, but that really hasn't occurred. No shareholder has tried to start a revolt or anything like that.

They do want to know what's going on, though, and we tell them through the annual meetings and our annual report. Or if they call, we visit with them on the phone. That's one of the reasons why I've always said that we need to pick up the phone. Most of the people who call are shareholders, and we need to be available to them.

I've always looked at my position as that of a caretaker. The franchise belongs to the fans, and I owe them the answers and the information they need to get. We are the only ones in the league who send out an annual report to thousands and thousands of people showing where every penny goes. No other club has to do that. There are no secrets about us.

I love that part of it. During the referendum people would say, "I don't want to pay this tax. The players are already making too much money." And I'd tell them the money isn't going to the players. It's going into the facilities, and that's all it's going into.

We turned our first $2 million profit in 1986, and 20 years later our profit was more than $25 million. A big reason for that is a national television contract that just gets more lucrative all the time. Television continues to this day to be our largest single source of operating income. It was worth $87.3 million in 2006, which was 41.9% of our total operating income. Every time we negotiate a television contract, I think it's never going to be this good again. Then the next one comes up four years later, and it's better.

Of course, another thing that really changed us was the stadium renovation. When we moved into the new stadium in 2003, our revenue jumped to $18 million, and the next year it was $22 million and then $25 million. And it happened because we're open all year, instead of 10 days a year.

We ranked ninth in the league in revenue the year we won the Super Bowl, but we dropped all the way to 20th in 2001 as we launched the stadium project. Then we started right back up, and now we're seventh.

There is an array of things going on constantly at the stadium. The main thing we have going for us now is business seminars. Different companies will come in and set up displays in the atrium for a weekend.

But we've also had high school proms, homecoming dances and weddings. The very first wedding we had was a young lady from the Dakotas whose fiancé had never been to Green Bay in his life. But she convinced him to get married at Lambeau Field.

We're especially proud of the very first event we held in the new Lambeau Field atrium, a black tie inaugural ball with the proceeds going to the St. Mary's Hospital Medical Center in Green Bay. Not only did we raise more than $500,000 for the hospital's endowment, but we got Brett to wear a tux, and I'm not sure he even did that at his own wedding.

The ball was such a momentous occasion, in fact, that I e-mailed Curly Lambeau to tell him about it. I have Madeline to thank for that.

When I told her I was going to speak at the event, she said, "Well, make sure you don't just stand up there and say, 'Thanks for being here. Let's have a nice time.' You have to do something different."

So I turned my speech into an e-mail to Curly. I told him I wasn't sure he even had e-mail where he was, but I just wanted to bring him up to date on what had happened to this little franchise that he started in 1919. I thanked him for the six world championships he'd won for us and told him how Vince Lombardi had added five, and how Ron Wolf had coped with free agency to bring us another one. Then I described the beautiful stadium we were sitting in that night and how it had come to be renovated and how it had saved his franchise. After I wrote the speech, I sent it to the public relations director at St. Mary's, and she loved it.

Madeline had no idea what I was going to say when I stood up that night, but I think she liked it, too.

We just keep trying to find new ideas and to appeal to new groups that will help us take advantage of the stadium. Some of the additional revenue we have gotten from Lambeau Field goes into the Packers Franchise Preservation Fund. The exact figure changes every year, but we now have more than $150 million in total corporate reserves. And it has to grow because who knows what's going to happen next?

I tell people on our staff to go back 12 years and think of the things that have gone on in this franchise that we never anticipated. We never thought we'd have to leave Milwaukee. We really didn't know that we were going to have a football team that all at once was capable of going to two Super Bowls and winning one. We didn't know that we would have a stock sale that would raise $24 million, and we didn't know that we would have to totally renovate Lambeau Field to save the franchise. All of those things happened in the last 12 years, so what's going to happen in the next 12?

Somebody might say that having more than $100 million in reserves is enormous, but it's really not. In today's world, it could cost $35 million just to sign a marquee quarterback, so you can go through that money in a hurry.

That's how we explain it to our shareholders, and they understand it. It's not like we're getting people who are asking us what we're doing with more than $150 million. They know that what we make all comes from football and goes back to football. I would guess that if we weren't making a profit, the shareholders we have today would want to know why not.

Not counting coaches and players, there might have been 15 people working for the Packers when I got here in 1971, and that included secretaries. Now we have about 150. A lot of that has to do with the fact that we're open every day of the year. We have a team store that has a lot of part-time personnel, and we have a huge staff that provides security around the stadium 24 hours a day. Just think about coaching staffs. They were made up of five or six people in the early 70's. Now there are 18 or 19 people on a staff.

We've become much more corporate, but we had to become much more corporate because the game just keeps getting bigger. There's so much more money involved now and so many more sources of revenue.

The Visitors and Convention Bureau does economic impact studies once in a while, and so does the Chamber of Commerce, and they show that we're worth about $3.5 million a weekend to local businesses when we play at home. That's why I told our architect during the renovation that we couldn't leave town for a whole year while they finished. Those businesses budget enormously for those 10 weekends.

The thing I notice is that when I go on the road for a game at a large city, the fans there will come in the morning, spend an hour or two in the parking lots, see the game and then stay maybe an hour afterwards and go home. That's it.

At Lambeau Field cars and RVs with license plates from all over the country start rolling into the parking lot on Friday afternoon, especially since the renovation because there is so much for people to do here now. They're around all day Saturday and all day Sunday and a great deal of the time on Monday. Our team store does a huge business on Monday mornings before people start going home. A Packers game at Lambeau Field is not just a game, it's a four-day event. It's as close to a college atmosphere as any stadium in the NFL.

I've always said that two things saved the Green Bay Packers. First of all, there was Commissioner Pete Rozelle convincing the other owners in the early 60's to share revenue. Then in the early 90's, when we knew that free agency was going to be a part of the NFL, we got a salary cap. Total free agency without a salary cap would have devastated us.

My biggest concern about the future is that the system stays in place. Even with a great stadium this franchise would face serious problems if the league didn't continue to share revenue and have a cap. The key is to have 32 competitive teams. You have to keep yourself interesting to the TV networks, to the sponsors and to the fans.

Football has a huge advantage because we play only 16 times a year, and we need a system in place so that some clubs can't run away and hide from the rest of us. Revenue sharing and the cap are vitally important to that.

I remember talking to Bud Selig when we were doing the collective bargaining agreement in the early 90's, and he said he didn't think we'd ever get a salary cap. But we did, and I give Paul Tagliabue credit for that.

I guess you're always concerned about keeping the system, but if you took me back into the 80's I was concerned then, too. I don't think I'm any more worried now than I ever was. Other leagues wish they had what we have, and we should always be thankful that we have this great system.

But we need to be even more thankful that we have such loyal fans. The system works for us only because of their dedication to this organization. They've shown their support in so many ways, whether it's the stock sale, the way they fill Lambeau Field on Sundays or the calls and letters that we get here every day. I'm probably more familiar with that last part than anyone.

CHAPTER NINETEEN

Politics and Religion —
Our Incredible Fans

I was coming back from Communion and praying to my good friend St. Jude, when a woman came up and tapped me on the shoulder. I was at Mass in Door County, and I guess she was planning to leave right after Communion. When I turned around, she handed me a pencil and a piece of paper and asked, "Would you please sign this for my son?" And so I put St. Jude on hold for a second, signed it and then went back to him.

That's how it is with Packers fans. I've talked to some who will say three rosaries during a game or sit next to a statue of the Blessed Mother thinking it will help their beloved team win. One time a fan sent me a rosary with every other bead either green or gold.

I know every team has fans who love and suffer with them, but I'm convinced that Packers fans are different. Many of the people I hear from have never even been to Green Bay, but they love the Packers anyway. Those who have been here tell me they're already saving for their next trip. Of course thousands of our fans have a share of stock, and so they own the team. And by gosh, they expect good results on Sunday.

The parish I belong to, St. Agnes Catholic Church, is just a couple of blocks from Lambeau Field. Candles in a Catholic church might be red or white, or sometimes they're blue, but at St. Agnes they're green and gold. The pastor there is Father Richard Getchel, the priest who married Brett and Deanna Favre.

Years ago during Masses in the fall, he'd say, "Let's all pray that the Packers play well." That went on for a couple of years, and then he started saying, "Let's all pray that the Packers play well," and he'd pause for a minute and say... "and win." And now he just comes out and says, "Let's all pray that the Packers win this weekend."

I have fans who send me color photos of a room of their house where every surface, vertical and horizontal, is layered with Packer memorabilia. I often hear from a lady who has a life-sized cardboard statue of Brett Favre that she keeps in her living room. I even had a fan send me a statue of myself that he called "Super Bob" after we won the Super Bowl in New Orleans. I was dressed in a Superman outfit with a cape and a big "S" on my chest.

Betty and Tom Sweeney are two of my favorite fans. They live in western Wisconsin. She calls herself "Granny Packer." She and Tom wrote a poem about me entitled simply "Bob Harlan." They put it on a very nice plaque and sent it to me. It has nine verses, and the second one goes:

> You've always been there for us
> Your smile shines so bright
> And so as your dust begins to settle
> We love you with all our might.

A couple of summers ago I was driving out of the parking lot during training camp, and a car pulled in that had a big Kansas Jayhawk on the front of it. My son Kevin lives in Kansas, so I knew that was a good 12 or 13-hour drive. There were four people in the car, and I just stopped for a minute to see what they were going to do. The driver was probably in his late 60s, and he was wearing shorts and a T-shirt, and he had a camera and binoculars around his neck. When he got out of the car, he went down on his hands and knees and bowed three times to the stadium. Then the three passengers got out and just started walking around the stadium, stopping every 10 yards to take pictures.

I've gotten a kick out of the reactions some of the politicians have had to Lambeau Field when they've visited us. President Bill Clinton came in the early 90's, and he made a request to see the stadium before he left the city. When Ron Wolf, Mike Holmgren and I greeted him, the very first thing he said was, "Boy, I never thought I'd get a chance to see this place." I thought of all the places that man had been, and still it was important to him to come and see Lambeau Field.

When Vice President Dick Cheney was in town recently, his Secret Service agents called our security staff and said he'd like to see the stadium. We walked him down the tunnel and took him into the locker room. When we went to see the Hall of Fame, he stopped us and said,

"I've got to pay for this." The people behind the counter laughed, but the Secret Service agents just stood there not saying a word. He didn't hesitate. He handed over his $10, and so did the Secret Service agents, and then we took them on the tour.

Senator Teddy Kennedy was in town last fall, and the Secret Service people called from the flight coming into Green Bay and said he would like to visit. As I was taking him down to the field, he reached into his coat pocket and said, "Bob I want to show you something." Then he pulled out a letter that he had gotten from Lisle Blackbourn when Liz was coaching the Packers. Senator Kennedy had played football at Harvard, and the letter was an invitation to a tryout. It looked like it had been mailed yesterday.

We're totally bipartisan here. If prominent people want to make sure that when they come to Green Bay they see Lambeau Field, we're delighted to show it to them. We're very proud of the place.

We hear from a lot of former players, too, and we try to keep them in the family. One of the calls I got made me feel really sad. Jim Carter, who is someone I like a lot, was here in the early 70's when I first came to town. He was the linebacker who took over for Ray Nitschke when Ray retired, and it was almost as if some people couldn't forgive him for that. Jim was a brash young kid at the time, and if the fans didn't like him, he let them know that he didn't care. When he called me about something not too long ago, I asked him if he ever came back. He said, "No Bob. I'm not sure I'd be welcome." I told him that just wasn't true, that people now understood what he'd gone through trying to replace a legend. Jim is a very successful businessman, and he has grown tremendously through the years. But he's never come back to where we could introduce him on the field for alumni weekend. I really hope that some day he will.

I have been taking my own telephone calls since the day I got here. It wasn't just something I started when I became president. I've always felt that there's not a fan, good or bad, who shouldn't be able to reach someone here.

In the mid 70's I started getting calls from a barber in New York named Mario. He was a big Lombardi fan, and he got very concerned when things started to go bad after Vince left us. He would call me at least once a week, and when I called him back, someone would answer the phone, "Barber Shop." I'd say, "Is Mario there?" And they'd say, "Yeah he's busy with a customer, I'll just put you on hold for a minute."

I'd sit for maybe five minutes while Mario finished shaving somebody before he'd get on the phone. Then I'd answer a couple of his questions, and he'd yell the answers to everybody in the barber shop.

Unfortunately, I get a lot more calls when we're losing than when we're winning. If I get through Monday after a loss without the phone ringing off the hook, I know I'm in pretty good shape for the rest of the week.

When I hear from fans, it's usually because they're concerned about something, particularly if they've had a bad experience in the stadium. A lot of them will say they're surprised they got through to me, but I want them to know that if they're unhappy, they're going to hear from us. I do know this: When I talk to one fan there's a good chance that he'll tell 20 other people about it. So I'm not just talking to one fan, I'm talking to 21.

I want to have that reputation for being available, but not everyone knows about it, and sometimes people will call in and ask to talk to my secretary. Margaret Meyers has been my secretary for 28 years, and she's done a terrific job. She doesn't get my telephone calls, but when I'm away for a long time she will open my mail. So she's seen some of the mail and a lot of the gifts.

I don't get a lot of calls at home, but I do remember getting one at about 3 o'clock in the morning when we were looking for a coach to replace Forrest Gregg. The guy was obviously calling from a party because you could hear a lot of yelling and carrying on. He was demanding that we hire Bill Parcells, and the sooner the better. That's when I took my name out of the phone book.

When I can't get someone to stop talking, when they won't let me have my say, I'll tell them, "If you're not going to let me tell my side of the story, this conversation is going to be much shorter." But I'm willing to listen and I'm willing to admit it when we're wrong.

Public relations is very important with the Green Bay Packers, and there's never going to be a day when it's not important. Our fans deserve that. They're the ones who make this franchise so very special.

CHAPTER TWENTY

For the Love of Mike

As we got ready for the 1998 season, I thought Mike Holmgren was becoming a different person.

He was quieter than he'd been in the past, not as outgoing. He'd get on the team plane and kind of be by himself. There was a different demeanor and a different personality there. He was just more distant. It seemed to me that he knew it was about to end for him in Green Bay.

He talked about the fishbowl here. He would tell me about times when people would find out where he lived, and he'd come home from work and find a car in his driveway and people standing on his front porch waiting for an autograph.

That's something you have to learn to accept in Green Bay. I saw it with everybody we had, whether it was Dan Devine, Bart Starr or Forrest Gregg. When you held that job, you became the most visible person in this part of the state or maybe the whole state. But it bothered Mike, and he never got used to it.

He was such a hero. Some coaches hide. They just don't go out at all. But Mike liked to go out. And he had to watch where he went and who he was with.

Of course he was the hottest name in coaching. As we became successful and went to two Super Bowls in a row, he became a bigger and bigger individual in the league. Whenever there was any kind of opening, Mike Holmgren was always mentioned as a candidate. In a way it makes you proud that your coach has done such a great job that he appeals to everybody else. But he had grown, and he wanted more authority, something he would never have as long as he was in Green Bay with Ron Wolf.

The Seattle rumors had been rampant for a while, and I had the impression they were very much on Mike's mind. He really wanted to run his own team, and I understood that. I think Ron understood it, too.

The relationship between the two of them was kind of running its course at that point. When they first came here, they were both so anxious to be successful. Mike would tell me this was such a great place for him because he knew Ron would get the players and all he would have to do was coach them. That worked out very well at first.

But later I think they each wanted to feel that it was their football team. And they probably should have. They both did such a marvelous job for the Green Bay Packers. They were a great duo, but that bond wasn't as strong in their last year together.

I almost always dealt with them individually. I would have Mike come into my office and sit and talk to me, and later on Ron would come in. Even when we were on the team plane, Mike might come over and sit with me for awhile, and then Ron would come over. It just happened that way. It wasn't something that I did intentionally. I wasn't trying to keep them apart. My only intention was to make sure that each of them had what he needed to be successful.

At the end I didn't see the same communication between them. There was a distance that hadn't been there before. There wasn't any bickering or anything like that. I don't want to paint that kind of picture. I never had to referee. These were just two highly successful men, each in his own capacity, and I think Ron could feel that Mike wanted to grow and move on. He didn't hold it against him, but it did affect their relationship.

Ron started talking to me early in the season about who the next coach would be, so obviously he'd had a lot of time to think about it. He brought up Ray Rhodes' name for the first time while we were sitting by ourselves in a small booth next to the press box before a game at Lambeau Field in mid-October. I was a little surprised by that, and I told him so. Ray was coming off a 6-9-1 season as the head coach at Philadelphia, and the Eagles were struggling again in 1998. They would finish the season 3-13.

But Ron said that he was concerned that our team was losing its toughness, and he believed Ray would bring that back to us. I had great confidence in Ron. Of course I trusted his judgment. That's why he was here, and I was prepared to let him do whatever he thought was best if the time came to replace Mike.

We got hit really hard by free agency in the 1998 off-season. Doug Evans, Gabe Wilkins, Craig Hentrich, Edgar Bennett, Eugene Robinson and Aaron Taylor all left, but I still believed we had a very strong team.

As we neared the draft, Reggie White had been talking to Mike quite a bit, telling him he was thinking about retirement because of a chronic disk problem in his lower back. So I wasn't surprised when Mike met with the press on the second day of the draft and announced that Reggie was going to retire. Less than 48 hours later, though, Reggie changed his mind and said he would be back for his 14th season.

He said that when he signed a new contract the previous year he had promised the Packers that he would play two more years, and he was a man of his word. Somebody asked him what had changed his mind, and Reggie said that God had spoken to him and told him to play. It was kind of an interesting twist on the pre-season.

Another interesting twist came in August when we played the Kansas City Chiefs in Tokyo. It was our first trip overseas in the 80-year history of the franchise, and neither Ron nor Mike was thrilled about it. They liked having an extra pre-season game, and if it had been played in Mexico City or Canton, Ohio, or somewhere like that, they would have been fine. But this was a major disruption.

We were chosen for the game because we were such a big attraction nationally. The league was looking for teams that were coming off of great seasons and had great stars. We'd just played in two Super Bowls, and we had Brett Favre and Reggie White. It was a tremendous compliment, but it was not an easy trip.

I was standing down on the field with Carl Peterson, the Chiefs president, toward the end of the game, and then it went into overtime. We were both sick when we saw that. The flying time home was more than 12 hours, and both of us were saying that somebody had to win that thing so we could get out of there. We finally won it, 27-24, but it was daylight in Wisconsin when we got home.

We got off to a great start in the regular season despite all of our free agency losses. In fact we were 4-0 for the first time since 1966. We beat Detroit, 38-19, by holding Barry Sanders to 70 yards and breaking his string of 100-yard games at 14, and then we sacked Trent Dilfer six times in a 23-15 victory over Tampa Bay at Lambeau Field. Reggie got three of the sacks and passed Tim Harris for the career franchise record with 55½. When we won, 13-6, at Cincinnati and 37-30 at Carolina, it looked like we were going to be every bit as good as we'd been in the two Super Bowl years.

But then we played at home against Minnesota on a Monday night, and it was a tough night in every way. We had had a driving rainstorm all day long, and it just did not let up that evening. It was too wet for the fans to tailgate, and they didn't want to get into their seats any sooner than they had to. So everybody was standing in the concourse before the game, and we almost had a panic down there. It was so crowded that no one could move.

I got calls later from people who said they couldn't breathe. One woman said she was actually lifted off the ground by the crowd, and she got so panicky that she called 911. At that time we had just the one concourse at Lambeau Field, which was one of the things that prompted us to put in two when we designed the new stadium. When the team had started out there in 1957 the stadium had a capacity of 32,500. But we were seating almost 60,000 that night, and there were so many people in the concourse that we had to send in the police to control things.

It was a horrible situation, and the night never got any better. Somebody approached me just before the two-minute warning of the second quarter and said that the police were going to announce that everyone had to stay in their seats at halftime because they didn't want a repeat of what had happened before the game. And I thought if we tell the people not to move they're really going to get alarmed. What will they think is going on in the stadium?

Fortunately it was Almuni Night, and so I went up to the fourth level of the press box and told the police, "You know these people are already scared. Instead of telling them they can't move and starting more panic, why don't we just ask them to remain in their seats to honor our alumni?" So we did that, and it worked out pretty well.

The game wasn't much better. Randall Cunningham passed for 442 yards and four touchdowns, breaking a record against us that Joe Montana had set at 411 yards in 1990, and we lost, 37-24. We also had our home winning streak end at 25 games that night.

We lost the next week, too, at Detroit, and then we beat Baltimore at home and our defense had a spectacular night a week later when we sacked Steve Young nine times in a 36-22 victory over San Francisco at Lambeau Field. We hadn't had that many sacks in 33 years. Brett broke the Packers career passing yardage record in that game, too. His 279 yards gave him 24,720 in just his seventh season. Bart Starr had taken 16 years to set the old record of 24,718.

We were up and down after that. We lost to the Steelers, beat the Giants, lost to the Vikings, beat the Eagles and lost to the Buccaneers before we made some history at home against Chicago. The Packers and the Bears had played 155 regular season games against each other, and when we beat them, 26-20, it marked our ninth victory in a row over them. The Bears had set the series record at eight from 1985 through 1988.

That started a season-ending, three-game winning streak that left us with an 11-5 record and our seventh straight winning season. We also placed Reggie, LeRoy Butler, Mark Chmura, Antonio Freeman and return specialist Roell Preston on the NFC Pro Bowl squad, while Brett became the first quarterback in the history of the league to pass for 30 or more touchdowns in five different seasons. But Minnesota won the division with a 15-1 record, and we had to go on the road for the NFC wild card game.

We played it at 3Com Park in San Francisco, and it turned out to be Mike Holmgren's final game as the Green Bay Packers coach.

We lost, 30-27, and in my mind it was as disappointing as the fourth-and-26 game we lost five years later in Philadelphia. With 6:12 to play, Wade Richey kicked a 40-yard field goal to give the 49ers a 23-20 lead, but we came back with an 89-yard drive that ended when Brett threw a 15-yard touchdown pass to Freeman, and we went ahead, 27-23.

Then the 49ers took over. Young completed a pass to Jerry Rice on our 41-yard line with 46 seconds to go, and replays showed that Scott McGarrahan stripped the ball from Rice just before his knee touched the ground. Bernardo Harris fell on it, and we were ready to celebrate. Rice was ruled down on the play, though, and the 49ers kept possession and moved to our 25. But with only 8 seconds left on the clock, we thought we were still in great shape. They were down to their last play.

I remember Young went back to pass and kind of stumbled as he took the snap. Terrell Owens went straight down the field and then turned left. He leaped at the goal line as Young delivered the ball, and Pat Terrell and Darren Sharper both hit him at the same time. We had him well covered, but he came down with the ball and held on. It was a heck of a throw, and he made a heck of a catch.

I was stunned. I had gone down to the sidelines early in the fourth quarter because it was one of those close games where I just couldn't sit still in the press box. I was convinced that Rice had fumbled, but even with that call we had had a great chance to win. I was ready to see us go into the locker room and celebrate. Owens had to make a great catch with a lot of people around him and a lot of bumping after he caught the ball. I mean, he was sandwiched between Terrell and Sharper.

When the game ended, I just kind of stayed where I was. I wasn't out by our bench, I was closer to the tunnel where you step down into this area that leads to the visitors' locker room. It seemed to me that Mike got there very quickly. I know he went across the field and congratulated Steve Mariucci, the 49ers' coach, but he got off that field in a hurry. When he walked by me the look on his face was shock at what had just happened. I think he knew that this was his last game with Green Bay.

The Seattle rumors that had started the previous year never really went away, and Ron just assumed if Mike didn't go there, he'd be going someplace. Mike seemed to know in his own mind – and I don't know who was telling him this – that the Seahawks were still interested and were definitely going to come after him.

Ron had given him a 21-day window immediately after the season to seek a dual role with another team. I'll say this about Ron. No matter who he had working for him, whether it was a coach or some very good personnel people, when they got a good opportunity he let them go. He wanted people to be able to fulfill their dreams.

On January 8, 1999, just five days after our loss at San Francisco, Mike resigned and was named executive vice president of football operations, general manager and head coach of the Seattle Seahawks. He got exactly what he wanted. He was given total control of the football operation, and he signed the highest contract in the history of the league.

The next thing I knew, he was in Seattle getting out of a car all dressed up and going to his first press conference. To be honest, it was kind of a tough thing to see. This guy who had done so much for us was now doing it for somebody else, and it hurt a little bit.

But it was all done on friendly terms. He came to see me after the announcement was made that he was leaving and said that if all he'd wanted was to be a head coach, he would have stayed in Green Bay. But this was like a dream job for him, and I understood totally. I would never hold it against him. People ask me now if it bothers me to see Mike having the success he's having in Seattle, and I tell them absolutely not. We parted on very good terms.

In fact if I had known that Ron would be leaving after the 2001 season I would have tried to persuade Mike to stay. It's still not my favorite way to go, but given his abilities, I would have offered him both jobs when Ron left. If I had thought I could hang on to part of that package we had with the two of them, I'm sure I would have talked to Mike about it.

Could we have offered the same financial deal that Paul Allen did in Seattle? Probably not. They gave him $8 million a year for eight years, and we couldn't have come close to that. But I'd never say he didn't deserve it.

We had extended Mike's contract through the 1999 season, and because he had a year to go on it, the Seahawks had to give us a second-round draft choice as compensation. The pick was the 16th in the second round or the 47th overall, and we used it to draft Fred Vinson, a corner-back from Vanderbilt. Vinson played for us for one year in 1999, and then the next April we traded him to Seattle. The trade brought us Ahman Green, so you'd have to say that worked out pretty well.

When Mike left, he took a lot of his assistant coaches with him. He also took Mike Reinfeldt and Ted Thompson. He wanted Reinfeldt to oversee his salary cap and do his contracts, and he wanted Thompson to come in and build a ball club for him.

Ted was a key guy for Ron. He was his right-hand man, and he had promoted him twice. But when I asked Ron why he let him go, it was the same thing. He said it was a big step up for Ted, and he didn't ever want to hold anybody back.

Reinfeldt, meanwhile, was a very big loss for me. When I'd hired him eight years earlier I had told him that he was part of my succession plan. But I couldn't compete with the money that he was being offered in Seattle. I kept going back to the Executive Committee and increasing his contract, but eventually we had to make a final offer, and he told me, "Bob, I appreciate it, but I think I have to go." He said the Seahawks' offer was so phenomenal he just couldn't turn it down.

I remember the day I knew our relationship with Mike Reinfeldt was going to end. Ron and I had been talking about a contract, and we went down the hall together to see him. When we walked into his office he was having a very quiet conversation with Mike Holmgren, and I thought this was definitely not a good sign. Ron told me, "Bob, you know he's going to take Reinfeldt from us." Right after that, he was gone.

Mike Reinfeldt and I still talk several times a year. It was just one of those career moves that you know is going to happen. A couple of years ago, there was a rumor that he was going to be interviewed for the president's job with the Cleveland Browns. That was the year I was looking at Ted Thompson as our general manager, and the word was that if Reinfeldt had gotten the Cleveland job he would have taken Ted with him.

The year before Mike left, he had turned down another great opportunity, and that was enough to get me thinking that he wasn't going to stay with us forever. There was a ladder out there, and he was going to climb it, and again I understood that. So I started thinking about who we could bring in to replace him.

I had known John Jones from the time he was in Green Bay working on Ray Nitschke's *Packer Report* in the 70's. I was familiar with his background with the league's Management Council and with the time he had spent in the Jacksonville Jaguars front office. He also had a Wisconsin background. His wife was from Wisconsin, and he had gone to the University of Wisconsin. I just kind of kept his name handy as someone I could call if Reinfeldt did indeed leave.

I thought if John wasn't interested I'd ask him if there was somebody he might recommend in the Management Council who was very familiar with the collective bargaining agreement and the salary cap and who was ready to advance. But I didn't have to do that because John accepted the job.

I told John that I wanted someone here who could grow with the organization and be ready to take over when I left. I liked his experience as an administrator with the Management Council, and I liked the fact that he'd worked on the team level with Jacksonville. I thought with his Wisconsin background, the opportunity would appeal to him.

In the meantime, Ron worked very quickly to fill the vacancy left by Mike Holmgren. He had known almost that whole season who he was going to bring in, although he did talk about some other people. Steve Spurrier's name was mentioned, for example. Spurrier was the top guy in the college game at the time, but that wasn't the direction that Ron had chosen to go.

He focused on Ray Rhodes and basically stuck with him because he thought Ray would restore the toughness he said we were starting to lose. He couldn't explain why we were losing it, but he'd noticed it, and it bothered him.

So on January 11, just three days after Mike Holmgren had left, Ron held a press conference and introduced Ray Rhodes as our new coach.

CHAPTER TWENTY-ONE

Hard Times

I got a call two days after Christmas from the nursing home in Des Moines where my mother was recovering from falling and breaking her arm. They told me she had suffered a brain stem stroke and been put in a hospital.

This was one day after we had lost to Tampa Bay in the second-to-last game of an extremely disappointing 1999 season and less than a month before we would announce our plans for a stadium referendum that absolutely had to pass to save the franchise.

Obviously, when I got the call from Des Moines, Madeline and I had to leave immediately to be with my mother. I went to Ron Wolf's secretary and told her where I was going to be, but I said I couldn't tell her how long I would be there. I just gave her my cell phone number and told her to have Ron call if he needed me.

This was on a Monday. The next time I heard from Ron was the following Sunday morning before we played the Arizona Cardinals at Lambeau Field. He said he was planning to fire Ray Rhodes. I told him to do what he needed to do.

We hadn't had a losing season in the seven years that Ron and Mike Holmgren had been together in Green Bay, and now we were going to have to win our last game just to finish 8-8. We still had good talent, which was proven by our success in the seven previous seasons and by the fact that we took right off again with a 9-7 record and back-to-back 12-4 years after Ray left. The 1999 season was a blip, and it was a blip in Ron's career as well.

One of Ron's great qualities is that he's not embarrassed to admit his mistakes. We all make mistakes and he was always quick to correct his before they could fester. There was never any denial. He was very disappointed in himself and in what had happened to his team, and he wasn't going to live with it. Ray was gone before Madeline and I got back to Green Bay.

"He's a different coach than I thought he was," Ron told me.

We had signed Ray to a four-year contract on January 11 of what would become a tumultuous year. The biggest news of the off-season was provided again by Reggie White, who finally did announce his retirement. But then he decided in 2000 to play one more season with Carolina, which I always thought was too bad. Reggie was a shadow of himself with the Panthers.

We went undefeated in the pre-season, but once the regular season began we were totally inconsistent despite the fact that we won three of our first four games. Brett had to come to our rescue in the last couple of minutes in all three.

We were behind by 10 points with 10:52 to play against Oakland in the season opener before he threw two touchdown passes to give us 28-24 victory. We lost our second game at Detroit and then came back to beat Minnesota, 23-20, when he threw another scoring pass with 12 seconds to play. And we were down, 23-19 with 1:45 left against Tampa Bay in Game 4 when he did it again in the last couple of seconds.

I remember walking out of the press box after the third time and Bob McGinn of the Milwaukee *Journal Sentinel* asking me, "Does that guy have any miracles left in him?" And I said, "I'm not sure."

From that point on, we were wildly unpredictable. We had a three-game losing streak, and then we had a three-game winning streak, and then we came right back with a three-game losing streak. We could never settle down and become the club we should have been.

Ron was on the road scouting during most of that time. He would come in on a Friday night or a Saturday morning and look at videos of practices the previous week. Then he'd sit with me at the games on Sunday. As the season wore on and we were hanging closer and closer to the .500 mark, about the only thing he would say was that he was not going to make a change. And I'd tell him, "Fine. You don't have to if you don't want to."

I really didn't see much of Ray during the season. He wasn't someone who would come in, sit down and talk. If he wanted to visit, I think he went directly to Ron. Mike Holmgren and I had been much closer. I would see Ray on the weekends, though, and we would talk then. I liked him very much. He is a nice man, but it just wasn't happening for him.

We would be going through losing streaks and not playing good football, and when I'd walk through the locker room in the middle of the week he'd be sitting at a table playing dominoes with the players. And I thought, "Is that what we want to put out in front of everybody?" I didn't know if it was what we wanted our head coach to be doing.

I thought Ray had great rapport with the players when he was here as a defensive coordinator, and I think he was a popular choice with them when he came back as head coach. In fact, I'm not sure that he wasn't still popular when he left, but he had lost his authority. And that's what got to Ron. It was almost like what Ron had seen when he'd gone onto Lindy Infante's practice field and called it a country club atmosphere.

But he pretty much stuck with Ray the entire year until we got into December. And then his whole attitude changed. The college football season had ended, giving Ron time to go down to the practice field where he could watch the team during the week. After we lost back-to-back games to Carolina and Minnesota, alarm had really set in with him, and he told me, "I think we're going to make a change, but let's see where we are."

I asked him what had changed his mind, and he said, "I think we have to have a disciplined, hard-nosed football team here. That's how you're successful in this business, and we didn't have that this year."

He told me that things looked good when he watched the team during training camp, but there was a different pulse on the practice field now and it was being reflected in our play. He didn't hear or see any noise or emotion during the practices, and that shocked him.

"You've got to have some fun when you're playing this game," he said. "You've got to enjoy what you're doing. These players aren't having any fun. There's no drive down there. Ray has lost the team."

Then we went to Tampa Bay and lost our third game in a row, 29-10. And the next day I got the call from Des Moines.

As it turned out, Madeline and I spent the entire week there because things were so much in jeopardy. We were even going to the funeral home and making arrangements. I didn't know how serious this was going to be, and since we lived 400 miles way, I had to do everything I could then. My mother couldn't move and she couldn't speak. She would stare at me, but she didn't know me. We spent the day of the Arizona game at the hospital, so I didn't know how it came out until Ron called me back later in the afternoon. We had gone to get some dinner, and he reached me just as we got to the restaurant. I asked him how we did, and he said we had won the game, but he was still going to make the change.

In fact, he was going to see Ray right after he got off the phone with me, but he wanted to check with me one more time and make sure I was okay with it.

And so Ron let Ray go just hours after the game and basically told the press the same things he had been telling me for the last month. The 8-8 record just wasn't good enough for the team we had; the players weren't having any fun; and there had been a huge change in the ball club that he just couldn't put up with.

Ray had the four-year contract, but that didn't create the same problem we'd had when Lindy was fired. Ron had put a buy-out clause in the contract, partly because of our experience that time. Not that Ray would have done what Lindy did, but those clauses were already becoming more prominent in the league.

Madeline and I returned to Green Bay after my mother was moved across town to a nursing home. She had just kind of stayed in the same state, and so we decided to go and then come back every weekend to see her. I dealt with Dr. Jose Angel, and he was very direct. He said a brain stem stroke is about as bad as it gets. He couldn't promise that my mother would ever get better.

I would call the nursing home every morning to get an update, and they would give me a report that never got any better. Then on August 8, I got a phone call at 1:40 in the morning from a nurse telling me that my mother had passed away. As soon as I heard the phone ring, I knew what it was. You know that call is coming, but when you get it, there's still a finality that hits you.

When I hung up, I didn't know what to do. I was all alone because Madeline had taken our granddaughter to Door County. So I lay down and thought I'd just say some prayers for my mother. A couple minutes later, I got another call from the funeral parlor asking me about arrangements. I told them they'd have to let me think about it overnight and talk to my wife. It was a tough time. My mother and I had been very, very close.

In the meantime, the Packers were not only fighting problems on the field, they were facing a serious financial crisis.

During the season, our treasurer, John Underwood, kept giving reports to the Executive Committee and to the Board of Directors, and he was going to present one to the shareholders the following summer. Basically, John's message was that we were having major problems and they were going to get much worse in the 2000 fiscal year.

After making a profit of just over $7 million in 1998 and just under $7 million in 1999, we had lost $419,000 in the 2000 fiscal year. John got everyone's attention when he said it was our first operating loss in more than a decade.

Our cash reserves were being drained, and unless we developed new sources of revenue from our stadium, we would have to borrow almost $10 million just to fund our normal operations by 2005. Our reserve fund at the time was at $49.8 million, but he projected that it would fall to $7.9 million in 2004, and it would be gone by 2005.

This is when John became famous for his three-legged stool talk. He said the long-term viability of the franchise depended on three legs. The first leg was a substantial level of revenue sharing in the NFL. The second was a hard salary cap. And the third was an ability to generate new revenue from the stadium. We had the first two legs, but we needed the third to succeed.

What was happening to us was that other teams were moving into new stadiums, and we kept dropping below them in revenue. We had been ninth in the league in revenue in 1997 when we won the Super Bowl, but we had already fallen to 17th, and John was telling us we'd probably be 25th by 2003.

Player salaries and bonuses were climbing higher and higher, and teams were depending more than ever before on stadium revenue for income. As more teams played in new stadiums, we slid closer to the bottom of the league. Our own payroll was up substantially because we were coming off of two Super Bowl years. And we didn't have the resources that everyone else was going to have.

This was a huge panic for our Board of Directors and our Executive Committee, and it showed when we sent our annual report. Normally we started the report with a review of the football season, and then we went into our community involvement and at the very end we gave the treasurer's report. But this time we wanted to make sure our shareholders knew just how dire the financial situation was, and so we opened with a letter from me telling them that we were facing our greatest challenge off the field since the mid-1950's when Curly Lambeau had asked the fans to pass the hat to save the team.

Now we were asking a new generation of Packers fans to save the team by supporting a referendum that would provide $295 million to redevelop Lambeau Field. We unveiled our plans for the renovation at a press conference on January 22, 2000, and now my problem was getting people to believe how desperate we truly were. We had to let them know that this had to get done, and it had to get done right now.

We were already talking about borrowing money to keep the franchise going, and there was absolutely no relief in sight because we were operating in a stadium that was open only 10 days a year. What were we going to do with it? There was no other way to save ourselves than to do the stadium.

We were starting this referendum coming off an 8-8 season, and the media's question to me was always, "What is that season going to do to you? How is it going to hurt you with the voters?" And I always told them that we weren't talking about a year when we went 8-8, and we weren't talking about the year when we were Super Bowl champions. We were trying to save 80 years of tradition. This was about that tradition and saving the Green Bay Packers.

As concerned as Underwood was, he became my biggest cheerleader during the eight months we spent campaigning for the referendum. He would always come up to me and say I was the guy who had to win this thing. I was the one with the credibility. It was up to me. Then he'd try to comfort me by saying, "We're going to win it. It's on your back, but we're going to win it."

It was an extremely difficult period both professionally and personally. We were fighting our problems on the field, we were fighting our financial problems off the field where I had to convince people that I was being honest with them, and Madeline and I were driving every weekend to Des Moines where my mother was in a nursing home unable to move. Those were three pretty big problems to deal with all at once, which is why I've told people that the worst time of my life here was the eight months of the referendum.

Madeline was my trouper. She went through everything with me. She would take care of me after my battles with the politicians, and she would help me get through the trips to Des Moines. She was our strength.

I was concerned that there was so much turmoil involving the team in such a short time. And I have to be honest, I was surprised when Ron came to me with the idea of replacing Ray Rhodes with Mike Sherman. I had been very disappointed when Mike Holmgren left, and I was even more disappointed with how quickly we had deteriorated after he'd gone. Sherman wasn't really an established guy, and I wondered if we didn't need somebody at that point who had a big reputation in the league. Somebody like Marty Schottenheimer.

Marty was the one person who was really prominent in Ron's picture during most of that time. They were talking back and forth to each other, and I really felt the offer was going to go to Marty.

I was at the office one day, walking in the hallway down by the locker room, and I ran into Mike Sherman and Ron. Mike had been an assistant coach here, so I just kind of welcomed him back and never saw him the rest of the day.

I went home later, and that's when Ron called me and said Mike had just blown the socks off of him. He said Mike had a program, he had tremendous respect for the game of football, he understood the tradition in Green Bay, and he'd make an excellent coach for our team. He was everything Ron wanted. So Ron slept on it that night, and the next morning he hired Mike and held his press conference.

I never got the impression from talking to Ron that Schottenheimer had much interest in Green Bay. He just didn't seem overly anxious to get the job, and I think it bothered Ron that he wasn't. Ron feels this is the best place in the league to coach, and people ought to be knocking on our door. Marty never showed that kind of enthusiasm.

And then Mike Sherman came in and showed all kinds of enthusiasm, not only for the job but for the tradition, and that swayed Ron tremendously. Ron never called me at home, but he called me at home that night. If Marty had shown the same excitement as Mike, there's a good possibility that he would have been hired. But he never displayed any warmth for the job.

On January 18, just a little more than two weeks after Ray was fired, Mike became our head coach. It was eight months after that when the voters approved the referendum and allowed us to begin renovating Lambeau Field. And as I've said many times, thank the Lord that we did it when we did it.

Our net income in 2003 when we moved into the redeveloped stadium was $18.9 million, and we went to $22.9 million the next year. In 2005, instead of having to borrow money, we made $25.4 million. I still believe that Lambeau Field is the best stadium in the National Football League and the most historic. I love its history, and I kept telling people that it was going to save this franchise. It truly did.

I can't begin to think where we'd be right now without it. One of our Board members asked me at a recent meeting what the stadium means to us today. Rather than go through all the numbers, I said the simplest way to explain it is that we're seventh in the league in revenue right now, and we would probably be 31st or 32nd if we hadn't done what we did.

I still remember the night the referendum passed and the party that we had to celebrate that 53% to 47% vote. The first guy to come across the room and give me a big hug was John Underwood.

CHAPTER TWENTY-TWO
GMs, Coaches and Cancer

Mike Sherman came to see me in January of 1999 before he left Green Bay to join Mike Holmgren's staff in Seattle. Mike had been our tight ends coach, and this may have been the only time all year that we had had a conversation. He came in to thank me and say what a marvelous place this was to coach. He said his only regret was that he couldn't have stayed longer.

So when Ron Wolf told me a year later that Mike was one of his candidates to replace Ray Rhodes, I told him about our talk. I hadn't had many assistant coaches do what Mike had done. Some might come in and say, "Thanks. Good luck," and then leave, but Mike was the only one I could remember having made it a point to say how sorry he was to go. I told Ron, "This place is very important to Mike Sherman."

I wouldn't say I was dubious about Ron's decision to hire Mike, but I was definitely surprised. Ray Rhodes had been a bad call, and I didn't know enough about Mike to know whether he might be or not. I still had a lot of faith in Ron, though, and I admired his ability to correct his mistakes immediately. The Executive Committee felt the same way. They never tried to block any of his decisions.

Mike showed up for his interview with a program. He is a very, very organized person, a detail guy and a good guy for younger coaches to learn from. He had the entire year laid out when he talked to Ron. He knew what the Green Bay Packers needed to do in July, and what they needed to do in August, September, and October. You name it, and he had it already planned. Ron had interviewed a lot of people in his life, but he'd never seen anything like that.

He still had a few doubts after the interview, but not many. And after sleeping on it for a night, he hired Mike Sherman.

We went 2-2 in the pre-season, and that's when Mike surprised the team one day by canceling practice and taking everyone to a bowling alley. He had a great knack for knowing when the players needed a break to get their minds off of football for a while. I think some of the traits he brought to the game came from his recruiting days as a college coach. He would change the pattern a little bit once in a while, and it was well received by the players.

The regular season was kind of up and down. We'd win a couple and lose a couple. We could never get any kind of a string going until the very end when we were 5-7 with four games to go. Then we won all four games, and all against division opponents.

We beat the Bears for the seventh straight time at Soldier Field, which was the longest streak by either side in a 79-year-old rivalry, and then two games later we went into Minnesota and beat the Vikings, who had been 7-0 at home. We were playing our best football at the very end, and I thought that was a great tribute to Mike. It was a big factor with me in giving him the general manager's duties after Ron came to me on February 1 and told me he was going to retire.

We had played so well during those last four weeks, and I thought that would be a great help to us going into the 2001 season. I didn't want to disturb that momentum. And then when Brett Favre came out of the locker room after the last game and said that we had the best chemistry he'd seen in all his years with the team, I thought that was another tribute to Mike. I was also very concerned about bringing in somebody over him with whom he might not be comfortable and who might want to tear apart a very good, young personnel department and bring in his own scouts.

A general manager leaving creates a terrible problem for a team. You are so much better off when a coach leaves, and you can let the general manager pick his own coach, set up what he wants to do and move on. When Ron and I would sit in the press box and talk about him retiring, I kept holding out hope that he was going to decide to come back after all.

I had no one else to talk to about his retirement because Ron and I had decided to keep his plans totally quiet in case he changed his mind. I gave a lot of thought to different people I could hire as a general manager, but I didn't have anyone else I really wanted to bring in. There's no doubt that I could have gotten somebody, but the No. 1 thing that concerned me was how that guy would work with Mike. If Mike was going to succeed, I didn't want to derail him after one season. If I brought in someone new, I could hurt two people, making it tough on both the coach and the GM.

I made my decision the day we sat down with the Executive Committee and discussed different options. When Ron said that giving both jobs to Mike was the way to go, he confirmed my thoughts, and we gave Mike the dual roles.

Once Ron was ready to leave, Mike started to totally reorganize and strengthen his personnel department. The first thing he did was give three-year contracts to John Dorsey as Director of College Scouting and Reggie McKenzie as Director of Pro Personnel. Then on May 17 he made a very good move and hired Mark Hatley as Vice-President of Football Operations.

Mark's duty would be to assist Mike with player personnel decisions and to oversee both the college and the pro scouting staffs. Both Dorsey and McKenzie knew Mark from the past, and they were very comfortable working with him. There was no talk about "Why is this guy coming in over us when we were here before he was?" They accepted it very well, and a lot of that had to do with Hat's personality. He didn't see himself as the authority figure. He was just here to work with everybody.

I don't know that I was overly enthusiastic when he was first hired, but he turned out to be a super addition to our staff because he was the total opposite of Mike. Mike was such an intense individual, and it was sometimes difficult for him to relax. Hat was a laid back guy who always had a smile on his face. He got along with everybody, and he brought a calming effect to the entire personnel situation.

Mike had told me if he couldn't get Hatley, there was nobody else he wanted. But if he could get him, he'd feel comfortable that he could handle both jobs. I thought that was a pretty heavy statement.

Two days after Mike named Hat, we had the groundbreaking ceremonies for the Lambeau Field renovation. I loved watching the stadium being rebuilt. I'd drive around the parking lot every night and just look at the progress. Once I stopped by the trailer where all of these heads of different areas were meeting and said, "I just want to tell you fellows that there's no sport in the world where teamwork is more important than football, but I'm amazed at the teamwork I see going on outside this stadium every single day."

Picking out the brick for the stadium was fascinating. The project manager had slabs of brick laid out in the parking lot, and one below-zero February day he asked me to come and look at them so I could see the brick under all conditions — when it was sunny, when it was cloudy, when it was wet, when it was dry. I kept thinking we've got to pick the right brick because this stadium is going to be so enormous. If we make a mistake, it's going to be as ugly as it can be. I knew I wanted a red brick to go with the green wrought iron, but the stadium people kept warning me to make sure it didn't look too orange.

So I went out there with John Jones, Mark Schiefelbein and Ted Eisenreich. We were looking at these bricks, and I kept telling them that we had to get it right because of how big this was going to be. What I didn't know was that the three of them had decided that whichever one I picked, they were going to pick something else. So I chose the one I liked, and somebody said, "No, this one's better." And then somebody else said, "That's okay, but I prefer this one." And I just looked at them thinking, "How can you even consider that?" Then they all started laughing.

When I finally chose the one I wanted, the project manager, who had not said one word during this whole process, said, "You picked out the perfect brick for this climate." And I asked him, "Why didn't you just tell me that in the first place?" He told me it was because I was the one who had to be happy with the color.

Later on, when the head of the project called to say they were starting to put up some brick on the west side of the stadium, I couldn't wait to get over there. I was delighted with what I saw, but I watched for a long time to make sure it didn't turn orange.

Of course Madeline makes all the decorating decisions at home. If she changes the color of a room, I just walk in and say it looks nice. I'm lucky if she lets me start the lawn mower. But she's been very happy with the brick, and so have I.

We opened the 2001 season by beating the Detroit Lions, and then two days later the world changed dramatically. I was driving to work and listening to the car radio on September 11 when I heard that a plane had crashed into one of the towers at the World Trade Center in New York. The announcer said it looked like a private plane might have had some mechanical problems and couldn't avoid the building.

I had an early-morning meeting with Pete Platten and John Underwood of the Executive Committee that day, and as I got to my office I turned on a little television I had in the back of the room. That's when I heard that a second plane had already hit the building, so now there was a major scare. John and Pete came in and closed the door and we met for a little more than an hour, and by the time we broke up someone came to the door and told us there had been two more crashes, one at the Pentagon and one in the field in Pennsylvania. It was obviously a very compelling time.

After two days of consultation with the league and the Players Association, Commissioner Paul Tagliabue called off the 15 games that were scheduled for the following Sunday and Monday. It was the first time in the history of the National Football League that games were canceled for reasons other than a players' strike. I don't think there was ever much chance that we would play those games. Three thousand lives were lost, and I just didn't see how anyone could possibly ask people to get enthusiastic about football when the whole world was in a state of shock. It was Tagliabue's call. He acted on it very quickly and did the right thing.

We were scheduled to play the Giants that Sunday in East Rutherford, New Jersey, which is just across the Hudson River from Manhattan. When we did travel to New York to make up the game at the end of the season, we didn't go to the World Trade Center, but I did ask the bus driver on the way from the airport to our hotel to point out the area where the buildings had been. He did, and there was just this big open space in the sky.

We played the Washington Redskins at Lambeau Field on Monday night of the week after the Giants game was postponed, and we held pre-game ceremonies to pay tribute to the victims. We chose Chris Gizzi, a young linebacker, to run out of the tunnel with the American flag and lead the team onto the field. Chris was a graduate of the Air Force Academy, and he came out of that tunnel and ran to the other end of the field like he was totally driven. It was a very dramatic moment for us.

As the season went along, we found that we were a much better ball club than we'd been the year before. We were able to put together three, three-game winning streaks, including the last three, to finish 12-4. Mike was establishing a pattern for being tough at the end of the year. When we won at home against Cleveland on December 23, we clinched our first playoff berth since 1998.

We opened the playoffs by beating San Francisco, 25-15, which made us 11-0 in the post-season at Lambeau Field and made Brett 31-0 at home when the game-time temperature was 34 degrees or lower. That set us up to play the top-seeded Rams the next Sunday at St. Louis, where we had a terrible day.

Brett threw six interceptions, four of which were tipped and three of which were returned for touchdowns. Antonio Freeman and Ahman Green both had fumbles that ended drives, and Allen Rossum saw a 95-yard kickoff return for a touchdown wiped out by a penalty. It was just a long, frustrating game from start to finish.

The 2002 season didn't start out very well either when LeRoy Butler announced his retirement because the shoulder blade that he'd broken the previous season still hadn't mended. The doctors couldn't guarantee that it would be sound enough for contact by the time training camp ended, so he just stepped aside. Not only was LeRoy a great player, he was a great leader. We missed him tremendously.

We beat Atlanta in the opener at Lambeau Field and then lost at New Orleans before we went on a seven-game winning streak. In the seventh game of the season, against Washington, Brett was sacked by LaVar Arrington in the third quarter, and if there was ever a time that I thought his consecutive game-starting streak was in jeopardy, that was it.

He'd had his left knee twisted under Arrington, and he was down for several minutes before he had to be helped to the bench and then driven from the field on a golf cart. Doug Pederson quarterbacked us for the rest of the game, and we won, 30-9, but it was a scary time at Lambeau Field.

The doctors said Brett had a sprained ligament. When nothing new showed up on an MRI the next day, we knew surgery wouldn't be needed, and we caught a break because we had the bye week coming up. We had 14 days before we had to play a Monday night game against Miami at Lambeau Field, and Brett had time to heal. But if we'd had to play right away, that might have been the end of the streak.

The seven-game winning streak was our first since 1963, so the team was really playing at its peak. But we lost at Minnesota and then we went to Tampa where Mike Sherman had some strong post-game words for defensive tackle Warren Sapp.

We lost the game, 21-7, and we lost our left tackle, Chad Clifton, for the season when he suffered a severe pelvis injury midway through the third quarter after a blindside hit from Sapp. Brett had been intercepted, and Sapp threw a block at Clifton on the opposite side of the field, completely removed from the play. Chad was taken from the field on a cart with numbness in both feet and legs, and after the game Mike approached Sapp as the teams walked off the field.

Mike thought the hit was unnecessary because it was so far from the play, but what really upset him was seeing Sapp celebrating after he'd turned and seen Chad was down. Jerry Parins, our head of security, was walking off the field with Mike when the confrontation took place, and he told me the next day that it was really spooky to be up close to Sapp.

He said Sapp was just so big, and his eyes were popping out of his head, and he was screaming at Mike. And Mike was firing right back at him. All Jerry wanted to do was get Mike off that field. He was afraid he was going to have to separate them because Mike was adamant about saying something. He'd stand up for his players in a heartbeat. I think they were really proud of him for that.

We clinched our first division championship since 1997 by beating the Bears in Green Bay, and shortly after that we had five players named to the NFC Pro Bowl team, including guard Marco Rivera, who was the first Packers offensive lineman to make it since center Larry McCarren in 1983. We finished 12-4 again, and Brett missed winning his fourth Most Valuable Player award by four votes. Oakland's Rich Gannon got 19, and Brett got 15.

The season ended on a very disappointing note when we lost, 27-7, to Atlanta at Lambeau Field in the first round of the playoffs. Nobody was expecting that. We had won all 12 of our previous playoff games at home, and we just didn't imagine losing this one. Home field advantage in the playoffs was what you played for all year long, but the game was basically over at halftime when the Falcons took a 24-0 lead. I didn't know much about Michael Vick at the time, and I certainly didn't know he was as good as he showed that day. We just couldn't stop him, and the season was over.

A nice thing happened to the organization about halfway through the year when *ESPN The Magazine* ranked the Packers No. 1 among 121 NFL, Major League Baseball, National Basketball Association and National Hockey League franchises. The magazine looked at things like fan relations, affordability, stadium experience and how well the team performed on the field measured directly against the money it received from its fans. I found out about the honor when a newspaper man called me after he got a press release from New York. The magazine hadn't even told us we'd won. We were also named "America's Team" in a Harris poll that year, which I thought was pretty good because we'd always claimed that title anyway.

When we opened the 2003 season I learned something about ceremonies as we lost to Minnesota on the day that we dedicated the new Lambeau Field. We were behind, 20-3, after the second quarter, and my first thought as I got up to go to the field for the ceremony was "Why in the world did we ever schedule this thing for halftime? We're never doing this again."

After we lost the game, 30-25, I ran into Jim Irwin, our radio play-by-play man, and he said, "You're not going to let this dampen your enthusiasm for today, are you? You still have a beautiful, beautiful stadium." I told him I wasn't, but it still hurt a lot.

We had unveiled 14-foot statues of Curly Lambeau and Vince Lombardi in the stadium plaza outside the Atrium on August 27, and then a week later I was very honored when the plaza was named after me. That had been instigated by the Executive Committee after we'd won the stadium referendum. Don Harden and John Underwood told me about it, and I was just delighted. My boys came home for the ceremony, and it was such a thrill to be able to share an area with two great names like Lambeau and Lombardi. That is the ultimate.

I would get another very nice surprise the following January when Mike Gage, the president of the Packers Hall of Fame, called me out of the blue. He told me I had been nominated for election to the Hall in July. It was a great honor, and to have it happen before I retired was especially rewarding.

The 2003 season showed once again that Mike was very tough down the stretch, winning six of our last seven games. We won the division with a 10-6 record, and there were some very interesting games in there.

We beat Detroit in the second week, but then we lost at Arizona, which put us at 1-2 going into Chicago. The week of the Bears game I decided to have a couple of skin areas tested, one on the back of my right shoulder and the other on the right side of my neck just under my ear. The area on my neck had been treated previously by Dr. Michael Smullen, who removed something that wasn't cancerous. But sometime after that, the skin had turned brown.

I'd gone to a meeting where I was sitting next to Pete Platten. Pete called me at the office after the meeting and said he hadn't wanted to bring it up when everyone was there, but he wondered if I had had my neck looked at. He had had skin cancer in the past, and he said it just didn't look good. I made up my mind to get the area examined.

At about that same time, Madeline walked by me one day while I was shaving and had my shirt off. She saw the mole on my right shoulder and said she didn't remember it being there before. She wanted me to get it checked out. So I went to Dr. Smullen, and he took a small sample from each area and sent it over to a clinic. He told me they'd let me know.

A big group from the Executive Committee made the trip to Chicago that Saturday, and we had a great weekend. We had a wonderful time at Mike Ditka's Restaurant the night before the game, and then we beat the Bears, 38-23. I was feeling terrific until I came into the office the next day and got a call from Dr. Smullen.

He called around 8:30 a.m. and told me that both of the areas that had been checked at the clinic were melanoma. The word came as a real shock to me. I guess "scared" certainly describes it. He was very blunt, saying, "I've called Dr. Gray, and we need to do something right away."

Dr. John Gray is the Packers' associate team physician and our family doctor. He came to see me very quickly. When I asked him what I needed to do, he said I was going to have to have surgery immediately, and he wanted to get me in to see Eugene Schmitt, a dermatologist and surgeon, the first thing the next morning. He also wanted Thomas Geocaris, a surgeon, involved in the operation.

I called Madeline, and she jumped on it pretty fast. Being a nurse, she obviously recognized how serious this was. She asked me what John wanted to do, and I told her I was going to see Dr. Schmitt the next morning, and we'd take it from there.

I was at Dr. Schmitt's office at 6:30 on Tuesday morning. He looked at the areas and wanted to know if we had had any other melanomas in the family. As it happened, Kevin had had one removed from his leg a few years before, and when I told him that, he was very concerned.

I spent the rest of the day undergoing tests. They put me in these tubes to check out different parts of my body and see if the cancer had spread. I must have been in one of those for a couple of hours. It's funny what goes through your mind during something like that.

I'm lying in this tube on a Tuesday morning finding out how severe my cancer is, when just two days earlier I had been having a great time in Chicago. I was feeling wonderful when I went to work on Monday, and then I got that phone call and all at once I didn't feel so wonderful.

I never really thought, "Why me?" Instead, the thing that hit me was how fast your life changes. I've told people since, "Appreciate your health, because once it goes you don't think of anything else."

When I went to see Dr. Geocaris, he described the surgery, the part he would play in it and how they were going to do it. He told me that they were going to go as deep as they could and make sure they got all of the cancer out of there. I had a brief meeting with an oncologist after that.

Dr. Schmitt and Dr. Geocaris performed the surgery the next day, and they did a wonderful job on me. The operation lasted about 3½ hours, and they came in together the next morning to tell me that things were looking very good. Both areas were stage one, and nothing had spread to the lymph nodes. They were going to be able to send me home. I was in the hospital one day and home the next, although I did have to watch the next two games, against Seattle and Kansas City, on television.

They forwarded all of the test results to the oncologist after the surgery, and he called me back and said, "I don't consider you a patient," which was a huge relief.

While I was in surgery Madeline had spent most of her time alone in the hospital chapel. We didn't want the boys to know about this right away, and so she waited to call them until after the surgery when we knew I was all right.

My biggest problem afterwards was that I had lost some strength in my right arm, but Dr. Gray and Dr. McKenzie, our team physician, worked with me a lot, and I felt pretty good after a while. I asked Dr. Schmitt how something like this could have come up, and he said it might have been dormant for a long time, and then just appeared. I know when I was a kid I caddied a lot, and when I played golf I never wore a hat. We never knew the dangers of the sun in those days. Or at least I didn't.

Now I'm extremely cautious about it. I use a lot of sunscreen, and I wear a hat constantly when I'm on the golf course. In fact I almost have a fear of the sun, which isn't real good either. But that's working out better now. The first couple of years after the surgery I went back to see Dr. Schmitt every three months, but that eventually dropped to every four months, and now it's every six months. It's been almost four years now, and they tell me the longer I go the better my chances are that it won't come back.

While all of this was going on with me, we were having our troubles on the football field, too. After winning in Chicago, we beat Seattle, but then we lost to Kansas City and went into St. Louis on October 19 with a 3-3 record. We not only lost the game, 34-24, but Brett suffered a hairline fracture of his right thumb on his second pass of the day. He never left the game, but I was really worried that this would be the injury that he couldn't get over.

The idea of a quarterback playing more than half a season with a broken thumb is amazing, but everything Brett does is like a new dimension. Still, you wondered about his effectiveness. But it was just like the Arrington thing. We had a bye the next week before we had to play at Minnesota. I thought the only thing that was going to save him was the calendar, and it did.

We beat the Chargers, 38-21, in San Diego in our 14th game, and Brett threw a second-quarter scoring pass to Donald Driver that marked the 23rd straight game in which he'd thrown for at least one touchdown, breaking Cecil Isbell's record set in 1942. We set two other franchise records that day. Ahman Green gained 75 yards to give him 1,538 on the year, breaking Jim Taylor's 41-year-old single-season rushing mark. And Ryan Longwell became our all-time scoring leader with 824 points, passing Don Hutson, who had held the record for 58 years.

And then a week later we went to Oakland for a Monday night game the day after Brett's father died. Brett's friends and family encouraged him to play against the Raiders, and Brett himself said that his dad would have wanted him to play. And so he proceeded to turn in one of the greatest performances of his career.

It was a very emotional night. Deanna met him as he was coming off the field, and there were a lot of tears and a lot of hugs. It had to be very tough on Brett, but he handled it so well. That was the night his teammates showed him with their play what they thought of him. Everybody did it that night for Brett.

We beat Denver, 31-3, in our last game of the regular season at Lambeau Field, and by the time it was over, nobody was watching. The fans were all listening to radios or straining to see the televisions in the private boxes. While we were beating the Broncos, the Vikings were playing at Arizona in a game they were heavily favored to win. By the end of our game, there was a lot more interest in what was happening in Tempe than there was in what was happening in Green Bay.

The Cardinals upset the Vikings, 18-17, on a 28-yard touchdown pass on the last play of the game that knocked Minnesota out of the playoffs and gave us the NFC North Division championship. It was just fascinating to look out into the stands and watch all of those people straining for a glimpse of a TV to see what the Vikings were doing. I was standing in the top row of this little booth with Mark Hatley, and we were just kind of waving at people and they were waving back at us. We all started jumping up and down like crazy when the Cardinals completed that pass.

So we were in the playoffs, and we had a home game with the Seattle Seahawks, coached by Mike Holmgren and quarterbacked by our former backup, Matt Hasselbeck. The game was tied, 27-27, at the end of regulation, and the captains came out onto the field for the coin flip to determine who got the ball first in overtime. The Seahawks won the flip, and Hasselbeck said, "We want the ball, and we're going to score."

I think if Mike had been out there with him he would have strangled him. I had known Matt when he was here, and I liked him very much. He was just a young kid who was speaking out of turn. You wanted the guy to feel that way, but you didn't want him to say it at that point. He was a great kid, but I was thinking, "Oh Matt, just be quiet." But he said it, and he had to be very sorry afterward. The fact that you knew him and you knew what he was really like helped you to accept it a little bit.

And then he threw an interception. I remember his passing into the left flat for Alex Bannister, and Al Harris jumping in front of Bannister and taking the pass 52 yards for a touchdown. That was the first time in NFL history that a defensive touchdown ended a playoff game in overtime. We won, 33-27, and went to the divisional playoff game in Philadelphia.

The Eagles had had a lot of injuries going into that game, and we were favored to win. We had a 14-7 lead at halftime, which could have been more if they hadn't stopped Ahman on a fourth-and-one at the goal line late in the second quarter. Then they just kept coming back at us. Their final drive should have ended with 1:12 left in the game when they faced fourth down and 26 yards to go on their own 26. Instead, they pulled off the famous fourth-and-26 play that I'm afraid we're going to hear about for the rest of our lives.

As usual, I had left the press box in the fourth quarter. I went down to the field level and found this little storage area off our locker room with a TV in it. There was a security guy, and I just showed him my pass and went in there by myself. When it got to fourth and 26 I couldn't have been much more confident. I mean, you figure, "Fourth and 26, what are the chances?" I was ready for the celebration.

And then Donovan McNabb completed a 28-yard pass to Freddie Mitchell for the first down. That set up David Akers' 37-yard field goal with five seconds left, tying the game at 17 and sending it into overtime. We ran just one play in the overtime when Brett threw a pass for Javon Walker under a lot of pressure, and Brian Dawkins intercepted it. Akers kicked a 31-yard field goal 4:48 into the overtime, and the Eagles won.

I was as devastated as I've ever been at a football game. That ranked right up there with watching Steve Young throw for the final touchdown to Terrell Owens and losing the Super Bowl in 1998. I was in that little room by myself. I had nobody to talk to, so I just stared at the TV.

The locker room afterwards was as quiet as I've ever seen it. Often after a tough loss, the players will come in grumbling and swearing and maybe throwing some stuff, but not this time. They just walked in and sat down at their lockers like it still hadn't set in. Nobody said a word. There was just shock on their faces, like, "What the heck just happened here? How did this get away?"

Mike fired our defensive coordinator, Ed Donatell, after the season, which surprised me a little bit. I happened to be in the office a couple of days later on a Saturday. I thought nobody was there, but when I went down the hall to make some copies, who should I see but Ed? I couldn't believe it. He was trying to print something, and when he saw me he just came over and gave me a big hug and said thank you. I thanked him, too, but I was so shocked to see him that it was very awkward. I told him, "You're going to be fine," and he said, "Yeah, I know. I've already had some calls."

I think Atlanta was one of those calls, and that's where he wound up. I don't know if he thought he'd been made a scapegoat for fourth and 26, but if he felt that way I don't think he would have said it to me. Jeff Jagodzinski, our tight ends coach then, was let go at the same time.

I've seen Ed a couple of times since then when we've played Atlanta, and he's come over and talked to me. He has always been a real gentleman. I just wished him all the best that day, and that was the end of it.

We had a new defensive coordinator when the 2004 season began. And we had a new general manager when it ended.

CHAPTER TWENTY-THREE

Time for a Change

Mark Hatley had gone golfing with several of our coaches. As he was putting his clubs in the trunk of his car, he told Tom Rossley, our offensive coordinator, that he felt some tightness in his chest. Tom asked him if he had seen a doctor. Mark said no, it was probably indigestion, he'd be fine. And he went home.

When Mark didn't show up for work in the morning, we sent Marc Lillibridge from our pro scouting staff to check on him. Mark Hatley lived in a townhouse in Green Bay while his wife stayed at their home in Tulsa. She would come to visit him, and he'd go out there to visit her, but she hadn't moved here permanently. So he was alone from the time he left the golf course that afternoon.

I was talking on the phone with someone the next day when I looked up and saw Melanie Marohl, the salary cap analyst in our Personnel Department, standing in my doorway, and she was crying. I told the person I was talking to that I'd have to call back, and when I hung up, the first thing Melanie said was, "I think Mark Hatley is dead." She said he'd been found at his house, and she didn't know any more details.

I went down immediately to the football offices on the third floor where I found out that Marc Lillibridge had knocked on Mark's door, and when he didn't get an answer he tried his cell phone. When that didn't work, he just beat the door down. Marc is a big man, and he was very close to Hat. In fact, he told me once that Hat was like a father to him. He said he found him in his bed just lying there, and he knew immediately that he was dead.

Mark died on July 26. The Brown County medical examiner said he'd suffered a sudden heart attack brought on by clogged arteries. It was an immense loss for the Green Bay Packers on both a professional and personal level. He was not only very good at his job, but he was somebody you just loved to be around. I always marveled at how much Mark thought of Green Bay and the tradition here even though he'd come to us from the Bears, a division rival. He would tell me this was the best place in the league, and he'd been in some pretty good places. He loved it here. It was a crime that we lost him because he was such a good man and such a big part of the organization.

I've always wondered what might have happened if Mark had lived. When I was dealing with Mike Sherman and the general manager's duties, would I have bitten the bullet and said, "Hat, you take over" even though he had worked under Mike? I would have had to give him serious consideration in that situation, and it might have changed everything. It would have been a hard call, but after I'd watched him work with Mike and the staff, he was the one guy I thought could do it. When he passed away, it was a tough loss in so many ways.

Mike Sherman is a very intense guy. He's going to give you everything he's got, and I appreciate that. But I thought he was becoming extra intense and feeling more pressure going into the 2004 season. And my concern grew as I watched him deal with cornerback Mike McKenzie's holdout.

It was just before the draft in April when McKenzie called our personnel department and said he wanted to be traded unless something was done about his contract. He had three years left on a five-year extension that he had signed in January of 2002, but he believed he was being underpaid, and he said he wouldn't come to training camp unless the deal was renegotiated.

The McKenzie situation was a matter of principle with Mike Sherman. He is a very ethical man, and the fact that McKenzie could sign an extension and be satisfied two years earlier and then suddenly be totally unhappy and make all of this noise bothered him deeply. That's just so anti-Mike Sherman, and Mike could be pretty stubborn.

We opened the season by winning at Carolina, 24-14, and two days later McKenzie and his agent, Drew Rosenhaus, came to Green Bay to meet with Mike. McKenzie was back on the practice field that afternoon, but he was still saying his contract was under market value, and Mike was still insisting he wasn't going to rework it.

That's when we started having problems in the locker room. You can't have somebody as upset as McKenzie was down there with 52 other players and make it a positive situation. Meanwhile, it was obvious to me that McKenzie was driving Mike crazy, and he was spending a lot more time worrying about him and his agent than he was about the next game.

Our drafts were showing some bad signs as well. I remember the day in the draft room when we were considering Ahmad Carroll. Mike was talking to the University of Arkansas coach on the phone, and I kept looking at this guy who was 5-10 and thinking, "Is that what we need?" We had always talked about how this division had big receivers, and it just seemed like somebody better should have been there in the first round.

We lost our next two games after winning at Carolina, and I had three meetings with Mike in the week before Game 4 against the New York Giants. That was very unusual for us. They weren't really formal meetings. They were more happenstance, and they lasted only about 10 minutes apiece. But all Mike could talk about was McKenzie.

I stopped down to see him twice that week, and when I was down in the breakfast room with the team on a Saturday morning, he came by and asked if I could sit down with him. I said sure, and we had a cup of coffee and talked about McKenzie some more. He was just so totally frustrated with the way things were going. He couldn't get the agent to do anything, and he was having trouble getting New Orleans to make a decision on a trade.

I asked him if there was anything he'd like me to do. I offered to step in at any time, but he said no, he had to handle it. I think he just wanted somebody to listen to him. It was the kind of situation that when McKenzie was out of camp he was getting all of the headlines, and when he came back he was so disgruntled Mike worried about what he was doing to his locker room.

Seeing Mike so preoccupied with general manager duties while our football team wasn't playing well at all convinced me that that dual role was too big a burden to put on one guy. That's when I put in a call to Ron Wolf.

I told Ron I wanted to hire a general manager to totally run the football program, which is what I would have liked to have done in 2001 if I hadn't been so worried about bringing in somebody who could work with Mike. I was still concerned about that, and ironically the thing that I had feared then proved to be a legitimate concern. He did have trouble co-existing with a new man.

I asked Ron if he could suggest a name for the general manager's job, and he didn't even hesitate. He said, "Absolutely. Ted Thompson." He told me that Ted had built the Seattle team, he was ready and he'd do a good job. I didn't even tell Ron that Ted was who I had been thinking about the whole time. I just said, "Thank you. You've made my day. I'll talk to you soon." And we hung up.

I also called Willie Davis, our Hall of Fame defensive end and a member of the Board of Directors, whose judgment I trust a great deal and told him what I was thinking about doing. I said, "You've watched us play all year. What are your thoughts?" He gave me a very simple answer. He said, "Bob, it's the right thing to do. He needs help."

So I had really made my decision before we even played the Giants. We were playing bad football, and every time I met with Mike, it was "Mike McKenzie, Mike McKenzie, Mike McKenzie," and I just thought, "I've got to help this guy." The idea was always to help him.

I knew he wasn't going to see it that way, but my responsibility was to try to put the best group out there, and we had to have someone else participating to make us the best group. I needed to do what was best for the organization, obviously, but at the same time I felt what was best for the organization was not to hurt Mike Sherman.

Then we went out and played a very flat game against the Giants. We lost it, 14-7, and a couple of weeks later, on October 19, I went to the Executive Committee and asked for permission to go after Ted Thompson after the season was over.

I told the Committee members that I'd watched Ted for the eight years he had worked here, starting in 1992 as an Assistant Pro Personnel Director before Ron promoted him to Pro Personnel Director in 1994 and then to Director of Player Personnel in 1997. He had gone to Seattle with Mike Holmgren in 2000 as Vice President of Football Operations. I told the Committee that I didn't like having one person in both jobs, and I thought it was becoming really troublesome to Mike. And they gave me their approval.

Ted's name was starting to become prominent around the league. He'd been interviewed by Miami the previous season, and I had heard through other sources that the Dolphins were still interested in him. This was at the same time as the rumor was going around that Mike Reinfeldt might have a chance to take over the top job at Cleveland, and if he did he would make Ted his general manager. In 2007, Mike did get the general manager's job with the Tennessee Titans.

Ted was the only one I had in mind for our job, and if he hadn't been available Mike Sherman probably would still have been the general manager the next year. So we just went through the season, and I figured when the year was over, I'd see how we were doing and move on.

In the meantime we were having other problems off the field. We played very badly in our fifth game, losing at home to Tennessee, 48-27, and after the game Tom Rossley said he wasn't feeling good. He still didn't feel good when he came in the next morning, so Mike insisted that he go to the hospital. After Tom had some tests, he underwent an angioplasty to open a blocked artery.

A couple of weeks later, Brett acknowledged to reporters that his wife Deanna was undergoing treatment for breast cancer and that she had had a lumpectomy earlier at the Sloan Kettering Cancer Center in New York. She was scheduled for a lot of chemotherapy over the next several months, but the doctors were convinced she would be fine.

This was coming on the heels of Mark Hatley's death in July, and then in early September, we had lost another great part of this organization when Red Cochran died of heart failure after undergoing hip replacement surgery. Red had been associated with us as an assistant coach or a scout for 42 years. He was 82, but he was as feisty as ever, and he was still doing some part-time scouting for us in the Midwest.

Then two days after we had played Minnesota on Christmas Eve, we learned that Reggie White had passed away at age 43. There were just so many tragedies, and it got so you were thinking, "When does this end?"

At least we resolved the McKenzie problem on October 4 when we traded him and a conditional sixth-round draft choice in 2006 to New Orleans for quarterback J.T. O'Sullivan and a second-round pick in 2005. That second-round pick turned out to be Nick Collins, a starting safety for us now who should play a prominent role in the future. From that standpoint, we got a pretty good player in that deal.

McKenzie was a tough situation. Now whenever a player is disgruntled, people are going to go back and look at what happened there. It's a matter of who's in charge of the team, the players and their agents or the coach and the general manager? Our fans will love you as long as you're a Green Bay Packer, but if you turn your back on the team, you become public enemy No. 1 in a heartbeat. Once McKenzie had started complaining about his contract and then failed to report to training camp, he was not a popular guy here. He's still not a popular guy here, and he never will be.

Interestingly enough, we started to get better very quickly after he left. We lost the Tennessee game the following weekend, but we broke our four-game losing streak in Game 6 at Detroit. Mike gave the team a rousing speech that week, and we won, 38-10. I don't know what he said, but the team that had been so flat suddenly came to life, and we won six in a row. But even though we were winning those games, I still felt Mike needed help. Once I started looking at Ted, I never changed my mind.

The winning streak ended when we lost, 47-17, at Philadelphia. We beat Detroit, but we lost again at home against Jacksonville to make us 8-6. But we won our last two games on the road against Minnesota and Chicago, clinching our third straight division title by beating the Vikings, 34-31, on Ryan Longwell's 29-yard field goal. Ironically, we had beaten the Vikings by the same score at home on November 14 on a 33-yard field goal by Longwell.

We played the Vikings again in the wild card playoff round at Lambeau Field, and the game was a train wreck. We were heavily favored because we had beaten them twice and because they were 3-7 over the last 10 weeks of the season. But Daunte Culpepper had a big game for Minnesota. He completed 19 of 29 passes for 284 yards and four touchdowns with no interceptions, while Brett threw four interceptions, and we lost, 31-17. But the outcome really had no effect on Mike's status. My mind had long since been made up at that point.

The Vikings playoff game was played on January 9, and on the previous day Seattle had lost to St. Louis in its wild card game. So the Seahawks were finished, and the way was clear for me to call them and try to get permission to talk to Ted.

I sat down with Mark Schiefelbein, our Administrative Affairs Director, after we lost to the Vikings and told him what I was working on. I asked Mark to try to get a private plane from somebody on our Board of Directors to pick up Ted and bring him back to Green Bay if I could work out something in Seattle.

Then I called Ron Wolf and asked if he'd been hearing any rumors about what was going on with the Cleveland Browns or anyone else who might be interested in Ted. Ron still had a lot of sources in the league, and he said everything was quiet.

The next day I had to fly to New York for a meeting of the NFL Management Council's Executive Committee, and when I got to my hotel room on that Monday night, I called Mark and asked if there was anything I needed to know. He said nothing was happening.

The Management Council meeting was January 11, and I planned to leave New York the next day and start working on the Ted Thompson situation. I still hadn't talked to Ted because I hadn't even asked permission yet, and I wanted to visit with Mike Sherman first. The next day I flew out of LaGuardia and into Detroit where I had a little layover.

While I was there I called Mark to see if anything was new, and unfortunately something was. He said he'd gotten a call from Ron Wolf, who told him we had to get Ted out of Seattle as quickly as possible because they were having a power struggle within the Seattle organization. Ron said it could be Mike Holmgren, or it could be Bob Whitsitt, but the sooner we got Ted out the better because it was hard to tell what was going to happen.

Here I was in the Detroit airport, and for the first time, I was nervous. We got on the plane, and when we landed at Green Bay the pilot announced that they were having trouble finding someone who could drive the jet bridge out to the plane. All I wanted to do was get to the office, and I was stuck on a plane in the Green Bay airport. I was ready to break a window and jump out. We sat there for at least 15 minutes before we could get off the plane.

When I finally got to the office, the first thing I did was write a fax for Bob Whitsitt, requesting permission to talk to Ted Thompson about making him our Director of Football Operations. I gave that to Jason Wied, our Corporate Counsel, to send to Seattle for me. In the meantime I went directly to Mike Sherman's office on the third floor and told Mike what I was planning to do.

I told him this had nothing to do with his record. It was just a feeling I had that the two jobs were becoming very burdensome for him and I wanted to make a change. I told him I was going to ask for permission to talk to Ted, and Mike's first reaction was, "I'm not sure you can get Ted Thompson."

I said, "Maybe I can't, but I still owe it to you to let you know what I'm trying to do. If I don't get him, I don't get him. But I'm trying to, and this is why. I think you need help, and I think I can take some of the burden off you. I don't think it's good for your health, and I believe you need more time for your family. This is not to hurt you, it's to help you."

Mike was obviously surprised. He wasn't pleased about it, but there was not a big argument or anything like that. I told him, "You know Ted, and you know how he works. I've always been concerned about somebody coming in and working over you, but I feel you two can make this work." He said he could make it work with Ted. Then we shook hands, and I left his office.

I'm sure he took it personally. No matter how many times I said I was trying to give him help, I don't think he ever bought it. But that was exactly what I was trying to do. We had a system that I wasn't really fond of anyway, and we were getting into trouble with it. It was changing Mike. I heard that from a lot of people on the staff.

Mike and I had seen a lot of each other the year he worked with Ron and in the first few years when he was doing both jobs. I was probably as close to him at that time as I'd been to Mike Holmgren. But that definitely cooled after I gave the general manager's duties to Ted. We rarely talked in that last year after Ted got here.

I couldn't help thinking, "But Mike, I'm the same guy who gave you the chance to be a general manager. You might not like what I'm doing now, but maybe nobody else would have ever given you that chance. I did, and now it's my choice to change it."

Mike's salary didn't change at all when we hired Ted. We didn't take one penny away from him, even though he was doing half of what he'd been doing before. That was another sign that we were trying to help him, not hurt him.

Mike is a very nice guy. I liked him a great deal. I really did. But sometimes you're not fond of doing things you have to do. And I had a responsibility to the organization.

Within 45 minutes of sending the fax to Whitsitt, I got permission to talk to Ted, which was very surprising. Sometimes it can take a day or two for that to happen, but I got the permission right away. Whitsitt was Mike Holmgren's boss, and I've heard a lot of rumors about that.

One of them was that Whitsitt thought letting one of Mike's best people go might have been a way for him to get back at him. Holmgren used to tell people in Seattle that while he had the final say on players, everything was given to him by Ted. He said Ted deserved a lot of credit for putting together a successful team. I've talked to Mike a lot since then, but I've never really asked him what went on out there.

I had Ted's cell phone number, and I called him immediately after we got permission to talk to him. I reached him on the sidelines at an East-

West Shrine Game practice and told him what I wanted to do. He said he would be interested, but he had scouts all around him at the time, and he needed to get to another location so we could talk.

We visited a couple more times that day, and I went through the parameters of the job. The next day was January 13, and we decided we would get together on the telephone the first thing that morning and start working on it.

I got a copy of Ron Wolf's contract, and I basically offered Ted the same perks and the same responsibilities that Ron had had and assured him that he would have total authority over the football operation. While Ted and I were talking on the phone, Jason Wied was down the hall talking to an attorney friend of Ted's. The attorney wasn't an agent, just somebody who was helping him with the wording of the contract.

Of course we weren't paying Ted as much as we did Ron. Ron was established as the best general manager in the league when he left here, while this was Ted's first shot at running an operation. I had an idea of where he should be in the market, and his representative knew the market, too. So we got together fairly rapidly on the numbers.

In the meantime I had Mark Schiefelbein call Ron Sadoff, a member of our Board of Directors who had a private plane, to see if we could use it to go to Seattle. Ted still hadn't agreed to take the job at the end of the day, which made me a little nervous. He said he wanted to sleep on it, and that he'd call me at 9 o'clock the next morning. I really don't know why he was hesitant then, and I've never asked him. He just said, "Can I sleep on it tonight?" And I remember thinking, "Yeah, you can, but I wish you wouldn't."

But the next morning Ted called at 9, right on the button, which was 7 o'clock his time. I had Jason and Mark in my office at the time, and Ted said, "If that job is still open, I'd like to accept it." That was great news.

I went down to Mike's office and told him I had just talked to Ted Thompson and that he had accepted the job. He said, "Fine," and that was it. It was a very, very brief conversation. He never showed any resentment or anger. It might have been inside, but he didn't show it.

We got Schief on Ron Sadoff's plane right away. He went to Seattle and picked Ted up at the airport and turned around and came right back, because I wanted to get him out of there. While they were flying back, we got word in the office that Bob Whitsitt had been relieved of his duties as President of Football Operations in Seattle.

We held a press conference in Green Bay while Ted was flying here on the afternoon of January 14, and we announced that we were hiring him. Basically we just said that in the modern salary cap environment where rosters were being overhauled every year, the jobs of both the coach and the general manager were becoming very demanding, and we were very pleased to be moving into the future with two highly-regarded men at the top of our football operation.

Ted got into town at about 5 p.m., and we had his press conference the next day.

I felt very good about getting Ted because I liked what he had done at Seattle, and I liked what he'd done in Green Bay. He was a guy who was getting recognized by other teams as a talent, and it wouldn't have been long before he got this job some place. I thought he was the ideal guy to bring in to work with Mike. But I didn't think it was going to be easy, and it wasn't.

CHAPTER TWENTY-FOUR

An Uneasy Truce

The season was in trouble immediately. We lost our first four games in 2005, and I didn't see a lot of connection between Ted Thompson and Mike Sherman. I remember one day in particular when I stopped by the practice field and saw Ted talking to Mike, and Mike was just looking off in another direction. I wondered, "Is he even listening?" It was a body language kind of thing, and I thought this was not a real close partnership.

You need that communication between a coach and a general manager. I remembered how Ron Wolf and Mike Holmgren would stand on the practice field and talk for a long time. There was a lot of back and forth between those two, but it wasn't like that with Ted and Mike Sherman. It just seemed like there was a strain there that I always feared would exist.

I chose Ted because I thought he would be the one man who could come in and work with Mike. To this day I still feel that way. If anybody was going to do it, Ted was the guy. He had a quiet personality and didn't show a lot of intensity, while Mike was very intense. There were other people who I could have considered, but they would have made it harder to co-exist than Ted did. Still, it was tough for Mike to accept that change. We tried to make it as smooth as possible, but I think Mike just couldn't accept the fact that some duties had been taken away from him.

When I hired Ted, I was as confident in him as I had been in Ron Wolf. I had gotten to watch him work with Ron for eight years, so I knew him much better than I'd known Ron when I hired him.

Then Ted went to Seattle, where he put that team together. Mike Holmgren was making the final decisions there, but someone had to give Mike the material with which to make those decisions, and that some-body was Ted. I felt we needed a retooling, and Ted was a great guy to get that done for us. He was at an age to do it, and Ron told me that Ted had grown tremendously in the years he had worked for him.

And then he had gotten to work for a very demanding guy in Mike Holmgren and succeeded in putting together a team that got to the Super Bowl. I knew what I was getting in Ted, and that's why I felt so strongly about him. This is a guy who lives and breathes the game. He devotes his entire life to this football team. He has never been married, so going on the road or sitting in that dark room day after day and looking at video is something he has no trouble handling. I'm very impressed with his work ethic.

He didn't begin with an easy off-season, either. We didn't know whether Brett would be back that winter, and we lost some key players to free agency.

I don't think people understood how much Ted wanted Brett to come back. He sat down and talked with him for an hour before Brett left the city following the 2004 season, and he exchanged phone calls with him almost every week. I would ask Ted after some of those conversations if he had gotten a feeling about what Brett was going to do, and he would say, "Not really. He talks about a million different things, but I just don't think he's ready to make a decision."

Both Ted and Mike took trips individually to Hattiesburg to visit with Brett. They were recruiting the guy. Brett was wavering because Deanna had been diagnosed with breast cancer. But after undergoing several months of chemotherapy, she was making good progress and seemed to be getting better all the time. I think that more than anything convinced him to return. It took him a long time to do it, but it really was a family decision. He was very cautious about it.

Of course as Ted and Mike were making their plans in the off-season, they wanted to know if they were going to need a veteran backup quarterback. Those people were being signed by other teams. So it was a concern as they were trying to build a roster, but they never came to me and said Brett just had to make a decision. They were very patient.

And then on March 10, Brett called Mike, and they had a long talk. That's when he said he would return for the 2005 season. I wasn't surprised. The general feeling on the administrative side of the building was that he wouldn't be coming back, but I always thought he would. He is just such a competitor.

Meanwhile, both of our starting guards signed as free agents with other teams, and we released safety Darren Sharper. Mike Wahle went to

Carolina and Marco Rivera went to Dallas, while Minnesota took Sharper. To lose two veteran offensive linemen was difficult, but they were offered such enormous signing bonuses by the other clubs that it was hard for us to decide that guards should get that kind of money.

Marco said he was shocked by the Cowboys' offer. He thought he was going to get about $3 million to sign, and he got almost triple that. I never had the impression that Mike Sherman resented losing those players. I think he could look at the salaries and understand that if you did something for one or two people it was going to affect all of the others. If Mike had any misgivings, he didn't voice them to me.

Brett never talked along those lines, either. He has always been good about staying back and working with what he's given. He's not the kind who's going to cry about what's around him.

Ted conducted his first draft for us in April, and there was a lot of excitement in the room when California quarterback Aaron Rodgers was still available with the 24th pick. He had been projected as the top pick in the draft by some people in the media, and the scouts were extremely pleased. Ted was calm, very well-prepared and totally in control at the draft. He knew exactly where he wanted to go. He's very committed to the draft. He's had a few free agents who have been good for us, but he won't just go into free agency hog wild. He knows rounds ahead of time what he wants to do. Mike tended to move up and change a lot, and I think Ted's approach is sounder.

I didn't see Mike making a lot of appearances in the draft room that year. He was kind of in and out, but he wasn't there all the time. Ted would pose questions to him, but it was obviously Ted's draft, and Mike understood that. I didn't see any conflict there at all.

On August 23, after a long wait, Ted announced that Mike had accepted a two-year contract extension that would keep him as coach through 2007. Ted would come to me frequently before he offered the extension and say that he wanted to make sure that Mike was happy with him, and he was happy with Mike. Mike had a year to go on his contract, and Ted was a little concerned about him going into a lame duck year. I told him if he wanted to wait four or five games into the season to see how the relationship would go, that would be fine, but Ted said he thought it was going to work out. And so he did the deal.

The season itself was very difficult. We finished 4-12, giving us our first losing record since 1991. That 13-year winning streak meant an awful lot to me. It started during free agency when people were saying that the Packers were going to suffer because the franchise was small, and the weather was too cold and nobody would want to come here. But then we went through 13 straight years of above .500 football. The franchise record is 14, set between 1934 and 1947 when Curly Lambeau was coach, and I thought it would be a great accomplishment if we could tie or break that record.

But when we lost to Philadelphia in the eleventh game on November 27, it not only knocked us out of the division race, it ended our string of non-losing seasons, which was the longest in the league at that time. Still, we were very competitive all year long. Eight of our losses came by seven points or less. We lost three games by three points each, one by two points and one by one point. The only blowout came on a Monday night when we lost, 48-3, in Baltimore in the 14th game of the season. Every other week we had a chance to win, but we just didn't get it done.

The season bothered Ted a great deal. He came to me a couple of times and said he was sorry that things were going the way they were in his first year on the watch. He hadn't had a lot of opportunity to see us when he was in Seattle, and after he'd spent time around the team and looked at a lot of tape, he admitted that he'd thought we were a little better than we were.

The way the year started gave us an indication of where we were headed. We had 14 penalties when we lost the opener at Detroit, 17-3. It was the fewest points we had scored since 1992, and it was also the game when we started our injury jinx. We lost Javon Walker, our best receiver, in the third quarter.

I don't know that anyone saw that 0-4 start coming. It was a feeling this organization hadn't had since 1991, and it was scary. Everyone thought we had a better ball club than that. Of course I had been around in the 70's and 80's when we had only three full winning seasons, but I really felt if we had the right football people in place we would never sink to that level.

I had seen other great organizations fall to 3-13 and go through some of the things that we were going through. I saw Dallas do it, and I saw Chicago do it, and they bounced back a few years later and became strong again. So my hope was, if we were going to run into this, let's make it as short a bump as we possibly can and start winning again.

The strangest game of the year came in the seventh week when we lost, 21-14, at Cincinnati. We were behind by seven points with less than a minute to play, but we were on Cincinnati's 28-yard line and moving the ball well. Then all at once, a fan jumped out of the stands behind our bench and ran out on the field where he took the football out of Brett's hands. He ran 50 yards to the opposite end of the field before the security guards caught him and threw him down.

We were in our hurry-up offense at the time, and the incident seemed to rattle us. Brett was sacked on the next play, and the drive died. Even the Cincinnati players admitted that the fan gave their defense a chance to get organized. Anyway, Brett threw five interceptions that day, and we lost the game and four of the next five.

I would sit with Ted at both home and away games during the season, and he never really talked about his thoughts on Mike. But I had a feeling the relationship wasn't what he had anticipated, and it just brought back to me what I had thought a couple of years before when I gave Mike both jobs. I'm pretty well convinced now we would have unraveled no matter who I would have brought in above him. And that bothers me because my fear came true. I don't know if it's out of my mind yet.

As the year went on, I heard from people in the scouting department that Mike was becoming more distant. Obviously, the season weighed on him tremendously. We kept losing all of those close games. Not only were the 13 straight winning years coming to an end, but it was one excruciating loss after another. That had to be a terrible burden on Mike.

We were 3-10 when we went on the road to Baltimore, and that game was awful from the start. It was the one time all year that we were never in it, and that may have been the breaking point with Mike.

We lost the following Sunday to Chicago, 24-17, and then a couple of days before our last game of the season against Seattle, Ted came to me and said he'd decided to make a change in the head coaching situation.

I asked him what happened, and he just said it hadn't worked out the way he'd expected it would, and that the team needed to go in a different direction. He said he wasn't basing it on the record or the way the players were playing. It was more a matter of where we were then and where we needed to go.

"We're all accountable," he told me. "I've made mistakes. There are things I wish I could have done differently. There are players on this team who could have played better, and there are things maybe our staff could have done better. This is a big boy place, and I'm not saying it's all

Mike's fault. I just think we need a change."

He said he'd rather sit in a dental chair than go through what he was going through right then, and I understood what he meant. This was not an easy thing for Ted to do. It was his first year; it had been a difficult season; and this was the first time he'd ever been put in a position where he had to make this kind of a call.

In the beginning, I think both Ted and Mike really tried to work together. I give them both a lot of credit for doing that. I know Ted wanted to see it work, but Mike kind of went into a shell, and finally Ted came to me and said he thought it would be in the best interest of the organization to make a change. I asked him when he wanted to do it, and he suggested we have a meeting right after the Seattle game and he'd do it then.

It was the first time all year that he'd brought up the subject of making a move, but then that's Ted's way. He's very careful about making decisions. He isn't one to talk a great deal about them until it's time to do something.

I can't say that I was totally shocked because of the way the season had gone and because I didn't see much communication between Mike and Ted. Interestingly enough, the first time Ted really admitted that that was a problem was the following year after we had hired Mike McCarthy as our new coach.

We had gone to Detroit in the third week of the season and won the ball game. It was Mike McCarthy's first victory, and obviously everyone on the team plane was excited on the way home. Ted was sitting in front of me, and Mike was sitting directly across from me. I noticed Ted get up and sit with Mike, and they talked for a while and had some good laughs.

When Ted went back to his seat, I said to him, "That's something I never saw last year." He asked, "What's that?" I told him, "You going over there and sitting with the head coach."

He looked at me and said, "I wanted to, but I never felt like I was welcome." I thought that told an awful lot about what their relationship had become.

We had a press conference on January 2, the day after the Seattle game, and Ted announced that Mike was being relieved of his duties as coach. He basically told the press that it was his job to watch and learn and see where we needed to go, and he'd decided it was time for a new coach to lead the team.

Then Mike had a press conference a couple of days later to say good-bye to everybody. I was truly sorry that it hadn't worked out. I liked Mike. He was good for us, and his family was good for the community.

Ted started interviewing coaching candidates immediately, and he talked to some very good people. The list included our defensive coordinator Jim Bates; Cleveland offensive coordinator Maurice Carthon; New York Giants defensive coordinator Tim Lewis, who was a former player for us; Dallas offensive coordinator and assistant head coach Sean Payton; and defensive coordinators Wade Phillips of San Diego and Ron Rivera of Chicago. And of course Mike McCarthy.

Ted brought most of the coaches into Green Bay, although he went to Chicago to talk to Rivera and to New York to interview Lewis. When the candidates first got here, I would lead them down into the football area and take them on an hour tour of the facilities. I enjoyed the tours a great deal because they gave me a chance to get to know the people and to let them see a little bit about what we had here. A number of them had played in Lambeau Field, but they weren't familiar with the weight room, the locker room and the other facilities. Ted wanted them to see all of that, and he also wanted to get my reaction to everybody we had in town. I was impressed with the caliber of people Ted had coming in.

Bates was the very last name on his list, and after he visited with him, Ted came in to see me and said Jim had had a heck of an interview. He said he thought he was finished talking to people, but he wanted to be very cautious. There is always a tendency to go with the last person interviewed. He told me he wanted to walk the hallways a little bit and think about it. He expected to have a decision the next day.

When he left my office, I honestly felt that he was going to go with Jim Bates. I didn't see Ted the rest of the day, but he came in the next morning and said he'd made his decision. He was going to hire Mike McCarthy.

As always, I said, "Fine, it's your choice." But I told him I was a little surprised. He never did tell me why he hadn't picked Jim, but I think his decision was based more on what Mike had to offer than it was on negatives about anybody else. I don't think he had a negative on anybody interviewed.

I had no reservations at all about Mike McCarthy. I remember when we had finished our tour of the facilities and I was about to take him upstairs to see Ted, he said, "I'm ready." And he was.

He gave me the impression that he had come here determined to do whatever he had to do to get the job. He loved what Green Bay represented, and he was very confident. I liked him very much. He struck me as bringing the kind of toughness that this team needs, and I liked his approach to the offense.

The announcement of Mike's hiring was made on January 12, so it didn't take Ted long. He had been very organized and very diligent in his search. He had a schedule set up, and he stayed with his schedule. He wanted to make absolutely sure that he had the right person for our situation.

Ted has never talked about "rebuilding," and neither has Mike. I think that's because both of them look at rebuilding as something that takes years to accomplish, and that's not what they're expecting here.

The system with free agency and the salary cap is set up so that one day it's going to hit you. The key is not to stay down too long when it does. We have been very fortunate. Since 1993, the start of free agency and the salary cap, the Packers are tied with the Denver Broncos for the best won-lost record in the league. We had 13 straight winning seasons, we have been in the playoffs 10 times, and we have had two Super Bowl appearances and one Super Bowl victory. We have really elevated this franchise to where we wanted it to be and to where the fans are expecting it to continue. A 4-12 season was as tough for them to accept as it was for us in the organization. You know the system is going to get you, but it's still a jolt when it does.

I think the team showed great improvement in 2006. It's a very young team, and if we can keep taking steps we'll get out of this situation and start winning again. We could be back over .500 as soon as this year. That's why Mike and Ted don't use the term "rebuilding." They see that as a long, laborious process.

You hope your football people are capable enough to avoid that, and I'm convinced that ours are. They think we're going to get back in a hurry, and that's the key.

CHAPTER TWENTY-FIVE

Bouncing Back and Looking Forward

The Jets game last fall was a nightmare. We were down, 31-0, at halftime, and I was wondering, "Is this really happening?" It was as bad a half as I'd seen in years. Ted Thompson even came down to see me and apologized for the way we were playing. Somebody said to me that it reminded him of the 70's and 80's, and I thought that wasn't far off. We lost the game, 38-10, and the fans were booing as the team left the field.

I spoke to a crowd of about 300 people in northern Wisconsin later that week, and while they were very good to me, their attitude was, "Well, let's see what happens next year." You could just tell they thought this year was over. We had a 4-8 record, and there was every potential for a second straight 4-12 season.

That possibility concerned me a great deal. You know the free agent and salary cap system is going to get you. You're going to fall, and the key is how quickly you can bounce back up. I thought, "We're not bouncing back."

That's when Mike McCarthy really stepped forward and proved himself. Mike knows what he's doing, he believes in what he's doing, and he has convinced the players that what he's doing is the right thing. It showed when we won our last four games.

A lot of young guys could have thrown it in at that point, but our players came back and played extremely good football. When it looked like they had nothing to play for, they got better on both sides of the ball and fought like crazy to win.

I know people say we played three weak teams down the stretch and then finished against the Bears when they had already locked up home field advantage in the playoffs, but I believe it was very important that we won those four games. It meant that we were on our way back. We finished 8-8, and that was with losses to New Orleans, St. Louis and Buffalo in games we could very easily have won. Those three games haunted us all year; just one more victory would have put us in the play-offs.

Now we have a good nucleus of players, and I have a great deal of confidence in Ted's ability to continue to surround Brett Favre with capable players on both offense and defense. I was thrilled when I learned that Brett would be returning for at least another year because the leadership that he brings is vitally important to this franchise.

I feel we're a much better team with him here, and that's not to put Aaron Rodgers or anybody else down. It's just that Brett has been our leader for so long, and we've got people playing for us right now who were probably in grade school when he was already a three-time MVP. When they see him run down the field after a big play and put Donald Driver on his shoulders, I think that sends a message to all of them. I wasn't surprised when he decided to come back in 2007, but then I wasn't surprised when he did the same thing the year before. Most people in our building were expecting him to leave, so I guess I was kind of the odd man out, but I just think his competitive nature keeps bringing him back

I first learned of his decision to return for the 2007 season when I got a call at my office from the sports editor of the Green Bay *Press-Gazette* at about 11 o'clock on the Friday morning before the Super Bowl. He asked me if I knew that the newspaper in Biloxi, Mississippi, had reported that Brett was coming back, and I said I didn't but I wasn't surprised. As soon as I got off the phone, I called down to Ted's office, and Ted told me he had just talked to Brett a few minutes earlier, and he was on his way up to see me. Brett had called Ted and then hung up and called his friend at the Biloxi newspaper immediately. They put the story out in Biloxi before Ted could even get upstairs.

Our fans were delighted to get the news. Calls and faxes came in from people all over the country. A lot of people had been convinced that Brett was leaving after watching his tearful TV interview following our last game against the Bears, but that didn't really throw me off.

I had been standing down by the players' tunnel after the Bears game, and so I didn't see or hear any of the interview. The first time I knew about it was when I got on the team bus where Madeline and several of the other wives were waiting to leave. They said, "Well, he's finished, isn't he?" I asked them why they thought that, and they told me about the interview. I said I had missed that, but I had just watched Brett in the locker room, and he was acting just like he always acted. If this was going to be the end, he would have certainly told his coaches and teammates then. But he hadn't said a word.

Brett is the heart and soul of this franchise, and I think it would be a sin if he left too early. I just don't think he's going to walk away until he knows he's finished. I also pray that he does know when that is. I don't want to see him embarrassed, because he's too big for that. I would be very disappointed if he held on too long and went out on a sad note. But I think Deanna will help convince him when it's time to go.

I really wouldn't be surprised if he came back for more than one year. He knows he still has a great arm, and now he can see a competitive team forming around him, thanks mainly to the extremely productive winter and spring we had before the 2006 season.

Ted's first move at that time was to sign Ahman Green to a one-year contract. Ahman was scheduled to become an unrestricted free agent, but he was coming off a torn tendon in his right leg. Ted kept telling me that nobody works harder to rehabilitate and make himself ready for the season than Ahman does, and he was right. Ahman proved that by having another 1,000-yard rushing year. Unfortunately, we did lose him to free agency in 2007.

Shortly after we signed him, defensive end Aaron Kampman and nose tackle Ryan Pickett also signed deals, and they both went on to have great seasons for us in 2006. And then on May 1, Ted made a major splash in the free agent market when he signed free agent cornerback Charles Woodson to a seven-year contract.

We did lose place-kicker Ryan Longwell to the Minnesota Vikings, however. Ryan was convinced in his own mind that he wanted to go to either a warm weather city or a dome, and we didn't get much of a chance to negotiate with him. He got his offer from the Vikings, and he was gone.

The 2006 draft went very well. In the first round we took linebacker A.J. Hawk, who became an instant starter for us, and then in the second we chose offensive lineman Daryn Colledge and wide receiver Greg Jennings. We also traded Javon Walker to Denver for more draft choices. Walker's situation was similar to Mike McKenzie's a few years ago. He was unhappy with his contract and didn't want to come to camp, and

Ted and Mike had made up their minds that they weren't going to let him put the organization through what McKenzie had put it through.

Colledge and Jennings became immediate starters, too, and then in the third round we picked Abdul Hodge and Jason Spitz. Hodge turned into a great special teams player and Spitz was a starting guard.

Ted traded down in the draft to get more choices, something he had also done in Seattle and something that Ron Wolf liked to do, too. Ted was very positive about the draft. He said there was a position or two where he would have liked to take someone who was already gone, but there were a number of places where he got players he never dreamed would be there.

A week after the draft Ted signed veteran wide receiver Donald Driver to a contract through 2009. Donald and Kampman were later named to the NFC Pro Bowl squad, which I thought was very impressive. Aaron was the only fifth-round draftee to be named, and Donald was the only seventh rounder, so there were two guys we drafted late who proved to be among the best players in the league.

When we made the cut for the final roster we had 14 rookies on the team, which was the most in the league. We had a young ball club, and Mike was making his NFL head coaching debut, so it really was a brand new team taking the Packers into the future.

The season started out very up and down. We lost the opener to Chicago, 26-0, at Lambeau Field, and Brett said after the game that maybe we just weren't very good. I guess I was higher on the team at that point than he was. The Bears were coming off a great year, and they were headed to the Super Bowl. It concerned me a little bit that Brett was that upset, but remember he was the same guy who had said during the summer that this team had as much potential as any he'd ever played on. I think those kids proved themselves to him.

We played New Orleans at home in the second week and forced three first quarter turnovers to take a 13-0 lead. If we had taken better advantage of their early mistakes, we would have had a great opportunity to jump on a young ball club and win the game. But we didn't get it done.

The next week Mike got his first victory as a head coach when we won, 31-24, at Detroit. Brett had an outstanding day, completing 25 of 36 passes for 340 yards and becoming only the second NFL quarterback in history to throw at least 400 career touchdown passes. Dan Marino had 420, and Brett finished the day with 402.

We lost at Philadelphia, 31-9, to go 1-3, but I think we sent a message to our team and to our fans after that game when we cut cornerback Ahmad Carroll, who had been our first draft choice in 2004.

Ahmad had blown the coverage on a 45-yard touchdown pass and committed a penalty that set up another touchdown, and Mike came out the next day and said we just felt like it was time to go in another direction. He was absolutely right. Mike and Ted served notice that they weren't going to put up with inadequate performances. If somebody wasn't getting the job done, they were going to deal with the problem and make the ball club better.

Game 5 was another one that got away from us when we lost to the Rams, 23-20, at Green Bay. We were trailing by only three points with less than a minute to play and the ball on their 11-yard line with a second down and 10. But then Brett was hit by two players as he took the snap, and the ball popped out of his hand. Colledge dove on it, but it squirted out from underneath him. The Rams recovered with 36 seconds left and were able to escape with a victory.

We lost wide receiver Koren Robinson after the St. Louis game when the league suspended him for violating its substance abuse policy. Koren had been released by the Vikings during their training camp, and when Ted first came to me to talk about signing him I was concerned. I had a feeling he'd come and see me about Koren because we had talked quite a bit about bringing in people with baggage. You have to be extremely cautious, and Ted knows that.

I have had fans call me and say they would rather lose games with good people than bring bad people to town, and I totally understand that. We expect bigger things from our players here, and if we had been considering someone with a real criminal past, I would have said no.

But Ted had faith in Koren. He knew him, and he guaranteed that he was a good kid who deserved a chance. He told me if Koren made one mistake here he wouldn't keep him, and that's what convinced me. You would be surprised at how little I heard from the fans about it. Koren behaved very well while he was here. I have no idea what's going to happen in the future, but I do know that he enjoyed playing here tremendously.

We came back from the St. Louis game to win, 34-24, in Miami, marking the first time in seven tries that we had beaten the Dolphins at home. But then we let another one slip away from us when we lost at Buffalo,

24-10. The stats were unbelievable. We had a 427-184 advantage in total yardage, a 26-11 advantage in first downs and a huge difference in time of possession. But we also had four turnovers.

With 4:47 to play we had one final chance to send the game into overtime. We were behind, 17-10, but we had a first and goal at the one when Brett threw a quick pass to Driver in the end zone. It was deflected right into the arms of Buffalo safety Ko Simpson, who ran it back 76 yards. Three plays later the Bills scored. We wound up getting beaten by two touchdowns in a game where we thought we would at least get a tie.

Brett was sensational the next week when we won, 23-17, at Minnesota. He finished with a 100 passer rating in a huge victory for us. I thought it gave the team a lot of confidence to beat the Vikings at their place, but then we suffered three tough losses in a row as New England beat us, 35-0, at Green Bay, Seattle beat us, 34-24, on the road, and then we had that terrible game with the Jets.

I was getting a lot of calls and letters at that point, and I think it's interesting that I haven't gotten another one since the season ended. Occasionally when people called and really started ripping us, I'd ask if they'd ever called during the 13 straight years when we finished over .500. Invariably they'd say no. But that's going to happen. The bar has been raised, and the fans expect more. Of course the bar needed to be raised. We needed to get better, and fortunately we have the right football people to make us better.

I liked Mike McCarthy from the very beginning, and the thing I keep going back to is that day I was showing him around the stadium, and he was so ready to get upstairs and start his interview with Ted. He was just so positive, and I think that carried through the season.

His players have great respect for him. He'll jump on them if he has to, but he's at an age where I think he can have a really good relationship with them. I watched him in the locker room after the final game in Chicago, and he went around from locker to locker, shaking hands and saying something to every player on the team. A couple of the players stood up and gave him a big hug.

I give Mike a great deal of credit for keeping everyone together after we'd been beaten badly by New England and the Jets. A lot of teams don't bounce back, but as a first-year coach he really proved that that was one of his strengths. Mike Sherman could do the very same thing. He had a lot of strong finishes, and his first year went the same way. It's great to have that quality back.

Every once in a while you'll read about a coach losing his team because everyone has thrown in the towel, but we had all these young kids and they didn't do that. People talk about college players coming in and playing a 16-game schedule and hitting the wall when they get to Game 12 or so. Well, we were 4-8 after Game 12, and that didn't happen.

Instead, we won in San Francisco, and then we beat Detroit and Minnesota at home before going to Chicago and finishing the season by beating the Bears. I was very pleased with that Chicago game because it got us back up to .500 and took us to where we had had only one losing season in the past 15 years. I salute the football people for that because they're the ones who did it. It's just so good for this franchise to be back to where it gets respect and to where it can be one of the elite teams in the league.

In my 18 years as CEO we had only three losing seasons, and that's important to me. I've taken the calls for years, and I know where the fans are coming from. All they want to know is what we're going to do on Sunday. If we get better in football, the rest of our business blossoms.

I've been told that as long as Ted Thompson is here, my fingerprints are going to be all over this organization, and if that's true, I'm proud of it. I was proud to hire Ron Wolf, and I was proud to hire Ted. If he's given time to keep building this ball club and make it strong, he's going to do just that.

I know that was a major hire for me, and I'm comfortable with it. I watched him for a long time before I hired him, and I thought about him for a long time before I finally went to the Executive Committee with his name. He's very sound.

Most people have said to me that my main legacy will be Lambeau Field, and if you were to ask me what I'm proudest of during my tenure as president, I'd say that on the business side it's the renovation of Lambeau Field. We had to have that stadium. I don't know what we'd do now without it.

We just barely won the referendum in 2003, and we couldn't possibly get it passed today. Bob Dunn, who was our project manager for the Hammes Co., has told me that if we wanted to do the very same $295 million project now, it would cost us $600 million. The building costs have doubled in that short period of time, and there's no way in the world we could get the public to approve a $600 million project.

People talk about a window of opportunity for a football team to succeed. Well, we had a window of opportunity to get the stadium done. I think God tapped me on the shoulder one day and said, "You'd better do it right now and get it over with." And we did. Now it's in place for the future, and we can move forward. If we didn't have the stadium, there wouldn't be a future.

On the football side, I take the greatest pride in our Super Bowl championship because even some diehard Packers fans in the late 80's and early 90's thought it was never going to happen again. You look at that lineup and that roster and you realize what a wonderful ball club that really was. But I don't think we're too far away from reaching that level again.

The NFC may not stay like it is today, with all those .500 teams, but I think we could plug some holes and get back in the next few years. And Ted is the right guy to take us there. Of course we have to have good health, and some bounces have to go our way, but it can be done. It's not like everybody's at 12-4 and we're chasing them.

My biggest regret is losing that second Super Bowl to Denver. We were a big favorite, and we really were the better team, but we just let it slip away. You regret that because it's so tough to get there, and you wonder when you'll be back. We still had some very good teams after that under Mike Sherman, but so many things have to happen to get back to the Super Bowl.

Of all the decisions I've made in this job, the one I have the most trouble with when I look back is giving both the coaching and general manager's jobs to Mike Sherman. A lot of people will say I was wrong about that, but when I think of the reasons I had for doing what I did, I'm still not convinced that it wasn't the right thing at the time. It helped me when Ron Wolf confirmed my decision. I feared that somebody coming in over Mike wouldn't work out, and I was right, but that came back to haunt me anyway. If it was ever going to work, we had the perfect guy in place in Ted Thompson.

Now those will be John Jones' calls. John is very capable, and I know he'll do a good job for us. He's surrounded by an excellent administrative staff and good football people. He just has to move forward and protect a very sacred franchise. And he'll do it.

I really don't have any great words of advice for John because he and I have worked together for so long, and he understands that the most important thing we do is on Sunday afternoons. We're obviously always looking for new sources of revenue and new ways to make Lambeau Field work for us, but everything is easier to do if you have a winning football team.

I still have an office at Lambeau Field now that I'm retired, and I intend to use it very carefully. I want to stay out of John's way. I'll only be in on weekends and nights when there aren't a lot of other people there. I'd like to help our community relations department and participate in certain projects where I can be a goodwill ambassador for the organization. And I'm very pleased that I am on the Board of Directors of the Packers Hall of Fame. I treasure the tradition of this franchise, and most of the players we are going to be electing to the Hall in the future played here during my tenure as president.

I'm still going to go to all of the home games, but I won't be traveling with the team. Madeline may choose to miss some of those home games, and that's fine. I've dragged her to almost every baseball park, basketball arena and football stadium there is for 47 years. She has been at my side and given me everything she has, and she deserves some time off.

I remember when I worked at Marquette and I had to load all the office machinery we used for statistics in the press room into the trunk of my car to take down to the Milwaukee Arena for the games. Afterwards Madeline and I would haul those machines up a couple of flights of stairs, put them back in the car and drive them to campus. She'd have one machine, I'd have another, and we'd be carrying them up and down those stairs. So if she'd like to stay home from a game once in a while, I will be a very understanding man.

I'm really not worried about filling my time, although I know Madeline's a little concerned about that. I have to make sure I eliminate that fear. I'm looking forward to taking off with her to see our kids and spending more time with the grandkids. I'd also like to pack up on some Saturday mornings and drive down to Madison for a football game where we can tailgate and have a good time at Camp Randall.

I love the atmosphere at college sporting events, and we've been very fortunate to have a wonderful relationship with the University of Wisconsin athletic department from the time in the 80's when Elroy Hirsch called and asked us to schedule a preseason game there every year to help them with their finances. We did it, and it carried over to a strong relationship with Pat Richter and Barry Alvarez. I have a lot of admiration for what those people have done with that athletic department.

I'd like to spend more time at our home in Door County, too. We've always been on kind of a short string up there. Now we don't have to be, and Madeline is thrilled about that.

I wouldn't mind playing a little more golf, either. I've only been able to play about ten times a year, and I know the boys would like to do more than that. It's a great togetherness thing for us. I won't be the guy who's out there five or six times a week, but a couple of days a week would be nice. As my grandson Robert gets older I hope he'll want to play more golf. There's just going to be more family time, and that's very important to us.

Madeline loves to go to Chicago where we can see Bryan. She likes to walk up and down Michigan Avenue, but I have to put blinders on her so she doesn't see the stores. That's a great visit for us, and so are the trips to Kansas City. Those grandchildren are growing up awfully fast.

My health has been good except for the melanoma, which of course has been the main concern. The physicals have been fine, and I don't weigh a lot more than I weighed when I was in high school. I work out every day, so there's no problem with that.

I know the cancer can come back, and I keep going in for checkups. I think about it most when I'm closing in on my six-month appointment. I'm always a little anxious that day to get it behind me. I'm a lot more cautious with sunscreen and hats and things like that. I cover up as much as I can.

I will miss the contact with the fans. I'm so proud to have represented this organization, and I admire their passion for the franchise. I know every team has fans who are devoted to it and suffer with it, but I think these fans are different because so many of them actually own the team. They love that, and they expect good results. And they deserve them. I will also miss my friends in the Packers organization. I feel very close to people in this building, and they have been a big part of my life.

The stadium is in place, we're making money, the football team is on its way up, and that's how I was hoping to leave things. I've had a long time to look at age 70 when I knew I would have to go. I hope I've made the most of my chances and left everything in good shape.

Now it's somebody else's turn.

A Few Words from
Madeline and The Boys

I think Bob is worried that he's going to drive me crazy. He's such a disciplined person and so high energy that I may have to find some little jobs for him now that he's retired. But I'm looking forward to this time in many ways.

I hadn't counted on so many emotions coming out when we were doing things with the Packers for the last time this past season. It's been such a pleasure and a privilege to be involved in this special situation, and we're going to miss that.

I wish I'd taken a picture when Bob got on the team bus to the airport after the last game in Chicago. He had this big smile on his face when he told me, "You know, in my 18 years as CEO we had only three losing seasons, and I'm proud of that."

Hearing people coming up to him saying wonderful things has been very rewarding. Everyone seemed sad that he was leaving, so I guess that's a compliment. He was an extremely popular boss, and I think that's because he had a way of putting value on every person's efforts. I've never seen him be abrupt to people when he feels down. He's a very fair person. Fair to a fault perhaps. There have been times when I've wished he'd just put his fist through a wall.

There were a lot of sleepless nights for him during the referendum, a lot of hours at the office and a lot of soul-searching. I was worried about his health, because he got so pale and thin. But it all turned out for the best. We would have been in big trouble trying to keep this team in Green Bay if the vote had failed.

When Bob and I met, neither of us could have dreamed that he would become President and Chief Executive Officer of the Green Bay Packers. Of course I thought he was the greatest thing that had ever happened then, and as he went from job to job and moved up, anyone could see that he had a lot to offer.

We just thought it was wonderful when we moved to Green Bay. The summers were free, and while the season was very demanding, it wasn't anything like baseball had been in St. Louis when Bob was traveling almost every week. Bob played golf with the boys whenever he could, and that was one way he got close to them. Now all three of them are better at the game than he is, but credit him for teaching it to them. They'll get to play more now.

The boys all played different sports when they were growing up, and Bob did have to miss some of their games, but I tried very hard to make all of them. Kevin was a hockey goalie, and Bob used to get up early to take him to practice. Bryan played football, and one of our fondest moments was going on a bus trip to Oshkosh to watch his Premontre High School team win the state private schools championship. Michael played soccer. They were all good players, and they loved what they did.

I really wasn't much of a sports fan before I met Bob, and I had to learn a lot. Sometimes I surprise myself. People will say, "How do you know that?" and I'm thinking I would have to be a total idiot if I hadn't picked up some of these things just by osmosis.

All of the boys are involved in sports now. I think it's just in their blood. Kevin does pro football play-by-play for CBS-TV and the Packers' preseason network. He also does college basketball on radio and television and pro basketball on TNT. Bryan started his own company in Chicago called Harlan Sports Management, which represents more than 50 pro and college football coaches and sportscasters. Mike is an account executive for the University of Wisconsin's Badger Sports Properties, which manages the athletic department's media rights and corporate partnerships.

Kevin has four children, and those four wonderful grandchildren are at the top of any list of the high points in our lives. Abigail is 18 and on her way to college. Haley is 17, Olivia is 14 and "King Robert" is 11. They're all beautiful both inside and outside.

Kevin's two oldest girls are on their high school varsity cheerleading squad. We took a trip to their home in Kansas City in January to see the girls cheer at a basketball game, and it was a special night. We're really anxious to make more trips there.

It will be nice to get away for a weekend and not have to worry about getting back on Monday. When he was working Bob would never think of taking any extra time. That's just his nature.

Having Michael at Wisconsin will be exciting. I've been to the Kohl

Center, and I'm looking forward to going back and to seeing Camp Randall Stadium now that it's been remodeled. And of course there are always a lot of great things to do in Chicago with Bryan. He knows all of the best restaurants.

I traveled to most of the road games in the first 14 years when Bob was president, and we had some wonderful trips. We always took the Executive Committee and our team chaplain, Fr. Jim Baraniak, to dinner on Saturday night before the game. But I learned when Bob first became president that it was not a good idea to develop really close friendships with the coaches and general managers' families. They eventually leave the organization, and it hurts to lose friends and feel the bitterness. So I've learned to protect myself and not get too close to people.

I socialized in a group with Jeri Braatz, Lindy Infante's wife and our team physician's wife. We had some fun times, but eventually all of those people left, and some of the decisions that precipitated their leaving came from Bob. I never saw those friends again. I was close to Karen Sherman, too. Their suite was next to mine, and so I saw her at all the home games and got to know her children. But when Mike left, that was the end of our friendship. I wrote Karen a note, but I never heard from her.

Bob and I talked about everything when he was president, and that was really fun when they were doing the stadium. At one point, I remember saying, "You know what, Bob? It needs a great big 'G' on the back of the scoreboard at the north end that you can see when you're driving east on Lombardi Avenue." And he agreed. Now we have one there, and every time we drive by it, we say, "There's our 'G.'" I'm sure the architect would have figured that out on his own, but we thought of it first.

I suppose I knew more than I should have about Bob's work, but I always understood that it was a confidential thing. He asked my opinion, and I think he respected it, which of course made me feel great. I think he would admit that sometimes another point of view is helpful. Maybe a little softer point of view.

Now we can enjoy a less stressful time. Bob has his own ways of dealing with stress. He's on that treadmill every morning for one thing. And if there's a problem, he just attacks it head-on. He doesn't let it consume him.

But the highs were very high, and the lows were very low, and I think the lows were that way because everybody tried so hard. I don't care what people were doing in that organization, they were all trying very hard. It just seemed like it should all work, but of course everybody else in the league was trying just as hard.

The year Bob's mother died was probably the most stressful for him. He was exceptionally close to his mother. Whereas his father was extremely successful and someone to emulate, his mother was probably the one who had more to do with forming his values. When she became sick, Bob worried so much about her. She had become frail before she got really ill, but she was very strong and stubborn. He tried every which way to get help for her, but she didn't want it, and that worried him. She would have felt so bad if she had known that, too, because the last thing she wanted was to get in the way of Bob's job or his success. It was hard to watch when she became very ill and went into the nursing home.

Then there was the selling of her house after the funeral. Bob never went back to that house. He couldn't face it, so Bryan and I handled all of the details. That was probably my time to be the strong one.

Of course another tough time for our family came when Bob was diagnosed with cancer. At about 8:30 on the Monday morning after our game in Chicago, Dr. Smullen called the house and asked where he could reach Bob. I knew Bob had had some biopsies sent to Madison, and when the doctor said he had to reach Bob right away, I had a feeling that that was not good. When Bob called me back later, I tried not to let him know what I was thinking. I tried to downplay it, saying things would be fine, but that time from when we first found out that something was wrong until after the surgery seemed like weeks.

Waiting for that surgery to end was rough. It took something like 3½ hours. I was in the waiting room for most of it with Jerry Mortell, who was a special friend whom we lost last summer. He was there with me the whole time, and then I went to the chapel for awhile.

We didn't tell the kids until it was over, and of course, they were furious about that. I just felt there was plenty of time to be upset and feel sad, and we could just talk all that out when the surgery was over. But we were able to give them good news. We were very lucky.

The Packers have given Bob an office at Lambeau Field to use in retirement. He will make some goodwill appearances on behalf of the organization, and he is on the Board of Directors of the Packers Hall of Fame. That's great, because he will still feel a part of the Packers family.

Missing his co-workers at Lambeau Field is his greatest concern.

I plan to continue to volunteer as a fund-raiser for a number of causes that are very close to me. I started working with the Friends of St. Mary's Hospital Board in Green Bay years ago, and it has gradually become my passion, maybe in part because of my nursing background. It's something I'll probably never give up, especially when I see all the good that can be done for charitable health care. I'm also on a fund-raising committee for a drug and alcohol treatment center for adolescents called Libertas, and Bob and I are trustees of the Veritas Society for Wisconsin Right for Life.

We used to do things more quietly. If we were involved, we did it sort of behind the scenes, but it was mentioned that it would be best if we let it be known. If that might lend something to the cause and to the recognition of the Packers giving back to the community, so be it.

Recently, Bob and the boys and I were extremely honored when we were selected as a YWCA "Family of Distinction." The award is given to families in the Green Bay area who make a difference by living their lives in exemplary ways. Later, St. Norbert College in De Pere presented Bob and me with an honorary Doctor of Laws degree. We love this community, and it has been very kind to us.

Bob officially retired after the May Board of Directors meeting, and the timing was perfect. It gave us the summer in Door County to get used to the idea before the fall when we could make plans to go to some games in Madison if we liked. And of course there is the Packers season. I'm sure Bob will want to go to all of the home games, but if there should be a game on Christmas, it would not be the worst thing if he missed it.

Christmas has not always worked out so well for us because Kevin has a busy schedule at that time, and the NFL has been playing around the holidays. Our big holiday has been Thanksgiving when we get together with the boys and the grandchildren for a three-day celebration. We also have a family reunion on Father's Day.

We're really looking forward to spending more time at our place in Door County. Kevin has a home there, too. Our grandchildren live there during the summer, and we love it. It will be even better this summer. We can stay longer and savor those golden moments.

***

For most sons, their fathers are larger than life. They are the first male role models, serving as this incredible influence that lasts a lifetime. The fact that my father has been a very public figure has only added to the pride I felt as his son. He has always done and said the right thing, something I'm sure most sons say of their fathers. But his life has been so chronicled and public that the rest of the world has had a view.

I've always said there isn't a man alive who has cherished his profession more than my dad. He has felt privileged to be in his position and honored to lead this historic Packers organization. We were always included, whether at spring training for the Cardinals or as ball boys for Packers training camps and games. He guided me in my early broadcasting days and there isn't a moment in my adult life now that I don't first ask myself, what would my dad do?

He's always been a great listener. Very caring. Sympathetic. Interested. Always available and never too busy. Family first. The kind of dad I try to be.

Relationships, of course, change with age and as I grew older, he has confided in me and asked opinions. There may be no more empowering moment than having your father, a famous one at that with a litany of accomplishments, bouncing a thought off his son, surveying for another opinion, valuing input. I've had a front row seat for much of his life and have, with the rest of my family, been his biggest fan.

His father was a tremendous success, my father has been a tremendous success and I take pride in my attempt to fall in line. I've never felt pressure, only pride, and love.

-Kevin Harlan

***

My father's accomplishments in restoring the winning tradition of the Green Bay Packers are a great source of pride to our entire family. But I'm most proud of him as a person. He treats everyone with respect, humility and sincere warmth.

His professional legacy will be as the consummate sports CEO and a key figure in the Packers' success on and off the field. To me, though, he'll always be my role model and a loving supportive father.

-Bryan Harlan

***

My father has been extremely instrumental in my life and in countless ways he has molded me into the person I am today. Growing up and living in Wisconsin and watching him work for and eventually oversee the entire operation of an entity as influential as the Green Bay Packers has been an amazing ride.

Working in professional sports can make anyone very susceptible to public scrutiny, but it has been just the opposite during my father's tenure. He has been praised for his work and beloved by Packer fans across the country. I am appreciative and thankful from the perspective of being his youngest son when people say to me how much they appreciate him for what he has done for the Packer community, but even more importantly, how much they respect him as a person.

My response to those people is that he is an even better dad, and his family means the world to him. He and I have many unique Packer memories together and certainly, like any family, some better days than others. But it is those times when he worked with me on my golf game, drove me to practice, gave me lasting advice while in high school and college, and just generally provided a solid family life for my brothers and me growing up that carry the most weight. I cannot be more proud and thankful to have that man as my father.

-Michael Harlan

"It has been such a tremendous honor to serve the Green Bay Packers and all of the people who care so much about them for these 36 years. The fans have thanked me over and over again for the new Lambeau Field, for bringing our Milwaukee friends with us to Green Bay, and most of all, for helping to restore the dignity of the team on the field. Their kindness gives me more pleasure than I can ever express. The Packers are an elite franchise again, and there can be no greater reward than that for the years I've devoted to this uniquely American team and its incredibly faithful supporters."

-Bob Harlan